Planning and Housing in the Rapidly Urbanisi

Throughout the world there is an increasing movement of populations into urban areas and cities. As a result the demographic, economic, social and cultural characteristics of urban areas are changing, particularly in countries undergoing rapid urbanisation.

Planning and Housing in the Rapidly Urbanising World explores a range of international approaches to this trend within the fields of housing and urban planning, with a particular focus on countries in the South. The impact on land use and housing is described and analysed with reference to the related issues of poverty, health and the environment.

Jenkins, Smith and Wang investigate the evolving relationship between development strategies and urban issues using a series of international case studies of planning and housing in Latin America, Asia and Sub-Saharan Africa. Particular consideration is given to how the discourse of 'sustainability' is used within the context of continuing urbanisation, and developing policy and practice.

Providing an accessible introduction to the key issues as well as enhancing current theoretical debates and exploring practical applications, this book will be an essential resource for students and researchers in this area.

Paul Jenkins is Professor of Architecture and Human Settlements and Director of the Centre for Environment & Human Settlements (CEHS) in the School of the Built Environment, Heriot-Watt University.

Harry Smith is a Lecturer in the School of the Built Environment, Heriot-Watt University.

Ya Ping Wang is a Reader in Urban Studies, School of the Built Environment, Heriot-Watt University.

Housing, Planning and Design Series
Editors: Nick Gallent and Mark Tewdwr-Jones
         The Bartlett School of Planning, University College London

A series of books examining the interface between housing policy and practice, and spatial planning. Various facets of this interface are explored, including the role of planning in supporting housing policies in the countryside, the pivotal role that planning plays in raising housing supply, affordability and quality, and the link between planning/housing policies and broader areas of concern including homelessness, the use of private dwellings, regeneration, market renewal, and environmental impact. The series positions housing and planning debates within the broader built environment agenda, engaging in a critical analysis of different issues at a time when many planning systems are being modernised and prepared for the challenges facing twenty-first century society.

Planning and Housing in the Rapidly Urbanising World
Paul Jenkins, Harry Smith and Ya Ping Wang

International Perspectives on Rural Homelessness
Edited by Paul Milbourne and Paul Cloke

Housing in the European Countryside
Rural pressure and policy in Western Europe
Edited by Nick Gallent, Mark Shucksmith and Mark Tewdwr-Jones

Private Dwelling
Contemplating the use of housing
Peter King

Housing Development
Edited by Andrew Golland and Ron Blake

Forthcoming
Rural Housing Policy
Tim Brown and Nicola Yates

Decent Homes for All
Nick Gallent and Mark Tewdwr-Jones

Including Neighbourhoods in Europe
Edited by Nicky Morrison, Judith Allen and Arild Holt-Jensen

Planning and Housing in the Rapidly Urbanising World

Paul Jenkins, Harry Smith and
Ya Ping Wang

Routledge
Taylor & Francis Group

LONDON AND NEW YORK

First published 2007
by Routledge
2 Park Square, Milton Park, Abingdon, Oxon OX14 4RN

Simultaneously published in the USA and Canada
by Routledge
711 Third Avenue, New York, NY 10017

Routledge is an imprint of the Taylor & Francis Group, an informa business

Typeset in Galliard by
HWA Text and Data Management, Tunbridge Wells

British Library Cataloguing in Publication Data
A catalogue record for this book is available from the British Library

Library of Congress Cataloging in Publication Data
Jenkins, Paul, 1953–
Planning and housing in the rapidly urbanising world / Paul Jenkins,
Harry Smith, and Ya Ping Wang.
    p. cm. – (Housing, planning, and design series)
    Includes bibliographical references and index.
1. Urbanization. 2. Community development, Urban. 3. City planning.
4. Housing. 5. Urban policy–Developing countries–Case studies. I. Smith,
Harry, 1963– II. Wang, Ya Ping, 1957– III. Title. IV. Series.
HT361.J46 2006
307.76–dc22   2006003292

ISBN10: 0–415–35796–9 (hbk)   ISBN13: 978–0–415–35796–8 (hbk)
ISBN10: 0–415–35797–7 (pbk)   ISBN13: 978–0–415–35797–5 (pbk)
ISBN10: 0–203–00399–3 (ebk)   ISBN13: 978–0–203–00399–2 (ebk)

Contents

About the authors

Paul Jenkins, who directs the Centre for Environment and Human Settlements (CEHS), is an architect and planner by training and practice, with over 30 years' experience working in Sub-Saharan Africa in a wide range of central and local government, NGO, private sector, international aid and community-based organisations, in urban development, planning, housing, architecture and construction. Apart from leading on this publication, he is the principal author for Chapters 2, 3, 4, 7, 9 and 12, as well as the Introduction and Conclusions, co-authoring Chapter 8 with Harry Smith.

Harry Smith, also an architect and planner by training and practice, has worked in the private, NGO, and academic sectors in Spain and the UK, and has been involved in research and training in Latin America and Sub-Saharan Africa. His areas of interest and expertise include planning, housing and architecture, with a focus on community involvement in development. As well as co-authoring Chapter 8, he has authored Chapters 5, 6 and 10 and undertaken the main final edit for the book.

Ya Ping Wang, a geographer and planner, has been studying urban planning and housing problems in China and other East Asia countries for 20 years. His contributions have included Chapters 1 and 11 and final manuscript preparation.

While the various chapters have different main authors, all the authors have worked collaboratively throughout this process, and take collective responsibility for the argument.

Foreword

This is a timely and challenging book of global relevance. As President of the Royal Town Planning Institute, I attended the UN Summit on Settlements in Istanbul in 1996, at which nations from all across the world undertook to work for adequate shelter for all and sustainable human settlements. In 2000, I became President of the Commonwealth Association of Planners, and in the years since then I have taken every opportunity to try to raise international awareness of the significance of urbanisation as one of the greatest challenges facing this generation.

Rapid urbanisation is under-researched, inadequately understood and too often ignored by policy makers. The world's urban population will continue to increase by around 65 million people a year for the foreseeable future. The bulk of that increase is in poorer countries. The urbanisation of poverty is happening on a scale and at a rate that confounds conventional mind-sets. The fate of the planet will be hugely influenced by how well the environmental, economic, social and political aspects of this transformation are managed. Yet the models that continue to inform policy interventions are frequently based on untested assumptions about the political economy of territories and the potential for transplantation of 'best practices'.

The book explores the vital question of how to make sense of this surge of urbanisation. The text introduces, probes and demonstrates the relevance of theories from international political economy which provide insights into what is happening. Theory matters, and policy makers depend on theories more than they imagine. The authors of this book have reinvigorated some of the important theoretical debates. They redefine what is meant by the 'developing world', putting the focus squarely on the issue of rapid urbanisation.

Of course, theory generalises and in that process of abstraction there is the risk of glossing over specificities and differences that are critically important. The authors are acutely aware of these dangers and have undertaken a very focused but also wide-ranging study of the situations in Sub-Saharan Africa, East Asia and Latin America. These are regions that they know well; they have been able to study first hand and in depth what is happening in planning and housing in these places. This breadth of vision, critical analysis, linking of theory and practice and of planning and housing add up to a uniquely valuable contribution to the literature. The book has been designed as a teaching text. It will be useful on a range of courses, in many different countries, that address contemporary urban development in an international context. Practising planners grappling with the challenges of informality and rapid urban change will find it relevant and a valuable support to their work. The book also makes an important contribution to the research literature.

I have been privileged to work with the authors over a long period, first in the School of Planning and Housing in Edinburgh College of Art, and then after 2002 in the School of the Built Environment at Heriot-Watt University. Therefore, I cannot claim to be a detached commentator on this text. I learned a lot from them and so will those who read this book.

Cliff Hague
Edinburgh
March 2006

Preface

Why a book on planning and housing in the rapidly urbanising world? Although there is a growing literature on the general nature of rapid urbanisation worldwide (which we draw on in the initial part of this book), there are in fact few recent books which specifically describe approaches to this in the fields of planning and housing, other than descriptions of case studies and best practices. Those that do exist tend to have been based on either conferences or compilations of research, and as such have a limited focus for teaching, which needs to cover a broader spectrum. Some other books have a macro-regional focus, but even these are somewhat dated, as is the last key general textbook in this area (Devas and Rakodi 1993). The last books which examined theory as well as practice in urban planning and housing in the 'developing world' are also from this period, the early 1990s. This is despite the growing demand for higher education and professional training in urban planning and housing in many parts of the world which struggle to deal with the effects of rapid urbanisation, as well as the need for existing practitioners to continue professional development.

We, as academic teachers and researchers with professional practice experience, believe that there are significant differences between the contexts for the activities in planning and housing in situations where rapid urbanisation is taking place, or has recently, and those where this has been consolidated for some time. We argue that the needs and appropriate professional responses in situations where large-scale urbanisation is (a) a relatively recent phenomenon, (b) established but still consolidating, or (c) established but undergoing major re-structuring, are thus distinct from those developed and continually evolving in areas of the world which urbanised some time in the past, and where urbanisation has already been consolidated, albeit recognising that urban re-structuring is still taking place in these situations.

For various reasons, theory and analysis tend to have developed in the urban areas created and consolidated earlier, and have then usually been transferred and applied to areas which are more recently urbanising. We argue that this has led to many policies and practices based on these which are not appropriate to the actual context, and subsequently to a tendency for policy and practice in these areas to be increasingly divorced from theory and analysis. This has led to the promotion of practice with an implicit, and generally unquestioned, theoretical basis, and indeed the latest trend in sectoral development is largely based on dissemination of 'best practices', with minimal contextual analysis and explicit evaluation.

In this book we suggest a new approach which is grounded on a clear analysis of the context and not simplistic transfer of either theory or practice, and that is therefore more endogenous than exogenous, or 'home-grown' than 'imported'. We recognise that this approach is not an easy option, but one requiring more rigour than that involved in the theory and practice transfers of the past, and thus that this represents a significant challenge. However, we believe that it is only through such a process that theory and analysis can re-engage with policy and practice in mutually beneficial ways.

This approach to the subject, which is consequently built in to the book's structure, draws on the authors' practical experience trying to comprehend the relevance of – and apply – theories, analyses, policies and practice from the planning and housing literature of the 1970s through to the 1990s which focused on the 'developing world'. The stasis in analytical development in this literature in the 1990s led the authors to study the parallels with the evolution of development theory, policy and practice, also perceived to be in a state of 'impasse'. It is no coincidence that there has been no significant continuation of urban planning and housing analytical literature for 'developing countries' as the concept of the developing world has been contested since the 1970s and particularly so in the 1980s, with a perceived 'crisis' in development studies in the 1990s.

Unlike in the shelter sector, in development studies this situation has eventually led to a resurgence of broader analyses as well as a continuing pragmatic focus on practice transfer. The latter at least has not only been a north–south flow but also south–south and even south–north. Overcoming the impasse also led to a literature focused on specific development themes and regional or area studies. This reflected not only that the concept of development was challenged theoretically and in practice – as for example in the newly industrialising countries – but also the structural changes in the so-called 'developed world', where there was growing evidence of 'under-development', and thus the concept of the nation state as the development 'container' has been fundamentally undermined, with some new approaches thus being termed 'post-development'.

One of the analytical strands to emerge in later development studies is that of a new international political economy analysis which is global in its scope, but recognises the differential effect of its key concepts in macro-regions, nation states and sub-regions, including rapidly growing urban areas. This approach argues that there has been a qualitative change in how the global economy operates since the creation of the post-war consensus which spawned the concept of 'development', and as such development is less of a national phenomenon but one affecting people everywhere. Development in this sense is thus not only divided by geography in broad terms, but also fundamentally by political, economic, social and cultural factors within societies, whether these are in geographic areas considered to be 'developed' or in areas that are seen as 'less developed'. This essentially means there are no standard answers – on the contrary there is a need for many more answers to problems clearly analysed within their contexts. Equally, unlike previous forms of political economy analysis, the structural aspects of the political economy are not seen as predetermining action, but the approach recognises that there is significant space for different action within the broad parameters analysed.

We believe this form of analysis permits a different approach to shelter issues in what we conceptualise as the 'rapidly urbanising world' from those advocated in relation to the 'developing world', which inherently implied models of development related in some way to the 'developed world's' experience. In this, the new political economy approach we advocate stresses the need for political and economic, as well as social and cultural analysis, as we consider that any appropriate approach needs to be based on a realistic assessment of these factors. It also permits a linking of such localised or national analyses to broader global trends, thus providing a more realistic contextual basis. This book thus attempts to apply such an international political economy approach to the planning and housing sector within the context of rapid urbanisation, which is seen as largely a product of the globalising social and economic trends.

Much of what we write about in the book draws on our research and teaching experience in professional practice and academia. The book initially was conceived as a support text for distance learning in specialised courses provided in the Centre for Environment and Human Settlements (CEHS) within the School of the Built Environment, Heriot-Watt University in Edinburgh, where we work at the time of writing. It is our hope that the book will serve this end in as wide a way as possible through use in teaching, but also inform new forms of research and practice.

Paul Jenkins, Harry Smith and Ya Ping Wang
Edinburgh
October 2005

Acknowledgements

The authors would like to acknowledge their debt to John Leonard in setting up the Centre for Environment and Human Settlements (CEHS). John was involved in the delivery of postgraduate overseas planning courses at the Town and Country Planning Department of Edinburgh University until this closed in 1989, when he opted to move to the School of Planning and Housing within Edinburgh College of Art to create CEHS and continue this tradition of teaching and research degree provision. We have all worked with John within CEHS, Paul eventually taking over from him as Director when he retired in 1996, and subsequently managing the transfer of CEHS to become part of the new School of the Built Environment at Heriot-Watt University. Through the book we are thus effectively continuing some four decades of work based in Edinburgh higher education institutions on international planning and housing issues. While John's teaching has been the basis for some of what is presented in this book, this has been considerably expanded and, as such, is fully the responsibility of the authors.

Abbreviations

ASEAN	Association of South East Asian Nations
BOT	Build, operate and transfer
CAFTA	Central American Free Trade Area
CDS	City Development Strategies
CEHS	Centre for Environment and Human Settlements
CEPAL	Economic Commission for Latin America
CPF	Central Provident Fund
DDA	Delhi Development Authority
DFID	Department for International Development (United Kingdom)
EMR	Extended Metropolitan Region
FTAA	Free Trade Area of the Americas
FUPROVI	Foundation for the Promotion of Housing
GDP	Gross Domestic Product
GIS	Geographical Information Systems
GNP	Gross National Product
GPS	Geo-Positioning Systems
HDB	Housing and Development Board
ICT	Information and Communication Technology
ILO	International Labour Organisation
IMF	International Monetary Fund
LDC	Least Developed Country
MDG	Millennium Development Goal
NEPAD	New Partnership for Africa's Development
NGO	Non-Governmental Organisation
NIC	Newly Industrialising Country
NIEO	New International Economic Order
OPEC	Organisation of Oil Producing Countries
SAP	Structural Adjustment Programme
SEZ	Special Economic Zone
TNC	Trans-national Corporation
UK	United Kingdom

UMP	Urban Management Programme
UN	United Nations
UNCED	United Nations Conference on Environment and Development
UNCHS	United Nations Centre for Human Settlements
UNDP	United Nations Development Programme
UNHSP	United Nations Human Settlements Programme
USA	United States of America
USAID	United States Agency for International Development

Introduction

This chapter introduces the core argument of the book, how we understand the concepts of planning and housing, and summarises the structure of the book.

A 'post-developmental' approach to planning and housing in the rapidly urbanising world

Development discourse evolved in the post-war dispensation in the middle of the twentieth century, and was closely associated with that period in its basic concepts. At this time, some countries were seen as being more developed and others less developed, with little analysis of how this had happened historically, and the developing countries were seen as needing to 'catch up'. It was believed possible for all countries to do so if appropriate measures were undertaken – a belief with no real foundation but one that conveniently underpinned de-colonisation and subsequent neo-colonisation. Exactly how development would lead to 'catching up' of course was deeply debated (in the non-communist world) between conservatives who favoured the trickle down of growth via market-based economics, and the centre left who promoted state leadership and management of the economy and redistribution. Both were criticised for not addressing the notion that development, as so defined, is essentially a zero-sum game and that to have a chance at competing there was a need for less dependency to begin with, and hence more self-sufficient development.

These three basic positions to 'development' were played out and developed over a 30–40-year period in development studies, covering theory, policy, practice and (perhaps more importantly) ideology – a range of spheres that can be referred to as 'development discourse'. This was manifested through a series of different approaches to development such as modernisation, Keynesianism, basic needs, 'dependencia', world system theory, with a range of 'alternatives' spinning off which queried the nature of development itself, usually with a more social than economic focus, but had limited impact in terms of real economic, social and political improvements. However, it was only as the redundancy of previous arguments began to be seen as widespread – in the diverging success or disaster stories of the so-called developing world – and when social science techniques of deconstruction began to be applied to the subject, that the prevalent concepts of development began to be questioned more widely and their underlying contexts became more of a focus.

This crisis in development studies was eventually superseded in two ways: a diversification of 'development' approaches being successively applied and adapted in pragmatic and often rather superficial ways; and a deeper analysis of how we ended up thinking of development in the first place, including 'post-developmental' approaches. A key approach within the latter tradition is based mainly on an international political economy analysis of globalisation which places the post-war settlement within a broader social, economic, political and cultural context, and permits a clearer understanding of how this played out in different macro-regions and how this continues today. This is the approach we have drawn on in this book.

The characterisation of rapidly urbanising contexts as 'recent', 'establishing' and 'consolidating' and initially re-structuring *has* a relationship to the concept of 'development', which is still widely used (and which continues to be predominantly measured economically), but not always directly so. We have deliberately tried to avoid the nomenclature of the 'developing world' in this book, although this is impossible to avoid throughout as so much of what the book covers has to do with how we have understood 'development' previously – and how theory, analysis, policy and practice have been created as a result. We see the creation of a distinct body of sectoral approaches to urban planning and housing in the 'developing world' as having generally been a process of adoption and adaptation from the 'developed world' of theory (to a limited extent), policy (to a greater extent), ideology (to a significant extent) and practice. We thus propose a more nuanced approach to analysis and theory, and subsequently policy and practice, which is based on actual context, arguing that situations of rapid urbanisation create contexts for which theory, policy and practice cannot be transferred simplistically from the already 'urbanised world'.

Planning and housing in the rapidly urbanising world?

Understanding the concepts of urban planning and housing needs to start from their historic evolution, and not only from the period when these became a more specific government function, or when they became part of the 'development discourse'. Housing is a process and product that goes back to the early development of forms of shelter, and we initially look at this from the point of view of how housing has related to various aspects of the broader social, economic and cultural context in the 'pre-capitalist' past, as we believe aspects of these traditions are still embedded within housing provision today, especially where rapid urbanisation is taking place. Thus while we use the term housing to mean both the production of houses and the processes associated with this, we also view this widely within its political, economic, social and cultural context, where the more generic term 'shelter' is often used. An international approach to shelter has to recognise the limitations of the capitalist system for many across the world – and hence how housing is produced and used in these contexts – as well as analyse the widespread impact of the capitalist system.

Likewise, the evolution of planning is linked to the evolution of forms of land use and land rights, which have evolved in different social, economic, political and cultural systems. Land use allocation has been a fundamental historic feature of these systems, whereas forward land use 'planning' in the modern sense of the term reflects the relatively recent growing role of the state over individualised land use rights, largely to compensate for the reduction of controls embedded in previous social formations, though also linked to the increase in scale and complexity of urban areas. As with the development of housing, capitalism has structured planning, and especially urban planning, in certain ways – yet these systems are of marginal relevance in many situations of rapid urban development, where traditional forms of urban land management, including forms of forward 'planning', are still embedded within pre-capitalist cultures and institutions. As such we argue that 'planning' needs to be de-constructed from its manifestation arising from its Northern origins and reconstructed within the parameters of the realities of rapid urbanisation, to be of relevance.

We thus examine early forms of urban land use management and shelter provision as the basis to establish how these were related to the social, economic, political and cultural systems of their 'pre-capitalist' period. This allows us to be aware of both how these systems still have relevance, and how they might be the basis for new approaches which are more appropriate to the reality of the majority in situations where rapid urbanisation is taking place, and where the approaches developed for regions which urbanised earlier, and continue to dominate resources worldwide, are not effective or equitable. We argue that we need to understand this to be able to see more clearly how the 'modern' systems of planning and housing may or may not be relevant, and thus create the possibility for other forms of practice which are not predicated on adopting and adapting the practice evolved in situations where urbanisation took place some time ago and under different conditions.

To further clarify this argument we also examine how urban planning and housing evolved under colonial rule during the period when the capitalist form of social system began to dominate internationally through imperialism, and then after the Second World War when this system of domination began to change, with de-colonisation and neo-colonisation. In these periods we examine the contexts and practice of urban planning and housing, and the changing approaches to adoption and adaptation of theory and practice developed generally in countries which dominated economically, if no longer directly in a political and administrative sense. It is during this latter period that 'development' as such, and different approaches to urban planning and housing in the 'developing' world began to be more specifically promoted and hence we investigate these in more detail, referring to the earlier discussion on development itself.

The above chronologically structured part of the book takes the reader up to the period of the 1990s and the first years of the new millennium. Here we review key issues in current thought on urban planning and housing in the rapidly urbanising world using a similar form of analysis that draws on development studies. While theory has continued to evolve based on analyses in the so-called 'developed world', this is potentially more open to analyses from the previously so-called 'developing world', as the distinction between these 'worlds' is seen as changing, with elements of convergence. To what extent this change has led (or not) to new analyses and theories, as opposed to policy and practice recommendations is investigated, with some analysis of why this has happened.

To illustrate the arguments in the above chapters, we apply these to three specific regional contexts. We stress that these are not the only regions undergoing rapid urbanisation, nor do we assume that there is complete homogeneity within these regions in relation to context. However, we argue that there are broad similarities within these regions concerning urbanisation and development and which affect urban planning and housing, and that these are broadly different from each other. The regions are Sub-Saharan Africa, Latin America and East Asia; all regions within which the authors have worked and undertaken the research which informs these chapters. The main objective of these chapters is not to provide a complete regional analysis or any form of overall typology for urban planning and housing, but to illustrate the approach which underpins the book of contextual analysis.

The book does not aspire to provide the definitive answer to what form of planning and housing is appropriate in different rapidly urbanising contexts, but to suggest the analytical approach to permit professionals and academics to seek such answers. This approach is outlined in the concluding chapter, with some reflection on how theory and analysis develop, and how policy and practice have more recently been divorced from this. To assist with this process, key texts are identified where possible, in addition to wider references in the extensive bibliography. In addition, we also include a glossary of terms used throughout the book.

The structure of the book

Part One of the book examines what we understand as rapid urbanisation, and the relationships between this and current global trends in development – often termed globalisation – as well as demographic and other social and economic tendencies which are associated with these contexts (Chapter 1). This is followed by an overview of the evolution of 'development' discourse, and how this has evolved up to the recent period (Chapter 2), followed in turn by Chapter 3, which provides a basis for a fresh look at how urbanisation has been affected by political economic trends at a global level, and how this has conditioned the responses in terms of the focus for theory, analysis, policy and practice described in the following chapters.

In Part Two of the book, we use this analytical framework to examine how approaches to urban planning and housing in the 'developing' world have evolved, and the essential differences between these and those in the 'developed' world. This section starts with a review of pre-colonial urban planning and housing (Chapter 4) and subsequently the colonial period (Chapter 5). This sets the scene for the link between development and planning and housing in the post-colonial period (Chapter 6: planning and Chapter 7: housing), and subsequent reflection in Chapter 8 on recent issues in planning and housing internationally.

In Part Three the essential macro-regional differences that we suggest have evolved are used as a basis for reviews of how urban planning and housing have developed and are continuing to develop in three major macro-regions: Sub-Saharan Africa (Chapter 9), Latin America (Chapter 10) and East Asia (Chapter 11), as initial examples of the analytical approach proposed. This leads us to Part Four, where Chapter 12 concludes with a discussion on how a context-based analytical approach to policy and practice in urban planning and housing can continue to develop worldwide in more appropriate ways.

Inevitably a book of this nature draws extensively on previous authorship, updating and making new links in various ways. We have tried to be explicit about this in the text, but have opted not to pepper the text itself with excessive references and trust that we have not, as a result, omitted important reference material.

Part One:

General Context

Chapter 1
Urbanisation and globalisation

Introduction

Over the last 50 years, the world has witnessed a dramatic growth of its urban population, from about 29 per cent of the world's population in 1950 to 48 per cent by 2003. A recent United Nations projection indicated that from 2000 to 2030 the world's urban population will grow at an average annual rate of 1.8 per cent, nearly double the rate expected for the total population of the world, and that the 50 per cent mark would be crossed in 2007. Indeed, the world's urban population is expected to rise to 61 per cent by 2030. Population growth will be particularly rapid in the urban areas of so-called 'developing world', averaging 2.3 per cent per year during 2000–30. The speed and scale of this growth pose major challenges, and monitoring these developments and creating sustainable urban environments remain crucial issues on the international development agenda (United Nations 2004).

This chapter aims to review the definitions, trends, components, and implications of the urbanisation process, noting the differences between the early stages of urbanisation, which started in what has been termed the 'developed world', and the current processes in the rapidly urbanising world. It will also discuss the linkages between urbanisation and globalisation and the increasing de-linking of urbanisation from economic development, as well as general approaches in managing the urbanisation process.

The meaning of urbanisation

Urbanisation normally refers to the demographic process of shifting the balance of (usually) national population from 'rural' to 'urban' areas; *urbanisation rate* (or *level*) indicates the proportion (e.g. percentage) of the population living in urban areas at a given time; and *urban growth rate* is a measurement of the expansion of the number of inhabitants living in urban settlements (expressed usually as per cent change per annum). These terms seem to be well defined, but the study of urbanisation is complex, particularly in relation to the definition of 'urban' and 'rural' settlements.

    Despite the fact that the world is becoming increasingly urban in nature, the apparent differences between 'urban' and 'rural' or town and country are actually not straightforward. The definition of urban itself changes over time and space (Cohen 2004), each country tending to adopt its own definition in an often arbitrary way that reflects different economic and cultural situations. Definitions are usually based on criteria that may include any of the following: size of population in a locality, population density, distance between built-up areas, predominant type of economic activity, legal or administrative boundaries and urban characteristics such as specific services and facilities. Table 1.1 shows examples of the diversity in criteria and definitions in various countries. In general, however, the traditional distinction between urban and rural areas within a country has been based on the assumption that urban areas, no matter how they are defined, provide a different way of life and usually a higher standard of living than those found in rural areas. In many industrialised countries, this distinction has become blurred and the principal difference between urban and rural areas in terms of living circumstances tends to be a matter of the degree of concentration of population (UN 2002).

    Linked to the problem of defining urban areas is the difficulty in identifying the population of a given city. This is because the size of a city's population is a function of how and where the city's administrative boundaries are drawn (Cohen 2004). Urbanisation levels can be affected by so-called 'under-bound' and 'over-bound' cities. In the under-bound city the administratively defined area is smaller than the physical extent of the settlement, while in the over-bound city the reverse is true. Obviously, any reclassification (e.g. changes in urban definition, city boundaries, etc.) could change a city's official population (and the national urbanisation rate) without any actual demographic change (Oberai 1987). Lack of reliable and up-to-date demographic data can also make analysing urbanisation difficult. National censuses are usually the principal sources, but they could be several years old. There is also a tendency for censuses to undercount urban populations, because of a large mobile population (Cohen 2004). The urban/rural definition has been made all the more difficult by the fact that the reality, and consequently the concepts, of what is urban is not static but is subject to change. All this means that the urban–rural division is an excessively crude dis-aggregation. Because there is no global standard, one needs to be very careful when making cross-country comparisons regarding the extent to which particular countries are urbanised.

Trends in urbanisation

The most commonly used urbanisation data come from publications produced by the United Nations Statistics Division. The UN collects, compiles and disseminates data from national statistical offices on population density and urbanisation

Table 1.1 Definitions of urban settlement in selected countries

Country	Minimum number of inhabitants of localities	Other conditions
Zambia	5,000	The majority of whom all depend on non-agricultural activities
South Africa		Places with some form of local authority
Swaziland		Localities proclaimed as urban
Canada	1,000	Population density of 400 or more per square kilometre
Costa Rica		Administrative centres of cantons
Mexico	2,500	
United States	2,500	Population density of 1,000 persons per square mile or more
Peru		Populated centres with 100 or more dwellings
Venezuela	1,000	
India	5,000	Towns, and other places having 5,000 or more inhabitants, a density of not less than 390 inhabitants per square kilometre, pronounced urban characteristics and at least three-quarters of the adult male population employed in pursuits other than agriculture
Mongolia		Capital and district centres
Pakistan		Places with municipal corporation, town committee or cantonment
Albania	400	Towns and other industrial centres of more than 400 inhabitants
Czech Republic	2,000	
Norway	200	
Spain	2,000	

Source: United Nations 2002: Table 6.

through the *Demographic Yearbook*, which includes a set of tables on estimates and projections of urban and rural populations based on the national census definition, which as indicated above differs from one country or area to another. Despite the problems of different definitions, these data provide some useful information on the trends and characteristics of urbanisation in the world. This section draws mainly from the UN data sources.

Urbanisation is not new and its roots go back to early history (see Chapter 4), but it only started to grow in a significant way following the industrial revolution, particularly in Western Europe and the United States during the nineteenth century. Industrialisation and the development of modern transportation such as the railways contributed to the process. For example, from 1801 to 1911, Britain's urban areas accounted for 94 per cent of the country's population increase. One-third of the urban growth was due to net immigration from rural areas (Lawton 1972). The world's population increased three-fold between 1800 and 1860 but the world's urban population increased thirty-fold. It has been estimated that before the start of the nineteenth century only some 3 per cent of the world's population lived in towns of over 5,000. At the beginning of the twenty-first century, the figure is probably about 40 per cent (Carter 1995).

During the first half of the twentieth century, urban population continued to grow fast, particularly in Europe and North America. At the beginning of the century, 60 per cent of the American people lived on farms and in villages, but by 1970, 69 per cent resided in metropolitan areas. Clearly, metropolitan concentration was the dominant feature of population redistribution in the so-called developed world during the first half of the twentieth century (Berry 1981). In the so-called developing world, urbanisation started later, being limited in the nineteenth century in both scale and extent to the areas of Western colonial expansion. During the twentieth century this situation changed dramatically. In 1920, about a quarter of world's urban population lived in 'developing' countries; by 1950 this had increased to 42 per cent.

Between 1950 and 2003, the world's total population increased from 2.52 billion to 6.3 billion, while the world's urban population increased from 0.73 billion (29 per cent) to 3.04 billion (48.3 per cent) (Table 1.2). In the more developed regions annual growth of urban population was 2 per cent, while in developing regions it reached a startling 3.91 per cent. From 1975 to 2000, urban population growth in developed regions slowed down to less than 1 per cent due to counter-urbanisation in the United States and Western Europe, while less developed regions maintained a high rate of 3.55 per cent per year. Thus, while in 1950 more than half of the world's urban population lived in developed regions, by 2003 over 70 per cent lived in developing regions, and hence the term 'rapidly urbanising world'. Looking at it from the point of view of urbanisation levels within these rapidly urbanising regions, while in 1950 less than 18 per cent

Table 1.2 Total, urban and rural populations by development group, selected periods: 1950–2030

Development group	Population (millions)					Average annual rate of change (%)		
	1950	1975	2000	2003	2030	1950–75	1975–2000	2000–30
Total population								
World	2.52	4.07	6.07	6.30	8.13	1.92	1.60	0.97
More developed regions	0.81	1.05	1.19	1.20	1.24	1.01	0.52	0.13
Less developed regions	1.71	3.02	4.88	5.10	6.89	2.29	1.92	1.15
Urban population								
World	0.73	1.52	2.86	3.04	4.94	2.91	2.53	1.83
More developed regions	0.43	0.70	0.88	0.90	1.01	2.00	0.91	0.47
Less developed regions	0.31	0.81	1.97	2.15	3.93	3.91	3.55	2.29
Rural population								
World	1.79	2.55	3.21	3.26	3.19	1.43	0.92	-0.03
More developed regions	0.39	0.34	0.31	0.31	0.23	-0.46	-0.40	-1.05
Less developed regions	1.40	2.21	2.90	2.95	2.96	1.82	1.09	0.06

Source: United Nations Department of Economic and Social Affairs, Population Division 2004: 7 (Table I.1).

of the population there lived in urban areas in 1950, by 2003 this figure was over 42 per cent (UN 2004). In terms of absolute numbers, there are now more than twice as many urbanites in developing regions as there are in more developed countries. Fuelled by changes in the countryside, high rates of fertility, falling death rates and rapid city-ward migration, most developing countries have been transformed from rural to urban societies in two or three decades. The larger cities, in particular, have been expanding rapidly, often doubling in size every 15 years (Gilbert and Gugler 1992).

There are marked differences in the size and proportion of the urban population among major areas of the world (Table 1.3). In 2003, Africa and Asia's urban population was just under 39 per cent; Europe and Oceania were at 73 per cent; and the Americas had the highest levels of urbanisation, with Latin America and the Caribbean at 76.8 per cent and Northern America at 80.2 per cent. However, the combined number of urban dwellers in Europe, Latin America and the Caribbean, Northern America and Oceania (1.2 billion) is smaller than the number in Asia (1.5 billion), one of the least urbanised major areas of the world. Of course, these broad figures conceal considerable variations within each area, particularly in developing regions. Most parts of Africa are far less urbanised, containing many countries where more than 70–80 per cent of the population still live in rural areas. Asia appears to be a little more uniform in its urban characteristics in comparison to Latin America and Africa.

A feature of contemporary urban population growth is the way in which the largest cities appear to have been growing at the most rapid rates, a phenomenon which has given rise to the concept of *urban primacy* – the demographic, economic, social and political dominance of one city over all others within an urban system (Drakakis-Smith 2000). Once a large city is created, then the attraction it offers in terms of supplies of labour and capital, as well as the concentration of infrastructures, will of itself promote growth and initiate a rising spiral of development. This is partly why the largest cities tend to grow fastest. In the largest cities the greatest opportunities are perceived in education and training, in heath care and in general improvement of living standards (Carter 1995). At the beginning of the twentieth century, only 16 cities in the world contained at least a million people, the vast majority of which were in industrially advanced economies. At the beginning of the twenty-first century, there are around 400 cities around the world of such size, about three-quarters of these in low- and middle-income countries (Cohen 2004: 24). In many rapidly urbanising countries, most large-scale modern activities, forms of social infrastructure and centres of decision making are found in a single major city which, in many cases, is the capital city (Gilbert and Gugler, 1992). This high degree of urban primacy, with a large proportion of the national population living in a single city, is mirrored in the way one city dominates all others.

In recent years, some observers have suggested that the nature of the

Table 1.3 The distribution of the world's urban population by region: 1950–2030

Development group	1950	1975	2000	2003	2030	1950–75	1975–2000	2000–30
	Urban population (millions)					*Average annual rate of change (%)*		
Africa	33	103	295	329	748	4.57	4.21	3.10
Asia	232	575	1,367	1,483		3.63	3.47	2.22
Europe	280	446	529	530	545	1.86	0.68	0.10
Latin America and the Caribbean	70	197	393	417	602	4.14	2.76	1.42
Northern America	110	180	250	261	354	1.98	1.32	1.16
Oceania	8	15	23	24	31	2.75	1.51	1.07
World	*Percentage of urban population*					*Rate of urbanisation (%)*		
Africa	14.9	25.3	37.1	38.7	53.5	2.12	1.54	1.22
Asia	16.6	24.0	37.1	38.8	54.5	1.47	1.75	1.28
Europe	51.2	66.0	72.7	73.0	79.6	1.02	0.38	0.30
Latin America and the Caribbean	41.9	61.2	75.5	76.8	84.6	1.52	0.84	0.38
Northern America	63.9	73.8	79.1	80.2	86.9	0.58	0.28	0.31
Oceania	60.6	71.7	72.7	73.1	74.9	0.67	0.06	0.10

continued…

Table 1.3 continued

Development group	1950	1975	2000	2003	2030	1950–75	1975–2000	2000–30
Percentage of the world's population living in region								
World	100.00	100.00	100.00	100.00	100.00			
Africa	4.50	6.79	10.33	10.81	15.13			
Asia	31.65	37.93	47.85	48.72	53.88			
Europe	38.20	29.42	18.52	17.41	11.02			
Latin America and the Caribbean	9.55	12.99	13.76	13.70	12.18			
Northern America	15.01	11.87	8.75	8.57	7.16			
Oceania	1.09	0.99	0.81	0.79	0.63			

Source: United Nations Department of Economic and Social Affairs, Population Division 2004: 7 (Tables I.4 and I.5).

urbanisation process has been changing, with various terms being used to describe the settlements associated with this process, such as *mega-cities* and *extended metropolitan regions* (EMR). These agglomerations are not the same as *world cities*, a term which describes the key command and control points of the global economy, such as New York, London, or Tokyo (UNCHS 1996) – see below. EMRs are a product of the globalisation of the world economy but refer more specifically to a pattern of urbanisation and city structure that is claimed to be fundamentally different from earlier types of urbanisation (McGee and Robinson 1995). EMRs represent a fusion of urban and regional development in which the distinction between urban and rural has become blurred as cities expand along corridors of communication, by-passing or surrounding small towns and villages which subsequently change in function and occupation (Drakakis-Smith 2000: 21).

In some geographic regions (e.g. Southeast Asia), urban and rural activities are interpenetrating. Rural economies and lifestyles increasingly assume characteristics that were formerly considered urban. More residents work outside agriculture; rural economies are increasingly diverse, mixing agriculture with cottage industries, industrial estates, and suburban development; and many rural residents are linked to city life through spells of migration and commuting. In some rapidly urbanising regions, mega-urban areas have emerged in which it is difficult to say where a particular city begins and ends. The reconfiguration of urban space is manifested in the outward spread of urban activities, such as industry, shopping centres, suburban homes, and recreational facilities, which are penetrating what was once rural territory (Montgomery *et al.* 2004: 23) – Figures 1.1 and 1.2. In short, the functions and roles of cities that connect them to surrounding territory are changing in ways that threaten the relevance of administrative boundaries. By blurring boundaries, such changes are causing researchers to question the value of urban/rural dichotomies, which appear increasingly simplistic (McGee 1991; Champion and Hugo 2004).

It is clear from current predictions that the fast growth of the world's urban population will continue, particularly in developing countries, as is shown for example in *World Urbanisation Prospects: the 2003 Revision*, produced by the United Nations Department of Economic and Social Affairs (Population Division) – see Box 1.1.

1.1 Incipient urban development in the rural area of Arraiján, near Ciudad de Panamá (Harry Smith)

1.2 Low-income development in the peri-urban area of Luanda, Angola (Harry Smith)

Box 1.1 Urbanisation prospects

The main findings and predictions of the United Nations Department of Economic and Social Affairs (Population Division) (2004: 5–8) on the urbanisation process over the next 30 years are the following:

- During 2000–30, the world's urban population is projected to grow at an average annual rate of 1.8 per cent, nearly double the rate expected for the total population of the world. It was estimated at 3 billion in 2003 (48 per cent of the total population) and is expected to rise to 5 billion (61 per cent) by 2030, while the rural population is anticipated to decline slightly from 3.3 billion in 2003 to 3.2 billion in 2030. By 2007, for the first time, there will be more people living in urban areas than in rural areas.
- The process of urbanisation is more advanced in developed regions, where 75 per cent of the population was living in urban areas in 2003. This is expected to increase to 82 per cent by 2030.
- However, population growth will be particularly rapid in the urban areas of developing regions, averaging 2.3 per cent per year during 2000–30. Almost all growth of the world's total population in this period is expected to be absorbed by urban areas in developing regions, with the proportion of urban population there expected to rise from 42 per cent in 2003 to 57 per cent by 2030.
- With 39 per cent of their populations living in urban areas in 2003, Africa and Asia are expected to experience rapid rates of urbanisation, so that by 2030, 54 per cent and 55 per cent, respectively, of their inhabitants will live in urban areas. By 2030, Asia and Africa will each have more urban dwellers than any other major area, with Asia alone accounting for over half of the urban population of the world.
- At that time, 85 per cent of the population in Latin America and the Caribbean will be urban.
- In Europe and North America, the percentages of the population living in urban areas are expected to rise from 73 per cent and 80 per cent, respectively, in 2003, to 80 per cent and 87 per cent in 2030. The increase in Oceania is likely to be from 73 per cent to 75 per cent over the same period.
- The proportion of people living in mega-cities (urban agglomerations of 10 million inhabitants or more) is expected to remain small, rising from 4 per cent in 2003 to 5 per cent by 2015. Almost 3 per cent of the

world population in 2003 was estimated to live in cities with 5 million to 10 million inhabitants, rising to nearly 4 per cent by 2015. About 25 per cent of the world population was living in urban settlements with fewer than 500,000 inhabitants in 2003, ranging from nearly 40 per cent in developed regions to just over 20 per cent in developing regions.

- The number of cities with 5 million inhabitants or more is projected to rise from 46 in 2003 to 61 in 2015. Among these, the number of mega-cities will increase from 20 in 2003 to 22 in 2015. In 2003, 33 of the 46 cities with 5 million inhabitants or more were in developing countries, and by 2015, 45 out of such 61 cities are expected to be in developing regions.
- Large urban agglomerations are not necessarily experiencing fast population growth. Of the 20 mega-cities identified in 2003, almost half experienced annual population growth below 1.5 per cent between 1975 and 2000, and only six grew at rates above 3 per cent.

Components and causes of urbanisation

Urban population growth has two main components: migration and natural growth. There is a considerable literature on migration to urban areas. Conventional economic theories of urbanisation and migration, based on the nineteenth-century experience in Europe and North America, see urban growth as a function of economic development, emphasising demand and supply factors. On the demand side, income inelasticity of demand for rural products and income elasticity of demand for urban products are the main reasons given for migration; on the supply side, technical development of agriculture releases labour from land (Tolley and Thomas 1987). Traditional social theory of migration emphasises the 'push' and 'pull' factors and believes that labour moves from areas of low opportunity to areas of high opportunity, with the choice of area being influenced by distance. In the early stages of development, positively selected migration (i.e. by the relatively better off, responding more to 'pull' factors) tends to predominate. But as development proceeds, intervening obstacles reduce, making it easier for the poor (negatively selected) to move (Rhoda 1979; Oberai 1987). Later migration is also influenced by stronger 'push' factors resulting from socio-economic change in villages.

Most recent studies of migration seem to concur with Todaro (1994) that migration is primarily motivated by perceived economic opportunities in the city. Migration persists from rural areas without unemployment to urban areas showing high unemployment on the basis of expectations of long-term income – i.e. temporary unemployment prospects are offset by attraction of higher urban wages. A strong association between economic and urban population growth has emerged from such theories. However, the precise nature of this link varies over space and time, and there are many contradictions (Drakakis-Smith 2000), as is shown in the following examples from around the world:

- in Ghana migration continued in the face of declining urban job opportunities and declining income differentials, with educational attainment becoming a key factor (Godfrey, in Sinclair 1978);
- in Venezuela, for the less educated, migration correlates with wage differential, but for the more educated it is linked more with employment level (Schultz, in Rogers and Williamson 1982);
- in Malaysia there has been little migration from the poor northeast to the rich west coast (Sinclair 1978; Rogers and Williamson 1982).

Apart from economic considerations, there are many other factors which can influence migration patterns in developing countries. Education (for migrants or their children) is an important factor, which could be related to longer-term economic motives. Disaster, famine and war can also be the main causes for migration in some regions. Although not backed by empirical studies, the 'bright lights hypothesis' (the attraction of the colourfulness of city life and entertainment) is also a motive given for migration (Connell *et al.* 1976).

There is very little direct evidence from migration surveys that the availability of housing or community facilities other than schools attracts migrants to urban areas independently of economic incentives, with researchers having noted that migrants may leave behind housing with better physical and environmental quality and security of tenure. However, an expanding urban housing supply that reduces housing costs (i.e. increases 'real' wage) can be expected to increase the attraction of an urban area. In addition, densely populated areas that are close to the city and areas that are well connected to the city through transport corridors provide higher than average numbers of migrants (Friedmann and Wulff 1975), with distance being less of a deterrent the higher the income or education level of the migrant (Connell *et al.* 1976).

Urban in-migrants rarely conform to the stereotypes that they are poor and uneducated slum dwellers, ill-adapted to urban life and given to so-called social deviance. On the contrary, in-migrants tend to be drawn from all classes, tending to be at least equal to native urban inhabitants in education, job status and income. Research has shown that out-migrants to urban areas often tend to be of well above average education and income background in the area of origin, while poorer and less educated out-migrants tend to go to other rural areas (Connell 1976). However, situations of war or natural disasters (which are not rare) may bring lower socio-economic status in-migrants to cities.

Rural–urban migration is of declining relative importance as a component of urban growth in most developing countries, as opposed to other types of migration and natural growth. A substantial component of in-migration to large cities may be made up of migrants from other cities (urban–urban) or of step migration patterns (rural–urban–urban, etc.). In addition, not all moves to the city are permanent, and net migration flows are usually small compared with their inflow (in-migration) and reverse (out-migration) components. The migrational component of urban populations has also become much more difficult to identify with the rise of circular migration, a temporary move to the city by those who retain a formal, census residence outside it. Such long-term commuting has increased markedly in recent years as transportation has become cheaper and more regular (Drakakis-Smith 2000).

The contribution of natural increase to urban growth has become an important factor. The two components of urban population growth – migration and natural increase – vary in relative importance through space and time, but in general, migration is more important in the early stages of urban population growth when the proportion of the national population living in towns and cities is low. As the urban proportion rises, so does the contributory role of natural growth, although only up to a certain point. Beyond this point, which is related more to the demographic cycle than to the absolute size of urban population, urban fertility begins to decline and migrational growth once again becomes more important, albeit at a drastically reduced level (Drakakis-Smith 2000).

Sustained high fertility combined with declining mortality has caused fast population growth in rapidly urbanising regions resulting in urban growth either directly through urban population natural increase or indirectly through migration of growing rural populations. Soon after the end of the Second World War, rapid declines in mortality occurred throughout much of the developing world, due to the use of drugs and medical practices. Gains in life expectancy that took 50 or 100 years to achieve in the developed world required little more than a decade or two in parts of the developing world, where natural increase may now account for well over half of total urban population growth. As is well known, urban residents face many constraints and opportunities that influence their childbearing. They typically want fewer children than their rural counterparts. Urban couples are probably more apt to appreciate the advantages of having fewer but better-educated children, choosing to make greater investments in their children's schooling and adopting childrearing strategies that place heavier demands on parental time, thus resulting in lower fertility rates in urban areas (Montgomery *et al.* 2004).

Despite substantial reductions in fertility in most regions since the 1970s, population growth in the less developed regions has remained high, as a high proportion of younger and more productive migrants has contributed to the high level of natural increase in cities.

Apart from migration and natural urban population increases, there are many other factors which contribute to the growth of official urbanisation levels. Reclassification, whereby urban status is conferred on formerly rural residents and territory, is an important one. This can happen when a settlement passes beyond a minimum size or density threshold, thereby qualifying to be termed an urban place, or when a government changes its definition of 'urban', as did the United States in 1950 and China in the 1980s. Cities can also annex neighbouring territory (Montgomery *et al.* 2004). Reclassification can also be related to new forms of urban development, for example researchers have found that population growth in rural areas is leading to the expansion of villages and sprouting of homes amidst fields. With this form of growth, population densities in vast rural regions exceed official thresholds for defining urban settlements. This is happening in vast stretches of rural India, Bangladesh, Pakistan, China, Indonesia, Egypt, Rwanda, Burundi, Nigeria and other developing countries. This is the phenomenon of urbanisation by implosion, which builds up urban spatial organisations through the densification of human settlements and the coalescence of villages. Applying the widespread criterion for defining urban settlements of 400 persons per square kilometre to these countries, Qadeer (2000, 2004) found that most of rural Bangladesh and a large band of territory in India, from West Bengal to Delhi, have rural densities exceeding the urban threshold. Qadeer (2000) called these regions *ruralopolises*, a hybrid settlement system that is spatially urban but economically, socially and institutionally rural. These densely populated rural regions are vast bands of territories beyond urban regions, extending over thousands of square kilometres, but studded with towns. Often agriculture and household production are the bases of their economies, but they are not insulated from the technological and social currents of modernisation. It is the combination of agrarian economy and high density that defines these regions and differentiates them from the high-density countryside of developed countries, such as Japan or the Netherlands (Qadeer 2004).

Urban centres in the world and their rate of change are influenced by external factors and by factors related to each particular local context. These include the quality of the site and availability of natural resources (especially fresh water), demographic structure, existing economy and infrastructure (the legacy of past decisions and investments) and the quality and capacity of public institutions. External influences range from the natural resources available close by, to trends within the regional and national economy, to decisions made by national governments and the 30,000 or so global corporations who control such a significant share of the world's economy (Satterthwaite 2002).

Understanding urban change within any nation is complicated, requiring consideration of changes in the scale and nature of the nation's economy and its connections with the global economy, the structure of government (especially the division of power and resources between different levels of government) and the extent and spatial distribution of transport and communications investments. For virtually all nations that have urbanised rapidly during the last 50 years, these changes have included long periods of quick economic expansion and large shifts in employment patterns from agricultural and pastoral activities (dispersed among rural areas) to industrial, service and information activities (highly concentrated in urban areas). The internationalisation of world production and trade (including the very rapid expansion in the value of international trade) has been an important part of this and has influenced urban trends in most nations, as is discussed in Chapter 3. Many cities owe their prosperity to their roles within this increasingly globalised production and distribution system (Satterthwaite 2002). International immigration and emigration has strong impacts on the population size of particular cities in most nations, but it is not only changing patterns of prosperity that explain these vast flows of people. Many cities have felt the impact of war or disaster, or of people fleeing such events. Major demographic change has also been apparent in all nations during the last 50 years which, in turn, has influenced urban change. As seen above, this includes the rapid population growth rates in much of Latin America, Asia and Africa after the Second World War (although in virtually all nations these have now declined significantly) and changes in the size and composition of households and in age structures (Satterthwaite 2002).

The pace of urbanisation is usually associated with that of industrialisation and economic growth. As countries develop, their economies undergo changes, some of these predictable, such as the relative importance of agriculture declining while that of manufacturing and services rises. Industrialisation and economic growth are almost always accompanied by urbanisation (World Bank 2000a), and urbanisation has been viewed as a measure of progress towards industry and services (Davis 1965; Montgomery *et al.* 2004). In some parts of the world, however, and particularly in Sub-Saharan Africa, cities have been growing without a concomitant expansion of economic activity. In Africa, high rates of city growth owe more to high rates of national population growth than to economic development. On this point, a comparison of Africa with Southeast Asia may be instructive. At first glance their urbanisation experiences appear to have been remarkably similar over the past 35 years. In 1950, some 14.7 per cent of Africa's population lived in urban areas, as did 14.8 per cent of the population of Southeast Asia. The level of urbanisation then rose in Africa, reaching 20.8 per cent in 1965 and 37.2 per cent in 2000. Southeast Asia recorded nearly identical changes, with its level of urbanisation reaching 19 per cent in 1965 and 37.5 per cent in 2000 (United Nations 2000). However, the economic experiences of these regions could hardly have been more different, with incomes per capita in Southeast Asia shooting up while in Africa they have stagnated or declined (World Bank 2000c). Such different experiences of urbanisation require different responses in relation to urban planning and housing as is discussed elsewhere in this book.

The impacts of globalisation

Chapter 3 provides a detailed analysis of globalisation and its impacts on urban development. This section provides an initial analysis of its links to urbanisation. To begin with, therefore, although the term 'globalisation' began to become commonly used from the 1960s and early 1970s onward, the phenomenon can be traced back to earlier periods in history. After an initial mercantilist wave of global economic expansion during the phase of capitalism (1500–1800), a further wave of globalisation during the nineteenth century involved the promotion of urbanisation as centres of colonial control – in both centre and periphery (see Chapter 2) – which underpinned industrialisation in the core countries. Such industrialisation required steady and secure raw materials, as well as markets for products, and was closely linked to colonialism and imperialism. New forms of exploitation needing new infrastructure and new bases for control, transport and processing emerged, with implications for how the geographic areas linked by these processes urbanised – major urbanisation in centre, minor (and dependent) urbanisation at periphery. Later, in the second half of the twentieth century, in a further wave of expansion of global economic and political interdependence, particularly between Western countries, much discussion was generated on the inadequacies of orthodox approaches to thinking about politics, economics and culture which presumed a strict separation between internal and external affairs, the domestic and international arenas, and the local and the global (Held and McGrew 2003). Following the collapse of state socialism in 1989 and the consolidation of the capitalist market economy worldwide, academic and public discussion of globalisation intensified. Information technology and changes in world governance (e.g. deregulation of currencies) led to the spread of industry and dominance of the financial sector. These developments appeared to confirm the belief that the world was fast becoming a shared social and economic space.

In many parts of the world, urbanisation is seen to be driven by a new global economy that is literally changing the face of the planet. Increasingly, urban growth is being influenced by continued global economic integration and the struggle for countries – and indeed individual cities – to be competitive in the global marketplace. According to Savitch (2002) the five essential components of globalisation are: (1) new technology, (2) the centrality of information made possible by instant communication, (3) an increasing trend towards the standardisation of economic and social products, (4) growing cross-national integration, and (5) mutual vulnerability stemming from greater interdependence. He identified some positive and negative implications of the globalisation process on cities – the positive impacts including rising prosperity, the enduring importance of urban cores, and increased democracy, while the negative implications consist of sharpening imbalances, increased social disorder, and greater citizen expectations.

Drakakis-Smith (2000) also summarised the impacts from globalisation, setting out various key arguments around this process: (1) that nation states are being transcended by higher-level organisations such as supra-national political entities and trans-national corporations; (2) that economic integration is a driving force linking resources from around the world into a global network of production and marketing; and (3) that convergence of cultures is leading to a hybrid to a great extent dominated by Western culture. Together with advancing communications technology, this would appear to support the notion of a shrinking world with intensified linkages worldwide, but Drakakis-Smith (2000: 3) warns that the 'process of inclusion or access to, and exclusion from, the means by which the world has allegedly shrunk has, in the view of many, widened the gap between the haves and have-nots, whether at the household or national level'.

UNHSP has also identified some general impacts of globalisation on cities (UNCHS 1996). In cultural terms, it sees globalisation as of both diversifying and enriching cultures, sometimes leading to vibrant fusions, but also leading to fear, racial tension and polarisation in some cities as a result of immigration. Another significant impact of globalisation has been standardisation, as people all over the world increasingly have access to the same cultural products. In relation to economic aspects, there could be a race to the bottom in economically dependent countries, with lower wages in the industrial sectors, job losses, unstable jobs and incomes, and inability to afford housing and other essential services. The consequent patterns of social exclusion vary across cities, but they often are reflected in other social cleavages as well, such as along racial and ethnic lines (Figure 1.3). This in turn accelerates and increases the process of 'informalisation' of the urban economy, with increasing shares of incomes earned in non-formally regulated employment (Figure 1.4). The twin processes of informalisation and deindustrialisation demonstrate how competition intensifies between and within urban labour markets.

What is clear is that cities will be reshaped by global economic forces over the course of this century. Newly globalised circuits of finance, trade, and information exchange are linking rich countries with some poor countries, and connecting some residents of poor countries to their counterparts elsewhere. Many poorer countries are industrialising rapidly, while advanced economies are taking steps away from manufacturing into the sectors of finance, specialised services and information technology. These changes are forcing countries – and industrial cities – to rethink their comparative advantages. To be competitive in global markets, cities are finding that they need to establish themselves as strategic nodes in international networks of exchange, increasingly competing against each other, striving to present the image and provide the infrastructure demanded by international firms so as to attract greater foreign investment and generate new jobs. As they link themselves to global markets, cities are increasingly exposing their residents to the risks, as well as the benefits, of being more tightly integrated into world networks of finance,

1.3 Informal vs. formal housing in Luanda, Angola (Paul Jenkins)

1.4 Informal vs. formal vending, downtown Johannesburg, South Africa (Paul Jenkins)

information and production. But cities vary greatly in their exposure to such risks and benefits, and the implications depend on national contexts and levels of development (Montgomery *et al.* 2004).

Globalisation has had a very uneven impact on various parts of the world. While the restructuring of global production has brought numerous benefits to some countries, previously thriving manufacturing cities in industrially advanced economies have lost many factory jobs and have been forced to restructure their economy. The region that appears to have benefited most from globalisation is Asia, while large parts of Africa have effectively been bypassed (Cohen 2004). Very few African cities, for example, have benefited from direct foreign investment in manufacturing, whereas foreign capital has increasingly gone to a number of cities in Asia and Latin America. New loci of economic activity can be expected to emerge, with some areas experiencing rapid growth while others decline (Montgomery *et al.* 2004). Because foreign direct investment is usually distributed unevenly across national landscapes, patterns of migration are likely to be reshaped. Cities are a nation's gateways to international markets, and city populations can be among the first beneficiaries of the waves of technological change that stream through these markets, though they can also find themselves among the first victims of price spikes and exchange-rate crises. Engagement with these markets may well come at the price of urban economic volatility.

Worldwide economic restructuring and the growing interdependence of countries and regions around the world has also led to the emergence of a new urban hierarchy. Some cities such as New York, London and Tokyo are considered to have become 'world cities' (Sassen 1993; Cohen 2004). Globalisation is also changing the roles and responsibilities of local and state governments. It has allowed individual cities to break away from the fate of their national economies. Increasingly, success or failure depends on the ability of municipal governments to capitalise on the assets of the local environment and to provide the modern infrastructure, enabling environment, and low-wage, flexible workforce demanded by modern businesses. Thus, cities are not just growing in size, they are also gaining in economic and political influence (Yeung 2002).

Urbanisation and development

Cities are the sites where diverse social and economic resources are concentrated, and that concentration can generate substantial social and economic benefits in the form of innovation and income growth (Jacobs 1969). Over recent history, it has generally been assumed that urbanisation goes hand in hand with industrialisation and 'development', and that the processes of urbanisation, structural change, development and industrialisation are all fundamental correlates. It has been argued that urbanisation is one of the most significant processes affecting societies in the late twentieth century and beyond (Devas and Rakodi 1993; Potter *et al.* 2004). Cities are also identified as sites of diverse forms of social interaction, whether on the staging grounds of neighbourhoods, through personal social networks, or within local community associations. There is good reason to believe that urbanisation itself might stimulate economic growth, and moderate rates of urban population growth have been taken as emblems of success (Montgomery *et al.* 2004). Mera (1978, 1981) also stresses some other positive links between urbanisation, particularly between the growth of large cities and social indicators such as school enrolments, literacy, declining infant mortality, nutritional intake, life expectancy, falling birth and death rates, etc.

However, the relationship between urbanisation, industrialisation and development has become more problematic in relation to developing countries which have experienced very rapid urbanisation in recent history. Some of them, many in Africa, have become more urbanised without much – if any – industrialisation. South America, with a similar urbanisation level to Europe, is largely still an economically developing region (Figure 1.5). On the other hand, urban population growth in most of the richer developed countries has slowed down. There is also generally growing apprehension about population increase, high levels of unemployment, poverty, slums, soaring infrastructure demands and costs, ecological dangers, etc. in cities, and about further decline of rural areas and 'lagging' regions. Responding to these trends, politicians and planners often

1.5 View of La Paz, Bolivia, where 'informal' development has massively spread uphill merging with the new unplanned city of El Alto (Harry Smith)

focus on what they perceive as 'urban problems', which they often see as including excessive in-migration and the limits to urban absorptive capacity.

During the twentieth century many attempts to 'explain' rapid urban growth relied heavily upon the apparently clear-cut links between the level of gross national product (GNP) per capita and the urban proportion of total population. However, this approach has been questioned because GNP per capita has been argued to be an indicator of economic growth rather than development (see Chapter 2), and urban population levels do not reflect the complexity of the urbanisation process (Drakakis-Smith 2000).

Managing urbanisation

The UN Department of Economic Affairs found that three-quarters of all governments reported that they are dissatisfied with the spatial distribution of their populations, developing countries (79 per cent) being more likely than developed countries (65 per cent) to report dissatisfaction. Developing countries are also more likely to have adopted policies to ameliorate spatial distribution. For example, almost three-quarters of developing countries have enacted policies to reduce the flow of persons moving to metropolitan areas, but only 12 per cent of developed countries have done so (United Nations Department of Economic and Social Affairs – Population Division 2004). In the past, urban primacy in developing countries was seen as illustration of serious developmental problems. Affected countries were alleged to be 'overurbanised' or possessing abnormal urban hierarchies very different from the more balanced rank-size hierarchies found in European and North American urban systems. Such comparisons revealed the weakness of these concepts – they were and are heavily based on Eurocentric 'norms'. This is, of course, not to minimize the real problems that rapid urban growth had posed for many cities in developing countries, but it does indicate that they must be assessed in their own regional and national contexts rather than measured against an inappropriate and often mythical European or North American standard (Drakakis-Smith 2000).

Many different strategies for controlling or limiting urban growth, and especially large or metropolitan city growth, have been attempted or proposed since the 1950s, mostly focused mainly on migration. Planners tend to stress the importance of the migration variable because it is felt to be to some extent practically controllable. The first group of strategies involves policing measures: returning rural–urban migrants to home or other rural areas (e.g. the Sapang Palay case, Dwyer 1975) and prohibiting migration to cities (through population registration, resident permits and charges, food and other material rationing, etc. – e.g. the practice in China). These approaches have usually been based on the questionable assumption that 'pressure' on urban and metropolitan areas is due entirely or mainly to in-migration; they were rarely politically acceptable, but have been effective in China and Burma, albeit with little success in Indonesia (Oberai 1987).

The second group of strategies provides incentives to keep population in rural areas: reducing the flow of migrants at source through rural development measures, land reform, etc. Rural development programmes and the 'Green Revolution', however, may have effects such as increasing rural employment only marginally and often in fact expels labour through displacement by larger farmers and capital-intensive farm modernisation, as well as reproducing urban sector conditions and disparities in the countryside. In addition, such measures may reduce the physical and socio-cultural distance between rural and urban areas, through schooling, new roads construction, and so on, thus encouraging out-migration to urban areas (Rhoda 1979; Oberai 1987). Another measure is redirecting the flow of migrants to rural frontier areas through resettlement schemes, etc. Spontaneous colonisation is very important in some areas where new land is still available, but official schemes tend to be expensive and failure-prone, with quantitatively negligible results (Rhoda 1979; Oberai 1987).

The third group of strategies promote the development of alternative urban centres: redirecting migrants to intermediate urban 'growth poles' or 'new cities'. Such programmes tend to be high-risk and expensive with little to negligible overall impact on the growth of major cities. Practice has often ignored the 'leading industry' requirement of 'growth pole' theory, leading often to the mere building of expensive industrial estates in cities with little industrial potential. Brasilia was seen as a successful case, with central government as a plausible leading industry, but impact on former capital Rio de Janeiro's growth is uncertain (not measurable). Growth poles appear to work best if there is an existing local entrepreneurial group ready to take up central government incentives (Oberai 1987; Renaud 1981; Brookfield 1975).

Besides attempting directly to control rural to urban migration, some countries have tried disincentives within cities, such as constraints on urban/metropolitan job creation, especially through negative controls (planning controls, permits, etc.) on industry. These policies have tended to be ineffective because simple efficiency criteria may demand full use of economies of scale in metropolitan areas' availability of skilled labour, technical services, access to transport, markets. Other national policy measures (e.g. general economic development planning and controls) may have created enormous (but often unnoticed) pressures for industry and other sectors to stay close to government in the capital city – to negotiate licences, political favours, etc. Finally, the objective of restricting big-city growth tends to conflict with those of import-substitution industrialisation strategies (see Chapter 2).

Many countries adopted urban development policies to restrain unwanted concentration of urban growth in the 1960s and 1970s, but policies were rarely carried through to a significant extent due to lack of awareness of the strength of forces encouraging urban growth, and lack of serious political commitment. Where more actively pursued, there has been little consensus about the effectiveness of such policies, or indeed their appropriateness. In some countries the rate of growth of the 'primate' city has declined, some secondary cities have begun to grow faster than primate cities, and core-periphery disparities appear to have narrowed. However, it is quite unclear whether these changes have been the result of spatial policy (Richardson 1987). There is a growing conviction that spatial strategies may arguably not be the most efficient or effective route to greater equity.

Generalised objectives of past national urban development policies have aimed to reduce 'pressure' on large metropolitan cities and create a more 'balanced' urban system (or urban/rural system). But when is a city becoming too big? What kind of urban population distribution is a 'balanced' one? Is there an 'optimum' city size? Should the size consideration focus only on the scale of population? How about economic, social and local environmental factors? The environmental movement tends to be hostile to the large city, but there is some disagreement as to whether ecological problems necessarily grow with city size per se. Can factors such as, for example, increasing technical capacity, economies of scale and administrative efficiency, if associated with city size, overcome potential or actual ecological problems? Thus it is difficult to make a case for generalised assumptions that any particular metropolitan city size is excessive (or that any urban pattern is 'unbalanced').

Nonetheless there continues to be political pressure – and some degree of societal consensus (environmental lobbies, etc.) – to 'contain' the growth of large cities on the grounds that congestion and communication costs may become very high, and that shelter and services lags may become too severe and costly. However, in a climate of structural adjustment and globalisation, governments in most rapidly urbanising countries have withdrawn from pursuing intervention policies and become more sensitive to powerful market trends. There have also been concerns that efforts at macro-spatial planning may divert attention from the traditional role of urban development policy making, i.e. promoting, assisting and supervising equitable development within towns and cities. Linn (1983) notes that controlling city size is very rarely an appropriate policy instrument to deal with issues such as, for example, congestion and pollution, and that policy intervention should be directed at sources of inefficiency, through for example pricing of externalities (pollution and congestion charges) and removing subsidies from urban services.

More indirect but effective measures such as fiscal policies are increasingly employed rather than planning and policing. Measures include: using broad economic policy tools to favour, say, the primary sector (e.g. redirecting trade policy, price policy, etc., to support agricultural production); reducing open or hidden subsidies which may encourage unwanted city growth, especially in large/capital cities; reducing excessive concentration of non-cost recoverable infrastructure investment financed from national taxation; moving towards full cost pricing (i.e. progressively reducing subsidies) for public sector services such as water, energy and transport, which tend to be concentrated in cities; eliminating price controls exclusively or mainly benefiting large cities, for example basic foods, petrol, etc.; and generally establishing appropriate taxes on metropolitan life (wage taxes, higher and more efficiently collected property taxes, metro residential taxes).

These new approaches are essentially neo-liberal in approach: they rest on the core assumption of the prime role of the price mechanism (ideally market determined), with appropriate public sector taxation and management to achieve a 'near optimal' distribution of activities (and ultimately population) within the urban/rural network. Thus urban development policy-making increasingly relies primarily on economic and institutional factors rather than on the much-criticised more abstract planning approach of the post-war era.

Conclusion

This chapter has shown that the process of urbanisation, whereby the world's population is becoming increasingly and predominantly urban, has been and continues to be dramatic in terms of its intensity and its consequences for human well-being – both positive and negative. Urbanisation has been uneven both in time and space, with its 'take-off' in core countries in the nineteenth century being linked to the expansion of industrial capitalism, and its latter manifestations in the now rapidly urbanising world being linked to globalisation. However, the chapter has also shown that there is not a single and direct relationship between urbanisation and development, with some parts of the world currently undergoing urbanisation without corresponding economic growth. In order to more fully understand the connections between urbanisation and levels of what has been conceptualised over the last 50 years as 'development', we need to look at the evolution of development discourse in the following chapter, before returning to the phenomenon of urbanisation, seen from a political economic viewpoint, in Chapter 3.

Chapter 2
Development discourse

Introduction

This chapter introduces some fundamental concepts of development discourse as the basis for the critical analysis of the evolution of planning and housing policy and practice in what has been called the 'developing world', to be the foundation for an alternative approach. The chapter initially reviews the evolution of development theory and practice, and then looks at some alternative theories. The period covered is from the early 1950s, with the end of the Second World War, through to the early 1990s. This is followed by a section which looks at changes in development discourse in the 1990s and more recent trends. One of these trends is then further developed in the following chapter, and Chapters 2 and 3 together thus provide the basis for arguments in relation to housing and planning in subsequent chapters.

Concepts and origins of 'development'

The concept of 'development' essentially contains an element of directed or 'progressive' change – whether in political, economic, social or cultural spheres. Development theory is generally more concerned with change than conventional social science disciplines and is essentially interdisciplinary, although not always dealt with this way. As Hettne (1990) has pointed out, *development theory* refers mainly to the academic understanding of this change, but due to the normative nature of much of this theory, it has always been closely linked to *development policies and strategies* – i.e. deliberate action to specifically promote change. Development policy and strategy, as directed change or transformation, implies an actor or actors – and this has usually been assumed to be the nation state, with these policies and strategies generally being defined at national level. Because of this, these policies and strategies often in fact fulfil ideological purposes even after their theoretical basis has been queried, and this is why approaches to development have tended to accumulate rather than replace each other. *Development practice* is itself often based as much on ideology and pragmatism as on any theory, policy or strategy, and hence we have opted to use the term *development discourse* here, to incorporate theoretical, strategic, practical and ideological actions which are generated around the basic concept of 'development'.

Development is thus seen as progressive and deliberately directed, but also cumulative – i.e. it builds on itself and is also usually seen as irreversible. The conceptual underpinning of the term is seen as being based in the Enlightenment and the creation of nation states in Europe from the mid-seventeenth century, which in turn laid the foundation for the industrial revolution. This basis for the concept has been criticised as fundamentally Western, leading to the embedding of ideas such as backward and advanced; barbarian and civilised; traditional and modern – although some of these were of earlier origin (e.g. the Roman period). These concepts became institutionalised in the nineteenth century in the West, with the growth of the state and associated bureaucracy, professional elites and technological, industrial and military systems – later expressed in both socialist and capitalist societies, and closely associated with imperial conquest (see also following chapter). All the major Western economic development strategies have been based on this basic concept of progressive, deliberative, cumulative and irreversible development, including the liberal economic model, state capitalism, Keynesianism, the soviet model, etc., as briefly described below.

The *liberal economic model* relies on the notion of market forces and is characterised by the English development experience in the era of the industrial revolution – i.e. gradual industrialisation starting with light industry, high profits and low wages which, with technological advancement and expanding markets, led to increasing private investment and replication of this system. However, as replication became increasingly difficult with the emergence of a competitive capitalist world economy, this led to state power being used to protect newly industrialising countries as national sovereignty was seen to be threatened by possible economic subordination – i.e. the *state capitalist strategy* as developed in continental European countries and, later, America and Japan in the late nineteenth and early twentieth centuries. In reaction to the limitations to constantly growing markets, most clearly evidenced in the Great Depression of the 1930s, *Keynesianism* allocated the responsibility for stability and continuous growth of the capitalist system to state intervention and planned investment – so-called 'mature' capitalism. This became the dominant ideology in the industrialised capitalist world especially after the Second World War – particularly in those countries with social democratic tendencies. In the same period, the *Soviet model*, in contrast, to a great extent continued the state-capitalist model of pre-revolutionary Russia, but with a more dominant role for the state enforcing rapid basic accumulation. In all of these macro-economic development strategies, the state was expected to play a key role, albeit with varying degrees of concentration, and, while differing significantly with regards to the means to achieve development, the end – *modernisation* – was similar.

Development, as thus defined, became increasingly associated with *economic* development – directed at a national level. During this period, the contemporary alternatives of more localised models of social development – evidenced in nostalgic romanticism, but also in classical anarchism, utopian socialism and rural populism – became sidelined as social and political movements and confined to an ideological level. Only after the world economic crisis in the 1970s was the nation state's role in development again challenged. However, the role of the state in defining what is 'development' still continues to dominate, albeit with less direct control over economic development, which in fact has largely been taken over by global market forces. The relevance of this for social development has been continually queried in the past three decades, increasingly by those countries who, by the narrow definition of macro-economic development, are considered 'under-developed' in some form, as well as from sections of society within the so-called 'developed' world.

Overview of the evolution of development theory and praxis

An overview of development discourse in the 1950–90 period can be structured around four principal paradigms: modernisation; dependency theory; 'basic needs' and 'redistribution with growth'; and neo-liberalism. This does not necessarily signify a chronological progression as, although various theoretical positions have arisen as reactions to previous theories, many of these continue to exist in parallel. As noted above, development practice does not necessarily directly follow the evolution of development theory, although it is influenced by theory and, in turn, influences this, albeit often implicitly rather than explicitly. Typical accounts of the evolution of development discourse start in the mid-twentieth century, when the term began to be used specifically to refer to countries which were perceived as less developed, although this itself arose from the post-war re-construction effort, as is explained below.[1]

The modernisation paradigm

After the Second World War, following the Bretton Woods[2] meetings between world powers in 1944, the United States reluctantly accepted the role of supporting the political stability of nation states and international security, partly due to the perceived threat of the spread of communism. Post-War Europe was rebuilt through Marshall Aid from the United States, which had suffered little and gained much from supporting the war effort. The International Monetary Fund and International Bank for Reconstruction and Development (more generally termed the 'World Bank') were created specifically for this purpose – the former to provide short-term credits to correct deficits in current accounts, the latter longer-term credits for development. In parallel, there was a felt need to rapidly decolonise, albeit maintaining foreign policy interests in the face of international tensions created by the 'Cold War'. Reconstruction in Europe (and Japan) was achieved mainly by the end of the 1950s, after a period of highly financed, tariff-protected industrial development as the basis for regained internal macro-economic balance, which subsequently permitted more openness to international competitiveness in a 'liberal world market'.

During this period, former colonial powers either lost their international territorial possessions (such as Germany) or looked for ways to de-colonise and end the costs of maintaining colonial administrations while retaining economic advantage in the previous colonies. American foreign policy also supported decolonisation, although this was in order to get access to new markets in areas dominated by colonial powers. Despite East–West detente, the United States and its European allies continued to be worried about Soviet influence in newly independent states – following the imposition of Soviet development models on Eastern European countries – and thus Western aid was seen as a means to ensure peaceful decolonisation to new elites which were culturally conditioned by the colonial powers and less likely to opt for radical development paths. Marshall Aid and foreign aid were thus the background for early post-war social and economic development policies, and the assertion of mutual benefits between rich and poor countries led eventually to development economics as a distinct discipline. Despite some emulation of Western development as the model for modernisation, there was recognition that the problems in the so-called 'backward areas' were specific and qualitatively different from those of the 'Western' and 'Socialist bloc' worlds, thus leading to the appearance of the term 'Third World'.[3] Early development theory thus saw economic development as necessarily different for the 'Third' world from that for the 'First' and 'Second' worlds, but still based on the experience of Western economic history and its underlying concept of modernisation (Figure 2.1).

In this *modernisation paradigm*, development was equated with economic growth, which was measured in terms of Gross National Product (GNP) with the objective of expanding per capita GNP output faster than population growth. The bulk of development literature in this paradigm thus focused on population growth and increased investment capacity. As domestic savings were perceived to be limited, this led to foreign aid being seen as a key to economic development. This was the general theme of the first UN Development Decade (1960–70), as proposed during the 1950s. This envisaged global transfers of resources through international aid, permitting the creation of strong post-colonial states where rapid state-led modernisation would close the existing First World–Third World economic gap. The basic objective was to increase the share of employment and output of manufacturing and services while decreasing that of agriculture – i.e. following the economic development paths of Europe and other 'developed' countries. Concern for poverty and inequality was secondary in this approach, with income redistribution seen as coming subsequent to economic growth, mainly through

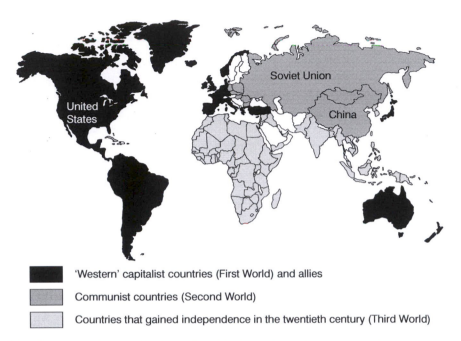

'Western' capitalist countries (First World) and allies

Communist countries (Second World)

Countries that gained independence in the twentieth century (Third World)

2.1 World map showing West and East blocks and countries that decolonised post-war (Drawing by Harry Smith)

'trickle down'. The maximum transferability of the factors of production – land, labour and capital – was considered a fundamental pre-condition for economic growth and thus the general commodification of goods and services was seen as an integral part of development; for example, traditional land rights were to be transformed into private property ownership to underpin investment and improve productivity through market action.

This initial approach in development economics from the late 1940s and 1950s was essentially a *liberal economic model*, as it was based on an assumption that deregulated international trade, free movement of capital and an international monetary system (based on the US dollar) would spread the benefits of development across the world through specialisation based on comparative advantages and division of labour enforced by competition, and that – once initiated – growth would be automatic and trickle down to lower income groups. In time, however, the continuing coexistence in reality of both 'advanced/modern' and 'backward/ traditional' sectors in most of the so-called Third World, led to a growing recognition of the importance of other 'non-economic' factors for development – i.e. sociological, cultural, psychological and political. Thus, by the 1960s, modernisation theory grew in complexity and become more inter-disciplinary. The initial exclusively economic focus was accompanied by theories of cultural modernisation which stressed the transformation of values. These, however, were again modelled on Western value patterns and thus the transfer of Western political, social and cultural values and institutions through the training of modern 'elites' was openly advocated, being seen as an integral part of the overall development process. This included a stress on the importance of formal education as a basis for new social status, and a focus on the nuclear family, as opposed to kinship networks.

The initial liberal economic approach to modernisation and development was replaced by *Keynesian* interventionist thinking, which had heavily influenced the redevelopment of Europe, stressing the importance of strong interventionist states and full employment for economic growth and material developments. This position was readily adopted by the modern, mostly Western-educated, elite power structures created in the developing world through the decolonisation process, as it both suited their modernisation aims and allowed the strengthening of their power base. Keynesian policies, as opposed to the free market approach of liberalism, argued that development problems were a result of insufficient demand, and could be remedied by government policies to stimulate demand through expansion of public expenditure, reduction of taxation and promotion of private investment through incentives. The state was thus to take responsibility for stability and continuous growth of the capitalist system through intervention and planned investment. Development in Keynesian economics was, nevertheless, still primarily seen as a process of capital formation determined by the level of investment. In parallel, development thinking on international trade continued to follow liberal economic lines with a 'global' perspective as opposed to a Keynesian national 'closed economy' perspective. However, less developed countries producing primary commodities came to realise they were subject to deteriorating terms of trade in relation to the importing industrialised nations, and this led to a call to reverse the trend by investing in industrialisation, reinforcing the Keynesian focus on 'closed economies'.

An alternative to these capitalist economic development models was derived from Marxist models of development dominated by the *Soviet model*. These to a great extent continued the pre-Revolutionary Russian state capitalist policies, albeit from an ideologically opposite position, as from the 1920s Stalin opted for a modernisation model based on basic accumulation enforced by state intervention and military force. This implied mandatory state development planning; a transfer of resources from agriculture to industry through the collectivisation of the former; and emphasis on heavy industry and large-scale technologically developed industrial investment. Russian development theory was imposed as ideology on the Soviet Union and neighbouring states. Although very different in political and social context, as noted above, these strategies also assumed the basic modernisation approach to development.

By the late 1960s modernisation development policies were seen as failing. Even despite high levels of growth of manufacturing GDP in some countries, the promised benefits were failing to materialise for a substantial (and growing) part of the population. Capital intensive industrialisation proved incapable of generating sufficient employment to absorb the existing labour surplus let alone its growth. At the same time there were limited improvements or stagnation in agricultural productivity, massive rural to urban migration and high rising under- and un-employment, increasing social dependency rates and widening income inequalities, with increasing numbers of the population living in poverty. Modernisation theory was therefore criticised from the political left, centre and right. On the left, in academic circles and in the 'developing world', *dependency theory* emerged in the 1970s, as did 'Redistribution With Growth' and 'Basic Needs' from the political centre, however the most influential critique came from the political right, through *neo-liberalism*.

Dependency theory

As early as the mid-1960s the Euro-centric modernisation approach to development began to be challenged – primarily in Latin America – and a theory dealing specifically with problems of 'under-development' was born. This approach, termed dependency theory (or 'dependencia'), stressed that structural development of one part of the world was usually linked to the under-development of another. Closely linked to this was the idea that the concept of development had been distorted by 'cultural' imperialism – i.e. Western values. Thus self-reliance required firstly the evolution of indigenous development thinking itself. The 'dependency' school emerged from the convergence of two main intellectual trends – initially a structuralist critique of development and later Neo-Marxism.

The former grew from debates on inflation in Latin America in the post Great Depression period and was led by the Economic Commission for Latin America (CEPAL) established 1948 in Santiago de Chile. The CEPAL position criticised the development of a centre-periphery model in international trade – stating that only the central nations benefit – and promoted state planned and supported import substitution (i.e. the 'closed economy') to break the peripheral position created by export of primary products and as the basis for industrial development – with a strong focus on regional integration. Later Neo-Marxism influenced dependency theory, emphasising the role of the peasantry in the struggle against imperialist dominance, as opposed to conventional Marxism which was based on the rise of an industrial proletariat. Importantly, the neo-Marxist approach did not require the prior development of capitalism for the industrial proletariat to evolve, but was based on a 'non-capitalist' path to socialism, through land reform and state sector industrialisation, as came to be practised in China and Cuba.

The essential elements of the dependency approach were that (Hettne 1990: 91):

- the most important obstacles to development were not capital or entre-preneurial skills, but the international division of labour (i.e. external not internal obstacles);
- the international division of labour was analysed in terms of relations between regions, of which the centre and periphery have particular importance as a transfer of surplus takes place from the latter to the former;
- as the periphery is deprived of its surplus, development of the centre implied under-development at the periphery, thus being inter-linked; and
- the periphery was thus doomed to under-development unless it managed to disassociate itself from the world market through national self-reliance – this requiring a revolutionary political transformation. When external obstacles were removed, development would be more or less automatic and endogenous.

Dependency led to distinct schools of development thinking in the 1970s, however, it was more a new viewpoint rather than a new theory as the concept of development *per se* was essentially similar to that of modernisation development theories. This was one of the main criticisms levelled against it – the ultimate causes of under-development were not identified other than the thesis that they originated at the 'centre'. The fact that a number of developing countries were at the time industrialising rapidly also contradicted the theory, as did the experience of those which tried to de-link and follow self-reliant strategies. Various Latin American countries which adopted dependency-breaking development strategies were not successful in the longer term, as technological and financial dependence on the West still remained dominant and their internal markets were limited due to the highly unequal nature of income distribution, thus leading to the use of higher subsidies for production. Overall, however, dependency theories assisted with the decline of the modernisation paradigm, pointing out its inadequacy to explain real developments in the developing world in the 1960s. They also influenced development policies and strategies in practice at both national and international levels,[4] and stimulated the later demands for a New International Economic Order articulated in the mid-1970s.

'Basic needs' and 'Redistribution with growth'

In parallel with dependency theory, Basic Needs and Redistribution with Growth development approaches evolved in the 1970s with the realisation that conventional development strategies (i.e. liberal economic, Keynesian or state-capitalist models) implied social or regional inequality as a necessary price for growth, and that economic growth did not necessarily eliminate poverty. These new development strategies were underpinned by relatively conservative 'supply-side' economics that grew essentially from criticism of the failures of Keynesian 'demand-side' economics. It was argued that, with the existence of 'supply-side constraints' and 'factor price distortions', stimulation of demand led to higher prices, inflation and unemployment. In addition, high labour costs and low capital prices, artificially maintained by political intervention, exacerbated this situation, not promoting the substitution of capital by labour. It was argued that the result was unequal income distribution, consumption and investment power, leading to a slow down in demand and hence the economy.

Redistribution with Growth development strategies, on the other hand, proposed that the objectives of growth and equity should not conflict, with a broader pattern of growth being generated through paying special attention to targeted poverty groups. This was to be achieved through the redistribution of new increments of growth towards the poor rather than through the redistribution of existing assets and income – regarded as politically and economically unacceptable. Lowering the relative price of labour and increasing that of capital would increase the substitution of capital with labour, and hence employment and output through labour-intensive technologies. Improvements in the incomes of the absolute poor would thus require transfers and subsidies and improved access to essential goods and services such as water, electricity, sewerage, housing, health facilities, schools etc. – i.e. the supply of associated *Basic Needs*.[5] The fundamental goal of these linked approaches was thus an improvement in the absolute incomes of the poor rather than redressing relative inequalities in income distribution.

The related Basic Needs and Redistribution with Growth development strategies were taken up in the mid to late 1970s by several international agencies such as the International Labour Organization (ILO) and the World Bank, although with different emphases. The ILO focused on employment, and offered a positive assessment of the so-called urban 'informal sector'[6] and recommended technical assistance for small-scale enterprises, deregulation of this sector and development of appropriate technology (Figure 2.2). The World Bank, on the other hand, focused on provision of basic needs for the poor and redistribution of new economic growth, arguing that these were not contradictory. The strategy inherent in this approach, however, was also still essentially a modification of previous Keynesian modernisation strategies in its focus on social engineering – i.e. balancing social and economic development as a planning strategy. While the importance of the political dimension was to some extent recognised in this approach, the means to achieve policy reform in non-supportive political circumstances was not very well developed.

2.2 Informal vending in La Paz, Bolivia (Harry Smith)

The key factors underpinning the 1970s macro-economic development strategies based on these approaches had the following goals:

- to increase productivity, output and incomes and redistribute income and investment increments derived from growth;
- to introduce strategies of public service expenditures in favour of the poor (i.e. infrastructure and social services) as a basis to alleviate poverty, inequality and unemployment;
- to deregulate the informal sector, develop labour intensive and appropriate technologies and improve the access of small-scale enterprises to finance, markets, technical and managerial assistance.

The neo-liberal reaction

During the 1970s the rise of trans-national corporations – made possible through improvements in communication, information and transport technology – changed the economic world order and reinforced the pattern of international investment in relation to labour processes. Skilled labour at the centre was thus increasingly replaced by unskilled labour at the periphery. As such, much industrialisation in the so-called developing world was no longer 'indigenous', but essentially tied in to global processes of production and hence simple centre-periphery models, such as dependency theory, were undermined. In parallel with this, the unilateral suspension of the Bretton Woods arrangements by the United States, the oil price increases of 1973 and 1979, and the transition from fixed to variable exchange rates, with a sharp rise in international interest rates, all represented major shocks to the world economy in the 1970s (Hoogvelt 1985). The aftershocks were a global tendency to recession and unemployment, rising debt levels, low and declining commodity prices, balance of payments deficits and increasing protectionism. Interest payment on the national debt, usually in local currency, became such a burden that it restricted the possibilities of government policies, as these switched to restrictive fiscal policy in order to restore budgetary equilibrium.

While fiscal restrictions were adopted voluntarily by most 'developed' countries, they were imposed on 'developing' countries. The national debt of these latter countries, as distinct from the former, was mostly expressed in foreign currencies. For these countries adjustment policies for reducing foreign debt and/or meeting debt service requirements generated not only fiscal, but also balance of payments problems. In general, developing countries initially reacted to the changing external context by implementing a variety of ad hoc domestic stabilisation measures, often supported by the International Monetary Fund (IMF), the World Bank and regional development banks. However, in order to alleviate the immediate debt problems, stand-by credits from the IMF were required and the IMF was only willing to provide such credits if certain conditions were met. While the IMF previously focused on currencies and international debt, and the World Bank on poverty and development, from the 1980s the two organisations began to co-ordinate their activities through Structural Adjustment Programmes (SAPs), addressing both debt and economic growth together, in addition to the promotion of longer-term programmes of economic adjustment tied to externally determined policy and institutional conditions. This was first applied to the most heavily indebted countries (Mexico and Brazil) in the early 1980s, but rapidly grew in importance, although in addition a number of domestic adjustment and liberalisation programmes continued to be initiated. In this way the approval of the IMF became a precondition for getting new loans from the World Bank and commercial banks, and getting official development assistance from developed countries.

During the 1980s the World Bank staked its institutional reputation on the proposition that the application of a standard package of measures, designed to remove policy-created obstacles ('distortions') to the expansion of output, would reconcile macro-economic adjustment with growth in developing countries. The resulting emphasis in development strategy was on policy changes, as opposed to previous emphases on boosting aggregate demand and better allocation of investment. The purpose of the policy packages was to remove economically damaging government interventions in markets, especially those for foreign exchange, credit, agricultural commodities and labour. The three pillars of Structural Adjustment Programmes (SAPs) were 'getting prices right, letting markets work and reforming public institutions', the private sector being seen as poised to take over (more efficiently) after state withdrawal. SAPs were thus fundamentally designed to adjust 'malfunctioning' economies to become viable components in a global economic system. By early 1992, 78 countries had accepted World Bank structural adjustment packages and many others introduced essentially similar policy frameworks without formal agreements.

The countries implementing SAPs were fundamentally altered through the change of the role of the state, food supply, urban–rural interaction and environmental strategies. Key elements of the resulting *neo-liberalist* development policies promoted by the IMF and World Bank were (and continue to be) market-oriented development strategies; minimal roles for the state; promotion of 'free' trade; financial discipline; seeking comparative advantage; and targeted prosperity through economic growth. A critical assumption of this 'new development orthodoxy', however, is that 'efficiently produced' goods will find a ready market, regardless of the nature of potential exports (often non-manufactured) and the particular national, regional or international context. However, in contrast, it has been argued that 'free' trade is little more than a myth, and that the existing, highly inequitable global relations of production and exchange reduce or eliminate the potential advantages of increased or more 'efficient' exports of primary commodities by most countries in the South.

In parallel with the above economic development policy changes, the conception of the role of government in the economy underwent a change around about 1980. The changing context for economic growth, together with the perceived failure of many previous state-led development approaches, led eventually to a fundamentalist reaction criticising the role of the state in economic planning and intervention, and stressing the positive effects of liberalisation of foreign trade as a basis for development. This theoretical counter-revolution came to a position of dominance in the 1980s in the context of the anti-Keynesian neo-liberal wave in the West and perceived success of the rise of free market ideology in the East. This neo-liberal position asserted that poor countries are poor due mainly to mismanagement, economic distortions and corruption, and stressed the benefits of markets which governments should not negate.

Neo-liberal policy in the North was based on monetarism and assumptions concerning the long-run efficiency of the market in resource allocation. This minimises the economic role of the state and advocates liberalisation of the economy, focusing on foreign trade as the engine of growth with a search for comparative economic advantage and promotion of indigenous entrepreneurial development. The strong states in the North thus increased their commitment to market-oriented international trade and encouraged developing countries to opt for export-oriented strategies (while not necessarily importing the resulting goods). The leading development agencies (especially the IMF and World Bank) argued that the principal cause of under-development was internal – not external – and thus focused on macro-economic re-structuring ('structural adjustment'). They also stressed the relative unimportance of physical capital compared to human development policies. Thus, while there was growing consensus among 'developing' countries that there was a need for radical reform of the international world economic order (see below), development agencies began to call for radical domestic reforms in developing countries.

The Newly Industrialising Countries (NICs) of East Asia (Hong Kong, Singapore, Taiwan, South Korea, Malaysia, Thailand, Indonesia and the Philippines) – which predominantly benefited from this development process – were widely cited as examples of the success of this approach, although it was argued that the generally high rates of growth and structural change that these economies have experienced blinded observers to the special circumstances of their development (Dixon *et al.* 1995). In particular, Hong Kong and Singapore were city states developed during the colonial period as trans-shipment and strategic centres (Figure 2.3); the basis for industrialisation was laid in Taiwan and South Korea during Japanese colonisation, and in the 1950s and 1960s they became key to American global and regional strategy, receiving large volumes of aid.[7] The 'ASEAN Four' (Malaysia, Thailand, Indonesia and the Philippines) are more typical of developing countries, but are also well endowed with a wide range of strategic products and most occupied key positions in American global and regional strategy, with attendant large in-flows of aid: Thailand in the 1960s, Indonesia in the late 1960s and early 1970s, and the Philippines since the 1950s.

In addition, it was argued that all the NICs and the ASEAN Four generally experienced long-term political and economic stability, and that they have constituted a self-reinforcing regional market. The reduction of absorption capacity for their exports in the United States in fact led to development of domestic markets and strengthening relationships between Japan and the NICs with the poorer economies of the region, leading to continued growth and rapid integration of these economies. Three waves of industrial development in the region can be identified – Japan after the Second World War, NICs in the 1960s and 1970s and

2.3 View of Hong Kong Island, Victoria Harbour and Kowloon (© 2003 Hong Kong Trade Development Council. Photographer: Graham Uden)

the ASEAN Four (particularly Malaysia and Thailand) since the early 1980s. SAPs in the 1980s, in fact, led to a reorientation to export industrialisation.

While the general applicability of the neo-liberal approach, and structural adjustment with export-led growth has been queried, it was also argued that the economic growth experienced in the Newly Industrialising Countries did not lead to eradication of poverty and that the environmental impact of economic development has also been negative – particularly in Taiwan and South Korea, with noxious processes and products being relocated to the poorer countries of the region since the early 1980s. Civil rights have also been long repressed in these countries with only recent liberalisation. In all, the state has actually played a major role in the economy and development process, with concomitant high levels of state expenditure, direct government involvement in production and high levels of tariff protection to stimulate import substitution industrial development. It can be argued that liberalisation was thus a product of, rather than the cause of, economic growth.

Other important development positions

Other important development positions in evidence up to the 1990s, while not seen as fundamental paradigms as such and of less influence in practice, include the globalisation of development theory, later Marxism and alternative development approaches.

The globalisation of development theory

Dependency theorists were primarily concerned with the effects of imperialism in peripheral countries, but implicit in their analysis was the concept that development and under-development needed to be seen in the context of world capitalism. The economic crises of the 1970s reinforced this, illustrating the extent to which an interdependent global economy had become reality. Dependence was thus increasingly seen as a world-wide phenomenon and subsequently trends to a more global analysis emerged. This was also reflected in the rise in international diplomacy oriented to global reforms. The globalisation of development theory thus evolved, based on an acceptance of interdependence – whether physical ('only one earth'); political ('new world order'); or economic (the 'global marketplace') (Hettne 1990).

The concept of global physical interdependence was based on physical, biological and ecological concepts of finiteness and wholeness which transcend national borders, and developed particularly in the 1970s through models such as 'Limits to Growth' (Meadows and Forrester 1972). Concerning the political world order, both the New International Economic Order (NIEO), originating in the South, and later the Brandt Commission Report originating in the North, proposed 'one world – one system' approaches. NIEO demands included global price stabilisation, increased aid, changes in the international monetary system, improved technology transfer and increased food security. The Brandt Report can be seen as a belated response to NIEO demands, which linked the needed resources for global redistributive transfers to the reduction and taxation of the arms trade. Both are aspects of global reform strategies in that they focused on the world as a single system, the former emphasising 'zero-sum' dependence whereas the latter stressed mutuality of interdependent interests. However, the need for supporting international political institutions to turn these positions into practice was never really confronted. On the contrary, the northern countries responded to the NIEO by variously applying 'alleviationist' strategies (quick actions on minor problems), or general acquiescence but delay (i.e. symbolic declarations) in anticipation of the erosion of 'developing world' group solidarity. The Brandt Report initiative was effectively blocked by the Reagan administration and the neo-liberalism which grew under this, underpinning the structural adjustment orthodoxy of the 1980s and 1990s.

These concepts of global interdependent development fall more generally under the term 'world development' and a series of 'world-system' oriented schools which emerged from the mid-1970s. These differ fundamentally from more state-centric concepts of development through conceptualising economic development at a global level. The world system approach asserts that the capitalist world economy has been essentially in existence since the sixteenth century, and from then onwards this system incorporated growing numbers of previously more or less isolated and self-sufficient societies into a complex system of power relations – this process of expansion having two dimensions: geographical broadening and socio-economic deepening. The result of this expansion was that a small number of core states transformed a huge external arena into a periphery – first Eastern Europe, then Latin America, Asia and Africa. Between the core states and the periphery, semi-peripheries are identified, each of these having different roles within the system, these changing as the system goes through periods of expansion and contraction. This approach assumes that remaining external areas will eventually be incorporated into the system (Hettne 1990).

Another manifestation of the world system approach is 'neo-structuralism' in which the world economy is seen as a structured whole, with its constituent parts all displaying various forms and degrees of interdependency. An example of this approach is the trans-national capitalist system approach, which states that the capitalist system has essentially changed from national to trans-national with trans-national corporations as the most significant actors. It hypothesises that a new trans-national community is emerging, made up of people from different nations, but with similar ideas and values as well as patterns of behaviour. On the other hand, national societies are undergoing a process of disintegration, including destruction of indigenous economies and concentration of property and income. The resulting process of marginalisation leads to increasing repression and authoritarianism in both under-developed and developed countries.

World system analyses strongly underline the limited possibilities of any nationally controlled development process. Development is thus basically a matter of changing the structural position from peripheral to semi-peripheral, a possibility limited in fact to relatively few countries. The world system theorists point to three options (Hettne 1990):

- the strategy of dedicatedly seizing the chance (e.g. state developmentalism as implemented in the Newly Industrialising Countries);
- the strategy of promotion by invitation and preferential access (based on comparative advantages such as low wages, high stability etc.); and
- the strategy of self-reliance, the most difficult in the current world system.

The book will return to this analysis in the following chapter.

Later Marxist approaches

Later Marxism differs from classical Marxism and Neo-Marxism in its definition of 'capitalism', which world system theorists define as a system of exchange operating at a global level. Such a definition of capitalism at world level renders standard Marxist definitions of class too rigid. Some later Marxist analysis thus differentiates between industrial and merchant capital – the former being capable of generating surplus value whereas merchant capital is created by 'unequal' exchange – while others see the world system as an aggregation of national capitalisms (and other non-capitalist modes of production) as opposed to one world system. This Marxist analysis points to the coexistence of several modes of production and their 'articulation' in specific social formations. This 'theory of articulation' developed from Marxist anthropology, but has theoretical links with dependency. Under-development is explained by the fact that the capitalist mode of production is articulated with non-capitalist modes and dominates these – large numbers of non-capitalist modes having been suggested, including Asiatic, ancient, feudal, colonial, peasant, statist, lineage, petty commodity mode, etc.

The problem of development in this perspective is thus the extent to which the capitalist mode dominates other modes, and how these latter are gradually undermined or dissolved – usually through processes of modification and reproduction of pre-capitalist structures. The process of 'articulation' involves an asymmetric relationship wherein the reproduction of the non-capitalist forms is subordinated to the logic of the capitalist forms, but not absorbed by them and not eradicated either. Non-capitalist activities are thus integrated gradually and in an uneven way into the sphere of commodity production, consumption and exchange through an increasing use of tools and raw commodities purchased as commodities, an expanded division of labour, increasing wage labour, and increasing commodification of land, labour and capital. The state is seen as having a key role in this process, particularly through policies which destroy the conditions for independent reproduction of the non-capitalist mode in favour of a dominant capitalist mode.

Alternative development

The term 'alternative development' has been referred to above in several places. While there is no one 'alternative development', Hettne (1990) defines the principal attributes of this as:

- human needs oriented (both material and non-material);
- endogenous (coming from within each society and thus expressing its values and visions);

- self-reliant (each society relying primarily on its human, natural and cultural resources);
- ecologically sound (both locally and globally); and
- based on maximisation of self-management and participatory decision-making.

In the 'developing' world the interest in 'alternative development' generally grew from the then elite's rejection of American or Soviet materialism, and is associated most with the first generation of Asian and African leaders who stressed cultural revival and preservation rather than modernisation. Modern elites in the developing world, however, have in recent times tended to opt for conventional solutions as these are associated with existing power blocs. In the meantime, interest in the 'developed world' in forms of 'alternative development' has increased, arguably due to the perception that conventional development, based on a world view of automatic growth and progress, has reached an impasse.

While there are various forms of 'alternative development', two are briefly described here – sustainable development and 'Third System' politics. The former – arguably the strongest manifestation of 'alternative development' worldwide – came from the new environmental consciousness emerging in the 1970s, sometimes also termed 'eco-development'. Conventional growth and development theory premised on modernisation had been relatively unconcerned with the problem of scarcity, while Marxist theory saw this as being socially determined by the forces of production of the capitalist system. However, in the mid-1970s the realisation that absolute scarcity can exist led to the proposal of 'Limits to Growth' – both physical and social – as an alternative basis for development. Initial doomsday predictions of physical limits were later revised, but while some believe that relative scarcity will lead to technological innovation, others foresee increased competition and even violence – both between and within states. Environmental interdependence is increasingly seen as transcending political borders, emphasising the importance of international action and institutions.

Referring to 'Third System' politics, the 'First System' is seen as the system of power comprised of the governing structures of territorial states, and definition of the 'Second System' generally being the structures of economic power, for example corporations and banks. The 'Third System' refers to non-governmental and non-profit structures through which people act individually or collectively such as voluntary institutions and associations. The nature of Third System power means this usually has a territorial base, but the political issues raised are often trans-local and issue-based and there are increasing global linkages across such non-governmental and community-based networks. In the 'developing world', however, the organisational base of the Third System is still relatively weak and linkage between various non-governmental movements is still northern-dominated.

This analysis has had extensive impact on more recent developments in development discourse, such as 'good governance', with an emphasis on state engagement with social groups as much as with economic groups.

Development thinking in the 1990s

The evolution of development theory in the previous sections has not been a smooth evolutionary process, but one characterised by theoretical contradictions and ideological polarisation. Failures of development strategies based on development theory in the 1960s and 1970s, and the unexpected successes in industrialisation and economic growth in other countries outside of any specific theoretically based strategy (i.e. the Newly Industrialising Countries), led to some marginalisation of development studies in the 1990s. This was accentuated by intellectual and political changes, characterised by mono-disciplinary trends in academia and neo-liberal trends in dominant national politics. In addition, conventional wisdom concerning the future of modernity in the 'developed world' was questioned (Escobar 1995), with the possibility of applying insights from the 'developing world' increasingly being considered. As such, through the 1990s there was more convergence in thinking concerning 'development' across the world, while recognising different contexts and histories, and less stress on different strategies for the 'developed' and 'under-developed' countries.

Different development strategies promoted in the 1990s – now within a global context – include (Hettne 1990):

- neo-Keynesianism, proposing a new interventionist role for the state in balancing supply and demand, at a national, regional and global level, as a means to manage economic fluctuation. This has largely taken over from socialist and social democratic strategies in stressing the role of the state sector in development;[8] and
- neo-mercantilism, which proposes a regionalised world economic system segmented in largely self-sufficient macro-economic blocs, large enough to provide (protected) domestic markets which could benefit from economies of scale, but avoid excessive specialisation.

Most countries, however, did not follow any one distinct development policy or strategy – and if they did it was not for long. During the 1990s, rather than development strategies geared to fundamental socio-economic transformation, there more often tended to be crisis management strategies, thus reducing the relevance of development theory.

This crisis of development in practice was reflected in the 1990s by a growing literature on a 'crisis' or 'impasse' in development theory. Schuurman (1993) attributed this to:

- the increasingly short-term nature of development strategies in developing countries due to the growing economic restrictions of the debt crisis;
- the realisation that the gap between rich and poor countries continued to widen despite a range of development theories and strategies, and that most developing countries were unlikely to be able to bridge that gap whatever strategy they followed;
- the growing awareness of inter-dependence and environmental implications at a global level; and
- the loss of the 'socialist paradigm' and growing conviction that the world (capitalist) economy is increasingly integrated and development strategies focused mainly at a national level cannot be effective.

Schuurman also saw this as partially the effect of the advance of post-modernism within the social sciences, undermining the 'great narratives' of capitalism, socialism, communism etc. (otherwise termed meta-theories). In parallel, greater understanding of the growing divergence within the 'developing world', based on research into different development options within a comparative-historical context, has also led to a changing focus in development theory from assumed homogeneity of development approaches to one of diversity (Schuurman 1993: 29). This provided a much wider empirical basis for investigation of the range of influences in each context and thus more nuanced or 'fine-tuned' approaches, with less emphasis on the need for new dogmatic meta-theory.

Recent positions in development discourse

Pieterse (2001) argues that in current development discourse we have a wide range of development theories which have been adapted and built on the development meta-theories of the past half century, which are still being utilised, although often in modified form. Examples of these are:

- Neo-liberalism suffered many critiques in its 1990s' manifestation of struc-tural adjustment, but continues to be a dominant theme for the Washington Consensus,[9] albeit with tensions arising between the more 'traditional' ap-proach of the IMF and the more recent 'populist' approaches of the World Bank, with a more nuanced approach to policy change including aspects of new institutional economics.
- Neo-modernisation theory re-evaluates 'tradition', seeing this as a resource and not an obstacle to development. This is closely allied to re-interpretation of what is meant by political modernisation and concerns for 'good governance'. Post-colonial studies have also promoted new conceptions of modernity which are different from Western concepts.

- New international political economy theory is seen as revitalising dependency theory and critiques uneven globalisation, both as a process and a specific political economy project, such as in neo-liberal policies, and critically analyses the rise of the newly industrialising countries.
- Alternative development has now become incorporated in the mainstream in many ways, such as through emphasis on participation of civil society, partnership working with NGOs, decentralisation and especially the institutionalisation of human development objectives including gender, environmental issues and the importance of culture.
- Critical post-development theory, which has developed out of the querying of the nature of basic development concepts in alternative development, and is also associated with the new international political economy in its critique of the impact of globalisation, as well as environmental movements. The main focus is de-linking and local autonomy.

What has essentially happened is that there has been a turning away from the exclusive, competing, 'meta-theories' of the past, with these various analytical approaches being absorbed into 'mid-range' theories. In other words, theories need to be seen within their intellectual context, and relate to other theories when applied to complex reality. This is also affected fundamentally as with growing globalisation and regionalisation, nation states can no longer be seen as the 'standard unit of development' as in the past. In fact, several analyses are often needed in combination in such 'post-development' thinking, which acknowledges the analytical crises but works within these, accepting that any concept of development will always have difficulties in application in practice. Different approaches to development theory can be based on:

- development seen as part of social science and hence related to social and economic thinking (e.g. Martinussen 1997);
- development seen as ideology influenced by politics (e.g. Hoogvelt 2001); and
- a sociological approach to development knowledge which accepts both (e.g. Leys 1996).

A way to deal with the complexity of what development studies has become, suggested by Pieterse, is to link the various development discourses to different stakeholders and actors as these typically hold different viewpoints of what is and should be development. For instance, international agencies such as the World Bank and IMF tend to stress neo-liberalism, albeit with different emphases. The World Trade Organisation emphasises neo-mercantilism, whereas the United Nations focuses on human development. International and local non-governmental organisations also focus on human development, but also on other forms of alternative development, as do local actors, who may also promote anti-development. Nation states still tend to promote modernisation or neo-Keynesianism, although as noted above, there are usually various development positions in evidence across different parts and levels of governments.

Conclusion

The objective of this chapter has been to present a short and concise introduction to development discourse as the basis for understanding how development theory and practice have influenced theory and practice concerning human settlements in the rapidly urbanising world. While much of the theory and practice developing in housing and planning in these situations has not been explicitly linked to development discourse (theory and practice), the book argues that in fact this had a dominant role to play – albeit usually implicitly – in the evolution of housing and planning thinking and approaches, including the increasing sense of impasse in the 1990s and the changed perspectives after that. A major aim of the chapter has been to show this form of linkage and use the more recently evolving positions on development as a basis for arguing for new approaches for the sector. In this it opts to follow the new international political economy approach, as we consider this the most appropriate. However, other forms of analysis are possible, and as such we are not espousing a new meta-theory, but ways to 'substantive' analysis as a guide for action, in that meta-theories are seen to be of limited value as a means to comprehend reality and direct action.

Chapter 3
A new international political economy approach to urban development in the rapidly urbanising world

Introduction

As Hoogvelt (2001) explains, a political economy approach focuses on how power relations within societies structure economic relations and are in turn affected by these – i.e. on the relations between politics and economics. Political economy analyses in the past tended to focus on the nation state, or specific modes of production within societies, but in the past two decades they have become more internationally oriented. One trend in these analyses is to focus on international economic competition and the global balance of power. A second trend focuses on political and economic inter-dependence across the world, stressing the role of supra-national institutions and macro-regional economic blocs – i.e. a plural world order. A third approach examines the structure of global economic changes, with a focus on the dominant capitalist forces, and the effect these have on individual nation states through global, or world, systems. What is termed the *new international political economy approach* (see Chapter 2) attempts to transcend the structuralism of most of these approaches, balancing political and economic analyses with analysis of how these affect each other, but also how they are filtered through social (and cultural) institutions. It also uses historical analysis to determine dominant configurations of ideas, institutions and material forces within which action takes place, thus drawing together structure and agency. Individuals and individual institutions such as governments (i.e. agents) are therefore seen to work within – and change – the parameters created by more general structures. The future is thus not pre-determined in this approach, but open to alternatives which can be influenced by action.

This book argues that a new international political economy approach to urban development analysis can help transcend some of the impasse and fragmentation in development discourse as reflected in the shelter sector, and permit a more inclusive approach to understanding how urban planning and housing is developing and could develop in situations affected by rapid urbanisation. It does this through helping us understand the structural impact of what we term 'globalisation' on urbanisation and on the parameters which have defined 'development' to date. The associated historical analysis looks at three broad periods of the now dominant capitalist political economy: the mercantilist period;

the colonial/imperialist and immediately subsequent neo-colonial period; and the current post-colonial period. It argues that to understand the most recent period requires an understanding of the previous periods and how these structured not only politics, economics and societies, but also the nature of analysis itself. This chapter reviews urban development in the light of this approach and thus leads on to how such an approach can be applied analytically to the development of planning and housing in pre-capitalist, colonial and post-war situations of urban development, and subsequently to how it can condition action today for the future.

Urban development in the mercantilist period

The development of capitalism is generally seen as starting in the fifteenth and sixteenth centuries in northwest Europe, involving global links from an early stage, which later grew into global markets and then into a global economy. The global economy was largely created by the end of the nineteenth century and continued to expand throughout the twentieth century, the last quarter of which saw a radical re-structuring, often referred to now as 'globalisation'. In fact, globalisation can be seen to be associated with each main period of capitalist development, with three 'waves' of globalisation linked to different technological options and governing structures (Robertson 2003). The first wave of globalisation occurred during the mercantilist phase of capitalism, between 1500–1800 approximately, with increasing dominance by northwest Europe in global trade, linked to shipping, financial (banking and insurance) innovation and military change. During this period core European nation states were formed and reformed, competing for access to, and dominance over, trade and the direct exploitation of natural resources, including labour, across the world. The economic surplus created was often used for continued nation state consolidation in northwest Europe, whether for military purposes or status, but increasingly also for investment in productive capacity – initially agricultural but then manufacturing – as the basis for the Industrial Revolution. This created wealth but also increased demand for labour and raw materials for manufacturing in the core countries,[1] as well as the need for food. The demand for industrial labour in these countries was to a great degree satisfied by rural re-structuring, taking tenant farmers off the land and applying new techniques to increase agricultural productivity. This process of rural change led to both urban influx, creating cheap labour for manufacturing and services, and migration, providing labour and skills for the development of colonies in the 'New World'.

Prior to the mercantile expansion of European nation states, urban areas existed in various parts of the world at various times, as described in the next chapter. In addition, a wide range of 'traditional' or 'vernacular' housing options developed over time, most of these being rural as urban populations were generally limited in size. Chapter 4 describes some of the contexts within which early urban areas developed, which are seen as pre-capitalist modes of production from a political economy viewpoint. Indigenous shelter forms are also closely related to 'pre-capitalist' modes of production – while reflecting environmental, cultural and other factors. It is important to emphasise, however, that within these pre-capitalist modes, first, there was enormous variation in the forms of production as well as the forms of shelter produced, and second, these forms of shelter production and associated forms of human settlement did not vanish with the penetration of capitalism. Rather, these forms were to a greater or lesser extent overlaid with capitalist forms, often adopting elements and commodifying these – becoming *articulated* with capitalist forms in subordinate ways, as argued by the Neo-Marxists (see Chapter 2). This process continues today, with forms of articulated pre-capitalist housing production and urban development maintaining an important position in many situations of rapid urbanisation across the world.

The nature of cities created in the core countries in the mercantilist phase of capitalism, with rapid urban influx (although not necessarily high urban natural growth rates due to high death rates), gave rise to severe gaps between needs and provision of basic services, which in time prompted mechanisms to respond to these: stronger government intervention at national and (later) local level, and subsequently the institutionalisation of public health measures including restriction of private action (e.g. public health requirements and building controls). However, during the mercantilist period, the number and size of urban areas was limited, even in the initial core European regions where industrialisation was beginning. This changed markedly as industrialisation spread and became more concentrated due to innovations in the sources of power (coal-powered steam engines) and transport (canals and later railways). This permitted not only the concentration of production in space – i.e. in cities and factories – but also a much wider and rapid expansion of the number and size of urban areas in the later mercantilist and early industrial periods (see below).

In the overseas areas of mercantilist penetration, limited urban development continued throughout the mercantile period. In the early mercantilist period much trade was carried on with indigenous populations overseas through small urban nuclei, and these served as key transport hubs for shipment of the commodities that were exploited (e.g. gold, spices, other natural products such as ivory and hides, and slaves (Figure 3.1)). The approach to urban development across the world varied between the early mercantilist powers, with limited investment in infrastructure by most of the northern European powers, but creation of new urban areas by southern European powers, such as in Latin America, albeit relatively small in size and number.[2] Many indigenous societies were severely affected by this phase of penetration, both in terms of subordination, enslavement and/or eradication, but also through the undermining of existing political and economic systems by

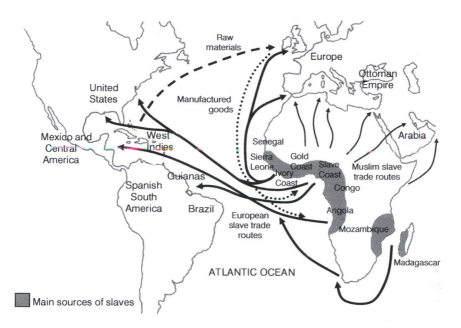

Raw
materials

Europe

Ottoman
Empire

United
States

Manufactured
goods

Mexico and
Central
America

West
Indies

Arabia

Senegal

Sierra
Leone

Gold
Coast
Ivory
Coast

Slave
Coast

Muslim slave
trade routes

Guianas

Congo

Spanish
South
America

Brazil

European
slave trade
routes

Angola

Mozambique

Madagascar

ATLANTIC OCEAN

Main sources of slaves

3.1 The African slave trade and related trade routes – fifteenth to nineteenth centuries
(Drawing by Harry Smith based on various sources)

the merchants, with metropolitan military backing, as well as of cultural systems
with the export of religion by missionaries. However, outside of Latin America
there was limited new urban development, with merchants tending to create small
settlements, often fortified mainly against other competing European nations, and
often based on existing indigenous settlements where these already existed.

Urban development in the industrial, colonial and neo-colonial periods

The second wave of globalisation is associated with industrialisation and colonialism,
or imperialism, and also with significant changes in technology and inter-state
relations. Industrialisation is closely linked to rapid urbanisation from the early
period of the nineteenth century (as noted in Chapter 1), as well as to imperial
expansion. From about 1800, the industrialising powers realised that they needed
to ensure raw material supplies, as well as markets, for continuing expansion of
production. Although colonial control was not necessarily the preferred solution,
this was what developed in the latter part of the nineteenth century as some
European countries began to annex territories for their exclusive, or dominant,
access to resources.[3] Between 1800 and 1878 the area of the world taken under the

control of European powers rose from 35 to 67 per cent, rising to 85 per cent by the outbreak of the First World War in 1914 (Hoogvelt 2001). This massive imperial expansion required new military and administrative controls, as well as centres for collection of production and its subsequent onward transport, focusing on ports. Hence urban networks were created as mechanisms for control and exploitation, sometimes building on the pre-existing urban trading centres but often creating new urban areas. These were usually situated at transport hubs, suitable harbours or good locations for control functions, or at specific sites for natural resource exploitation such as mines or harbours. These urban areas were predominantly for the benefit and use of the colonial powers, with limited acceptance of the subaltern classes they required to service them, and hence access to urban areas was often controlled, either directly or indirectly.

The first wave of globalisation was thus linked closely to early urban development, but relatively limited in scope and pace, except in the late eighteenth century in core European countries when urban development began to accelerate. The second wave of globalisation, however, was closely linked to growing urban development in both the metropolitan *and* the colonised areas – or core and periphery – albeit with different effects and different rates of growth. In the former, rapid urbanisation continued as both rural exodus was intensified and natural growth rates rose in urban areas (related to improved public health), and the widening gaps between urban growth and urban services led to the first state-decreed basic housing standards and land use controls, and the eventual emergence of land use planning. These government standards and controls were immediately exported to the new colonial urban areas, where there was more 'freedom' for their imposition as either the indigenous population was marginalised from decision making, or the population was predominantly colonial and newly resident. However, urban growth was not a rapid phenomenon in the colonies – although the number of urban areas increased significantly, colonial control maintained these at relatively small size. In many ways the imperialist colonial expansion provided state planning and housing with its heyday, albeit with highly differentiated provision for different social groups, even within colonial and indigenous societies.

The colonial period was also one of intense overseas investment for the main colonising powers, with large-scale investments in fixed infrastructure including urban infrastructure and housing. For instance, nearly 75 per cent of all British capital investments in its colonies were in transport (especially railways and ports), energy (e.g. electricity and gas) as well as other social infrastructure (water and sewerage, health and education, etc.), compared with some 10 per cent in direct production facilities such as mines and plantations (Hoogvelt 2001) (Figure 3.2). The nature of investment was thus long term and without necessarily any immediate overall returns.[4] This was possible because capitalist development in the core increasingly became concentrated and centralised and industrial capital merged with

3.2 Juiz de Fora railway station in Brazil – an example of infrastructure built with British capital in Latin America (Fondo de Imágenes Históricas de Ciudades Americanas (FIHCA), Universidad Pablo de Olavide, Sevilla)

banking capital to create financial capital markets. This process was paralleled by growing protectionism between the main competing European capitalist powers as capitalist enterprises began to manifest monopoly characteristics, which intensified the scramble for control of remaining areas of the world and friction between core European states, eventually leading to large-scale war. The massive investment in colonial and peripheral infrastructure was thus partly driven by political aims, to control resources and markets, but also by the inherent tendencies in the development of capital to seek returns.

The extent to which colonial urban infrastructure investment benefited the indigenous population (if at all) depended on the nature of the colonisation, the function of the settlement, and the attitude to governance. In some colonies the basic objective was to control, exploit and expand already existing production systems, with some new additions in direct natural resource exploitation. Here colonial settlements were relatively small, with a focus on major transport nodes for export, with some mining and fishing settlements. In others the colony was seen as the location for large-scale emigration from the metropole or other colonies, and here urban areas were bigger and more complex, with a bigger demand for indigenous labour. Mono-functional settlements such as mine or military towns were less complex but the demand for indigenous labour was very different – high in the former and low in the latter. Some colonising powers assumed that the indigenous population was essentially rural and therefore minimised urban residency rights and land/housing provision for such groups; others deliberately co-opted an indigenous ruling class for indirect rule, albeit separated socially and physically; and others promoted an indigenous ruling class as an adjunct to the colonial class. Each had different physical manifestations in terms of urban development and therefore different attitudes to planning and housing.

Approaches to planning and housing in different colonial situations are described in Chapter 5, and these need to be seen in the context of the broader penetration of core European-based capitalist relations and industrial mode of production, articulating with pre-existing modes of production and political, social and cultural structures. In general, limited and highly controlled forms of urban development were promoted, closely associated with new forms of capitalist economic expansion, which entailed significant infrastructure investments, with colonial governments having a predominant role in directing and controlling the nature of urban form. The nature of planning and housing provision within this mode of production was inherently unsustainable, however, as has been evidenced by subsequent events.

If the mercantilist period of capitalist expansion was characterised by limited urban development, and the colonial period by rapid urbanisation in the core countries, with gradually increasing, but highly controlled, urbanisation in the colonised world, the subsequent decolonisation process brought about forms of rapid urbanisation in the ex-colonies and peripheral regions, while at the same time consolidating urban development in the metropolitan areas. By the middle of the twentieth century two world wars had led to relative impoverishment in the core European countries, and the rise of the United States as the dominant world power, contested mainly by the Soviet Union. The core European nations could no longer maintain their colonies and the new global super powers wanted these opened up for their own influence and penetration. There was a rapid move to de-colonise immediately after the war, establishing an initial neo-colonial phase through to the 1970s, whereby colonial-created political and economic structures largely retained their net effect.

This was possible due to the continued control of key economic relations by metropolitan-based companies, and settler populations in some areas, as well as the continued basis of imported institutions such as legal and political systems. Most colonial powers also had deliberately groomed indigenous elites for managed hand-over of power, with deeply inculcated cultural values. Thus while political control was handed over at Independence in most colonies by the 1970s, economic power was largely retained in the core countries, with the additional involvement of the new global super powers (the United States and the Soviet Union). In this situation the newly independent ex-colonies continued to be dependent on the capitalist system based in the core, and produced primarily raw materials for manufacturing in these areas, importing the resulting products, with declining terms of trade – a form of 'resource bondage'.[5] However, manufacturing was also beginning to be decentralised from the core countries, following on from the response to local consumer demand in the Second World War period, and increasingly the core countries began to specialise in production goods as opposed to consumer goods. This transformation of productive power thus ensured the continued economic dominance of the core countries, with peripheral development dependent on the technologies controlled by these, applying 'technological rents'[6] as added value.

The neo-colonial period lasted from the 1950s to the 1970s, and as outlined in Chapter 2, was the period when 'development' began to be conceptualised as such, with the focus initially on modernisation, later opposed by dependency theories and policies. These disagreed on how development would be achieved, but agreed on the need for such social and economic development. While modernisation theorists and policy makers stressed the need for trickle down from the core countries and their companies' continued economic activity in the ex-colonies, the dependency theorists and policy makers stressed the need to break free from the dependent relations of production which had been built up through the late mercantilist and colonial periods. The former focused on selective economic and technological aid for development, with related political and socio-cultural modernisation, and closely associated this with Cold War geo-politics, while the latter focused on de-linking from the global system dominated by the core countries (including the new core countries) and protected development within nation states and macro-regions, often also promoting revolutionary political change. Both, however, assumed that the so-called 'developing world' could catch up in development terms.

These political economic changes were again reflected in the nature of urban development which took place in the immediate post-Independence period in many countries. One of the first effects was the rapid influx from rural areas to urban areas as colonial administrative controls over labour were removed, often initially with families joining heads of households who had already moved to an urban base. The post-Independence drive for widening social services such as education and health, and the initial urban location of these, provided a 'pull' effect for urban influx. Changing demographic patterns also had an important effect: life expectancy rose and fertility rates remained high and thus urban populations also began to grow quickly through natural increase. The neo-colonial period was characterised by rapid urban growth across the previous colonies, although with significant differences in impact. These related to the level of urbanisation already experienced, the structure of society developed in the colonial period and the levels and forms of economic development achieved and development policies adopted. Thus, for instance, Latin America had a long-established urban structure and the majority of the population was immigrant at some stage. In this macro-region, many countries had a relatively consolidated economic development structure, and these opted for a 'dependency' form of protected development, which reinforced already high rates of urban growth with most countries becoming predominantly urban during this period. On the contrary, Sub-Saharan Africa had very limited urban structures with the majority of the population indigenous and still based in rural areas. The relatively high level of economic dependency could not underpin strong efforts at independent and protected development, despite this being attempted in some countries, and thus, although urban in-migration began to rise rapidly from this period, the demographic effect of this overall remained relatively muted initially.

Urban development in the post-colonial period[7]

By the mid-1970s the post-war reconstruction boom had begun to diminish in the core countries as mass production began to saturate existing markets for consumer goods, and the oil crisis sparked a global economic downturn. As such, the post-war settlement of state-managed economies and related social welfare systems in the core, underpinned by corporatist social democracies (especially northern Europe), began to show signs of limitation for capital accumulation, with economic stagnation and recurrent crises. One of the first steps for corporations and firms based in these core countries (now also including Japan) was to restructure their production with parts of this moving to places where wages were lower, with this becoming possible with new communication and transport technology such as containerised shipping, as well as new flexible 'post-Fordist' production systems. This was the main driving force behind the trans-national firms moving part of their production to the so-called newly industrialising countries of South-East Asia and Latin America, and signalled a shift from nation state backed Fordist production lines based on the post-war settlement, to a new international division of labour, including increasingly 'flexible' integration of labour such as through sub-contracting and casual employment. Hence during the 1970s, while the so-called 'developing world' increased its share of global manufacturing exports by 3 per cent up to 10 per cent, two-thirds of this was based in eight newly industrialising countries (Hoogvelt 2001).

This change was the first phase of a major global macro-economic re-structuring which, unlike the previous mercantilist accumulation and subsequent imperialist geographic expansion of capital and its neo-colonial consolidation, began to turn in on itself. This was kick-started by the oil crisis in the 1970s,[8] which represented a form of economic nationalism such as that promoted by dependency theory and policies. This spurred on the re-structuring of core economies, but also provided a massive injection of capital into the financial institutions based in these, which was used to fund major loan portfolios to newly independent countries. The easy lending of the 1970s, together with the separation of financial from managerial accountability, led to high losses and spiralling debt in many 'developing countries'. This created a new form of dependence and extraction of surplus from these countries to the benefit of the core countries – termed 'debt peonage'[9] – which added to continued 'resource bondage' for many and 'technological rents' for most. The total outstanding debt reached about 30 per cent of the combined GDP of these countries by the end of the 1980s (Hoogvelt 2001).

This process affected countries and regions very differently, and together with the opportunity some had to adopt a role in the re-structured 'globalising' manufacturing economy, led to the challenging of the concept of the 'developing' or 'Third' world as a general category. It raised the possibility for newly industrialising countries to gain 'core' status, dependent on their ability to provide suitable bases for trans-national capital – and also led to the need for core countries to re-structure, as they lost their manufacturing dominance and had to compete for retention of other forms of economic supremacy. In this sense, therefore, 'development' in the original sense of the 'less-developed' countries catching up with the 'developed' countries was no longer seen as generally viable, as economic activity is no longer necessarily located in either the previous core or previous peripheral nation states. What is currently happening is a re-structuring of the basis for capital accumulation away from geographic expansion or consolidation of capital penetration in the 'periphery', to a socially differentiated form of accumulation which is less geographically dependent. In parallel with this, changes in production techniques have led to the rise in importance in knowledge as a key factor in capital accumulation, as opposed to land, labour or capital itself. This has permitted new forms of economic development, whether acting on these traditional factors, or completely new, such as that based on the internet.

This reduced importance of geographical space in economic development is evidenced in world trade, which is increasingly concentrated in relations between the core countries, with some growth in relations with the newly industrialising countries, but a relative withdrawal from other peripheral countries, where the terms of trade still deteriorate for most commodities (i.e. resource bondage still continues). 'Globalisation' is thus not an ever-widening inclusive phenomenon, but an increasingly exclusive one, as noted in Chapter 1. This is also reinforced by global financial flows: whereas up to 1960 the 'developing world' received 50 per cent of total direct investment, this dropped to one-third of this (16.5 per cent) by 1989 – and over half of this reduced proportion went to Asia. In the 1990s this turned around, with foreign direct investment in the 'developing world' rising again to 38 per cent by 1997, however one-third of this was going to one country, China, and mainly to its coastal provinces. If these areas are included with the nine dominant newly industrialising countries and together with the core countries of Western Europe, North America and Japan, this group of countries received nearly 90 per cent of all foreign direct investment in the 1990s, while containing only 30 per cent of the world's population. This trend to concentrate economic activity is reinforced through other financial flows such as private portfolio funds in the same period: 60 per cent going to six countries (Brazil, Mexico, Argentina, Thailand, Indonesia and China), and 94 per cent going to 20 countries, including four 'transition' economies in Central and Eastern Europe. It is important to note, however, that much of this is short-term speculative finance, as has been seen in the various financial crises in these regions in the 1990s (Hoogvelt 2001).

In addition to this renewed concentration of macro-economic inclusion, within countries there are marked disparities. According to Hoogvelt, some 200 individuals now have a net value equal to the income of more than 40 per cent of the world's population, illustrating that social inequality is not only geographically expressed. The financial services industry is very selective in whom it caters to, and this excludes the majority in many countries, whereas the minority who are bankable increasingly have their savings invested internationally and not locally, through the existing globalisation of portfolio investment. Thus, whereas in the colonial and neo-colonial periods a large proportion of core country finance was invested in the colonies and other peripheral regions, now even the investment created within these regions is generally directed elsewhere, especially as this is seen to be less risky. At the same time as these social and economic divisions are exacerbated in the non-core periphery, structural change is leading to widening social and economic difference in the core regions – albeit mitigated by continuing forms of welfare and wealth redistribution. Thus what is appearing in the current wave of globalisation is a concentration and deepening of capitalist accumulation where it has already taken root (geographically and socially), together with some contraction (again both geographical and social) from regions at the previous 'frontline' of capitalist penetration. This will preferentially benefit some 20 per cent of the world's population who are in effect the socio-economic elite, and exclude some 40 per cent who will be increasingly marginalised from core economic engagement, while the remaining 40 per cent can possibly benefit depending on political, economic, as well as social and cultural, options adopted.

The above scenario raises the question of what forms of urban development are possible and appropriate in these different forms of articulation with the new forms of the dominant international capitalist political economy. This book argues that there is a fundamental difference between previous forms of capitalist geographic expansion and consolidation, and the current form of re-structuring, and this is having a profound effect on the parameters for urban development and the possibility of urban responses in terms of land use management and shelter provision through planning and housing, mitigated by different national and local political economic parameters. Whereas the colonial and immediate neo-colonial period led to hope that 'under-development' could be resolved – albeit with no agreement on how – the re-structuring of capital to provide primarily for the existing elite in core regions and new elite in non-core regions through new forms of concentrated activity is fundamentally undermining the possibility of wider forms of socio-economic development for the world's majority, a few of whom may benefit but the majority of whom will not. The nature of urban development is in fact affected in all situations, as will be argued below, but the possible benefits of urban areas will only be available to a minority in the regions of the world which have recently urbanised, or are currently urbanising – at least for the foreseeable future. As such the urban solutions for land use management and housing that were mainly developed within the parameters of rapid and consolidated urbanisation, with associated relatively widespread economic growth of the past, are arguably not relevant for areas which will urbanise without such associated growth. In short, if we accept that a significant proportion of the world's population will be largely excluded from 'mainstream' social and economic development and the majority of the population in these will increasingly live in urban areas, what are the appropriate strategies for urban development for these groups? What appropriate actions can be taken in planning and housing within the parameters of a new international political economy analysis of global urbanisation trends?

Current trends in urban development

The current phase of globalisation affects urban development in two main ways: increasing urban growth and re-structuring of urban areas, with varying degrees in different parts of the world. Urban growth is stimulated by increased urban influx in the as yet not heavily urbanised areas as rural development opportunities are reduced due to contraction of investment and trade, and commodification penetrates more aspects of 'traditional' livelihoods, often undermining these. At the same time, natural (demographic) urban growth rates remain high in many rapidly urbanising areas – as well as those which have urbanised fairly recently – as the insecurity of livelihoods, together with cultural attitudes, continue to promote high levels of fertility whereas better health care leads to lower mortality rates. Thus areas of the world which had previous limited urbanisation are now showing the highest rates, such as Sub-Saharan Africa. In areas where rapid urbanisation has taken place already, socio-economic factors tend to bring about lower birth rates and then eventually demographic stabilisation can work through the age structure, such as is happening in Latin America. At the same time, economic opportunities can be attracted to secondary urban areas and thus urban networks change with the differential growth of smaller towns and cities, as well as other forms of settlements with urban as opposed to rural characteristics.

The opportunities for providing for the urban needs of populations affected by rapid urbanisation processes is closely tied, however, to macro-economic development opportunities, and although these are not homogeneous across global macro-regions, there are some broad macro-regional characteristics that can be explored. This is addressed in more detail later in the book, which is divided into three 'case studies' of planning and housing in three macro-regions: Sub-Saharan Africa, Latin America and East Asia. In each of these chapters the evolution of urban forms and planning and housing responses within these is briefly examined, with a more in-depth focus on the last five decades, relating to the analysis in Chapters 4–8 of the book. It is stressed again that the 'regionalisation' of the arguments in the book *vis-à-vis* opportunity for appropriate forms of planning and housing is not intended to reduce the complexities of each region and of the urban areas within these, or to overly determine how these might develop, but to illustrate essential differences of options within the broad parameters discussed above, i.e. in the light of a new international political economy analysis. The intention is to stimulate thought and more specific analysis related to the actual contexts – a process that is further elaborated in the concluding chapter.

In brief, the three macro-regional case study chapters focus on the following issues. The Sub-Saharan Africa chapter, given the relative marginalisation from the core economic development regions, looks at alternative forms of urban analysis that can develop as the basis of different approaches to urban development. While some urban areas of the region are articulated with the new global economy, this directly affects only a minority of inhabitants, and the rising trends in rapid urbanisation are seen as reinforcing the need for new approaches to planning and housing as formal approaches to date have had very limited positive impact, especially for the minority. In the Latin American chapter, the rich and relatively long urban history has produced a quite dense urban network that is now adapting to the opportunities for differential engagement with the new global economy. This is also leading to 'winners' and 'losers' in socio-economic terms, however the rise of new forms of political structure (at national and local levels) also potentially reinforces the possibility of wider distribution of urban benefits than has been the case to date. Thus new innovations in urban planning and housing provision in some cities and countries in this macro-region are reviewed as to their possible wider replicability – in the region and internationally. In the East Asia chapter, again a relatively long history of urban development, allied to strong traditions of governmental control, has led to the resulting developed urban structure now being seriously challenged by transition to even deeper engagement with the new global economy. This poses unique challenges in both quantitative and qualitative terms for the region, where traditional forms of urban development and housing – whether local or international – are unlikely to be effective. Here the challenge is whether the state developmentalist model can survive in the face of wider demand and greater competition for resources. Further brief analysis of the political economy context in each of these macro-regions is given in the following sub-sections, which serve to set the scene for the exploration and analysis of planning and housing issues in Chapters 9–11.

Sub-Saharan Africa

This macro-region represents enormous social and cultural diversity, yet significant economic and political conformity. While peripherally integrated into mercantilist expansion from the sixteenth century, especially in terms of exploitation of raw material and labour, the region was colonised relatively late, with the nature of colonisation depending on the nature of the colonising power and of the perceived economic potential. However, after a relatively short period of full colonisation, imperial rule disintegrated through the impact of two World Wars on the main European colonising powers, with a rapid and to a certain degree managed de-colonisation process leading initially to a strong form of neo-colonial development. This was briefly challenged in the 1970s by application of short-lived 'dependency' approaches to national development, but the dominant development strategies were all based on modernisation. The region did not benefit in absolute terms from significant inward investment after the colonial period ended. Its level of debt accumulation after global deregulation in the 1970s was relatively low compared to other macro-regions, but high in relation to economic levels, and thus the nation states quickly succumbed to international pressures as multi-national and bi-lateral agencies took over the private sector debt in the 1980s and imposed macro-economic structural adjustment.

The region contains a high proportion of the world's least developed countries, as measured by the UN. As Hoogvelt (2001) reports, whereas in the mid-1970s its primary commodities represented 7 per cent of world trade, this dropped to less than 0.5 per cent in the 1990s – manufacturing trade dropping from 1.2 to 0.4 per cent in a similar time frame. The share of global foreign direct investment dropped from 13 per cent in 1980 to under 5 per cent in the late 1990s, and 90 per cent of international inward funds are linked to international aid. The last two decades have seen stagnation and structural marginalisation of the region, at the same time as its accumulated foreign debt has continued rising three-fold from some $US84 billion to $US235 billion. Despite multi-lateral commitments to reduce this for highly indebted countries, with 33 of the 41 so-defined countries worldwide in this region, this has had little real effect due to the difficulties and lack of political desire or capacity to implement the associated political and economic agendas demanded by the aid agencies.

Structural adjustment not only seriously undermined fledgling national economies in this region, forcing them into new depths of subordination with the emerging new global economy, but also undermined the post-Independence political structures that had emerged. These had often become largely elite-dominated 'patrimonial' states, with strong leaders negotiating continued dominance with major political actors, for example the military, traditional rulers, opposing liberation movements and (in some cases) national bourgeoisies. The balance of power which had depended on the patronage of the leadership was undermined by the demands of structural adjustment economic policies, and when these were not adhered to, by the subsequent international insistence on multi-party representative democratic settlements in the 1990s. The social, economic and political structures that emerged from these processes in the new millennium (which in some cases were unsuccessful with countries descending into civil war and other forms of instability), were fundamentally aligned to adopting an extremely subservient role in the new global economy. This entailed returning to the limited opportunities to export commodities (raw materials or energy) with few opportunities for other forms of economic engagement, such as manufacturing. However, where this was structurally possible it tended to be labour extensive and highly mechanised, and thus did not contribute significantly to absorbing the rapidly rising economically active population. In parallel, the continuation – and intensification in some instances – of core world regions' subsidy for their agricultural output (driven largely by competition between themselves) undermined export-led agriculture from the Sub-Saharan African region, and indeed, through dumping of highly subsidised food, often the very viability of rural development. Fundamentally the region faces increased exclusion from the possibility of social 'modernisation' and increased economic marginalisation, with a limited political and economic elite benefiting from continued exploitation and forms of 'compradore capitalism', servicing those parts of the economy which are articulated with the new global economy, often channelled through regional access points in the region's relatively more developed countries, such as South Africa (Figure 3.3).

Latin America

Latin America has been characterised by relatively strong state regimes, but weak civil societies, since Independence was achieved in most countries nearly two centuries ago. This has led to a deeply engrained tradition of clientelism in politics, and to non-representative political elites dominated by economic interests. The main feature of political and economic life has in fact been the struggle between external and internal economic interest groups, and between factions of the latter, such as landed oligarchies and domestic industrialists. This has begun to change as authoritarian states are dismantled and as the effects of external articulation with the new global economy take effect. The main factors in the development of the region since the Second World War have been the various attempts to establish rapidly modernising development paths, initially through protectionist policies of import substitution industrialisation (cf. dependency), and then through forced engagement with the international economy based on anti-communist inspired military regimes and forms of state developmentalism. The former failed largely due to limited effective demand in regional markets, the continued need for technology

3.3 Johannesburg International Airport, South Africa (Dr Peter Clarke-Farr)

(and capital) from the core, and international pressure. The latter failed partly due to its repressive nature in the face of already substantial societal politicisation, but also the high and unsustainable levels of international debt it acquired in the 1970s when core financial institutions were awash with petro-dollars.

The neo-liberal monetarist policies established in the United States under Reagan led to the high levels of debt spiralling and creating a decade of stagnation and 'de-development' in the 1980s – with leading conservative regimes in the core countries ignoring continued domestic repression. The reaction to this under international agency pressure has generally been the dismantling of state developmentalism and adoption of neo-liberal monetarist policies, with promotion of privatisation and export-led growth policies. Across the region multi-lateral agencies applied structural adjustment programmes which enforced economic contraction and widespread reduction in social programmes, wages and living standards. This exacerbated social unrest and laid the ground for new levels of civil society organisation against social and economic, as well as military, repression (Figure 3.4). The process of building forms of democratic action within society based on experience of social movements took place well before this was re-established in formal ways within parliamentary constitutions and government, and this has permitted continued innovation in political forms, especially challenging

3.4 Protest in La Paz against export of Bolivian gas through multinational companies (Sayer Payne)

the deep-seated forms of clientelism which continued through the authoritarian regimes into the neo-liberal period. In addition, there is a strong current of anti-developmentalism in Latin America, maintaining the strong legacy of independent intellectual development (see Chapter 2). This queries and de-constructs the concepts of development, and sees this as '... the last and failed attempt to complete the Enlightenment in Asia, Africa and Latin America' (Escobar 1995: 221).

This tendency is, if anything, reinforced by the persistence of social problems even after economic growth has been re-instated during the 1990s. During this period the United States government has pushed for the creation of the Central American Free Trade Area (CAFTA), followed by the Free Trade Area of the Americas (FTAA), which would fully open up the continent to US investors and producers. In addition, privatisation of public utilities has continued to be promoted, meeting fierce opposition from civil society, which in some countries has succeeded in stalling or reversing the privatisation process. However, the proportion of the population in the region living in poverty was much the same at 36 per cent in 1997 as it was at the beginning of the 'lost development decade' in 1980, and income inequalities had increased (Hoogvelt 2001). With population increases this meant absolute numbers of the poor rising, and with the majority in all countries in urban areas, this has had a major impact on the possibility to reduce deficits in urban services, as well as employment opportunities, with a consequent trend to 'informalisation'. Thus, although Latin America has the potential for continued engagement in the new global economy, given the wealth of its elites, the size of its internal markets, and its relatively skilled labour force, whether it can rise to core region status is queried, especially as significant proportions of its population continue to be excluded socially and economically. It is also not clear whether the widening participatory democratic trends which have had their roots in opposition to national authoritarianism can rally sufficiently against global economic pressures with their current tendency to re-structure capitalism within the core and its intermediate regions. Thus the tendency for social and economic disparities continues to be still very much an issue in the region.

East Asia

In the 1980s and 1990s seven countries in East Asia showed all-time record development gains with fast and sustained growth, with average GNP/capita growth rates in excess of 5 per cent per annum[10]: Malaysia, Thailand, Indonesia, South Korea, Taiwan, together with Singapore and Hong Kong (the last four being the first to display this and initially called the four 'Asian Tigers'). This growth was export-led, but relied on high degrees of state intervention. Initially seen as a form of 'state capitalism', this came to be termed the 'developmental state' and seen as a replicable format for other countries. This approach has seen the state's engagement to promote rapid industrialisation as broadly beneficial and equitable, a form of 'guiding hand', providing for social welfare with economic development. Others, however, have stressed the repressive nature of the state, with strong limitations on labour organisation and closely controlled investment for national priorities that have in fact entailed significant levels of collusion. Other analysts have argued that the parameters for development were unique in the geo-political context of the Cold War, with high levels of un-accounted US support against communism, as well as the economic opportunity afforded by the seeking of lower wage options by core region manufacturing freed from regulation – and stress that these opportunities are no longer options in the way they were in the 1970s–1990s. Overall the combination of economic opportunity and political will permitted specific developmentalist policies to be followed without necessarily strong national backing from pre-existing economic elites and wider social groups, and the resulting economic success in turn permitted the re-adjustment to wider social inclusion over time on newly dictated state terms.

The unique opportunity that was seized by governing elites in East Asia has been challenged both from inside and outside. From inside, growing pressure from organised labour and other civil society associations for social improvements, including higher wages and greater environmental controls, has led to the loss of comparative advantage in terms of cheap manufacturing, with the re-investment of capital in cheaper locations within the region. Externally, the end of the Cold War led to withdrawal of US strategic support and growing protectionism within the United States against the newly industrialising countries, with ensuing punitive trade measures and currency de-stabilisation, including the disastrous 1997 financial crisis. In response different approaches are developing across the region, some opting for high technology development and increasing engagement with the new global economy (Figure 3.5), others for the widening of domestic and regional markets for production, and hence less global export orientation. For most countries there is a still a long way to go to re-establish pre-1990s economic buoyancy and social development aspirations, including reducing poverty. The sustainability of this model of development even within the region is questioned as the impact on the environment of past policies and of growing democratisation on the demand for more redistribution is realised, yet regional capital is increasingly invested in the international financial system and not within the region itself. Whether recent moves to strengthen a macro-regional economic bloc will succeed and provide a new platform for development is still unclear, as various different organisational structures exist. As important, if not more so, will be the role China opts to play in the region and internationally, and the response from Japan.

3.5 Young workers arriving at a factory in Shenzhen, South China (Ya Ping Wang)

Conclusions

This chapter has argued for, and outlined, a new international political economy analysis of urban development through different periods of global economic development, with more emphasis on the most recent phase and areas now undergoing rapid urban change. It argues that this is a more appropriate frame of reference than the 'development' paradigms which have underpinned theory and policies for urban planning and housing in the 'developing world', whether explicit or implicit, in the last three decades or so – as will be described in Chapters 4–8. If this basic premise is accepted, and the parameters outlined above are the starting point for analysis, what is the action that is appropriate within such parameters for planning and housing in this context? After all, it is argued that an essential aspect of the new international political economy is the relevance of agency within a clearly analysed political and economic structural context. This question is returned to in the concluding chapter to the book, but sketched out here is a guide to the more in-depth macro-regional analyses which follow in Part Three.

The main conclusions from the analysis outlined above can be summarised as follows:

1   Capitalism continues as the increasingly dominant form of economic engage-
    ment across the world, however the global aspect of this does not mean that
    all are beneficially affected by this worldwide. On the contrary (as in previous
    phases of capitalist expansion), capitalist economic development is highly
    exclusionary in its articulation with other socio-economic forms of interchange,
    but also (unlike during these previous phases) the proportion of worldwide
    populations benefiting is reducing to a smaller elite, both in the former 'core'
    and 'periphery' *and* in the new 'core' regions. In other words the new global
    economic order is stratified socially more than geographically, and this is being
    reflected in changing political structures.
2   The changes in economic production and consumption driven by capitalism
    have long been associated with growing urban development, although there
    have traditionally been gaps between urbanisation and the application of means
    to improve urban living standards, but the re-structuring of capitalism is now
    prompting forms of urbanisation with limited opportunity to provide for
    improvements to urban living for a rapidly increasing majority, while providing
    this for the elite. There is thus growing social and economic polarisation in
    urban areas worldwide, which is often reflected physically.
3   The older core regions have political and social systems which to some
    extent mediate the impact of the re-structured and more concentrated form
    of capitalism in urban areas, but these do not exist in any resilient way in
    the semi-periphery or often at all in the periphery, and hence the impact

of changes in core capitalism is often extremely harsh in situations of rapid urbanisation, with deteriorating urban economies and services in the face of growing urban populations.

4   Some of these mediating mechanisms have been forms of state, state-supported market, and socially based ways of providing shelter as well as managing land use for collective benefits – i.e. planning and housing – and these are now adapting to new situations in the core regions in terms of greater disparities of objectives and demands on their systems. Typical examples are privatising public housing and entrepreneurial municipal planning. While some of these new professional adaptations may have relevance for some of the objectives and demands in the rapidly urbanising world, most do not as they tend to preferentially protect values of, and promote benefits for, the socio-economic and political elite who are part of these 'formal' systems.

5   In the same way that new forms of conceptualising politics and decision-making through wider forms of governance have been emerging in core and semi-periphery regions, especially Latin America, there is a need for new forms of decision-making and resource allocation for urban land-based resources and shelter, not only in these regions, but also in the periphery, requiring new approaches to planning and housing which focus on social inclusion as well as economic growth.

6   These new approaches need to be developed from first principles in the actual political, economic, social and cultural contexts for which they need to operate, and not be imported and adapted from the core regions, whether recent or previous mechanisms. This poses a major intellectual challenge for the sector as these are new challenges which previous theory and practice have not had to face.

The following chapters of the book initially reinforce the summary argument in this chapter about the impact of changing global forces on planning and housing (Part Two), followed by more in-depth case studies in three macro-regions (Part Three), leading to conclusions on how theory and practice need to continue to evolve within this context. The analytical path used is the relation between planning and housing models and development models in the past 50 years, and the redundancy of these in the light of the changing impact of the new international political economy. First, however, the next chapter examines pre-capitalist forms of shelter and urban development, as in fact where capitalism has not penetrated fully, pre-capitalist forms continue to have great importance, and it is in this way we need to see 'extra-capitalist' action in urban development for those who are not part of the 'included' in globalisation today.

Part Two:

Planning and Housing in the Rapidly Urbanising World

Chapter 4
Pre-capitalist 'traditional' shelter and urban settlements

Introduction

This chapter looks at how traditional forms of shelter and urban settlements developed prior to the expansion and penetration of capitalism, as a basis to review the relevance of different forms of production for housing policy and practice in rapidly urbanising situations, some of which are peripheral to global capitalism. The majority of buildings in most human settlements were, and continue to be, composed of housing and thus house form has a predominant impact on settlement form. Housing is also probably the oldest built form, although not necessarily the most developed architecturally. In fact the overwhelming majority of houses produced world-wide have not been developed by architects, but by residents and their associates, albeit with an increasing specialisation of people with building skills in urban situations.[1] This chapter first examines traditional forms of housing and human settlement and then early forms of urban settlement.

Traditional forms of housing and human settlement

There is a fairly specialised study of traditional housing and settlement form from which this chapter draws. Approaches to 'vernacular architecture', as this area of study is sometimes called, initially tended to stress design and construction factors, but later focused on environmental factors. Mainly due to the separation of academic disciplines, such as architecture and anthropology, the cultural and social attributes of traditional dwellings only came to be studied much later, with the economic and political reality still arguably under-recognised (see Appendix A). Currently there is a more concerted attempt to bring together these various approaches in a more integrated way.

Drawing on such an integrated approach, traditional forms of housing and settlements can be seen to have four main influences:

- availability and utilisation of materials and technology, which are often based on local resources and knowledge;
- environmental considerations, and the nature of shelter in protecting from adverse and uncomfortable climates;

- socio-cultural influences, for example concerning how space is used and ideas concerning the meaning of shelter within a culture, including expression in decoration and artistic forms; and
- economic and political considerations, such as the nature of the broader social economy, productive, employment and work patterns, and the nature of accumulation (including forms of savings and investment), as well as how socio-economic interchange is governed – i.e. the political context.

Concerning socio-cultural influences, the nature of housing and settlement form is strongly influenced by the cultures of the inhabitants and their society. This is evidenced in the production of housing and settlements, including the location, layout, types of spaces created, materials chosen, methods of construction, and the decoration of dwellings, as well as ceremonies concerning building – all of which express cultural attributes. In terms of use of shelter, the way the spaces are used, including furnishings and other living 'equipment', again reflect cultural attributes. This position is strongly argued by Amos Rapoport in a series of publications and is examined in some detail here.

Rapoport distinguishes sub-groups of traditional building as being 'primitive', 'pre-industrial vernacular' and 'modern vernacular' (Rapoport 1969). He defines *primitive* buildings as those produced by societies defined as primitive by anthropologists on the basis of technological and economic levels of development as well as forms of social organisation. The term primitive thus does not refer to the builder's intention or capabilities but to the categorisation of the form of social development. In primitive societies there is little specialisation of activity except by gender and age, and most households have the available knowledge to build their own dwelling; however, for socio-cultural as well as technical reasons, this is often done co-operatively. The builder can include his or her own, and their household's, specific needs within a culturally defined set of 'rules' concerning the process of production which leads to quite a high degree of uniformity of design and form.

Rapoport defines the distinction between *primitive* building and *pre-industrial vernacular* building as being primarily the use of specialised skills. Through an often slow transition, skilled tradesmen developed part-time specialisations, while continuing more general productive practices. In many societies both these forms co-existed and in fact continue to co-exist to some extent, as is expressed, for example, in the strong collective definition of what is culturally acceptable, although more advanced skills in pre-industrial vernacular often permit much more individuality and differentiation than in primitive building. In pre-industrial vernacular, collective respect for authority is often expressed in the hierarchy of the settlement form as much as in the actual built fabric. As with *primitive* building, the models used for this tradition developed over many generations and are thus usually well adapted to physical and environmental conditions (see below). Arguably, the flexibility of this form of production also allows a very open-ended nature for building which means this is also adaptable to future changes in needs.

Increasing economic specialisation and social and political differentiation within societies and growth of larger settlements led eventually to the growing institutionalisation of traditional forms of shelter and settlement – whether through 'pattern books' for buildings, or the slowly growing application of building and planning codes and regulations.[2] This institutionalisation, with its functional attributes, is one of the key elements of transformation from *pre-industrial* to *modern vernacular* in building. It is expressed in increased specialisation of building types as well as spaces within buildings. Rapoport thus sees the *modern vernacular* primarily expressed in types of building, for example motels, diners and drive-ins in North America, which also have originated outside the 'design professions'. It is, however, also contemporarily expressed in the housing which is built without involvement of the design professions – which as noted above still include the majority of dwellings world-wide.

Specialisation in the use of space is argued to be one feature of the evolution of primitive, pre-industrial and modern vernacular. In the first category spaces are very basic and multi-purpose as there is little specialisation of social and economic activities – for example animals and humans as well as work and living activities, share internal and external space together. As economies and societies become more specialised, differentiation of space occurs within, outside and between buildings. The pre-industrial shelter and settlement form expresses this more clearly – especially within urban settlements, such as the medieval city (see below on early urban settlements).

Due to lack of spatial specialisation, traditional building forms are relatively limited in functional scope. In primitive cultures these are predominantly dwellings, with some religious buildings, chief's houses and storehouses or granaries. This predominance of dwellings continues in the pre-industrial forms also, both urban and rural, although specialised production-related buildings (e.g. mills and storehouses) and monumental building forms begin to assume important economic, social, cultural and political status (e.g. castles and religious buildings). Rapoport argues that these are not truly 'vernacular' as they are often 'designed' by specialists.

As this chapter is not concerned with vernacular architecture as such, but with traditional forms of *housing*, these other building forms and Rapoport's 'modern vernacular' are not a focus, and the rest of this section will refer to 'primitive' and 'pre-industrial vernacular' as 'traditional' for brevity.

Understanding traditional house form in its socio-cultural context

It has been argued above that traditional forms of dwellings have had certain similar basic characteristics in terms of evolving specialisation and differentiation of space and function across the world. Some of these are only visible 'historically' – i.e. in a ruined or specially conserved state – but some are still in use and continuing to evolve. It is also true that, despite certain common traits, there are enormous differences between traditional building forms. As noted above, the differences are essentially those of cultural values and social organisation; climates and environments; and materials and technology – much of the literature on traditional building focusing on these attributes. However, as economic specialisation increases, this also has had a growing impact, and thus economic – and related political – aspects are also of importance, and will be explored later in the chapter.

In relation to the aspects highlighted above, many of the approaches to analysis of traditional house form have been largely physical and deterministic in their orientation – i.e. focusing primarily on climate and the need for shelter, with house form seen mainly as a product of available materials and construction technology. *Climate is* important in creation of built form, but cultural aspects are arguably more important, as very different building forms have evolved in near proximity and similar climates. Again, while available *materials and construction technology* are important modifying factors, they are also not determinant – for example there are situations where a technology is known and materials available but this is only used for ceremonial construction, not in dwellings. Also, even when new materials or technologies become available they often do not change the basic built form, as cultural values are a strong influence.

Other analytical approaches have seen the nature of *the site* as determinant on built form – for example the hill villages of Italy and the need for defence. Again, while site is of great importance, both physically and culturally, it again is not a determinant, and adaptations to site often entail cultural aspects (e.g. Chinese Feng Shui). More specifically in relation to siting of buildings, defence has been used to explain dense urban patterns of settlement, however social preferences for collective living may be as important a factor (e.g. in Greek villages). *Defensive attributes* in dwellings may have had more importance in former times but largely survive in symbolic ways in later landscapes.

Religion is seen as another determinant of traditional built form, this argument being based on the fact that both humans and animals create shelter, but human beings endow built form with a spiritual aspect which is a uniquely human expression. While it is recognised that the house has symbolic and spiritual attributes endowed on it, this is rather different from the view that it is primarily religious in design. Finally, as noted above, the impact of *economic ways of life* is of great importance, but these do not in themselves *determine* built form as similar economic forms display different built forms.

Overall it is stressed that, while the above factors are all of importance in determining built forms, *none of them are solely determinant*. The physical factors (climate, material and technology and site) in particular create constraints and possibilities, but not imperatives. This is also true of the defence and economic aspects – in peaceful societies producing surplus there are different possibilities than in strife-filled societies on the edge of survival. However, again, there is no inevitability in the creation of built form.

> The different forms taken by dwellings are a complex phenomenon for which no single explanation will suffice. All possible explanations, however, are variations of one single theme: people with very different attitudes and ideals respond to varied physical environments. These responses vary from place to place because of changes and differences in the interplay of social, cultural, ritual, economic and physical factors. These factors and responses may also change gradually in the same place with the passage of time; however, lack of rapid change and persistence of form are characteristic of primitive and vernacular dwellings.
>
> (Rapoport 1969: 46)

The traditional dwelling is in fact primarily a social institution, created for a complex set of purposes and functions, not just a physical structure. Religious and cultural ceremonies have been associated with dwelling creation from pre-history and the form the dwelling takes to some extent expresses the cultural milieu to which it belongs as well as the functions for which it is used. Rapoport's main thesis is thus that traditional house form is the product primarily of a whole range of *socio-cultural factors*, modified secondarily by *physical factors*. He sees socio-cultural factors as including religious beliefs, family, kinship and clan structure, social organisation (e.g. castes), social relations but also means of livelihood, and thus economies (see Appendix B). Physical factors include climatic and site conditions, construction technology and materials.

When we consider the role of the house in relation to society, another important feature of primitive and vernacular built form is the relationship between house and general settlement form. The fact that in some societies the house building *per se* is limited in function to, for instance, sleeping and storage, makes this clear. Implicit in some of the above definitions are uses of dwelling space outside of the confines of the dwelling's built form, i.e. the immediate habitat around as well as within dwellings. The settlement in fact is a social and spatial system relating dwellings, other buildings, settlement and landscape, all within defined socio-cultural concepts and ways of living. Settlements can be classified in many ways, one of the most important being the distinction between dispersal and concentration. In dispersed settlements more functions take place within and immediately around the dwelling itself than in concentrated settlements (Figure 4.1), though the latter also vary between those where the dwelling is still the setting for most social activity, and those where the dwelling functions are minimised, with other functions taking place elsewhere in the settlement. These distinctions are visible from the earliest pre-historic settlements through to the vast variety of human settlements across the world today.

Understanding traditional house form in its physical context[3]

The physical context for traditional house form can be approached from two perspectives: the material and technological context and the climatic and environmental context. Concerning *construction, materials and technology*, as argued above, this does not generally determine the built form, but certainly modifies the choice. The biggest technological challenge is the spanning of space, and the material available naturally limited the possibilities of this. In primitive dwellings, space was spanned with materials with either compressive strength (bricks, stone, etc. used in beehive structures and actual vaults and domes) or tensile strength – typically organic materials of animal origin (bone, skin, felts) or vegetable origin (timber or woven, plaited or twisted vegetable). The shortage of

4.1 Concentrated settlement: Taos Pueblo (Mark Hollabaugh)

some of these materials has led at times to their being transported great distances, and re-used for many generations. While simple structures of load-bearing walls and timber and thatch roofs perhaps dominate, a wide variety of structural forms is in evidence across the world in primitive and vernacular building, including examples from pre-history. These include frame construction, curtain walls, continuously 'poured' structures (pueblos), prefabrication (roofs and walls), and tension structures (tents).

Concerning the *construction process*, as noted earlier, this can be non-specialised (most likely in primitive dwellings), employing specialised skills and/or also co-operative action. In a number of situations the preferred technological solution necessitates co-operation – such as lifting large prefabricated elements such as roofs into place. However, in many societies, even if more specialised trades are involved, building often continues to be a collective process: gathering materials, preparing them, carting water, etc. There are usually socio-cultural ceremonies closely associated with construction, both individual and collective. While locally available materials are more generally used in traditional construction, this is not always the case. Given that there may well be a range of possible materials available, again socio-cultural factors influence choice. This may be based on status, religion or technologies passed on from generation to generation. The close relationship of primitive and vernacular dwellings to the environment is also used in the construction process, when weathering is used as an integral part – sun-drying of adobe, curing of timber, etc.

Specialisation in traditional construction also permitted development of techniques over time, and often took place with increasing specialisation of building types. Most dwellings, however, remained of relatively simple construction – for instance using un-fired as opposed to fired brick or undressed as opposed to dressed stone – because of the extra labour involved. The lower investment in the initial material, however, often had to be balanced by higher maintenance of the material (e.g. periodic plastering). Thus the use of higher cost materials for roofing developed widely as the alternatives were even more costly in maintenance. In general, traditional buildings rely on materials encountered locally, including 'inert' and 'organic' substances such as soil, rock, timber, grass, etc., and derivatives of these (e.g. bricks, lime). The structures developed usually exploit simple forms of compression and tension, including post and beam constructions, as well as domes, corbelled roofs, A-frames, etc. Another area of technical expertise that develops is the relationship of the building form and materials to the local climate, which can include quite severe extremes.

Referring to *climate*, the major physical function of dwellings is thermal control, closely followed by protection from wind, rain and solar radiation, as well as adapting humidity, air movement and natural light. Some key responses to climate in primitive and vernacular dwellings are:

- Hot dry areas, with low night-time temperatures, such as arid zones, develop thick walls and roofs with high heat capacity materials to absorb solar radiation and re-radiate this throughout the night. These buildings are usually compact and closely packed together, with separate cooking and small openings. Cave and underground dwellings fit in this category. Courtyards are also used extensively, and living in the warmer summer nights also takes place in external spaces (rooftops, verandas, courtyards, etc).
- Hot, humid areas, with little daily or seasonal variation and high rainfall tend to maximise shade and minimise heat capacity. This leads to almost the opposite from hot arid zones, as the objective is to allow the body to lose heat. Ventilation is maximised, with long narrow forms and widely separated units, with minimum internal divisions. This affects privacy and often social controls may deal with this – otherwise screens are used. Buildings are raised to allow air flow from below and better catch breezes. The roof acts like a large umbrella on these houses, as well as protecting from solar radiation. Roof slopes are generally steep due to high rainfall levels.
- Cold temperature areas tend to maximise heat capacity, as with hot arid areas, but with internal sources of heat usually centrally located. Dark colours are used to capture solar radiation (as opposed to lighter colours in arid regions). Protection from the wind is also important.

The relation of the dwelling to the climate can include various seasonal solutions also – summer and winter forms of dwelling being different. Often this is tied in with other cultural and economic factors, such as seeking pasture, following game for hunting or working farmland on a seasonal basis (see below).

Understanding traditional house form in its socio-economic and political context

Schoenauer (2000) approaches traditional forms of housing in a slightly different, but complementary, way to Rapoport. He differentiates between pre-urban and urban forms, and within the latter category, different 'Oriental' and 'Occidental' forms. In his pre-urban category he sees traditional housing as '… an architectural response to a set of cultural and physical forces intrinsic to a particular socio-economic and physical environment' (Schoenauer 2000: 11). He stresses that accepting such an 'anthropo-geographic and socio-economic' approach leads to distinguishing between different dwelling categories on the basis of socio-economic structures, as follows.

'Ephemeral' or 'transient' dwellings, which are those of hunting/gathering nomadic societies. Relatively recent and/or current examples are the BaMbuti ('pygmy') and San ('bushman') huts in Africa and Arunta ('aborigine') huts of

Australia, which represent a form of shelter that was prevalent across the world in many different environments until perhaps 8000 BC, when cultivation permitted different forms of living. These shelters are rudimentary and based on simple construction techniques using locally available material and non-specialised skills. The small and non-hierarchical social groups are reflected in settlement size and form. Settlements were very temporary, as scarce natural resources in the regions they inhabited required frequent moves as part of longer seasonal migrations. Many of these peoples were gradually driven to the most inhospitable regions such as far north, deserts and in tropical forests, where limited natural resources have been a factor in preserving this way of life.

'Episodic' or 'Irregular temporary' dwellings were produced by advanced hunting/gathering nomadic groups in transition to pastoralist or agricultural economies, usually facilitated by access to a richer natural environment. Here settlements existed for weeks rather than days, although construction remained simple, albeit more technologically advanced and capable of greater environmental protection, sometimes with distinctive dwelling types related to seasonal opportunities and migration. While few advanced hunting/gathering societies now exist, contemporary examples from the northern hemisphere include the Inuit winter igloo and summer tupiq tent; and also Native American, Siberian Tungu and Northern European Lapp 'tepees' or tents. In the southern hemisphere examples include the shelters of the 'slash and burn' cultivators in tropical forest regions, such as the Indian groups of Latin American and South East Asian forests. These have more complex social groupings in tribal units, communal-based economies and more complicated communal buildings, including those for living. However, due to climate and predatory insects these structures tend to last a limited number of years, as do local food supplies, leading to frequent migrations. An example is the Wai-Wai communal dwelling (Brazil and Guyana).

'Periodic' or 'Regular temporary' dwellings are those of nomadic pastoral societies which are intermediary between hunting/gathering and sedentary agrarian societies. Examples include the Mongolian 'yurt', and the Tuareg and Bedouin tent. The social basis is often tribal with hierarchic sub-groups organised in hierarchic chiefdoms, and the economic basis generally domesticated livestock with some continuing hunting/gathering. These pastoral groups tend to inhabit large tundra, steppe or savannah areas, migrating with the climate. Shelters are thus often portable and, in adverse climates, quite sophisticated. The moveable structures mean that materials do not have to be locally available. Nomadic pastoral herders are more likely to take structural as well as covering components with them (usually frame and mat dwellings or tents), using pack animals. Many of these structures are similar to the above more temporary house forms – i.e. simple spherical, trapezoidal and conical shapes – although these can be expanded.

'Seasonal' dwellings are occupied by semi-nomads, who remain in one location for considerable periods as their socio-economic basis is mixed pastoralism and cultivation. These groups tend to move less frequently and are found in steppe and savannah regions which offer natural advantages for both forms of livelihood. Societies are tribal and hierarchic, and shelters for different periods/locations often differ in complexity, with summer shelters typically simpler, similar to those of true nomads. However, there is a greater perception of ownership in these cultures as areas of cultivation and pasture are often returned to regularly. Ownership rights are, however, still expressed in communal forms – for example in the name of the family or clan, which is the economic unit in terms of labour. Examples include the American Navaho 'hogan' and African Masai 'boma'.

'Semi-permanent' dwellings are used by sedentary societies relying on simple forms of cultivation. Their agriculture relies on leaving land fallow for periods and hence the dwelling forms are not fully permanent, lasting from a few to maybe more than 10 years. Concepts of land and property ownership in these societies are much more complex, as they have developed over long periods, often overlaid with class structures as inheritance has accumulated. Cultural groupings also have an important influence on dwelling form and settlement size, which are usually clusters of semi-permanent hut structures, with specialisation of use (e.g. storage, cooking, and even public use such as worship). Typical examples include a wide range of Sub-Saharan African traditional dwelling forms and those of the Central American peoples (e.g. Mayan, Mexican and Pueblo Indians). Some of these shelter forms have evolved over relatively long periods to form semi-permanent settlements of some size and complexity. Construction techniques are more developed, but the form of construction is still not highly specialised in terms of labour, techniques or materials.

'Permanent' dwellings require, above all, more permanent forms of economic sustenance. As such, the carrying capacity of the land largely determined the nature of settlement until relatively recently in historic terms – and still is of great importance in rural settlement forms in many parts of the world. The nature of rural human settlements is thus affected at the 'micro-economic' level – i.e. in specific local regions – but also at the 'meso-economic' level where the relationships between producers and others are established through, for instance, markets, which have wider geographic significance through trade. Agricultural development and fishing have historically been closely linked to evolving forms of sedentary (as opposed to nomadic and semi-nomadic) economic sustenance and forms of settlement. However, rural settlements vary enormously in size and form, varying from scattered kinship-linked hamlets, through linear villages, to relatively high density enclosed towns. This depends on the carrying capacity of the land, nature of resources and technology available (i.e. economic attributes); the forms of social organisation that have evolved in different cultures; and different political

circumstances – for example defence can still be a major influence where there is no overall political stability.

The nature of housing in more settled communities changes as these develop over time. Depending on the nature of the economic, social and political basis for settlement type these may need to change location at certain intervals or may be fixed over long periods. The nature of the construction varies to some extent based on permanence, as does the increasing specialisation in construction. In nomadic and semi-permanent settlement forms, house construction has often limited specialisation and most members of a society learn basic skills – although there may be gender or other social differentiation, and some people obviously will have better inherent skills than others, or develop these through practice. In situations where longer established settlements can evolve and change over time more permanent construction often requires more specialised skills – whether massive construction (e.g. shelter from adverse climates) or light-weight construction (e.g. frame structures to withstand earthquakes). Construction specialisation usually entails a more developed economic basis in society and can lead to protection of skills and skill transfer (e.g. through guilds).

Permanent dwellings thus tend to belong to agricultural societies with a degree of socio-economic advancement which permits permanent cultivation. The basic social unit in these societies is the household, often in extended form (especially if agricultural advancement is limited and requires extensive labour). Social structures are much more complex than in less permanent socio-economic groups, and include community and broader political hierarchies such as states as well as family/clan hierarchies (which are, however, weaker than in more migratory socio-economic forms). The nature of this socio-economic basis allows (and requires) a higher degree of specialisation and this is also reflected in forms of shelter and other specialised buildings, although farming is the dominant activity. There is thus more reliance on forms of social redistribution, governed by cultural and political forces, as opposed to direct inter-household reciprocity, which is an important feature of the less established socio-economic groups; however, intra-household reciprocity still plays an important basis for family life. In these more sedentary societies property ownership becomes more individualised, based on family lines. The nature of shelter also varies enormously – from cave dwellings in China to North American colonists' homesteads – as do traditional construction techniques.

Although the above pre-urban forms of settlement date back to the origins of humankind, and have evolved over long periods within specific environmental and cultural situations to display distinctive house and settlement forms, the majority of people across the world still live in dwellings or settlements that exhibit many of these characteristics, although they may be integrated into very different socio-economic and political contexts. Even in urban areas many people have either lived in these dwelling forms and/or settlements in rural areas previously, or maintain links with these. This is now changing as, for the first time in the history of humankind, the majority of the world's population is becoming urbanised and many more people are born and raised in urban settings, as noted in Chapter 1. However, pre-urban and pre-capitalist forms still have a strong cultural influence on how urban areas and dwellings are developed, especially as the majority of urban dwellers continue to rely on socially and culturally established traditions in terms of how they approach dwelling production. The next section of the chapter thus looks at early urban forms of housing and settlement.

The development of urban settlement form

Early urban civilisation

Schoenauer (2000) identifies what he calls 'early civilisations' as developing in sedentary agrarian societies occupying the fertile alluvial plains of great rivers in areas where protection from nomadic tribes was assisted by natural features – mountain ranges and/or deserts. These rivers included the Tigris/Euphrates, Indus, Nile and Hwang Ho/Yangtze river systems, the rivers themselves also offering relatively easy means of transportation (Figure 4.2). He terms this early urban settlement form the 'oriental' experience.

These early civilisations developed the first urban settlement forms, dating back perhaps to 4000 BC, evolving over a long period from previous rural settlement forms. Despite their geographical separation they share a common house form – the courtyard house – which Schoenauer argues essentially evolved from the simple collective groupings of nomadic and semi-nomadic societies. He argues that in urban areas the factors of privacy and safety (of inhabitants and possessions) became more important, leading to this distinctive form, although he also acknowledges environmental considerations, due to the prevailing hot dry climates of these regions.

These ancient civilisations consisted of various fortified city states which evolved elaborate systems of government and politics, as well as many cultural attributes (e.g. writing, mathematics and art) and highly differentiated systems of labour. The cities depended on the surrounding villages and farms to supply their food, although in time these diminished with growing trade, fuelling an early form of urban expansion. Nevertheless, the scale of this form of urbanisation was very limited – at its peak in 2000 BC the city of Ur in Mesopotamia had only some 34,000 inhabitants. Building technology also remained fairly simple with no use of arches, only wooden lintels, but elaborate systems for drainage were established in some cities, and forms of land use planning with strict limitations on growth were established in Chinese urban settlements.

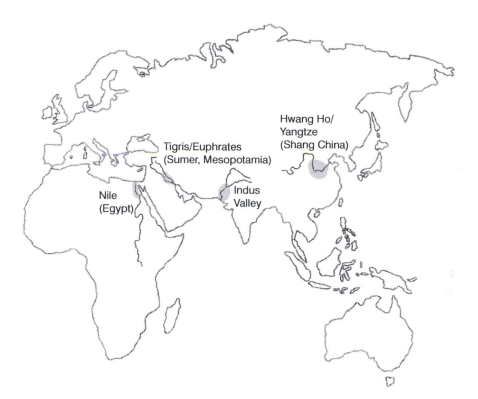

4.2 Map of early urban civilisations (Tigris/Euphrates, Indus, Nile, Hwang Ho/Yangtze) (Drawing by Harry Smith)

A second major period of oriental urban civilisation was developed by the Greeks and Romans from 900 BC to AD 500. Greek cities also had strict expansion controls, although their relation with the (less fertile) rural hinterland was different as these were part of the governing unit and not subordinate as in the earlier civilisations. Trade was also more important for these cities and the continued creation of new urban areas spurred this on, spreading Hellenistic civilisation. This urban form included grid street layouts, a new feature not previously developed in the earlier urban civilisations, where land occupation and house development had followed non-geometric patterns. The Macedonian empire reached into some of these earlier civilisations and the process of transformation of urban form was subsequently carried on in the Roman Empire which replaced it. The Romans fully embraced the Greek tradition of urban planning based on a geometric urban layout and institutionalised this with specific urban and street layout categories. They also perfected infrastructure such as communal water supplies and sewerage systems in larger cities. Rome itself developed multi-storey tenement flats for the labouring classes in contrast to the courtyard 'atrium' houses for the better-off, and reached the previously unsurpassed size of one million inhabitants by the first century AD. This resulted in traffic problems which required early forms of traffic control, as well as the need for food warehouses and public parks.

The Roman Empire collapsed about the fifth century AD, after which, in most of the Northern European areas where the Romans had expanded, urban forms were abandoned for many centuries. In Southern Europe, North Africa, the Middle East and Asia Minor, however, the Roman Empire was supplanted by the Arab Empire from the seventh through to the thirteenth centuries. Cities originally founded by Greeks and Romans became gradually adapted to Islamic social structure and culture and associated urban patterns, particularly changes to geometric street patterns. This also included the creation of neighbourhood-level social focal points as opposed to the dominant city centres of the previous urban form. Houses, however, remained inward-looking courtyard dwellings based on the family, with privacy being an even more important element than before, based on a strict division of public and private spheres which also applied to gender in Islamic culture. The exterior of houses remained simple and plain whereas the interior offered micro-climatic control and was decorated. The strict division between inner private and semi-public space was gradually reduced in Egyptian urban dwellings within this tradition when Turkish influences of the Ottoman Empire came to dominate from the thirteenth through to the nineteenth centuries. This Turkish influence is seen in displays of wealth in the exterior with decorated screened outer windows and projecting balconies and can also be seen in dwellings in Mesopotamia of the same period.

On the Indian sub-continent, similar settlement forms also dominated traditional cities from the twelfth century on, despite different religious and cultural influences. Courtyard-style dwellings were again organically grouped along irregular access pathways and slightly wider streets, all related to neighbourhood units with some provision of local services and open space. Privacy of the household home was again paramount, and although restrictions on women in public were less in evidence than in Arab societies, internal spaces continued to have gender role specialisation. Similar to the Turkish style above, upper stories also had windows projecting over the street, screened for privacy and climatic reasons. Later cities developed with strict planning controls administered by the founding ruler, including the nature of building on main streets, a hierarchy of street widths and other forms of social control – an early form of development control.

In China, urban areas existed from the eleventh century BC, however political unrest led to many of these being destroyed, to be rebuilt centuries later. Rather like in the ancient Mesopotamian civilisations, cities had a dominant role over the related rural villages, however in this case this was overseen by the central nation state, not the city state. The main urban areas were geometrically planned, although less rigorously so than Greek and Roman cities. Another difference was the high population and population densities (up to 320 inhabitants per hectare in Beijing in the fifteenth century). In these settlements there was considerable specialisation in land use and function, including commercial and production quarters, an aspect Chinese cities destined to continue to the present day. The courtyard dwellings housed extended families as married sons remained with their parents. Gender differences of use and privacy were also strong with women largely confined to dwellings as in most Islamic cultures.

To summarise, most early 'oriental' urban settlements developed organic forms, based on rural settlement traditions and dwelling forms. The cultural nature of the early civilisations led to a tendency for inward-looking dwelling units based on the household. The role of wider forms of governance was of great importance in managing cities (whether city-based or state-based), and relatively high degrees of urban management developed, including communal infrastructure and regulated development. In some civilisations the use of orthogonal geometry dominated town layouts, and these generally represented city and/or state power in physical terms. Overall a major difference in these urban societies from the pre-urban societies was the reliance on social forms of control which went beyond the family, tribe or clan, and were based on either the city state or the nation state. However, the majority of construction was relatively simple, with limited specialisation of labour and technique, and although few urban dwellers built their own dwellings exclusively, they had considerable input to these. The result was individual solutions following socially, culturally and politically acceptable norms within the technological and economic contexts of the time, which brought about considerable homogeneity at a wider level, including relatively low rise and the widespread use of the courtyard house form.

Early urban development in Europe

Urban development in the 'West', or 'North' (generically termed the 'occident' by Schoenauer) generally came much later, and was influenced by this through culture (e.g. Christian religion and Greek philosophy) and conquest (e.g. Roman and later Islam expansion). The Roman Empire brought the first urban forms to Northern Europe, however urban settlements more or less disappeared after its collapse, only to be gradually replaced by more 'organic' urban forms much later, after the so-called Dark Ages.[4] The unsettled nature of this medieval period in these regions led to dispersed rural settlements in small farmsteads and the development of the fortified tower for the elite, later developing into larger castles as feudal fiefdoms were consolidated. Settlements often grew near these castles and became towns (or 'burghs'), that were authorised by the feudal chief and also usually fortified. As in early oriental urban settlements, the urban dwelling form in these burghs largely evolved from the rural homestead form, but increasingly became multi-storey on long narrow plots, due to space restrictions within the city walls. These dwellings still often incorporated a form of internal yard, though this was a utility area as opposed to an outdoor living space as in the oriental dwelling. These forms of dwelling and settlement form continued in various forms of development in occidental urban areas until the eighteenth century, when political-economic change and rural transformation led to the commencement of rapid urbanisation (as outlined in Chapter 3), as well as growing spatial separation.

Box 4.1 Tracking the change from traditional to modern housing in Botswana

A useful analysis of the changes between vernacular and modern dwelling types in a developing country is the research of Anita Larsson into house form and settlement in Botswana (Larsson 1984, 1988, 1990). The initial study investigated traditionally built houses in villages and analysed these in relation to a number of functional aspects. The majority of these were decorated, mud-walled, thatched roof constructions grouped around outdoor living/functional spaces – including the 'lolwapa', which is an open air space enclosed by a low mud wall. These buildings were then enclosed by a hedge creating a 'yard', and the yards were grouped in various kinship-based neighbourhood 'wards', with a focal 'kgotla' or headman's court. A fully traditional house could be made from collected natural materials from the family's agricultural holdings outside the village. Building was generally undertaken by family members, with friends and relatives helping on a reciprocal basis, especially for the roof (see Figure 4.3).

A second study investigated the transition from traditional to modern housing in three main towns. This studied the nature of the changes in design of buildings and use of space, including domestic and work activities and building process/materials, and investigated the consequences for inhabitants. The study found that modernisation mainly involved building materials and some space and actually led to a decrease in utility in several aspects, as compared to traditional dwellings. Changing lifestyles and attitudes led to demand for more indoor space (e.g. indoor cooking and personal hygiene), yet this was actually more limited due to the higher costs of modern building provision. There was thus typically more overcrowding in modern housing, including mixed housing. The modern materials, however, required less maintenance and this particularly freed up women from this area of work. Larsson differentiated between what she termed the 'quasi-modern' dwelling which was a partial modern-produced solution, but lacked essential elements of provision (e.g. indoor kitchen or bathroom, or adequate space for the

4.3 A mainly traditional house in Botswana (Drawing by Viera Larsson, in Larsson 1988: 50)

household), and the 'developed traditional' dwelling which demonstrated partial modernisation of traditional dwellings (see Figures 4.4 and 4.5). The former is typically the product of state-supported sites and services and house provision for sale, whereas the latter is found in both villages and 'squatter' areas in and around towns, and the main difference was the nature of state regulation, as this did not permit traditional building forms in urban plots, except where these were being upgraded. Essentially the differences between these two transitional types can be interpreted as 'top-down' solutions, with state and formal private sector intervention; and 'bottom-up' solutions which evolve from, but continued to integrate, traditional built forms and although

continued...

Box 4.1 continued

using commodified materials and labour, this is not fully market based as it is process driven rather than provided as a product.

The third study in this series focused on modern housing provision and state intervention in this, especially state regulation of standards of building materials and space (room and plot sizes) as opposed to other aspects of housing quality. In this, cultural values – of householders as much as government personnel – conceptualised and prized 'modern' as opposed to 'traditional' qualities, reflected in the title of the report: 'Modern houses for modern life'. The study also identified and discussed cultural, gender and social class influences on, and by, housing.[5] Overall, modern housing is highly influenced by elite cultural values (actual and aspirational) and state bureaucratic intervention in wider market provision in the 'public' sphere of life, as opposed to being an aspect of social utility and cultural expression

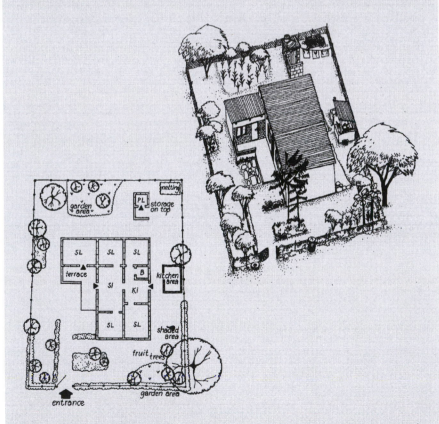

4.4 'Developed traditional' dwelling in Botswana (Drawing by Viera Larsson in Larsson, 1988: 64)

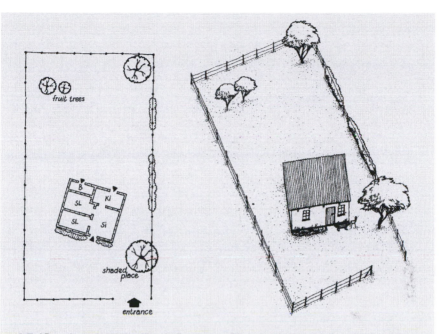

4.5 'Quasi-modern' dwelling in Botswana (Drawing by Viera Larsson, in Larsson 1988: 56)

largely within the 'domestic' sphere of life. The study also investigated the principal aspects of the political economy since Independence, and the nature of housing policy and practice in this period, leading to conclusions which characterised the dominant tendency in policy and practice in the capital, Gaberone, and the second principal urban area, Francistown, in terms of 'modern' and 'traditional' orientation and identified conflict between the use value of the home in traditional context and the house as predominantly a commodity in the modern context (e.g. through income generation by sub-letting). Larsson's research demonstrates the need for inter-linked approaches to analysis of housing, including the physical, social, cultural as well as the political and economic contexts. Her overall conclusions include a call for a different approach to 'modernisation' in housing which permits traditional socio-cultural values and material/technological methods to be integrated – a complementary alternative 'combination of tradition and modernity' as opposed to the perceived current conflicting relationship. This, she acknowledges, would require less rigid regulation and more household decision making, as well as more acknowledgement of women's role in housing in male-dominated decision-making, whether at household or government level.

Examining the nature of pre-capitalist housing and urban development

An analytical framework

There were distinct differences between the early urban forms that developed in oriental and occidental areas. The former was often (although not always) organic in settlement form and centred on the low-rise household-owned courtyard house, built with relatively simple processes and inputs. The latter, while starting in this format, developed different uses of outdoor space (to some extent due to climatic factors), and higher rise solutions (partly due to defence, but also socio-economic structure, including access to urban land). These factors in themselves did not produce the radically different urban settlement forms that developed, but created the cultural and technical context. The main difference between traditional oriental and occidental urban forms was in fact the rapid development of specialised land ownership patterns in the latter, and the subsequent development of industrialisation, with highly specialised forms of labour division as capitalism evolved from mercantile to industrial forms and as urbanisation became more widespread and rapid. The growing importance of property as capital led to the development of a house-building industry oriented to exchange as opposed to use value, which had been the main basis for oriental urban house and settlement forms, as well as traditional non-urban dwellings. Essentially what changed was from dwelling production within a socio-economic form of interchange based on social and socio-political redistributive structures, to a relatively anonymous market-based form of socio-economic interchange, with increasing involvement of a largely autonomous state.

Karl Polanyi provides a way for us to see how these pre-capitalist forms of socio-economic interchange relate to capitalist forms, including eventually in contemporary contexts. Polanyi was an economic historian whose studies drew on many areas, including anthropology. His writing concentrated on the relation of economy to society in 'primitive and archaic systems' and the origin, growth and transformation of nineteenth-century capitalism (see Polanyi 1944, 1977; Polanyi *et al.* 1957; Dalton 1971). His major contention was that different forms of socio-economic integration (or interchange) have been dominant in different situations (geographical and temporal) and that latter-day 'economics' became distorted as it became divorced from its societal context. He also argued that pre-capitalist forms of socio-economic integration continue to operate after the dominant development of capitalism, which is another way of understanding the articulation of capitalist forms with pre-capitalist forms.

Polanyi's studies in what were then termed 'primitive' and 'archaic' economies showed that the institutions through which goods were produced and distributed were 'embedded' in social institutions and thus the 'economy' functioned as a subordinate by-product of kinship, political and religious obligations. He contended that all communities institutionalise exchange of material items and services and systematise the allocation of rights to land and other resources, but most do this to ensure the sustained provision for continuance of social life. The economy, as a rule, is therefore subordinated to social relationships, and the economic system is thus a function of social (and related socio-political) organisation. In 'primitive' and 'archaic' societies, land and labour were typically allocated in accordance to these obligations and were seen as social and moral rights – and not commodities to be traded. Markets (i.e. in the sense of market 'exchange' as opposed to the market 'system') did develop in these societies, but for limited forms of exchange, and were controlled as part of the socio-cultural and political system.

Polanyi argued that political, religious and familial organisations 'traditionally' arranged production and distribution in basically two broad transactional modes that Polanyi called:[6]

- reciprocity – obligatory gift-giving between kin and friends, based on sym-metrical exchange in relationships; and
- redistribution – obligatory payments to centralised political or religious authorities, which used the receipts for their own maintenance, provision of community services, and emergency stock for individual or communal disaster,[7] in either homogeneous or hierarchical/stratified societies.[8]

These forms of socio-economic interchange were fundamentally different from that of systematic *market exchange*, which Polanyi argued was not a ubiquitous and invariable form of economic organisation. He thus refuted the notion that all economies could be transformed into market terms and that market-based economic organisation could determine social organisation and culture in all societies.

Polanyi's studies of the origin, growth and transformation of capitalism indicated that the Industrial Revolution had required wide-ranging institutional changes. These included acts of government to free up feudal and other pre-capitalist controls on land, labour and other resources, as well as creation and expansion of financial markets to provide freer movement of money and capital. This intervention was based on commoditisation of land, labour and capital (as well as other products)[9] and the development of 'free' market exchange processes for these. Free market exchange was a unique concept in that the pursuit of material self-gain became institutionally enforced as the dominant incentive to participate economically as opposed to socially. However, this eroded social and community life and thus quickly led to socially protective measures. Social control was thus (re)-instituted on labour, land, money and some product markets (e.g.

after 1860 in England), to protect workers, farmers, and businessmen. This was to ensure both economic protection (i.e. income) for specific groups (through unions, factory acts, agricultural tariffs and central banking) but also communal life (through safety requirements, planning and building codes, industrial accident insurance, etc). Thus Polanyi argued that a 'double movement' was created in the late nineteenth century – free market transactions of commodities were encouraged worldwide, while (incomplete) market controls were imposed in Europe and later America on transactions in land, labour and money in the interests of community stability and cohesion.

In Polanyi's analysis of the development of capitalism he argued that *reciprocity, redistribution* and *market exchange* often exist side by side on different levels and in different sectors of the economy and it may not always be possible to select one as dominant. He also stressed that each requires institutional supports as preconditions for their effective functioning. In other words, the systems of socio-economic interchange are not created solely by aggregates of individual activities, but develop within specific institutional contexts within society. He considered that reciprocity as a form of integration gains greatly in power through its capacity to employ redistribution and exchange as subordinate methods. However, he stressed that market exchange has become the *dominant* (i.e. most widespread) and *integrative* (i.e. primary) transactional mode in today's society, but redistributive transactions are very much present in taxes and government expenditure, as are reciprocal transactions (e.g. gift-giving and shared household activities). This early 'institutionalist' form of analysis was paradoxically returned to by capitalist economists in the 1990s when they developed 'New Institutional Economics'.

Applying the analysis to housing and settlement form

Applying this analysis to the relationships between traditional and modern forms of housing and settlement form, we can argue that non-specialised primitive dwellings can be associated with societies where socio-economic interchange was dominated by *reciprocity*, and this is reflected in both building processes (i.e. in shared labour) and settlement organisation (i.e. essentially organic and non-hierarchical). Early *re-distributive* societies, on the other hand, acquired some level of specialisation and surplus production, as well as social structure to undertake the redistribution of this surplus, and these permitted the development of more specialised building functions, with some separation of spatial functions, especially representing political and cultural hierarchies. These forms of socio-economic interchange have existed for long periods, across wide areas of the world in various structured civilisations, some of which developed early urban forms, as described above. The nature of socio-political organisation underpinned significant advances in developing building and climate adaptation technology, architectural expression and specialised building and residential space use – as well as urban infrastructure development and land use control. Thus, in societies which were sedentary and strongly structured, urban settlement was much more likely than in semi-permanent or nomadic societies.

The development of the wider *market system* of socio-economic interchange from the sixteenth and seventeenth centuries, on the other hand, led to undermining of the wider social control of economies and the increasing political control by elites as it became more anonymous. This was also characterised by commodification of space (land and buildings), as well as of the components of construction: materials, technological expertise and labour – eventually also including finance. This form of socio-economic interchange was associated with growing specialisation and promoted a wide range of building and settlement forms, with increasing specialisation in production. It included the commodification of dwellings, which eventually became mass produced by either capital interests or re-distributive states (or combinations of these). In this process the house itself has become transformed from something predominantly of 'use value' to the inhabitants – albeit transferred when necessary and even bought and sold – to predominantly something of 'exchange value' in a market as it became the largest single investment for most households. 'Housing' thus largely changed from being a social process to being an economic product – i.e. from something that was predominantly socially produced and modified, transformed etc., to something that increasingly became produced by the anonymous market and exchanged through market principles.

As argued in Chapter 3, modern forms of urbanisation and urban development are closely associated with this form of capitalist commodification – although, as described above, urban development took place before market-based forms of socio-economic interchange came to dominate other forms. As is argued in more detail later, the extent of global penetration of this form of market-domination of housing production and exchange is far from uniform, however, as capitalism has penetrated incompletely in many parts of the world. Thus while Northern European societies generally urbanised at a time when market socio-economic interchange was coming to dominate, and have since largely been dominated by this process, this is not true of many other parts of the world which are still urbanising. Here the reciprocal and re-distributive forms of socio-economic integration still co-exist with the market, and different groups operate in, and between, these forms of socio-economic interchange. As such, the primitive, pre-industrial and industrialised forms of shelter and settlements all also co-exist with different levels of articulation with capitalism – and different perspectives for evolution of this in future.

Effectively, in many rapidly urbanising countries, hybrid forms of socio-economic interchange, with associated hybrid forms of housing and settlement, dominate the urban development process. This is one of the principal reasons to commence a study of planning and housing policy and practice in the rapidly urbanising world with a study of traditional house forms and urban settlement patterns. It is important to learn from the way that these forms were clearly embedded within their social, cultural, economic, environmental, material and technical realities, as a means to better understand the hybrid situations of the increasingly urbanised societies of today. Many of these have not had the benefit of high levels of market investment of capital or state redistributed services that have led to the wider and deeper application of 'modern' economic forms of housing in the earlier urban development in the North. Thus, while this has been seen as the incomplete articulation of pre-capitalist forms by capitalism, there is a need to unpack what we mean by *pre-capitalist*, and not only in relation to different political, social and cultural contexts, but also to understand how other *non-capitalist* forms of interchange operate and underpin housing and planning in different contexts. This argument will be returned to in later chapters.

Chapter 5
Colonial and neo-colonial planning and housing

Introduction

This chapter provides an overview of the influence that European colonial powers had on urban development and housing in much of the rapidly urbanising world, both before and after rapid urbanisation took off in the industrialising period in Europe and North America – as discussed in Chapters 1 and 3. This chapter spans from the period of early expansion of the Spanish and Portuguese empires into the Americas and the Indian Ocean during the sixteenth century, to the major period of worldwide decolonisation that peaked around the 1960s. It thus covers urban development and housing during the growth and spread of capitalism from its origins in northwest Europe, touched on in the analysis in the previous chapter, to much of the contemporary rapidly urbanising world, including the mercantilist, industrial, colonial and neo-colonial periods that this has passed through.[1]

This chapter is therefore centred around the phenomenon and period of Western colonialism. In his analysis of urbanism and colonialism, King (1990: 46–7) uses a definition of colonialism provided by Emerson (1968): 'the establishment and maintenance, for an extended time, of rule over an alien people that is separate from and subordinate to the ruling power'. King (1992: 350) notes that this definition leaves much uncovered, emphasising political dominance and focusing on the coloniser rather than the colonised. In addition, he notes the different conditions the term 'colonialism' is associated with, ranging from the establishment of 'colonies' or plantations to which European settlers emigrated, to the conflation of colonialism with imperialism as in Marxist analysis, which links modern colonialism (from the nineteenth century onwards) with economic expansion in search of raw materials and markets and not necessarily with direct rule over land. This chapter takes a broad approach to colonialism, recognising that there was a period of expansion of (originally) European dominion and influence over large parts of the world, which started in the late fifteenth century and encompassed territorial rule and/or economic domination. This approach helps understand the transformation of pre-capitalist societies throughout the world that came under this colonial influence, and the concomitant transformations in the production of human settlements and shelter.

Previous chapters have identified the extent of European imperial influence, but non-Western societies did not come under European influence at the same time, nor did they achieve independence simultaneously; thus – for instance – it can be said that Latin America in fact entered a 'neo-colonial' phase before most of Sub-Saharan Africa was even fully colonised. The periods covered in this chapter are therefore predominantly meaningful from a global perspective, with reference to the new international political economy approach introduced in Chapter 3, as region- and country-specific histories vary considerably (as will be seen in Chapters 9–11), as do the actors involved and their objectives and motives. The main parts of the rapidly urbanising world which came under Western colonisation, and their respective periods, were as follows (see also Figure 5.1):[2]

- Latin America – this was occupied by Spain and Portugal from the sixteenth to the nineteenth centuries. Independence of mainland Latin America came about in the 1820s, though Brazilian independence from Portugal was only nominal until 1889 – see Chapter 10. While Spain mainly used cheap indigenous labour to extract precious metals, Portugal's colonisation of today's Brazil was linked to a series of productive/extractive activities over time, using slave labour mostly from Africa. Other European powers' colonies around the Caribbean became politically independent in the second half of the twentieth century.
- Asia – although Portugal had port enclaves in India dating back to the sixteenth century (followed later by Britain and France), and trading companies were active from the mid-eighteenth century, the main colonial period was British Government direct rule of India from the mid-nineteenth century to 1947. South East Asia came under the colonial control of Britain, France and the Netherlands at the end of the nineteenth century, regaining independence in the 1950s/1960s. The initial interest of these colonising powers was in trading, but in a later phase plantation agriculture also developed.
- Sub-Saharan Africa – after a long period of limited coastal settlement through trading posts (linked to the American slave trade and the trade routes to Asia) the main colonial period began with the 'Scramble for Africa' in the 1880s, when European colonial powers carved up Africa mainly in order to extract raw materials to supply their new industrial economies. European colonial administration in Africa generally ended in the 1950s/1960s.[3]

The chapter first looks at how the colonial powers affected the development of human settlements in these countries, which imported urban development and planning theories and practice, and then focuses on the transformation of housing forms and provision under the colonial influence.

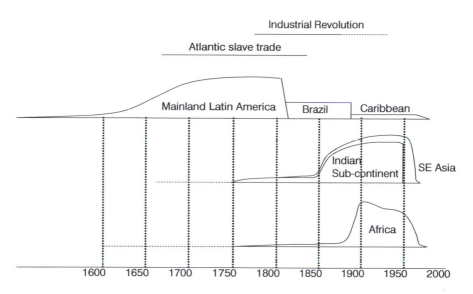

5.1 Periods and areas of European colonisation (Drawing by Harry Smith based on Lowder, 1986: 53)

Planning in the colonial period

The role of cities in the colonial empires

Home (1997: 2) argues that all cities are, in a way, colonial:

> They are created through the exercise of dominance by some groups over others, to extract agricultural surplus, provide services, and exercise political control. Transport improvements then allow one society or state to incorporate other territory and peoples overseas. The city thus becomes an instrument of colonization and (in the case of the European overseas empires) racial dominance.

The city was indeed used as an instrument of colonisation by Western powers, in different ways related to their main colonising objectives. Thus, during the sixteenth century the Spanish Empire established an urban system in Latin America based on cities founded in locations strategic for the extraction and transport of minerals back to the metropolis and for administration of the territory, sometimes obliterating pre-existing indigenous urban settlements. In contrast, in nineteenth century India the British developed their administrative centres mostly in already existing cities, into which they introduced new forms of segregation and 'improvements'. There are therefore different legacies in terms of urban development and planning in the various parts of the rapidly urbanising world. Some of these legacies are studied in more depth in the case study chapters (see Chapters 9, 10 and 11).

Generally, the colonies provided a source of cheap raw materials, land and labour, as well as markets for goods manufactured in the core countries. Urban areas were not usually seen as production centres, but rather as means to control and channel production that took place in rural areas. Urbanisation in the colonies took place largely without industrialisation, as opposed to the close link between industrialisation and urbanisation that was evident in western societies (King 1990). Colonial cities depended on trade between the colony and the metropolis rather than on their own industrial production, and in this sense urbanisation in this context has been termed 'dependent urbanization' (Castells 1977). Linked to dependency theory (see Chapter 2), this view of urbanisation sees urban areas in the colonies as enclaves underpinning penetration of their territories by the capitalist system, with the purpose of 'helping to maintain expanding levels of production and consumption in the home countries of advanced capitalism' (Friedmann and Wulff 1976, in King 1990: 50). Within this system of economic interaction, colonial cities played different roles, often non-economic, including:

- defence and military control;
- commercial ports oriented to trade with the metropolis;
- new capitals created almost entirely for administrative, political and social functions;
- new centres established with political, administrative and commercial functions (King 1990).

However, even when urban areas had a clear productive role, they were still most often considered by the colonial rulers as the natural abode of Europeans but not of the indigenous population. This was particularly the case in Africa, and had implications for planning and for the provision of housing, as is detailed later in this chapter.

In an attempt to systematise their study, King (1990: 20–2) identified criteria that permit the construction of a typology of colonial cities: (1) classification of societies and territories on the basis of the number of inhabitants and the nature and level of their economy and culture, including the existence of urban settlement; (2) motives for and circumstances of colonisation; and (3) numbers and degree of permanence of the colonising population, which affect the degree of coercion exercised over the indigenous inhabitants. These criteria are factors that influenced the physical, spatial and social form of the colonial city, with 10 possibilities being identified by King (1990), ranging from an existing site being occupied with little or no modifications, to a new settlement being built for the colonists' only and permanent settlement by non-colonial groups not being permitted. Some of these types have been more prevalent in certain areas, during certain periods, and under certain colonial rules, already becoming apparent during the early phase of globalisation associated with the mercantilist period.

Early influences on urban development during the mercantilist period – sixteenth to eighteenth centuries

During the mercantilist period two main ways in which colonial powers related to the territories they came in contact with can be distinguished: settlement of the land with creation of Western urban centres (particularly in the Americas) and trading with no or little settlement (much of Sub-Saharan Africa and South and East Asia).

In the former, the location and form of new urban settlements were determined by the colonising powers (e.g. in Latin America – see Chapter 10), which revived the grid pattern used by the ancient Greeks 2000 years earlier. Foundation of cities in the Spanish colonies can be seen as a continuation of the activities of the Christian kingdoms in the Iberian peninsula, whose advance on the Islamic southern part of the peninsula was secured and consolidated through establishing cities that marked a new 'frontier'. After defeating the last Muslim kingdom in the peninsula, the alliance between Christian state (i.e. the Crown) and 'warrior nobility' found a vast new territory in Latin America where this form of expansion was to an extent replicated. The Crown sponsored and regulated 'conquest' and colonisation, and later controlled the colonies through the application of mercantilist measures, while the nobility and other individuals effected such colonisation on the Crown's behalf with the aim of acquiring wealth and establishing landed estates.

Other parts of the Americas were settled later by emerging northern European powers through the initiative of a variety of actors – Crown-sponsored settlements, commercially driven ventures, and settlements established by groups fleeing religious persecution – which also took with them practices developed in their metropoles. In the eighteenth century, 'new towns' were planned and built in Europe drawing on classical urban and architectural forms, and separating socio-economic classes and functions. These were often located in extensions separate from the organic 'old towns', which was possible due to growing political stability, at least at the local level, although nation states were still in flux. Such new towns were also a strong feature of urban development in the 'New World' colonies, where classical grid-iron patterns were applied more comprehensively. Western European governments thus supported the establishment of settlements throughout the 'New World' colonies, and applied mercantile regulations to ensure they controlled trade and wealth originating in the colonies (see Figure 5.2). These encompassed activities such as excluding foreign ships from colonial ports; demanding that

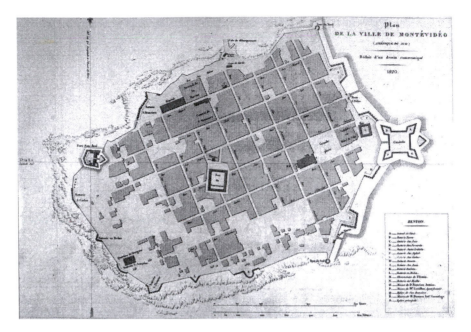

5.2 Map of Montevideo in 1820, showing colonial grid surrounded by fortifications (Carlos Martínez, Facultad de Ciencias de Montevideo, http://glaucus.fcien.edu. uy/pcmya/ecos/sodre/sodreen.html)

colonial trade pass through metropolitan ports; and protecting production in the metropolis from colonial competition (Fieldhouse 1965).

European colonial expansion in other parts of the world (Africa and Asia) during this period was based on intermittent trading. In the territories where colonial powers established trading links and outposts along trading routes, their presence tended to be restricted to port enclaves with limited indigenous impact, often comprising only a fortification to defend the port facilities and some residential development for traders. This predominantly economic exchange and limited physical presence would give way to economic and political domination in the period of industrial capitalism, with the physical and social impact of the colonial powers on urban development in these areas becoming much more pronounced.

Industrial capitalism and the export of planning approaches and practice from the metropolis to the colony

This section focuses mainly (but not exclusively) on the British colonial experience, and its interaction with the development of urban planning and housing in Britain. This is due to the fact that the British Empire was the most extensive colonial empire, and its influence on urban development and planning practices in what is now the rapidly urbanising world was widespread; and that it reached its maximum geographic cover and influence in the first half of the twentieth century, when 'town and country' planning in the 'modern' sense developed in the metropolis and was exported elsewhere.

As noted in Chapter 2, during the nineteenth century the industrialising cities in the metropolis grew at unprecedented rates, and pressing issues emerged around providing housing, sanitation, transport and other services for their burgeoning populations. The Industrial Revolution brought with it problems at increasingly large scales, as well as the development of new technology and institutional structures to tackle these. New professions such as civil engineering and public health started to influence heavily the development of cities during this period, and in the early twentieth century planning started to emerge in the UK as a distinct profession with a set of concepts and values, developed not only within the new professions but also by thinkers and activist from other fields. An influential example is that of Scottish biologist Patrick Geddes, who in the early twentieth century advocated an integrated approach to town planning based on civic surveys, the analysis of which would be the basis for reports for action (Geddes 1968). Although Geddes's approach to planning was proposed as an alternative to industrialism, seeking the 'harmonizing [of] relations between people, and between man and nature' (Hague 1984: 167), its clear 'survey–analysis–plan' sequence was taken up in general by 'rational planning' (see below).

The first town planning control legislation was passed in the UK in 1909, and further revised in 1919 and 1932. During the latter period of the Victorian age considerable investment was made in public infrastructure in urban areas with a view to improving public health. Part of the perception was that urban areas were 'evil' and inherently unhealthy, whereas rural areas were often romanticised as idyllic and healthy. This perception to some extent underpinned the 'garden city' movement instituted by Ebenezer Howard (1898), which led to the first garden cities at Letchworth and Welwyn in the early twentieth century (see Figure 5.3). Similar concepts were being applied by other contemporary 'enlightened' industrialists who provided healthy housing environments for their workers.

The garden city concept was widely used in planning in Britain after the First World War, and green belts were proposed around major urban areas as a means to limit growth and maintain some rural aspects of life near cities – although these would not be established by law until after the Second World War. In addition, the construction of improved housing for workers was expanded by housing associations/cooperatives and (increasingly) local governments from the end of the nineteenth century. This was of a small scale until between the two World Wars, when considerable central government finance was used for the first time to fund widespread local authority housing. This process of public provision of housing was

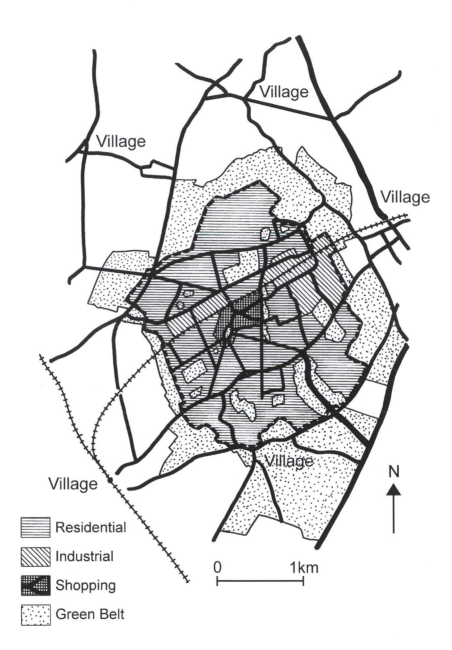

Village

Village

Village

Village

Village

N

Residential

Industrial

Shopping

Green Belt

0   1km

5.3 Letchworth Garden City, England (Drawing by Harry Smith)

accelerated after the Second World War with widespread demolition of inner city slum housing, mostly privately rented, and its replacement with public housing, mostly on peripheral estates.

The post-war period was also a watershed for urban planning in Britain, with the Town and Country Planning Act 1947 allowing planners effective powers to control urban development of all types. The Act required the preparation of development plans for all urban areas, and reflected the high post-war confidence in the public sector, which continued for the next three decades. The main precepts were that (McAuslan 1975):

- the public sector had a key role in urban development;
- private land rights were to be restricted in the public interest;
- professional planners (seen as 'neutral') within local government would adjudicate competing interests for land uses;
- different land uses should be separated – especially residential and industrial uses;
- rapidly growing vehicular movement would be facilitated and separated from pedestrian traffic;
- well ordered urban areas were seen as desirable; and
- the size of large urban areas needed containing, using 'green belts', new town development and regional planning policies to disperse development throughout the country.

Other planning mechanisms and models that were used in this period included:

- New Towns – which involved the creation of towns planned and built by central government as part of a regional planning approach, aiming to 'de-congest' existing cities, and building on the concept of garden cities;
- neighbourhood units – i.e. spatial organisation of new urban development into what was intended to be socially cohesive communities defined by the catchment area of the local elementary school, and provided with local services;
- the Ville Radieuse ('Radiant City') – a model that emerged from the Modern Movement (specifically proposed by Swiss architect Le Corbusier) which aimed to decongest city centres through demolishing the existing fabric and replacing it with high-rise buildings that would increase density while improving circulation and increasing the amount of open space. Functions were to be strictly spatially segregated, as was the mass-produced housing, according to employment and social level;

- inner city redevelopment – which often involved large scale demolition of inner city areas that were considered to suffer from 'slum conditions', with redevelopment of these areas mainly for public sector housing, as well as linked to the relocation of residents to new developments in the periphery of the city or in new towns.

The key actor in this 'rational' urban planning scenario was local government, which had risen to prominence in the provision and management of urban services from the beginning of the century. The balance of elected officers and professional staff such as planners was seen as ideal to implement the above aims, as was a high degree of local government autonomy. Central government's role was seen as broad policy guidance, approval of development plans prepared locally, and adjudicating appeals. However, by the mid-1960s this local government prestige and prominence waned, partly due to unsuccessful slum clearance and city centre redevelopment programmes and associated poor quality public housing provision. There was thus a swing from the technocratic solution, especially when there were conflicting needs, interests and priorities, to a less rigid approach that recognised cities as complex systems and focused on procedures to guide development through policies rather than through design (see Chapter 6). This swing was accelerated with a more general retreat from direct public sector intervention and a political stress on market solutions and entrepreneurship associated with Conservative Party governments, especially from 1980.

Many of the concepts, values and approaches to planning in the core countries, such as Britain, were 'exported' to the colonies. King (1980: 205) identifies three periods in the modern history of 'exporting planning':

- up to the twentieth century, when settlements and urban areas were laid out according to military, technical, political and cultural principles, the most important being military-political dominance;
- from early to mid-twentieth century, coinciding with the development of formally-stated 'town planning' theory, ideology, legislation and professional skills in Britain, which were conveyed to the periphery through the network of colonial relationships;
- neo-colonial developments after 1947 in Asia and 1956 in Africa, when cultural, political and economic links permitted the process of 'cultural colonialism' to continue, with the continued export of values, ideologies and planning models.

Thus in the early nineteenth century, urban planning in the British colonies was largely the responsibility of military engineers, with civilian professions such as engineers, surveyors and occasionally architects being recruited into colonial and technical administrative services from the mid-nineteenth century (King 1990). Planning legislation and institutions were adapted from the metropolitan models and established in the colonies, with the municipality being given key responsibilities. Certain influential planners from Britain (Baker, Lutyens, Geddes) also had a particular impact on urban development in specific colonial cities (see Figure 5.4).

After the Second World War links between the metropole and the colonies became more tangible: with funding from the Colonial Office, from 1940 UK town planning, housing and building 'expertise' was increasingly made available to the colonial territories. In 1948 a Colonial Liaison Unit dealing with housing, building and planning matters overseas was set up at the Building Research Station in Britain, and from the 1950s onwards growing international networks and new international organisations served as a means for diffusion of planning knowledge to colonial and ex-colonial societies. This was aided by the growth in the number of students studying planning in the UK, and of courses offered to them (King 1990).

Through these channels, Western 'expertise', with its assumptions, values and mechanisms, was exported to colonial societies. 'Techniques' and goals of planning were introduced, each according to the standards deemed appropriate to the various segregated populations in the city, without disturbing the overall power structure and basic divisions in society. The ideological and cultural context of British planning, with its primacy of 'health, light and air', combined with a set of social and aesthetic beliefs as a reaction to the nineteenth century industrial city, was transferred to urban areas in the colonies. In this approach there was an implicit environmental determinism which pursued physicalist solutions to social, economic and political problems, transferring standards and norms from the metropole where economic and cultural experience was radically different (King 1990: 55–6).

Although many of the objectives of municipal government can be seen as socially legitimate and necessary, their definition according to metropolitan cultural norms became another means of social control, often ignoring or deliberately destroying the religious, social, symbolic or political meaning of indigenous built environments. An extreme and overt case was the destruction of large parts of Delhi, Lucknow and Kanpur following the Indian Revolt against the British in 1857–8 (see Box 5.1 and Home (1997: 122–5)).

A key feature of colonial planning was segregation, mainly on racial lines. Sometimes the segregated city not only resulted from but created a segregated society. In central and southern Africa the indigenous population was deliberately kept out of cities. In India segregation was based on economic and cultural criteria governing occupation of residential areas, and South-east Asian cities were zoned into Asian and European areas (King 1990). In addition, in many colonial

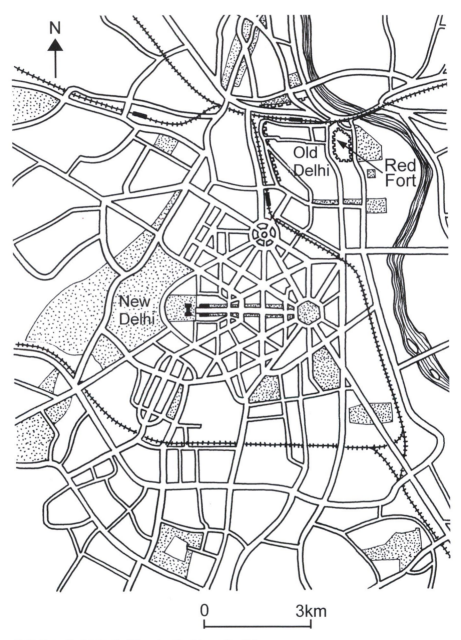

5.4 New Delhi, India (Drawing by Harry Smith)

and ex-colonial societies, a large proportion of formal housing was provided by government, and the design and allocation of housing according to occupation and income group was significant in structuring perceptions of social stratification, compounded by racial stereotyping. New urban environments, therefore, often deliberately ignored symbolic meaning of space in traditional settlement forms, and were based on income and occupational differentials which clearly affected the perception of social differences (King 1990).

Many developing countries adopted the British planning system and legislation during the post-war period,[4] and often transferred the system of local government, with its assumptions about local democracy and autonomy and clear division of roles between elected officials and professional civil servants. However, little consideration was given to the appropriateness of this, including the political basis and technical and administrative capacity. King (1990) argues that while planning emerged in the core metropoles in a political system that was to an extent democratic, in the colonies planning was imposed dictatorially. Although 'modern' statutory planning (law) is assumed to be formulated by representatives of a democratic society who supposedly express its 'collective will', control of use and modification of the environment is also affected by rules and codes based on shared values (unwritten law), but these were disregarded by the imposition of Western written laws and regulations. In the colonies, by definition, planning laws were enforced by the elites and were not the result of a democratic process. In addition, these usually conflicted with the indigenous cultural codes. Over time two processes took place: new laws and regulations were enforced by municipal or national government; and the lifestyle and cultural behaviour of some local inhabitants was often modified as they emulated the ruling colonial elite. However, for many – usually in fact a majority – the formal planning system had little impact as they lived in rural areas administered by traditional rulers or in 'informal' urban areas where 'traditional' socio-cultural values were paramount, albeit modified and subordinate to the colonial structures.

Legacies of colonial planning

Planning activities in colonial (and neo-colonial) urban areas undertaken under the control or influence of western planning institutions and governance mechanisms left the following legacy (see Home 1997):

- failure to manage the growing 'tidal wave' of urban growth and informal settlements;
- land policies which sought to exclude or limit the involvement of indigenous communities in urban life, helping to create so-called 'squatter' settlements;

- an expectation of public sector solutions to the pressures of urban growth;
- lack of financial and technical capacity in local government;
- segregation: racial segregation being replaced in many places by socio-economic segregation; and
- low density developments which are expensive to service, benefit a privileged minority and are often perceived as an aspiration for lower income groups.

The above account has stressed the British 'legacy' in planning. There are other legacies, such as that of other European colonial powers and the United States. For instance the American system stresses land use zoning and sub-division regulation and derives from a fundamentally different concern than that of the British system. This latter was based on concern about public health in the rapidly growing urban areas and the rights of the community over the individual, whereas the American system is fundamentally concerned with individual private property rights and the need to ensure adequate public services were provided in the rapid land development associated with urban expansion in America. As a result the American system views land use control essentially as a local, voluntary mechanism to *protect* individual rights and promote development. The British (also French and some other European countries') approach incorporates a high degree of public intervention and communal rights, and thus constrains individual rights, with development needing permission.

To conclude, the European (and later American) creation of, and influence on, urban development patterns in their colonies, and the exportation of Northern models of land use management and planning throughout the colonial and neo-colonial period, are key factors which help to understand and explain the existing conditions and processes in urban areas in the rapidly urbanising world. In broad terms, direct Western influences established mental models underpinning how actors conceive of, produce and manage urban environments, as well as organisational structures that undertake such production and management (in this period increasingly based on the state and the private sector as opposed to social groups). These influences directly reflected the penetration of capitalism and have continued in the post-colonial era through other mechanisms, as is seen in the following chapters. Such institutions (i.e. mental models and organisational structures), however, penetrated insofar only as was necessary to allow the expansion of the capitalist system, in some cases obliterating existing indigenous practices, in others ostensibly suppressing or marginalising them while in practice becoming 'articulated' with them. This argument is returned to in the concluding section of the chapter.

Housing in the colonial period

Changes in housing production and form during the colonial period

As urban areas in the colonies were established and/or expanded, new areas and forms of housing were developed. Particularly in the earlier periods of colonisation, indigenous populations continued to produce traditional forms of housing. However, the colonising populations took with them evolving practices in housing production and form, usually drawing on developments in the metropoles, though also adapting housing forms from the colonies themselves, and spreading their use to other colonised areas and, in modified form, to the core countries (e.g. the bungalow). Much of the early colonial housing development was to house settlers, leaving indigenous populations to provide their own housing. As colonial rule penetrated and the needs of the capitalist system evolved, the agents of colonialism (plantation and mining companies, colonial administrations, etc.) became increasingly involved in producing housing for indigenous populations who were economically engaged with the system (ranging from manual labour in plantations and mines to white-collar and service-based roles in the administration). This increasing engagement with housing-limited sectors of the indigenous population was accompanied by the penetration of capitalist forms of housing production, which commodified housing to varying degrees and became 'articulated' with traditional forms of production. See Chapter 7 for an analysis of this process. This section provides an introduction to significant changes in housing production and form in the rapidly urbanising world during the stages of expansion of mercantilist and industrial capitalism.

Forms of colonial housing during the mercantilist period – sixteenth to eighteenth centuries

In the early period of Western colonial expansion, the grid-iron urban patterns established in the 'New World' settlements provided a regular framework of plots which were developed individually following dwelling types that were adapted from European models. Thus, in Latin America a characteristic model was the courtyard house (see Figure 5.5), derived from the Mediterranean tradition seen in Chapter 4. Although there was some degree of racial segregation, this was not as pronounced as was the case in many Northern European colonies – indigenous and mixed race population tended to live in smaller houses built out of more traditional materials in the most peripheral blocks, as well as in the larger and more central Hispanic-owned houses in the case of servants and slaves. Northern American colonies, on the other hand, reflected developments in housing in the northern European

5.5 Courtyard house in Villa de Leyva, Colombia (Harry Smith)

metropoles. Here the 'Renaissance' urban form was most often expressed in what in the English-speaking world is known as the Georgian terraced 'townhouse', at times with imposing architectural facades across a number of dwellings. Rather than being produced by craftsmen as in the medieval times, these dwellings were planned and erected by speculative builders and the growing profession of architects. The houses were exclusively domestic, with employment (other than that of domestic servants) being in separate areas and buildings. However, in Europe this was so only for the upper and (fast growing) middle classes, with many workers still working where they lived, generally in the older parts of town where older medieval buildings were subdivided to provide minimal non-differentiated living and often working space for the majority of the poor.

Exporting and importing housing production and form in the nineteenth century

The Industrial Revolution dramatically changed housing production in the metropoles in the nineteenth century. Whereas early industrial developments in the eighteenth century tended to be near energy sources (and transportation) such as rivers, where the factory owner perhaps provided cottage housing, the advent of steam power based on coal in the early nineteenth century led to large new areas of residential development being created in previously existing towns and cities as production became concentrated. This process was facilitated by the demolition of city walls in an era where they had become obsolete. Residential expansion was often either in terraced row housing or in medium height tenements, the latter particularly in Northern European countries, but also in larger North American cities. The former dwelling form was an adaptation of rural cottage forms, whereas the latter was the (sometimes physical) adaptation of urban townhouse forms. With increased commodification of labour and financial services, the vast majority of this working-class housing was produced speculatively for rent. This was possible by expanding the building process developed previously for middle-class housing – i.e. financed by the elite and built by increasingly specialised building contractors – although there was a minority movement at the time to provide workers' housing through co-operatives.

Turning to events in the colonies, Home (1997) provides a comprehensive description of adapted and new forms of housing that were created throughout the British colonial world, mainly for migrant labour in cities, which this section draws on extensively. The evolution of colonial housing forms reflects how different cultures travelled to different geographic areas and interacted (or not) with other cultures. During this process building traditions and technologies were transferred and adapted, and climate considerations were sometimes taken into account and other times ignored, resulting in house forms that were not always well suited for their environment (see Figure 5.6). Crucially, there was a profound transformation in how housing was produced, as housing for the majority of workers who moved either voluntarily or in a forced manner to urban areas and other production centres was built either by the companies that provided them with employment (and much later by government), or by the workers themselves. In the former case, building technology and housing models were imposed by a different culture; in the latter, workers drew on their building traditions, but mostly without the same level of recourse to the social networks, support and building materials which were available to them in their places of origin.

Housing provided by colonial administrations and companies made obvious the stark differences in social, economic and political status between the European settlers and the colonised – whether indigenous to the area or arrived from other

5.6 Portuguese colonial houses in Huambo, Angola (Harry Smith)

colonies. The colonial settlers were provided with houses that were spacious, encouraged family life, signified their status, and were segregated from other social and ethnic groups in areas where generous space standards were used. Non-European worker housing, on the other hand, was a way of 'warehousing' labour, in Home's words. During much of the colonial period, both before and after slavery was abolished, non-European people were considered to 'belong' to rural areas, and the only reason for their presence in urban areas was for employment within the colonial system. In addition, labourers were wanted in the cities, but not their dependants. Thus, according to Home (1997: 89), non-European worker housing generally:

- was intended for temporary workers;
- was not intended for family occupation; and
- did not recognise social relations other than the work relationship.

The different requirements and expectations the colonial system had of housing for the European and non-European populations led to the development of differentiated new housing forms. Although especially in the early colonial period European colonisers tended to imitate house forms from the metropole, even when these were ill-suited to climate and available building materials, during the nineteenth century a new housing form, the *bungalow*, became a common residential unit. Apparently developed in India from the Indian service tent and the Bengali native hut, its use spread quickly to house the growing numbers of European settlers the colonial system required, and was also eventually adopted as a popular housing form back in the metropole (see King 1990: 100–29).

Probably the most widespread housing form supplied by the colonial system for non-European workers was the *barrack*, which had variants such as the *closed compound*. Barracks were used in the estates, mining camps and towns, were built by employers, and were encouraged by government regulations and public health specialists. These typically long, narrow, single-storey structures, with a communicating veranda or corridor, and communal cooking, washing and toilet facilities (where these existed), have their origins in military accommodation, and were first adapted by plantation owners in the Caribbean region. They were used to provide housing all over the colonies in different forms.[5] The closed compound was a variation on the barrack model, used primarily in the South African diamond mines of Kimberley, where barracks were arranged around a large open square and enclosed by a fence patrolled by guards. Barracks and their variations were essentially a way of keeping male workers under surveillance and control. They offered little or no opportunity for privacy and family life, and were often extremely overcrowded, leading to poor sanitary conditions and high mortality rates.

Another example of the segregationist approach to housing is the creation of *townships* and *native locations*. These developed in different ways in different places. For example, in Nigeria townships were created for European populations, as a development of the idea of the cantonment, though they could contain native reservations. Within townships, there were often European reservations with planning standards that established large plot areas and high construction standards, while standards in the native reservations were much lower. In South Africa the process of segregation involved allocating land on the edges of towns for the establishment of native locations, which would later be referred to as townships, while towns increasingly became the exclusive domain of European residents (see Home 1997: 125–39). Justification for such segregation included: safeguarding the European population's health; (in some cases) 'protecting' indigenous cultures from Western influence; and keeping populations of Western origin in areas which were out of bounds to indigenous administrations – the latter being seen as unsuitable for this task.

Home (1997) notes that other regional housing forms emerged in the colonies with the aim of controlling the migrant labour force, two examples of these being the *chawl* (tenement buildings of up to five storeys, typical forms of mass housing in Bombay and Calcutta), and the *shophouse* (a narrow fronted but deep, two to three storeys high house over shop, often arcaded, which evolved from the traditional house of mainland south China, and became common across much of South-east Asia).[6]

Housing in the colonies in the twentieth century

In the metropoles, government intervention in housing was prompted by the growth of slums for the urban poor and the working class, associated with the rapid urbanisation that was taking place together with industrialisation in the nineteenth century. Slums were central areas of town where subdivision of older housing, and often extensions to existing buildings, had led to high population densities, overcrowding and poor sanitary conditions. These processes were often associated with the flight of wealthier residents, leaving behind low-income populations. Slum conditions existed long before this in rural areas and smaller towns and villages, but the scale of these conditions in larger towns and cities brought with it new problems such as the greater likelihood and faster spread of disease, which affected all classes. A response to this was the development of urban regulation of building, and then land use, from the mid-nineteenth century – leading to early town planning (as we now understand it). As noted above, the emergence of town planning in the context of rapid urban growth, in response to poor urban conditions, led eventually to the concept of rural living becoming culturally idealised through Garden Cities, Green Belts, suburban Neighbourhoods, and eventually New Towns. In these forms of planning, different dwelling forms evolved, especially the semi-detached and detached house (evolved from the mid-eighteenth century middle-class villa, itself modelled on the aristocratic mansion), and then the detached bungalow (imported from the colonies). Changing socio-economic patterns in the metropoles underpinned this: whereas for much of the nineteenth and early twentieth centuries the main form of residential construction was still the individual landowner or speculator, with or without an architect, and small-scale building firms built limited numbers of units at a time, this changed with increased demand, and suburban expansion developed by specialised building firms on a speculative basis became the norm. In addition to the regulation of such building activities according to the various urban planning models mentioned above, government also took a direct proactive role initially through 'improvements' to areas in city centres based on the opening up of new and/or wider streets, and later through demolishing slums and building new housing, often on lower cost land on the periphery of the growing city.

Returning to the situation in the colonies, Home (1997) describes various examples of housing provided by employers in the early twentieth century of a standard higher than that of barracks, seen in the previous section. Some large-scale factory and plantation owners, and large government agencies in charge of, e.g. mines and railways, provided housing estates, sometimes with community facilities. These tended to be of a low standard, and were not the norm. Indeed, in general the twentieth century continued a trend that went back to the origins of colonialism, whereby non-European migrants to colonial towns had to provide themselves with their own shelter, sometimes on unoccupied land that incomers simply laid claim to, sometimes on land that was allocated by colonial landowners (who had themselves either claimed land that was, in their eyes, vacant, or taken it from the local population). Thus from early on in the colonial experience areas in or near the colonial urban centres were settled by migrant working populations (either local or from other colonies), who built structures that were not authorised by the colonial authorities. Depending on the sense of security of tenure that settlers in these areas had, as well as on access to materials and the building traditions they brought with them, their houses could range from shelters made out of scrap material, to houses built with lightweight materials that were easy to disassemble and move elsewhere if evicted, and to 'consolidated' houses made out of more permanent materials. A common characteristic of most of these *informal settlements* is the lack or poor provision of services such as sanitation, water, power, etc. (see Figure 5.7).[7] These settlements increasingly became a focus of state concern and intervention during the twentieth century (see also Chapter 7).

Reflecting events in metropoles such as Britain, government in the colonies also began to take an interest in housing conditions of workers, not as an employer but as an authority, in the late nineteenth and early twentieth centuries. This typically was done through establishing worker housing areas built to minimum

5.7 Dense unserviced informal settlement in Luanda, Angola (Development Workshop)

standards and, towards the middle of the twentieth century, on an increasingly massive scale. As in the metropole, government-funded building of new housing areas in the first half of the twentieth century was often linked to the demolition of existing housing which was considered to be substandard and overcrowded. These *slum clearance and redevelopment* schemes were based on similar programmes that were being implemented in Europe and the United States (see Chapter 7 for more detail on 'modernisation' in housing). In the British Empire the housing forms that these programmes produced ranged from three to five storey blocks based on the chawl in India, to cottage-style family accommodation in South Africa and the Caribbean (Home 1997). 'Neo-colonial' states such as Latin American countries also implemented such programmes, ranging from the construction of low-rise neighbourhoods based on single family units to modern high-rise blocks, sometimes close to the city centre (e.g. Caracas in Venezuela), though more often far from the centre and poorly serviced (e.g. Rio de Janeiro in Brazil).

An alternative approach to government provision of finished housing units also began to emerge in the late colonial period: *aided self-help*. This approach is based on government providing land, services, finance, and technical assistance to owner-builders, the mix of each of these 'ingredients' depending on the particular scheme or project. This approach would become mainstream in international agency housing policy from the 1970s onwards, following strong critiques of the modernist paradigm in the 1960s, which much of the literature points to as the starting point of public sector involvement in aided self-help (see Chapter 7). However, recent research has begun to show that during the colonial period some government agencies had already started to implement programmes and projects which provided support to low-income households in building their own homes. Home (1997) refers to *sites-and-services* schemes being recommended for Trinidad following riots in 1937. Harris (1998a, 1998b) has identified early examples of aided self-help schemes underway in India by the late 1940s, as well as the diffusion of this approach throughout British colonies in the Caribbean and Africa (including South Africa) during this period. Official backing for the approach from the colonial power seems to have resulted from US influence. Aided self-help theory and policy were elaborated and promoted internationally initially by Jacob L. Crane,[8] from the US Public Housing Administration, who helped set up the first initiatives in Puerto Rico, then a Territory of the United States. Puerto Rico seems to have been the first place to establish aided self-help at the core of its housing programme, with US sponsorship. The approach, based on 'self-reliance', was subsequently promoted by US agencies worldwide. In the 1950s it was being adopted in several Caribbean and Latin American countries. Harris (1998a) notes that many of the lessons learnt during this period were soon forgotten, and mistakes were repeated in the new wave of aided self-help initiatives from the 1970s onwards. These are described and analysed in Chapter 7.

The colonial legacy in housing in the rapidly urbanising world

Many of the housing issues that societies in the rapidly urbanising world are grappling with hark back to the colonial period, which in some parts of the world ended relatively recently. Particular legacies from this period include:

*   segregation: of homes from work (therefore also between genders), between ethnic groups and between social classes;
*   provision of housing by agencies external to the household (private sector and – particularly for low-income populations – the state);
*   modification of traditional social relations in the production of 'self-built' housing;
*   commodification of housing and components of housing;
*   homes becoming more a unit of consumption and less a unit of production.

Some of these trends, particularly commodification, have continued and intensified in post-colonial times. Others, such as the provision of housing by external agencies, have in many cases waned, though often not the expectation of this form of provision.

Box 5.1 Colonial planning and housing in Delhi and New Delhi

The development of Delhi as the capital of the British Indian Empire is arguably an extreme and untypical case of the export of British town planning to the colonies; however, it clearly illustrates key characteristics of the colonial legacy in planning and housing.

Delhi's history prior to British domination reflects the rise and fall of political units in the region. The city was the capital of the Delhi Sultanate in the fourteenth century, reaching an estimated population of 400,000, but then declined after being sacked and after the early Mogul emperors located their capitals elsewhere. The city flourished again, in a slightly different location, under later Mogul Emperors, with its population rising to around 150,000 in the eighteenth century. It was sacked again on several occasions during the decline of the Moguls. Mogul cities housed heterogeneous populations in terms of origins and religion. Construction, sanitation, trade and tax collection were the responsibility of an appointed secular governor, who co-opted community leaders to organise (and even fund) tasks that required community participation (Lowder 1986).

Delhi was not one of the main cities in the early British domination of India, which focused initially on port cities such as Mumbai, Calcutta and

continued...

Box 5.1 continued

Madras. However, Delhi drew the colonisers' attention after being closely involved in the Indian Mutiny of 1857–58, which led to direct colonial rule by the British government rather than by the East India Company. The mutiny created a lasting fear of revolt, with the colonisers ceasing to live alongside the indigenous population in Delhi (and elsewhere), and creating a separate settlement or cantonment for the European population. Cantonments were created here and in other cities through confiscating land and establishing low-density residential areas. In contrast, the troops were stationed within the walled city, with a wide fire zone around the fortification they occupied. More significantly for the indigenous population, the British demolished large parts of the city in order to remove dense areas with intricate street patterns which were seen as difficult to control, as well as places of public assembly, including many religious buildings. Straight wide roads were driven through the existing urban fabric and, in Delhi, the railway was built through the city also for security purposes (Home 1997).

The idea of the cantonment was taken further when in 1911 the British decided to transfer their capital of India from Calcutta to Delhi, thus removing the seat of power from the increasingly volatile climate in Calcutta while strengthening the connections of the British Empire with north India and Indian Muslims. This decision was announced at a *durbar* (a public ritual which was used by Mogul emperors to reaffirm their relationships with government administrators, adopted as a pageant by the British colonisers and used as a vehicle to manifest their dominion) in Delhi which was held to celebrate the coronation of King George V (Jyoti 1992). The symbolism of locating the new British imperial capital on the site of the former Mogul empire's capital, and of using a ceremony based on Mogul tradition to announce this, was carried through in the form of the development that ensued.

Essentially, New Delhi was a cantonment writ large, independent from the authority administering what then became known as Old Delhi, and designed on a grand scale following the Beaux Arts tradition (see Figure 5.4). This vast and monumental new settlement based on wide avenues laid out on a geometric pattern and built from 1911–40, with the Viceroy's Palace as its centrepiece, sought to express what the colonisers perceived as the superiority of their Western, rational, scientifically based form of town planning, and to achieve this the services of the newly emerging planning profession were enlisted. These Western planners and their employers did not consult with Indians in the design of the new capital, and indeed the lack of power sharing was expressed in the key administrative buildings included in the complex, which were all part of the British-run administration. In addition, the social composition of the new settlement was rigidly cast in the hierarchical physical layout of housing areas, with the largest housing plots located closest to the centre of power being for the colonial elite, while Indian clerks working for the colonial administration were relegated to smaller plots on the periphery (Jyoti 1992).

The transfer of the capital led to a rise in the cost of living in Old Delhi, compounding the worsening living conditions and resulting in protests. As a response to serious outbreaks of disease in major Indian cities at the end of the nineteenth century, and following the model of legislation passed in England and Germany, bodies called 'improvement trusts', which were independent from the city administration, were created in several Indian cities. These trusts, which were not directly democratically accountable, in general were given powers to control development, open new roads, reduce densities in established built-up areas, reclaim and drain land, build housing, etc. In Delhi, however, this mechanism was not implemented until 1937, due to opposition from the local British colonial administration (Home 1997).

Changes in the political economy of urban development and housing in the colonial and neo-colonial periods

Besides the issue of political domination and the imposition of Western models throughout the colonies, which is described above, a key transformation that is evident in both planning and housing in colonial cities is the penetration of capitalist modes of production and reproduction, and the marginalisation of indigenous forms of production and management of the built environment. King (1990: 42–3) notes that the introduction of planned towns by the colonial powers in many areas also implied the introduction of the notion of a market in land, thus replacing existing tenure systems which were controlled by social obligations. In addition, urban planning was often linked to the state becoming the main landowner, similarly sweeping aside, or subordinating, existing land tenure arrangements. Commodification of land during this period, together with the development of wage labour, contributed to the creation of surplus wealth that was accrued by the (initially exclusively) Western colonial elites and invested both in colonial ventures and back in the metropole, driving further commodification in this process.

The replacement of traditional forms of land tenure was accompanied by the replacement of traditional forms of settlement development and of housing provision. In relation to both, colonial masters (whether companies or the state) established new forms of production of the built environment that involved top-down hierarchical systems (particularly in the case of planning) and nominally 'free' market mechanisms (particularly in the case of housing). These imported approaches tended to affect the populations most directly engaged with the colonial economic system, and occasionally wider populations whose conditions were perceived to affect the system more generally (e.g. through propagation of disease, revolt, etc.). Fundamentally the broad colonial era examined here – albeit in different time periods and under different political economy regimes – served mainly to undermine indigenous forms of social and economic activity and regulation and replace these with that of the colonial powers – increasingly those of the capitalist European powers. This process thus served to underpin industrialisation in the North and destroy alternatives existing in the South, with all this being undertaken under the banner of 'development' – a concept that became more clearly defined at the end of the colonial period, with an associated discourse that was described in Chapter 2. This process of penetration by the capitalist system did not end with the end of colonialism and neo-colonialism, but has continued and deepened, also continuing the links to different forms of propagation of evolving planning and housing theory and practice, as is illustrated and argued in the following chapters.

Chapter 6
Planning in the period 1960–90

Introduction

Chapter 5 showed how colonial rule and influence by Western powers in what became called 'developing' countries introduced Western approaches to urban development in these, initially through direct interventions by colonial authorities, and later by importing planning legislation based on the emerging urban planning legal frameworks that were developed in the metropoles. The colonial period legacy extended into the post-colonial era, with both old and new planning mechanisms and models developed in the West continuing to be implemented – mostly unsuccessfully – in the rapidly urbanising world.

Planning approaches in the core countries can be seen to have developed under three paradigms during the twentieth century.[1] The first paradigm was design-based and reliant on a 'command and control' framework for implementation (the 'blueprint'), its key planning instrument being master plans, and the heyday of this being after the Second World War. The second paradigm focused on rational decision-making on the basis of large amounts of data, seeing urban areas as sets of 'systems' (transport, economic, etc.), which could be guided through e.g. structure plans, starting in the late 1960s. The third paradigm has emerged more recently (mainly in the 1990s), through the recognition that planning is a political decision-making process in which values are relative, knowledge socially constructed and contested, and which requires arenas for negotiation and dialogue – this being instrumentalised mainly through 'participatory approaches' to planning. Although these three paradigms emerged in chronological order over the last century, they did not supersede each other, and thus they co-exist to different degrees (Jenkins and Smith 2001).

This chapter introduces the critiques that emerged in response to the predominantly design-based planning approaches that had predominantly been introduced to the rapidly urbanising countries from the late colonial period onwards – mainly master planning. This is followed by a review of the above alternatives to this 'blueprint' approach that emerged mainly in the core countries, ranging from systems planning to urban management, several of which have been promoted in the rapidly urbanising world with the support of international agencies – though master planning is still widely prevalent in land use management. The chapter then discusses the development of participatory approaches in planning, and reviews the emerging recognition of urban planning and management as a negotiation process. The chapter concludes with a brief analysis of the above evolution of planning theory and practice from a new international political economy and institutionalist perspective.

Planning 'by design'

During the immediate post-Second World War years in Western Europe, political commitment to the modernisation paradigm and the welfare state reached a peak. This combination was partly the continuation of trends emerging earlier in the century, and partly a response to the ravages of the war and to the need for reconstruction (see Chapter 2). There was also a perception that industrialisation had been successful in the USSR through centralised planning, based on five-year plans, which had also been a feature of the war effort. Centralised planning, as a technical/scientific approach underpinning modernisation policy, thus became central to the organisation of economic and social policy, including urban and regional planning in the core world regions. Hence the increased prestige and application in the post-war years of two planning approaches that had developed in the inter-war period: master plans and regional plans.

Master planning – rationale and practice

During the inter-war period traditional physical planning – initially more concerned with town extension – developed into comprehensive 'master planning', based on the production of a detailed physical plan representing a desired future state. One of the principal objectives was often to limit city growth (e.g. Spengler 1967), based on the notion that there was an 'optimum size' beyond which growth would be counterproductive due to overcrowding and congestion, rising economic costs and social breakdown (see Chapter 1). Similar concerns underpinned the concept of rural–urban balance (e.g. Taylor and Williams 1982). These concepts continued a post-Victorian British anti-urban view and led to a stress on rural development programmes as an alternative to urban development in many countries.

Master planning focused mainly on land use in the future, although also included plans for infrastructure. The master plan tended to be very precise large-scale maps showing the exact disposition of all land uses, activities and proposed development, which were the product of the three-stage planning process proposed by Patrick Geddes – survey, analysis and plan (see Chapter 5). Their preparation and implementation were based on the precepts that applied in Western Europe at the time, key underpinning factors being that local government led urban development, private land rights needed to be restricted, and plans were prepared by professional planners who were seen as 'neutral experts'.

In the post-war years master planning in the core countries was closely associated to inner city redevelopment and the creation of new towns. A key aim of these urban development activities was to provide public housing, while limiting urban growth and improving health conditions in existing urban areas. Such new towns and areas of comprehensive redevelopment were laid out according to modern movement ideals, with a separation of land uses into zones with distinct functions and segregated transport routes based on the motor car. Through this approach, the public sector aimed to provide public housing on a large scale, often resulting in large un-serviced mono-functional areas. In addition, this undermined the provision of private rental housing, thus concentrating low-cost rental housing provision in the state.

In the rapidly urbanising world of the inter-war and post-war periods master plans were usually prepared by foreign planners and, increasingly, private consultancy firms. Significant examples of an incipient master planning approach combined with 'City Beautiful' principles in the inter-war period include, for example, French proposals for cities in its Northern African colonies, and plans prepared (often by French *urbanistes*) for cities in Latin America.[2] Fully 'modern' master plans were developed for various cities in the rapidly urbanising world from the 1930s onwards, a well-documented example being Le Corbusier's Obus Plans for Algiers (Lamprakos 1992), but, as in Western Europe, master planning activity here peaked in the two decades following the Second World War (see Box 6.1). This was linked to the need for reconstruction following the war, the redistribution of population related to partition and decolonisation, the creation of new capitals for the newly independent countries, and as a response to rapid population and urban growth. Following metropolitan experience, new towns were planned in many countries that were under British control or influence and which were trying to cope with large-scale population growth and political upheaval (Hong Kong, Singapore, India, Israel, Malaysia, etc.). New capitals, usually designed by Western planners, were also planned and built in an attempt to reconfigure the colonial urban systems – e.g. in Malawi, Nigeria, Tanzania, Punjab and Brazil (Home 1997) (see Figure 6.1).

Criticisms of master planning

There have been few successful examples of master planning in the developing world, notable ones being the city states of Hong Kong and Singapore, where 'national' resources have been made available in an intense way for urban development and there are acute land shortages. In some other countries (such as Zimbabwe and South Africa) there has also been some implementation of master

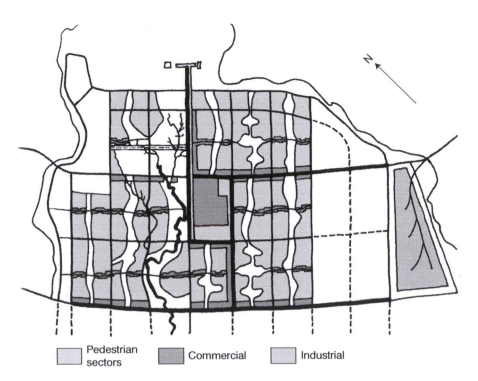

Pedestrian sectors   Commercial   Industrial

6.1 Plan of Chandigarh, India (Drawn by Harry Smith, based on Sarin 1982: 49)

planning; however, this has only benefited the minority community and hence cannot be seen as any form of success.

Major criticisms of the master planning approach which emerged in the 1960s in Britain, included the following (Devas 1993; Dwyer 1975; Lowder 1986):

- the professional focus being more often on the plan as a product rather than on its effects;
- the stress on spatial factors and land use compared to social, economic and environmental issues, resulting in a rigid (often immediately out-of-date) land use zoning plan unrelated to the rapidly changing forces which shape urban development;
- the failure to recognise the significance of spontaneous settlement and the practical issues involved in engaging with this;
- plans adopting inappropriate Western norms and ignoring indigenous traditions, thus leading to their unacceptability by local populations and often higher implementation costs;
- the often relative absence of effective land use controls (legislation,

administration, mechanisms, etc.) and hence the unlikely nature of practical implementation except in restricted areas (usually the city centre);

- the often implicit negative view of urban growth, with associated under-estimation of future urban population;
- the lack of financial analysis and the unrealistic assumption of sufficient economic basis for a relatively high level of public sector interventions;
- the poor institutional link between professional plan development, political interests, decision-making on city budgets, and other agencies involved in infrastructure and service provision.

This critique, and developments in planning theory, led to changes in planning legislation and practice in the North in the 1960s and 1970s (see below). However, despite these criticisms, master planning – or elements of it – continues to be a dominant approach in attempts to control or channel urban development in the rapidly urbanising world. This is mainly due to the nature of urban planners' training, much of which is still undertaken within a context of strong architectural and civic design traditions, and still underpinned by the political, social and cultural values of the North. In many countries the 'visionary' nature of the profession is accorded a high status. This is also reinforced by the tendency – especially by professionals and politicians – to adhere to high standards, generally unattainable in a widespread way.

The above reasons for retaining master planning approaches are compounded by vested interests within the planning profession, in both the public and the private sectors, neither of which want to change the status quo and threaten future job security or work. Problems with this approach are also inherent in the low institutional (and often legal) status of urban planning, which is in many places subordinated to administrative and budgetary departments as well as infrastructure and service agencies, each with their own objectives and interests. Finally, it may be in the politicians' (and donor agency) interests to have a plan, but it may not be in their interest to have it comprehensively applied (if at all).

Box 6.1 Master planning in Delhi

After achieving independence in 1947, India continued to draw on Western urban planning approaches. Delhi, the federal capital, grew massively in the late 1940s and 1950s through the influx of displaced population following the partition of the country. The colonial period had left behind an administrative structure based on separate authorities representing the old city, and the bureaucratic (New Delhi) and military zones. A unitary Delhi Development

continued...

Box 6.1 continued

Authority (DDA), established in 1955, engaged foreign consultants to assist in preparing a master plan for the city, which was amended in 1967.

The initial plan took three years to prepare. Its main objectives were putting a limit to the expansion of the city, and controlling land use so as to achieve a target physical structure by 1981. It proposed eight new towns outside the Delhi Union Territory, banning new large-scale industry in the city, and constraining city growth with a green belt. The state was to expropriate all developable land within the area designated to be urban by 1981, and develop integrated schemes comprising housing, infrastructure and land allocation for community facilities. Housing for the poor was to be provided by cross-subsidy from the development of high-income housing.

Although the state did expropriate a vast amount of land, the plan was not successfully implemented. Key failings were that:

- Delhi continued to grow and exceeded the projected population, while the new towns failed to reach their target populations;
- in 1975–7 the authorities forcibly removed around a million people from the city to its periphery, but this failed to eradicate 'unauthorised settlements' in and around the city;
- developers leapfrogged the green belt and development emerged as peripheral sprawl and ribbon development along roads, increasing transport and servicing costs, and transferring the problems of dealing with such development to neighbouring authorities;
- the majority of land allocations were made to high-income groups, the lower than expected levels of house construction went mainly to housing government employees, and cross-subsidies did not materialise.

Reasons for the failure of the Delhi Master Plan include:

- the plan covering areas beyond the Delhi Union territory – not covered by a common planning authority;
- lack of clear responsibility for implementing the plan, though the DDA had general responsibility for administering the area;
- consideration of Old Delhi as a 'slum' from which polluting industries and village-like trades had to be removed, and from which higher-income groups should be induced to move out;
- lack of awareness of immigrants' survival strategies based on existing kinship networks and proximity to casual employment opportunities, which were more abundant in the old city;

- lack of foresight regarding developers' response to development restrictions in the green belt;
- use of expensive and protracted land allocation procedures that favoured high-income groups, as well as the establishment of a monopoly over land use which turned the DDA into a speculator.

In summary, the Delhi Master Plan exemplifies the continuation of the importation of Western planning approaches, adding to Delhi's experience of inner city improvement and new town construction in the *city beautiful* tradition of the colonial period, the post-colonial spread of the 'modern' master plan. It thus also exemplifies the continuing penetration of socio-economic practices linked to the evolution and spread of capitalism, and the conflicts generated in its interface with traditional practices.

Sources: Dwyer 1975; Lowder 1986.

Regional planning

Another form of centralised planning, regional planning, emerged during the inter-war period in various forms and Western contexts, as a response to increasing complexity in urban development and its economic and social implications. One of its roots was the drive for 'decongestion' of cities which were seen as suffering from slum conditions due to densities that were regarded as being too high. In this sense regional planning was closely linked to housing policies, and was geographically focused on large cities whose housing problems were addressed by dispersing population to the region surrounding them.[3] Another strand leading to 'regional planning' was the growing complexity of interactions between economic activity and the provision of services to urban development in industrialised regions, which elicited the introduction of regulatory measures that cut across existing administrative boundaries.[4]

A brief overview of the development of regional planning in the United Kingdom helps understand how the concept evolved and was exported. In the United Kingdom, regional planning in its wider sense, including economic planning, had its roots in the aftermath of the Great Depression of the 1930s, when it became clear that economic recovery was not following the patterns of the previous productive distribution, with urban areas based on specialised heavy industry (e.g. the North of England) not recovering while new industrial areas were fast developing (e.g. in South-east England). This led to widespread unemployment despite significant migration. The government appointed special commissions to invest in designated 'development areas' to alleviate this problem, but it was only after a nationwide study (Barlow Report 1937–40) that regional development was planned in a broader way, following legislation enacted from 1945. The government thus sought to promote employment in certain areas through direct incentives and indirect regulation.

In the early 1960s planners become interested in the concept of 'growth poles' (based on work by a French economist, Perroux 1955). The idea was to identify which parts of a region had the best prospects of rapid industrial growth and concentrate (especially public) investment in these. In parallel the government increased its regulation of new work places through control of new office development though it did not deal with expansion in retailing. In the late 1960s the UK government developed a national plan, following the then trend in 'indicative planning' (as opposed to regulatory planning), and increased the investment attraction for under-developed areas through various differential taxes and grants. In the 1980s the new UK government drastically reduced spending on employment promotion and focused on decaying inner urban areas, where growing unemployment was related to structural changes in manufacturing and other previous industries. This was often implemented through specially created urban development corporations, such as had been used successfully for creating new towns (which received special grants); and 'enterprise zones' which received tax relief and simplified planning controls.

Faced with rapid urban growth (especially in major cities), many governments in the 'developing' world introduced 'Northern' planning concepts such as new towns and growth pole strategies, as part of regional planning, with the objective of redirecting growth from the fastest growing 'primate' cities. As noted in Chapter 1, in general 'growth poles' have seldom been successful, according to Parr (1999), because as a strategy they were:

- inappropriate, i.e. they did not address the nature of the regional problem (e.g. through attempting large-scale industrialisation rather than improving agriculture);
- unfeasible, e.g. requiring large capital outlays;
- unrealistic, usually lacking in adequate analysis; and
- inconsistent, often acquiring additional objectives unrelated to the logic of growth poles that undermined the strategy.

However, decentralisation is still promoted in more recent times through promotion of secondary and tertiary urban centres as alternatives to metropolitan growth.

In the North the ideas of national economic planning grew important in the 1950s and 1960s, often being translated into regional economic planning, and this process was also copied in rapidly urbanising countries; however, scope for implementation was much more limited. Many of the national development plans produced to promote this were, however, little more than politico-economic visions, with limited real implementation, though they consumed considerable government resources. In general – unlike in Europe – the spatial aspects of these plans were very limited. In addition there was a strong reluctance for governments of the time to invest in urban infrastructure, especially social infrastructure such as health and education facilities, as this was seen as consumption rather than production-related, following general modernisation development strategies.

Alternatives to 'blueprint' planning: systems planning[5]

Structure planning

A reaction against the rigidity and limited scope of detailed master plans in the mid-1960s in Britain led to a new level of urban planning being developed: *structure plans*. These were intended to produce a broad strategic framework within which more detailed local plans could be produced, taking into account a wider regional context, as well as transportation, housing and environmental issues (Devas 1993). These permitted the linking of city-region and socio-economic planning, and recognised the importance of transportation planning as a central element, as well as environmental quality (see Figure 6.2).

The introduction of structure plans coincided with the emergence of interest in planning 'systems', based on concepts from cybernetics, and aiming to model urban systems and identify optimum patterns of development to guide planning. The 'systems' approach to planning was more prevalent in the United States and relied on emerging computer simulation techniques to compute large amounts of data and test alternatives. The aspects of structure plans thus modelled included transportation systems and regional land use patterns. The results of using computer modelling in planning were not felt to be very useful in Britain, however, as the process was very lengthy and produced an enormous amount of data and options, yet the results seemed little better than inspired 'guesswork' (Devas 1993).

A key aspect in structure planning and the systems approach it drew on was acceptance of the view that urban areas are in constant change, and hence the perceived need to gather data on trends and interpret these in order to produce appropriate guidance. This required professionals with skills in economics and social sciences rather than in design (Taylor 1998), and a new type of professional planner became established in some Western countries such as the United Kingdom, with associated new forms of training, drawing more on geographical and social science traditions than on architecture and urban design.

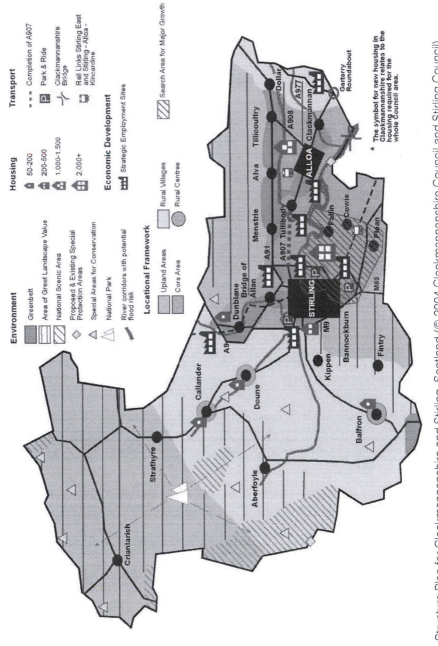

Environment

▓	Greenbelt
▓	Area of Great Landscape Value
▓	National Scenic Area
◇	Proposed & Existing Special Protection Areas
△	Special Areas for Conservation
△	National Park
∿	River corridors with potential flood risk

Locational Framework

▢	Upland Areas
▢	Core Area

Housing

⌂	50-200
⌂	200-500
⌂	1,000-1,500
⌂	2,000+

Economic Development

⊞	Strategic Employment Sites

○	Rural Villages
●	Rural Centres

Transport

═ ═	Completion of A907
P	Park & Ride
⊥	Clackmannanshire Bridge
▭	Rail Links Stirling East and Stirling – Alloa – Kincardine

▨	Search Area for Major Growth

* The symbol for new housing in Clackmannanshire relates to the housing required for the whole Council area.

6.2 Structure Plan for Clackmannanshire and Stirling, Scotland (© 2004 Clackmannanshire Council and Stirling Council)

In the United Kingdom these changes in approach entailed changes in institutional responsibility for planning, which was divided between different tiers of government: counties prepared structure plans, and districts were responsible for local plans and implementation. This led to conflicts and eventually marginalisation of the structure plan function. Structure plans' legislative base was land use planning, and as alternative interests for planners developed – e.g. urban regeneration – their use was seen as limited (Devas 1993). In addition, few countries in the rapidly urbanising world adopted the structure planning approach (Devas 1993) and master planning has continued to be dominant.

Action planning

Another response to master planning was developed by practitioners such as Otto Koenigsberger (Koenigsberger 1964), due to the practicalities of needing a more effective urban planning tool. This proposed an *action planning* approach which instead of attempting such a comprehensive set of goals would identify key issues which could be affected by immediate action, and interventions which would be within the resources of the relevant authorities to implement. The main steps in action planning were:

1. '*reconnaissance*: rapid appraisal of the dominant features of the area under consideration, identifying strategic issues and problems;
2. *guiding concept*: the principles to be applied in approaching the issues and problems identified, and the framework to be used for public sector and joint public/private/community initiatives on infrastructure, transport, housing, services etc.
3. *action programming*: selection of a series of interconnected development strategies concerned with investment, land use and other resource use, designed to tackle the identified problems and to make best use of resources;
4. *role casting*: specification of the roles of the various agencies to be responsible for implementation of the components of the action programme, including detailed planning, financing, controlling, legalising, etc.;
5. *monitoring and feedback*: an institutional arrangement for gathering information on the progress of implementation, on the problems encountered and on public responses, for feedback into the process of plan and programme revision.'

(Devas 1993: 87)

Action planning thus avoids the massive exercises in data collection required by structure planning, and permits the definition of priority and finite tasks, which not only is more realistic in management terms, but also allows the identification of these for funding. It does however, inevitably downplay strategic and longer-term visions, and hence specific action plans might not co-ordinate well. The risk is that – especially with donor funding – action planning can produce an isolated project approach and major strategic problems remain unresolved.

Action planning advocates have promoted and developed its amenability to community involvement in the process. *Community action planning* takes into consideration stakeholder interests and aims to put in place processes 'which are problem driven, community based, participatory, small in scale, fast and incremental, with results which are tangible, immediate and sustainable' (Hamdi and Goethert 1997: ix). Methods and tools from community action planning have been used in various parts of the rapidly urbanising world – often as part of international agency-funded urban planning and management projects – though the approach as a whole has not become a mainstream part of planning. Hamdi and Goethert (1997) describe some examples of community action planning in practice in a variety of scenarios, including new settlement planning, improvement of existing settlements, and capacity building, in both the rapidly urbanising and urbanised worlds.

Land management and guided land development

During the 1980s the difficulties experienced with master planning and the changes to 'support' housing strategies as opposed to 'supply' housing strategies (see Chapter 7), and the growing interest in urban efficiency as an element of economic growth, led to a focus on land management: land acquisition, allocation, transfer and registration. In the light of the restricted capacity for formal (administrative or market) land allocation for the growing numbers of urban poor, the majority of this group were accessing land informally, and this was becoming a major feature of urban land use. These 'informal' means of access have varied in time and geographically from traditional allocation through illegal subdivision to direct occupation, mostly ignoring established planning and land use regulations – as indeed these regulations ignore these (often prevalent) land access processes. However, as cities grow it proves increasingly more difficult for the poor to access land, and land becomes commoditised and bought and sold – however, often still in the informal ways mentioned above.

The focus on land management has included stress on the need for appropriate legal bases, as well as more appropriate mechanisms for land allocation, transfer and registration – such as addressage and Geographical Information Systems (GIS). The approaches to land management in the late 1980s focused increasingly on land markets, accepting that these could be both formal (accepted and at least practically administered by governments) and informal (without regulation). Private sector developers in fact often worked in both areas and a continuum of 'informality' ranging from illegal occupation through to legal occupation but unauthorised construction was accepted as existing. The international agency Urban Management Programme approach to land markets dominated professional attitudes initially, and focused on assessing land markets, formal and informal, as a means to defining appropriate government action to reduce market distortion. This assumed that the market was the most efficient means for land allocation. In time a more critical approach to land markets developed, following a political economy analysis – see Chapter 7.

While urban planners have focused on land use planning and regulation of development, in fact one of the most important guiding forces in land use is infrastructure provision. Thus while local authority planners developed detailed plans with various scenarios over long horizons, in practice municipal engineers have been instrumental in deciding some of the most important underlying parameters for land use without much co-ordination in many places. The realisation of this led to an approach to urban planning called *guided land development*. This basically meant planners working closely with engineering colleagues in the planning of new infrastructure, deliberately using this to guide future land use in a normative way. This approach, as with action planning, produced fundable projects, and has hence tended to be supported by funding agencies, especially as these projects and actions are finite and produce an easily identifiable product whose impact can be evaluated (see Figure 6.3). This, however, also can be susceptible to the difficulties mentioned above concerning action planning when viewed at a strategic level.

6.3 Guided land development in Curitiba, Brazil (Harry Smith)

Institutional co-ordination

In general the growing complexities of urban planning and housing and infrastructure development had led to a proliferation of housing and planning institutions in many developing countries through the 1960s and 1970s, often compounded by the direct involvement of national or provincial agencies as well as parastatals, in addition to the local institutions. In fact, in many countries the tendency was for centralisation of government functions, limiting local authorities' resources and legal powers. In the 1980s the creation of specialised implementing agencies for projects and programmes at the behest of donors – to ensure their projects were implemented – was also common, with resources going specifically to these agencies, thus bypassing local level agencies (which subsequently inherited the projects). The levels of co-ordination between these various agencies – and between them and government, especially local – was typically very low, partly due to limited capacity and weak communication lines, but also to vested interests and competition for resources.

Another feature of the increasingly fragmented nature of urban planning was the physical growth of cities. Many cities had far outgrown their boundaries and in some cases large areas of the functional urban area were governed through other neighbouring local authorities, or provincial or national authorities. This added to the institutional complexity of planning and in larger cities to the proposal to create metropolitan development authorities – either as a separate tier of government or as a distinct entity with development functions. These institutions often had wider powers and access to greater financial resources than local authorities, and this, together with support from donor agencies, gave them the ability to develop large-scale urban infrastructure projects.

During the 1990s there was a growing critique of this approach, as the creation of the metropolitan authorities tended to increase rather than decrease the number of institutions, as few previously existing institutions were actually closed down. Often overlapping areas of authority led to growing lack of co-ordination, and relations between local and metropolitan authorities were often strained. Metropolitan authorities also tended to act as project implementation agencies and then hand over the completed projects to the local level, where there was limited capacity (or interest) to maintain these. They were also seen as being less accountable to the political system and the public, and while this had advantages in implementation terms, it could create serious reactions. Eventually there was a growing stress on the need to strengthen local government, and in parallel with this, of strengthening the role of the private sector and organisations within civil society in urban development.

Urban management

During the late 1960s and 1970s new ideas about public sector management were being applied in the North, incorporating concepts developed within the private sector in North America and Europe. This entailed an emphasis on management with clearly defined organisational goals, objectives and strategies, and with corporate monitoring and co-ordinating of activities within the various departments within this framework. This became widely adopted in local government in Britain in the 1970s, especially after its reorganisation. Within the corporate approach the planner was often incorporated within the policy team.

In the 1980s the new attitudes to government stressed at national level in the USA and Britain led to more stringent controls on local authority resources, at the same time as these were required to be more accountable. One tendency was to create 'cost centres' with decentralised budgets responsible for identified areas of activity such as service provision. The objective was to ensure more *efficient*, *transparent* and *accountable* use of resources and growing commercialisation of these. Related to this approach has been the separation of the 'client' and 'contractor' roles within the local authority – with the local authority acting as client, defining the terms of reference for a specific service, and this being tendered for commercially by a contracting organisation (possibly within the local authority). This was meant to lead to a clearer relationship between services and costs of provision, as well as allowing competition. A variation of this system is the 'build, operate and transfer' (BOT) system where a contractor creates and operates for gain a particular service over a defined period, then transferring it back to the public. This has been used for major infrastructure investment such as bridges and roads where tolls can be levied. Other forms of partnerships can be joint ventures between public and private agencies or the re-establishment of public sector agencies as commercial undertakings. The World Bank has been extremely instrumental in promoting these forms of urban management, making this the principal focus of its urban sector lending since the mid-1990s. This is looked at in more depth in Chapter 8.

This approach to urban management has been allied to the stress on better and smaller government which has been a feature of structural adjustment programmes (see Chapter 2), a process still underway in many countries – some having just begun to address urban management problems very recently. In general the resources and skills available at local level are often far less than would be necessary for the increasingly complex tasks associated with urban management, especially in its partnership form. Again, vested interests do not adapt easily to such new forms of operation, and the objectives of efficiency, transparency and accountability are often not shared by local politicians or civil servants.

Whether this rather technocratic approach to urban management will have widespread success or not is still unclear, although it has been operational for well over a decade. In addition, how the impact of this approach affects the (often) poor majority of urban residents, and whether these systems of management best serve such groups, is open to question. Apart from this, at a more managerial level, there are practical problems associated with service provision in rapidly urbanising countries that are not the same as these in the already highly urbanised core countries. In many rapidly urbanising world cities there may be no or few private sector entities interested or able to undertake the service. In addition many public services either are natural monopolies (e.g. water supply) or tend to function as such due to the small size of the effective market. This undermines some of the basic reasons to privatise services to make them more efficient. Finally the problems of co-ordination and monitoring of service provision are much more complicated in such approaches, and many rapidly urbanising countries do not have the adequate skills levels in local government – especially after years of a drain on more qualified personnel due to structural adjustment.

Overall, the focus on urban management has led to a greater realisation that urban planning has to be an integral element of overall urban management, and has to be proactive in urban development rather than reactive. It is also clear that the role of government is not dominant, but needs to focus on co-ordination, both within government and with both private sector and civil society interests. Planning has thus become more focused on negotiation as opposed to regulation. This entails negotiation on the objectives of urban planning and management as well as on the mechanisms for implementation through partnerships.

Economic development planning

The much slower growth of the economies in rapidly urbanising countries (and in many cases, the post-Independence economic slow-down and even reversal of growth) led to employment in the 'formal' (i.e. legal, taxed) sector not keeping pace with the growth in active work forces, especially in urban areas. Alternative occupations were essential given the lack of adequate forms of state-provided social welfare and high levels of poverty, and this led to a rapid growth in the 'informal' sector, which was first conceived as such and documented from the early 1970s with support from the ILO (see Chapter 2). The basic approach advocated was that the informal sector was important and necessary and should be encouraged to grow, consolidate and become integrated with the formal sector, rather than be outlawed and restricted.

Urban planners, as well as most administrators and politicians, generally opposed this approach, looking on the informal sector as illegal and dangerous. This was supported by formal business, lobbies which saw unfair competition at least in commerce, services and small-scale production. Others saw the informal sector as a form of 'worker' exploitation and hence refused to support it on ideological grounds. Landowners also looked on informal land occupation as a threat to their investment/speculation opportunities. As such, there has been considerable debate on the pros and cons of the informal urban economy and how this can interact with urban planning and management.[6]

In general during the 1980s the importance of the urban economy in the national economy was seen as growing. As more rapidly urbanising countries either feed themselves and improve agricultural productivity, or have this wiped out through food aid and the impact of protectionist policies in the North, the tendency for urban-based economic activity begins to dominate. The importance of linkages within, and between, productive sectors has been realised and the added advantage physical proximity in urban areas brings has been increasingly recognised. Hence in the early 1990s international opinion began to stress the economic importance of cities and related urban management functions (e.g. global place-marketing). This has also brought about new roles for urban planners, both in improving the economic efficiencies of urban land, infrastructure and services management, and in participating in economic development promotion, as opposed to a principally regulatory role (see below).

Examples of economic development promotion roles undertaken by governments include (Devas 1993):

- using public funds in important infrastructure and environmental improvements to encourage private sector finance of various types of development;
- using public funds to stimulate enterprise through promotional activities, skills upgrading schemes, and providing seed money for new small-scale enterprise development;
- using public funds in high profile key projects which permit the attraction of international and other private sector investment – such as, e.g. airport upgrading and conference centre facilities;
- providing public funds to stimulate private investment in housing stock upgrading, thus avoiding more costly redevelopment;
- establishing institutional mechanisms and organisational forms within local government that permit the above – such as City Development Departments, which bring together economic development, estate management and urban planning functions.

Environmental urban management

In parallel with the economic focus for urban management above, wider awareness of environmental issues during the 1980s led to a new focus on environmental management within and around urban areas. While often originated at the international level, the impact of environmental regulation is felt at local level.

Environmental problems can be created by various forms of extractive and manufacturing industry which can be essential to the employment base of a city. It can be provoked by the wealthy through increased car ownership and solid waste production, but it also can be provoked by the lack of land and services for large proportions of the population. Examples of the latter include (Hardoy *et al.* 2001):

- pollution of underground water supplies (solid waste, sanitation and excessive extraction);
- occupation (especially residential) of unsuitable land (e.g. slopes, natural drainage zones and ecologically fragile areas);
- destruction of vegetation and forests for solid fuel and development, increasing flooding and erosion as well as decreasing natural bio-diversity;
- increasing atmospheric pollution through solid fuel burning;
- uncontrolled dumping of solid waste (see Figure 6.4).

Here the direct victims are often the poorest urban residents, but the nature of environmental problems often transcends the poverty ghettos and affects the wide urban area, and the 'ecological footprint' of the urban area in its hinterland.[7] Hence there is political motivation to improve environmental management yet few resources or mechanisms (e.g. legislation or institutions) to implement this.

Increased attention is being paid to the problems of integrating environmental issues with overall urban management, however rapidly urbanising countries have immense problems in dealing with these due to the difficulties of regulation and the often complex and interlinked nature of the issues. In many cases there is no adequate legislation or institutions that can undertake the environmental management functions, and there is little option for privatising many of these functions due to the adverse nature of much private sector activity on the environment. The means to address these issues more effectively in an appropriate way for many rapidly urbanising countries has not as yet been found. On top of this, it is the limitation of regulation that at times effectively provides the draw card for foreign investment which wants to avoid the environmental costs of production, and hence there can be direct conflict between different sectors and levels of government concerning environmental regulation and promotion of economic development.

Planning as negotiation

The third major paradigm in urban planning (after 'Planning by Design' and 'Planning Systems') has been planning as negotiation. Several of the approaches to urban planning and management seen in this chapter included some element of

6.4 Poor urban management: uncollected solid waste in the centre of Luanda, Angola (Harry Smith)

'participation' in the planning process. For example, the legislation that established the two-tier planning system in the United Kingdom, with structure plans and local plans, also set the legal requirement for consultation with the public during plan preparation, though in practice such consultation is often limited, procedural, reactive and relatively inaccessible to groups who cannot afford to hire consultants. Community action planning, for example, aims to be more bottom-up, with a scope that may be more meaningful and comprehensible to local communities than region-wide strategic planning, and methods that are simple and inexpensive.

Such attempts to widen participation in the planning and management of urban development responded to different agendas. In the core countries this was linked to a reaction against the perceived failures of modern planning in the two decades following the Second World War. Critiques of plan production by technocratic elites were the basis of the rise of 'advocacy planning' in the United States in the 1960s, where planning theorists started to argue that planning was not simply a rational process only requiring efficient data collection, analysis, and proposal-making by experts. Planning was also, and probably more importantly, a value-laden political activity which involved decisions affecting different interests. 'Advocacy planners' were therefore required to represent the interests of groups within the public, especially those who were not well represented in the formal planning process (Taylor 1998). In the United Kingdom, the influential Skeffington report (1969) recommended enhanced public involvement in the planning process, including a role for community forums that would have an input to this, though the subsequent legislation responded to such recommendations only partially, requiring minimum formal information and consultation to take place at specified stages.

In countries in the rapidly urbanising world, provision for public participation in planning has often been a result of either the direct importation of Western planning legislation or the funding of programmes and projects by international agencies. In this latter context, public participation was an ingredient in sites-and-services schemes and settlement upgrading projects in the 1970s, but was limited to contribution of labour in the least 'participatory' initiatives, and to forms of consultation, co-option and mobilisation in the most 'participatory' (see Figure 6.5). Thus participation here was a way of tapping local communities' resources rather than providing them with

6.5 Presentation of Integrated Development Plan for eNdondakusuka, Kwa-Zulu Natal, South Africa (eNdondakusuka Municipality and Christine Platt)

real participation in decision-making. Later UN-funded programmes and projects in the late 1980s and 1990s[8] focused on 'empowering' local communities and 'enabling' these to manage their own development, thus supporting the implementation of enabling strategies (see Chapter 7).

In the evolution from limited forms of participation that resulted from the first critiques of modern technocratic planning, to the increasing calls for involvement of other actors – be it through 'partnerships' in urban management or through 'community self-management' encouraged by the enablement paradigm – there has been a growing recognition of the role of negotiation. This follows on from the acknowledgment of the political nature of planning in the 1960s. At the time, such recognition resulted (in some places) in attempts to channel public views through the formal mechanisms of representative democracy, an approach that was limited in many of the core countries, and that often was dependent on weak traditions in representative democracy in rapidly urbanising countries (where attempted). More recently there has been a further recognition – particularly among some planning theorists, though also increasingly in practice – of the limitations of the mechanisms of representative democracy, and forms of 'participatory democracy' have been promoted and experimented with in various rapidly urbanising countries. A well-known example is that of municipal level 'participatory budgeting', which has been pioneered in Brazil. The implications of participatory democracy for urban planning and management are looked at in more detail in Chapter 12.

Whether through the influence of planning theory, such as the 'collaborative planning' approach that argues for discursive long-term engagement between interested parties in decision-making on 'level playing fields' (Healey 1997), or as a response to the reality that weak government agencies need to engage with the private sector and civil society in order to tackle the issues faced by rapidly growing urban areas, negotiation is gradually being recognised as an activity that is intrinsic to urban planning and management. Informal instances of such negotiation permeate, for example, the history of land invasions in Latin America, where clientelistic deals between community leaders and politicians have been well documented. Formal negotiations underpin the establishment and operation of partnerships, a linchpin of the urban management approach, as well as the deals that local governments strike with private corporations to secure the establishment of business in the locality, in competition with authorities elsewhere.

The rise and (near) fall of planning according to a new international political economy perspective

Taylor (1998) provides a good overview of developments in planning theory during the period this chapter focuses on. Some analyses of urban planning in

Britain from a political economy point of view undertaken in the 1970s, when the first two decades of post-war planning experience were under scrutiny, concluded that planning authorities were limited in their powers to initiate development and therefore to implement the plans they prepared and approved (Pickvance 1977, cited in Taylor 1998). It was primarily market forces that determined the pattern of land development – including through influencing planners' decision-making – and thus also the redistributive impacts of development. Pickvance's view was essentially one of urban planning acting in opposition to the market, but limited in its scope to act against it. Marxist critiques at the time took a different view, seeing planning – as part of state activity – as an integral part of the capitalist economic and social system. Decision-making in planning was thus seen as being determined by the needs of the ruling class. Some Marxist critics argued that the state used planning to address urban problems generated by the failures of the capitalist market system, thus aiming to minimise inefficiencies that might compromise its operation. They recognised that the working class in Western Europe and North America had been able to achieve some gains through the planning systems established in the aftermath of the Second World War, but also noted that such systems had respected existing (skewed) structures of private land ownership and property development, regulating private land development activities rather than replacing them (Taylor 1998).

Contemporary to the above Marxist critiques of planning was the revival of classical liberalism, which critiqued post-war social democracy in Western Europe (see Chapter 2), and underpinned a neo-liberal attitude to planning in the 1980s. Such neo-liberal critiques generally supported the view that urban development should be largely left to market forces, though some minimal form of planning and land use regulation (such as notional land use zoning) could support market-led development (e.g. Hayek 1960; Sorenson and Day 1981, cited in Taylor 1998). Neo-liberal policies in relation to planning in 1980s Britain reflected some of these positions, by attempting to 'streamline' planning and by-pass planning regulations through the creation of urban development corporations and enterprise zones (see section on *Regional planning* above). The Thatcher government did not significantly alter the planning system *per se*, but did impact on the way the planners operated, increasingly seeing these as partners to work with, and in support of, the private sector (Taylor 1998).

In the late 1980s and 1990s new political economy analyses of urban planning were developed: regime theory and regulation theory. Regime theory's starting point is the view that, in capitalist societies, 'many of the most significant decisions affecting people's lives are made outside government by firms operating within the capitalist market system' (Taylor 1998: 141–2). In a context of local government with declining or limited power, local authorities were compelled to adopt an entrepreneurial approach in order to tackle the problems generated by economic decline in their constituencies, and therefore to engage in partnerships with non-governmental agencies, especially in the private sector. Regime analysts therefore focus on the relationships between economic forces and political agendas and balances of power in local contexts, which give rise to different kinds of local government strategies, and therefore different kinds of 'regimes' or governing coalitions.[9] Regulation theory focuses on the strategies adopted by local governments as a result of the change in the 'mode of regulation' of capitalism since the 1970s, from 'Fordist' production that was largely embedded in national economies, to a 'post-Fordist' mode of production that is global in scope. Faced with the dis-aggregation of industrial production into discrete segments that are relocated to locations where returns on investment can be maximised (for instance through exploitation of cheap labour), local governments are forced to be competitive and to adopt negotiating strategies, which are studied by regulation theorists.

The above theoretical approaches have emerged in the North in response to developments in planning practice and in an effort to explain evolving contexts for urban planning and management in the core countries. As argued in Chapter 3, there is a need to develop theoretical analyses of, and practical approaches to, urban development within the rapidly urbanising regions, and some guides towards this are provided in Chapter 3 and in the macro-regional case study chapters. An initial broad-brush analysis can be provided here, however, on the basis of the account given of the development of approaches to urban planning and wider development strategies in the rapidly urbanising world in the period from 1960 to the 1990s.

The master planning and regional planning approaches that had been exported to rapidly urbanising countries in the first two post-Second World War decades, were integral to the modernisation development paradigm. The newly independent countries emerging during decolonisation sought to use Northern 'rational' planning processes to replicate the perceived success of post-war reconstruction which such processes appeared to have contributed to. However, the problems encountered by these approaches in the core countries were generally exacerbated in rapidly urbanising cities due to, among other factors: lack of strong implementing powers in local government; absence or scarcity of investors in the private sector to realise the developments envisaged on the blueprint plans; and low or no engagement of the local populations with formal local government activities including planning, thus leading to public disregard for the officially desired end-state. As noted above, continuing use of master planning in the rapidly urbanising world owes more to the vested interests of local elites trained in, or acquainted with, the technocratic traditions of master planning and of international consultants than with a track record of success, not to mention ruling elites whose real interests were served by capturing the added value of land which became 'urban' through the planning process.

The current revival of master plans, often associated with business and elite-oriented initiatives (both in core and periphery cities) in North and South, is linked to attempts to offer attractive and 'certain' opportunities to international investors, in the post-Fordist climate of increasing competition for investment. There are thus perhaps fewer examples of grand master planned schemes for whole new capitals and new towns, or for the expansion of existing urban areas, but increasingly smaller-scale initiatives aimed at elites and economic activities with high returns, e.g. on waterfronts. These smaller scale master planned schemes appear to be achieving some results on the ground in certain cities in middle-income countries, but have a much lower rate of implementation in low-income countries. In either case, they increasingly do not pretend to offer solutions for the majority of the population, but arguably provide means to ally national elites with international elites interested in urban investment, whether in land and property values or in large-scale construction projects.

Alternative planning systems have largely been implemented (where this has happened at all) in situations where planning authorities have had to recognise their limitations, following the initial post-colonial modernisation euphoria, and have been forced to seek other avenues to exert some control on urban development and to secure the attractiveness of their urban areas to foreign investors. Drivers for the different approaches have, again, been the need to strengthen competitive advantage, but at the same time the need to mitigate worsening conditions in urban living. Less resource-intensive approaches such as community action planning have been used for low-income populations, often in informal settlements, while more 'formal' planning approaches have remained in use for the 'formal' parts of towns and cities. Thus a dichotomy has to some extent developed between large-scale strategic plans such as metropolitan plans and structure plans, as well as infrastructure and broader economic development plans, and the finer-grained more localised actions around land and services provision, which may be planned or ad hoc and more or less involve affected communities.

The growing segregation in the use of planning approaches and instruments, ranging from formal and resource-intensive to informal and low-cost, reflects segregation and fragmentation in actual provision of infrastructure and services in urban development, with increasing polarisation between those parts of urban areas that are more directly integrated with global finance and the core capitalist system, and those that are increasingly less directly integrated with this – or effectively excluded – and whose relative poverty is also growing (Graham and Marvin 2001). This growing polarisation has been recognised in recent international agency statements and initiatives, and attempts to address this underpin some of the current approaches that are described and analysed in Chapter 8. However, the following chapter looks at the development of housing policy and practice in the 1960s to 1990s period, which parallels much of what has been described in this chapter for urban planning and management.

Chapter 7

Housing in the period 1960–90

Introduction

This chapter examines how housing policy and practice developed in the rapidly urbanising context of the period 1960–90 which is associated with neo-colonialism and parallels the previous chapter's focus on planning. It starts with a brief review of how housing developed in the post-war period in the North, as this largely influenced the policies and practice of housing in the South when many countries emerged from colonial rule into neo-colonial situations, as described in Chapters 2 and 3. The chapter takes a chronological approach, and relates the evolving policy and practice in housing in the situations of growing rapid urbanisation to development theories and praxis. It also looks in some detail at the so-called 'self-help housing' debate, and how this led to an impasse in theoretical development.

The post-war housing drive in the North and its effects in the South

The two World Wars were turning points in terms of housing delivery in Europe. Whereas the First World War saw the first significant intervention of the state in housing through freezing rents and thus reducing private rental supply, it did not lead to large-scale state investment in housing. The Second World War, however, reduced existing state and private housing investment dramatically through severe shortages of finance, labour and materials and thus created high pent-up demand. The solution in the post-war European nation states was generally to include state housing provision as a key component within the Welfare State, albeit with differing emphases and processes across Europe. In this paradigm of housing provision, the state was expected to provide basic housing for either the poor or any group which desired state housing, and large-scale 'general needs' and 'slum improvement' housing programmes were initiated, usually through local authorities with central government finance (see Figure 7.1).

The private sector was also involved in delivery – initially mainly for middle and higher income groups, but also for lower income groups with state subsidies.

7.1 Bijlmermeer, a model town built near Amsterdam in the 1960s, with high-rise housing blocks and segregation between road traffic and pedestrians (Harry Smith)

In some (exceptional) situations the state also intervened directly in the labour market through local authority direct-build departments. In addition, limited skilled labour availability led to the search for new low-labour construction solutions, such as prefabrication, which also sought more efficient use of scarce material. Prefabrication ranged from full emergency housing units, largely produced by the increasingly redundant aircraft manufacturing industry, to the mass production of components for construction of, for instance, large-scale high-rise blocks of flats. In general this was in line with the dominant macro-economic state management approach of the time – Keynesianism – which advocated the stimulation of economic growth through supporting increasing demand.

As described in Chapters 2 and 3, the post-war settlement also entailed rapid de-colonisation, but the creation of neo-colonial links, and it was during this period that 'development' was conceptualised – initially in the reconstruction of Europe, and then in the 'catching up' of the 'less developed' ex-colonies. In this context policy began to focus on the needs in housing and urban development of what began to be termed the 'developing world', as the lifting of colonial controls coincided with general demographic growth and resulted in growing urban populations. During this period development theory and practice largely focused on the need for modernisation, and this actively promoted urbanisation in the developing world as a basis for making adequate labour available for the growing modern and industrial sectors of the economy. In this approach, as with associated economic trickle-down, population growth was expected to adjust automatically through demographic transition, and hierarchies of urban areas were expected to develop naturally, as they had in the industrialised countries, with specialised functions.

In the initial neo-colonial period the approach to housing envisaged the provision of 'modern' housing based on Western cultural and technical standards, predominantly through conventional construction. These were mostly planned for new urban areas, and there was also some experimentation with prefabrication. As noted in Chapter 5, in this approach the supply of modern housing for growing urban workforces was to be financed by large employer organisations (e.g. mining companies) or governments (e.g. civil servants' and workers' housing), and a variety of new public housing agencies were created to this end (Wakely 1988). Thus, as in the core countries, subsidised public sector housing was seen as part of a general strategy of stabilisation of labour and the creation of skilled working and middle classes as a means to rapid economic development.

The associated visible achievement of 'modernity' in physical terms in urban areas was an important goal for many governments (Stren 1990), reflected in the dominant 'International' architectural style. Low urbanisation due to colonial control before de-colonisation (see Chapter 5) meant that the incidence of 'traditional' forms of housing in most urban areas at this time was not widespread, but where these building forms existed they were assumed to be unsuitable. This was partly due to imported standards from the North, but also to traditional forms of social, cultural, economic and political expression being considered inappropriate for the 'modern' world. The modern cultural values embedded in new independent economic and political elites during the later colonial period and de-colonisation, were thus intensified in some of these neo-colonial state-led processes.

In this context governments in the South, as in the North, used minimum standards as a basis for calculating housing deficit and subsequent targets for subsidised housing delivery for key workers, this being mainly middle-rise (tenement) blocks and individual dwelling units, often on the urban periphery where land was cheap (see Figure 7.2). International development agencies played a minor role in shelter activities at this stage, generally only providing limited technical assistance, with governments defining their own modern housing programmes, closely linked to continued development of urban master plans. However, economic development did not take off as expected in many countries, leading to pressure to reduce the fiscal burden of housing provision. In addition there was often a high rate of resale of the new state-assisted modern housing units to the better off as these did not provide the forms of space that culturally were desired, as well as carrying significant costs.

Continued fast growth of urban populations and the inadequate supply of conventional housing in relation to need and real demand quickly led to growing

7.2 Modern tenement blocks on the periphery of Huambo, Angola (Harry Smith)

'slums' and squatter settlements. Conventional housing was predominantly provided in peripheral locations often far from employment opportunities, thus diminishing the possibilities for household strategies which required other economic survival techniques – e.g. agriculture, use of the residence as a workplace, subletting as a source of income, etc. Households therefore opted for non-conventional solutions, such as squatting and illegal sub-divisions in slums. These were initially seen to be aberrations in development, contravening urban plans based on strict land use control regulations transferred from colonial powers, and many largely unrealised urban master plans prepared at the time proposed redevelopment of slums with conventional housing.

As development theories became more influenced by Keynesian policies, the role of the state in providing financial support for housing development was seen to be more effective in stimulating demand than direct supply. This was also seen as a means to raise productivity and even out fluctuations in the construction sector. Until this period, public housing investment had been seen by most governments as predominantly a consumption expenditure and was not highly prioritised, but it now began to be seen as a potential motor of wider development and employment generation. Accordingly, in the 1960s, housing policies were developed to adjust imbalances in effective housing demand in relation to the supply side, through increasing mortgage finance via savings and loans associations. However, limitation of public investment capacity was seen as a major drawback, and given the general fiscal difficulties in the 'developing world', with weak taxation, and the lack of indigenous capital resources for large-scale investment and mortgage systems, international aid was increasingly looked to as a means to bridge the gap.[1]

There were some exceptions to this conventional, commodified form of housing delivery, carrying on some of the earlier colonial forms of 'self-build' described in Chapter 5, also supported by international agencies. Aided self-build was, however, seen as an alternative means to conventional construction and not its substitution, with the objective of reduction of labour costs through the occupiers building the houses (or parts of these) themselves. This was also expected to increase the beneficiaries' commitment to modern forms of dwelling, as well as provide new skills to assist in broadening the capacity of the construction industry for other development activities.

These early ideas of 'self-build' housing gained some acceptance and support within national governments and began to be generalised, particularly in Latin America. Here (especially US-based) international agencies encouraged state-sponsored self-build housing programmes through the creation of new dedicated government housing agencies as a way to replicate the previous isolated projects – termed 'Alliance for Progress' agencies. In this context, in the 1960s, USAID significantly increased its support to these programmes with a series of family based self-build and mutual aid projects in several Latin American countries.[2] This international support also had a political objective, to offset tendencies for revolutionary political change following the Cuban revolution of 1959. However, after 1966 the levels of finance available from the United States in particular declined as the tense security situation eased and Vietnam became the principal preoccupation, and many Latin American governments subsequently discontinued their relatively high level of support for self-build housing supply. These projects, despite substantial funding, largely remained limited in impact, and in practice labour savings and productivity were low, and the time constraints and relatively high cost of housing investment for beneficiaries rendered these projects unattractive for wide-scale duplication (Burgess 1992).

In general the capacity of the state to supply the rapidly growing demand for low-cost housing in urban areas through conventional and self-build methods proved hopelessly limited in the 1950s and 1960s, producing a minimal number of units in relation to rapidly growing need, and exacerbating the situation through continued eradication of slums and squatter settlements. Both conventional and self-build forms of housing were expensive for the vast majority of the population and did not meet lower income groups' needs, but in fact tended to benefit growing middle classes. Thus, whereas in the North, industrial development increased wealth redistribution and democratic political forms had led to the state-sponsored housing drives which permitted the housing deficits from rapid urbanisation for lower-income populations to be substantially addressed at least in quantitative terms, this was not the case in the South. Here in most regions rapid urbanisation surged ahead of economic development and related urban infrastructure and housing investment capacity. In this context, growing gaps between supply and demand for conventional (or 'formal') urban housing developed, with 'informal' housing forms of housing provision filling these gaps. In relation to this, however, in the late 1960s a different approach to non-conventional housing supply began to develop – termed 'self-help' housing, which drew much on the self-build traditions.

The 'self-help' housing paradigm

What is 'self-help' housing and how did this term emerge and become a paradigm within housing in the 'developing world'? As seen in Chapter 5, governments in the colonial period had already experimented with forms of assistance for the future occupiers of housing in urban areas to build this themselves, or at least consolidate this over time, i.e. 'self-build' (Harris and Giles 2003). This was in fact something that governments in the core capitalist countries had resorted to in times of crisis, when there was inadequate state or private investment to provide needed housing stock, usually closely related to periods of rapid urbanisation (Harms 1982).[3]

The emergence of what came to be termed 'self-help' housing in the rapidly urbanising world was largely due to the widespread promotion of this in publications by John Turner, an English architect who was deeply influenced by Patrick Geddes' work in India and who worked in assisted self-build projects for the Ministry of Public Works in Peru. Here Turner developed his wider ideas on 'self-help' housing together with William Mangin, based on his experience in the 'barriadas', which he subsequently wrote about extensively. He argued that squatter areas were not a form of social malaise, but triumphs of 'self-help' effort which needed more 'dweller control' and 'autonomy', with limited government intervention (see Figure 7.3).

This alternative approach to the previous one that 'sub-standard' dwellings had to be done away with through modern conventional construction, albeit some self-built, was linked to a series of mid-1960s anthropological studies of life in slums and squatter settlements in the 'developing world', mainly focused on Latin America, but also India (e.g. Lewis 1961; Peattie 1968). Most of these studies stressed the potential for self-development inherent in many of these areas, using terms such as 'slums of hope' (Lloyd 1979), arguing against the view of these areas as 'marginal' (Perlman 1976 – see Box 7.1). Charles Abrams, in one of the earliest key texts on housing provision within this approach (Abrams 1964), had suggested the progressive provision of housing, based on 'sites and utilities', extendible core housing and 'roof-loan' schemes, though he remained sceptical of using self-help to provide fully conventional housing.[4]

7.3 Reconstruction of a shack under way through mutual aid in an informal settlement in San José, Costa Rica (Harry Smith)

Turner's proposals extended these ideas and promoted individual home-ownership and self-help involvement in progressive housing provision over time, initially stressing self-help mainly as labour (i.e. self-build), but later as self-management. Turner argued for reducing the government's role to ensuring security of tenure for land and housing, applying lower official standards, and providing access to financial and appropriate technological support. His arguments in support of 'self-help' housing were publicised through a wide range of publications including two influential books.[5] These ideas subsequently heavily influenced the 1976 United Nations Habitat Conference in Vancouver (UN 1979),[6] and later the World Bank and other international agencies.

Box 7.1 The critique of 'the myth of marginality'

Drawing on sociological studies on the 'culture of poverty' (Lewis 1961, 1966) and from the 'architectural-ecological school', policy-makers saw informal settlements as areas of social breakdown, with lifestyles that were 'marginal' and even threatening to the mainstream social system, and equated the problem of 'marginality' with that of substandard housing. Physical eradication of informal settlements and provision of 'adequate' low-cost housing was therefore seen as the solution to such 'marginality'.

continued...

Box 7.1 continued

Perlman's (1976) critique of the assumptions of 'marginality' was based on surveys she undertook in several informal settlements (*favelas*) in Rio de Janeiro, Brazil, in 1968–9. Her critique, which was a defence of the illegal squatter settlement, went beyond Turner's and condemned the socioeconomic system which produces the informal settlement. Perlman's structured field surveys undermined virtually every aspect of the 'marginality' stereotype:

- Social: rather than favelas being internally disorganised with residents who are isolated from the wider urban context, Perlman found in them high rates of community group membership, strong kinship networks, evidence of trust in mutual help, and that the majority made full use of the city.
- Cultural: instead of being an enclave of rural parochialism where residents develop and perpetuate a culture of poverty, in favelas there was change and openness to new ideas and to 'rational modes of thinking', with a widespread sense of optimism and a prevalence of 'rational mobility-related' aspirations.
- Economic: rather than being a drain on the urban economy, in favelas Perlman found a strong work ethic, with residents providing a constant supply of cheap labour to the city, while also participating as consumers.
- Political: instead of 'radical leftists' not integrated into city and national political life, social and political organisations abounded and maintained contact with the public sector and politicians.

Perlman's initial conclusions were that, in terms of 'economic integration', in Rio de Janeiro's favelas:

- residents form a 'reserve army', taking up the least desirable jobs;
- lack of 'upward mobility' and increasing unemployment in the period 1959–69 were related to (external) structural changes rather than to any negative changes in the characteristics of the favela residents; and
- there was internal exploitation such as a shopkeeper credit/indebtedness/ high prices nexus and some slum landlordism.

In terms of 'social and cultural integration', Perlman's initial conclusions were that favela residents were:

- not marginal but 'integrated' on unfavourable terms; and
- stigmatised by the rest of society.

Perlman concluded that the 'myths of marginality' are false and misleading. Marginality exists but it is the marginality of exclusion and exploitation rather than of low motivation and parochialism. It is misleading to assume that poverty is a consequence of individual characteristics of the poor rather than of the condition of society itself. The 'Functionalist model' of society was therefore seen as a myth, based on the false assumption that every functioning social structure is based on a set of shared values among its members, and therefore of necessity defines 'marginals' as outside that society. Perlman argued for an alternative 'conflict' model where the so-called 'marginal sector' is just one of many competing groups, although a particularly weak one, subject to coercion by stronger groups.

Source: Perlman 1976

The key tenets of Turner's argument can be summarised as follows (Mathey 1992). Housing users know their needs better than government officials, and high regulatory standards undermine rather than guarantee more adequate housing. Housing users can access and utilise resources in more effective ways than conventional housing solutions and mass production permit, albeit with wider variation in quality, and this is reflected in lower costs and better affordability. Self-help housing also produces better architectural solutions as its focuses on individualised household use values and not abstract market exchange values. So-called 'autonomous' forms of housing (i.e. autonomous from the state) provide better living and working relationships as well as assisting community development. Housing thus needs to be seen as a verb and not a noun – or in other words as a process and not a product. While Turner initially promoted maximising autonomy from the state and individual household self-building, he later emphasised self-organised or self-managed construction and an 'enabling' role of the state (Turner 1986, 1988). Thus in later publications his focus was increasingly on 'building community' and the role of intermediate non-governmental organisations between community-based organisations and the government.

The support and platform for these ideas given by the UN came at a time when modernisation development strategies were seen as failing. As was explained in Chapter 2, this gave rise to new development strategies, such as 'basic needs' and 'redistribution with growth', which came to dominate the lending strategies of international development agencies in the 1970s and 1980s in Latin America, Africa and Asia. This led to the direct promotion of 'self-help' housing policies as an alternative to conventional housing delivery, and a significant proportion of self-help housing projects became internationally sponsored. In particular during the early 1970s the World Bank promoted a range of self-help housing projects across the world, subsequently making a systematic attempt to influence national policy formulation to include this in the latter part of the 1970s, and becoming the principal international agency supporting housing.

A basic principle particularly promoted by the World Bank was cost recovery from beneficiaries – to render the investment replicable – and therefore the need for 'affordable' standards. The backbone of the World Bank's policies for low-income housing in the 1970s can be summed up as: home ownership and security of tenure in land and housing; the need for self-help contributions; progressive development processes for house consolidation; reduction in standards to assist affordability; improved access to financial resources; and appropriate technologies and materials. The World Bank published several key policy positions relevant to urban areas in this period, including urbanisation (1972) and housing (1975), and an Urban Projects Department was set up in 1975 to ensure adequate policy implementation. In all some 52 urban projects were developed by the World Bank between 1972–81, committing some $1.6 billion or nine per cent of total commitments to urban development and related infrastructure as well as small-scale enterprise promotion.

By the mid-1970s the 'self-help' approach to housing had become accepted by all the major international agencies and was firmly established as the official alternative to conventional housing supply for lower income groups (Burgess 1992). Pugh (1995) identified four phases in the development of what can be loosely termed the 'self-help' housing paradigm. In the early to mid-1970s this concentrated on provision of *sites and services* areas,[7] with varied levels of service, and state support to self-help house construction. However, this approach could not keep pace with continued growing urban housing demand and spontaneous occupation (or 'squatting') of land for informal housing continued to increase world-wide. In addition it was found difficult to provide new sites at 'affordable' levels for increasingly poor urban populations, based on full cost recovery, and hence by the late 1970s the emphasis shifted to upgrading of existing squatter areas in conjunction with provision of new sites for de-densification.[8] In the early 1980s this in turn was extended to include a focus on employment activities and community organisation, recognising that increased income-levels were often needed to make upgrading 'affordable' and community participation was essential to ensure project success in existing housing areas.[9] The last phase, from the mid-1980s to the early 1990s, continued upgrading and sites and services provision but focused more on 'programmes' rather than individual isolated 'projects', as it became clear that the effect of the latter was sporadic and often conflictive with overall urban and economic development.

This period when the self-help paradigm was dominant as an approach to housing in the rapidly urbanising world was termed by Pugh (1995) as the 'affordability/cost recovery/replicability' period. The approach was found to have weaknesses:

- substantial subsidies were inherent in the financing of the housing projects – e.g. through interest rates lower than inflation (Mayo and Gross 1987);
- cost recovery proved difficult – with often more than 50 per cent defaults in loans;
- the private sector was never adequately attracted to get involved; and
- there was 'downward-raiding' of projects, i.e. higher-income groups which were not adequately supplied by market mechanisms acquired the houses.

The World Bank thus decided that '... housing required more sophisticated and interdependent relationships among markets, the state, and self-help among households' (Pugh 1995: 66).

In addition to the operational problems mentioned above, and despite the concentration of the World Bank and other international agencies on self-help housing policies and projects, the results were still far short of actual housing demand in most urban areas.[10] In addition to governments' increasing economic limitations in developing wider programmes without international assistance, the relatively limited success of these policies also demonstrated the lack of commitment by many governments, arguably linked to lack of interest in socio-economic groups not considered a priority (i.e. not the dominant elites). In fact, while this approach drew on the proposals advocated by Abrams, Turner and so on, other more political aspects of self-help housing development which they advocated – i.e. dweller control and political devolution – were not promoted. It has been argued that self-help housing strategies, linked as they were to basic needs and redistribution with growth development strategies, were fundamentally geared to maintaining existing ownership and power structures, traditional financial procedures and free market operation, through stressing full cost recovery, affordability and replicability (Mathey 1992). These and other analytical criticisms of this approach sparked a lively debate in the literature in the 1970s and particularly the 1980s, as the next section describes.

Critiques of the self-help housing paradigm

Critiques of the 'self-help' housing paradigm have been made by theorists, professional practitioners and development agency personnel. Criticism of international agencies' support for self-help housing, as a means for social control and pacification, was voiced as early as 1972 in Peru, and from the mid-1970s by Colombian Emilio Pradilla, who argued from a Marxist position that self-help policies were being promoted in the interest of the dominant capitalist hegemony by reducing the cost of reproduction of labour and through the associated creation of new markets for the building industry and finance capital. This argument was associated with the 'dependencia' development critique (see Chapter 2), and was later taken up in Anglophone literature by Rod Burgess in the late 1970s, arguing that self-help housing was effectively a form of double exploitation.

Burgess developed his Neo-Marxist critique drawing on articulation theory (see below) and specifically opposed Turner's position in a series of publications (Burgess 1977, 1978, 1982, 1985, 1987, 1992), which Turner responded to (Turner 1978, 1982, 1986, 1988, 1992), collectively becoming known as the 'self-help housing debate'. This critique essentially focused on the need to take the wider political economic context into account when dealing with housing supply, including the wide range of vested interests: landowners, finance institutions, building firms, politicians, etc. Burgess agreed that self-help production can avoid some, but not all, of the factors contributing to the high cost of housing, but argued that it implied new forms of exploitation within general 'petty-commodity' relations, inevitably subordinated to the dominant capitalist system. In addition he argued that the advantages of 'spontaneous' self-help were often cancelled as soon as this became 'state assisted' self-help.

The analytical basis of this critique of self-help is rooted in articulation theory. As noted in Chapter 2, this basically argued that capitalist development in developing countries proceeds through the alteration and reproduction (i.e. 'articulation') of pre-capitalist formations in an increasingly subordinate relationship, rather than their outright destruction. Burgess argued that the adoption of self-help housing policies is an example of this, where non-capitalist activities are integrated to some extent into the sphere of commodity production, and are partially transformed in the process, to the benefit of capital. Evidence of this in urban housing policies is the 'eradication' of pre-capitalist 'traditional' construction and land use patterns associated with slums and squatter settlements and its (eventual) replacement with self-help housing. Articulation theorists also argued that redistribution with growth strategies emphasised the importance of the state's role in facilitating capital accumulation and valorisation through this articulation process (e.g. McGee 1979; Ward 1982).

The Neo-Marxist theorists argued that these policies were promoted as a subordinate way to underpin mainstream capitalist modes of production. This included the development of policies for stimulation of labour-intensive activities, such as the informal sector, small-scale enterprises and appropriate technology. In these they argued that the state attempts to improve small-scale enterprises' access to finance, markets and technical assistance, as well as encourage subcontracting arrangements with large firms, in an attempt to draw these forms of production towards the logic of capitalist accumulation. These articulation processes can also be seen in the consolidation and expansion of commodification of land, building materials, housing and finance; the generalisation of the principle of private property in land and housing; and the introduction or expansion of the capitalist division of labour and wage economy. The general objective was a lowering of social reproduction costs of labour power, such as housing costs. Self-help housing policies were thus, in this view, essentially aimed at increasing productivity and efficiency of housing production, and hence at leading to cost reductions, expansion of output and lower-income accessibility through gradually commodifying artisanal practices.

Articulation theorists argued that, contrary to their aims, self-help housing policies eventually limit low-income access and the further development of the productive forces on a scale necessary to deal adequately with the housing problem. Such state intervention always entails costs which effectively bar the majority of those housed in artisanal settlements from access, and prejudice the actual livelihoods of many in these project areas. This has been borne out through: the contracting of informal, below minimum wage labour as 'self-help', thus expanding capitalist relations and the wage economy; the regularisation of tenure which increased land costs, displaced the poor and consolidated capitalist markets of land and property; and the reduction of housing investment at national level by shifting the costs of housing provision over time to the poor. The reduction of standards was also seen as an expression of the new international division of labour, adjusting the costs of reproduction of labour away from 'the unrealistic surge of expectations that arose in the post-war period of decolonisation and national independence struggles' (Burgess 1992: 88).

While the critique above was the dominant one, some critics focused on other, more operational, aspects of self-help housing delivery, such as the comparative advantages (or disadvantages) of collective rather than individual effort, and the social heterogeneity of spontaneous settlements and how this influenced upgrading. In general the majority of these critiques referred to Latin American contexts, and the transferability of this experience was also questioned (e.g. Dwyer 1974, 1975). In time the so-called 'self-help housing debate' became broadened in scope by other practitioners and analysts, as well as applied to a wider global context (e.g. Gilbert 1986), including post-independent 'proto-Socialist' governments' approaches to housing (Mathey 1990). However, while some practitioners could see the validity of both sides of the argument, the debate essentially became by-passed in the late 1980s, as it did little to provide solutions to the enormous and rapidly growing housing needs in the rapidly urbanising world. Whereas self-help housing had been incorporated into international, and to some extent national, housing policies and practices, the Neo-Marxist critique was just that: critical without offering any valid alternative within the housing sector.

Post 'self-help' housing debate

As the above theoretical debate petered out, there was a swing in publications on housing in these contexts to concentrate more on empirical studies and operational testing and guidance, as opposed to theoretical positions (e.g. Cheema 1987; Payne 1984; Peattie 1983, 1987; Rakodi 1992). The new studies in the 1980s were partly the product of reflection on the international agency-backed projects of the 1970s which were by then being evaluated. Several of these studies suggested that the cost savings through self-help housing projects were either minimal or non-existent. Analysts associated with the World Bank in particular began to look at the 'affordability problem' which affected many of the Bank's self-help projects, and suggested that what was needed was stimulus to make housing investment by the private sector more attractive through higher profitability, which would lower costs in the long run through stimulating supply and eventual market saturation.

Other approaches stressed the need for savings and credit associations and wide small-scale landlord provision of rental housing as means to improve household investment capacity (Gilbert and Ward 1984). Further areas of concern investigated were the 'gentrification' effect observed in many self-help housing projects targeted to low-income households (Nientied *et al.* 1986). In relation to this, many project evaluation reports indicated that the poor either did not get access to the projects targeted to them, or were expelled by higher income groups. In addition the reduction in standards, based on the principles of full cost recovery, led to increasing difficulties in maintenance of housing areas and arguably in-human conditions (Burgess 1992). This has especially affected women, and the importance of gender in relation to self-help housing became a focus in the latter part of the 1980s (e.g. Moser and Peake 1987; Schlyter 1996).

Overall a large number of self-help housing projects – ranging from basic sites and services through to core housing and informal settlement upgrading – were implemented in the period between the mid-1970s and the early 1990s (see Figures 7.4 and 7.5), when the last comprehensive analysis of this approach was published (Mathey 1992). In general the impact of self-help housing policies and practice for the poor has probably been more muted than its proponents had expected, although forms of aided self-help housing eventually became part of the repertory of government action in housing throughout the rapidly urbanising world. The fact that some governments found political advantage in this approach, and that the private sector also adapted to this form of delivery in some instances, has arguably been the most important factor in success. Despite this, however, more urban residents live in informal settlements now than three decades ago, when the approach was first widely promoted. The fact that residents of these areas predominantly rely on (non-state-aided) self-help is still a key issue for housing policies and practice that still needs more specific attention. However, that was not

7.4 Self-help housing incrementally built by households through government loans funded by the Inter-American Development Bank in the early 1980s, San José, Costa Rica (Harry Smith)

7.5 Self-help housing built by households with NGO support and central government finance in the mid-1990s, San José, Costa Rica (Harry Smith)

the focus for immediate post-self-help housing policies and practice in the rapidly urbanising world, as the next section discusses.

The effect of early neo-liberalism on housing policy and practice in the 1980s

In Chapter 2 we saw that the dominant development strategy to emerge after the 1970s was the neo-liberal paradigm with its monetarism and structural adjustment focus. In line with this, in the 1980s a second major period of World Bank activity in housing emerged which has been characterised as that in which housing policies became closely related to macro-economic policies and early structural adjustment lending (Burgess 1992; Pugh 1995), and housing interventions became focused on finance. The World Bank increasingly drew on innovations in the creation of housing credit institutions earlier in the decade, and continued as the dominant international actor in housing development, increasing its influence over national policies and programmes as the debt crisis grew. As with other economic management issues in this paradigm, structural reforms were seen as necessary in housing finance markets, to deal with 'excessive' regulation and subsidised interest rates.

In some countries reform of the housing finance system was deemed necessary, but in many others, whole new housing finance institutions were required as market provision of housing had never become widely generalised. This differential led to more rapid disbursement of international loan funds in countries where housing finance systems had already been developed to critical thresholds, such as in Latin America and Asia, with others therefore generally lagging, such as in Sub-Saharan Africa. However, even in better-off countries the formal housing finance institutions generally ignored lower income groups and hence policy impact was uneven also within countries. This period of macro-economic adjustment and housing finance systems had the objective of reforming whole housing systems and thus increasing overall housing supply – i.e. not focusing on lower income groups *per se*. However, it did not necessarily replace the earlier, more project-related, form of housing delivery, but encompassed this within a wider policy framework, gradually phasing these projects out.[11] An indicator of this is that sites and services developments, as proportions of the overall World Bank housing loans, reduced from 100 per cent in 1972 to less than five per cent in 1990. In parallel there was a shift in lending strategy to larger loans.[12] Geographically this assistance became concentrated, as did much international finance, in relatively few urban areas in the newly industrialising countries (e.g. Brazil, Mexico, South Korea, etc.).

The new approach to the broader housing policy context ('whole housing systems') was characterised as a transition from housing supply to support policies for state intervention (Wakely 1986). The 'support approach' complemented the growing interest in urban management problems (see below), and also neo-liberal tendencies to privatisation, and was perhaps best expressed in the much publicised Sri Lanka 'Million Houses Programme' (Weerapana 1986).[13] This theme was then taken up by the United Nations in the *1986 Global Report on Human Settlements* and as the main theme in the 1987 International Year of Shelter for the Homeless. This in turn was the basis for the UN's promotion of Global Shelter Strategies, based on state facilitation, rather than direct implementation, through 'enabling' the private and community sectors to respond to housing demand. A basic concept in this approach was that human settlements contribute positively to economic as well as social development. Enablement was defined as providing legislative, institutional and financial frameworks for entrepreneurship of private sector, communities and individuals, and hence in this period the international agencies focused assistance on promoting the development of policies and programmes as opposed to projects.

The enabling approach as was defined initially by UNCHS (1987) differed from that which the World Bank (1993) later advocated in its policy paper *Housing: enabling markets to work*. In the UNCHS initial formulation of enablement the emphasis was on the key role of community and on the need to enable the community to 'help themselves', as well as on action at the local level. The later World Bank version of enablement hardly mentioned communities, conceptualising society rather as constituted by 'consumers' and 'producers', and focusing on seven instruments which were mainly related to economic aspects, and which overlapped with only a couple of aspects of the UNCHS approach. Thus, the UNCHS enabling strategy was originally based on community participation, while the World Bank's enabling strategy was couched in the language of economics and markets, with a predominance of macro-economic considerations and, implicitly, with a view of society as composed of individuals and individual households that should be given access to property rights, mortgage finance, etc. – see Figure 7.6 for comparison (Jenkins and Smith 2002; Smith 1999).

The UNCHS' approach to enabling strategies underwent important changes which have been analysed by Pugh (1997), becoming less focused on the 'grass roots' in human settlements and engaging more with the state–market–NGO–household relationship, viewing society as a whole. UNCHS (1990: 7) articulated enablement in more economically focused terms – '... to mobilize resources and apply entrepreneurial skills for increased housing and infrastructure production ...' – and shifted further towards what would eventually be expressed as the World Bank enabling strategy, based on housing markets. However, Pugh (1997) noted that with its new strategy the World Bank's approach to housing also shifted from strict neo-liberalism to the recognition of a new role for government, though poverty alleviation was implicitly to take place through the widely criticised 'trickle-down' effect, which needed to be supplemented with 'safety nets' for the most vulnerable.

UNCHS	World Bank
Prime purpose: 'to state the sets of measures that are to be used to enable communities to help themselves ... making conditions for self-help and mutual aid as favourable as possible, through sets of enabling action in support of locally determined, self-organized, and self-managed settlement programmes'	**Prime purpose:** 'the reform of government policies, institutions, and regulations to enable housing markets to work more efficiently, and a move away from the limited, project-based support of public agencies, engaged in the production and financing of housing.'
Instruments: *Settlement-wide action:* • spatial restructuring: not master plan; • organizational restructuring: community-based and neighbourhood groups with decision-making autonomy. *Actions at local level:* • increase access to basic resources for locally determined and self-managed programmes; • essentially, institutional changes in administrative rules and regulations. *Whole section on community participation:* • in decision-making, implementation and maintenance spheres of collective activity. COUCHED IN COMMUNITY DEVELOPMENT DISCOURSE. NO MENTION OF MARKET.	**Instruments:** *Demand side:* • develop property rights; • develop mortgage finance; • rationalize subsidies. *Supply side:* • provide infrastructure for residential land development; • regulate land and housing development; • organize building industry. *Other:* • develop institutional framework for managing housing sector. COUCHED IN MARKET ECONOMICS DISCOURSE. PREDOMINANCE OF MACRO ISSUES. NONE DIRECTLY ADDRESSING THE POOR.
Lessons learnt: • The poor have done more for themselves than governments. • More than sites & services and upgrading is needed. • Resource constraints are likely to make government intervention difficult.	**Lessons learnt:** • The informal housing sector has a role. • Project success is dependent on distortions in housing sector and the economy. • Typical projects are usually too small. • Governments have been diverted from regulatory & institutional reform to projects. • There has been a shift from physical to institutional reform. • A variety of approaches to lending emerged. • Past focus on lending to the poor should continue.

7.6 A comparison of UNCHS and World Bank enabling strategies, as initially stated (Smith (1999: 26) based on UNCHS (1987) and World Bank (1993))

This approach to enablement emerged during a third period of World Bank activity in housing starting in 1986, the main thrust of which was growth and development of the whole housing sector in urban and national contexts (Pugh 1995). Two key World Bank reports set out its new policy positions. *Urban Policy and Economic Development: an Agenda for the 1990s* (1991) focused on the rise in urban populations and rise in urban share of GDP in developing countries, stressing the link between urban economies and national productivity. *Housing: enabling markets to work* (1993) adopted the 'enabling strategy' terminology discussed above, promoted primarily policy intervention rather than project or programme activities, and emphasised the reduced role of the state and increased role of the private sector. This 'enabling markets' approach was adopted by most international agencies in the latter part of the 1980s and early 1990s as they strove to convince national governments to promote housing delivery programmes with a wider impact. However, the governments of many rapidly urbanising countries continued to be ambivalent to the promotion of such 'enabling strategies' for housing the poor, and in addition the type of institutions and skills needed were often lacking or limited in scope. The role promoted for governments in this context was to create appropriate institutions to manage the housing sector market overall with minimum interference, yet defend public interests through stimulating demand and facilitating housing supply using the 'instruments' shown in Figure 7.6. Apart from paying greater attention to the role of government and emphasising partnerships between government, private sector and NGOs (Pugh 1995), this later approach also accepted the legitimacy of subsidies, provided these are adequately targeted programmes limited to poor groups.

World Bank urban sector finance in the 1990s thus began to move its focus away from housing *per se* and to become increasingly tied to reorganisation of market-oriented delivery systems for urban development in general. In addition to the economic conditionalities for 'market enablement', the World Bank began to add political conditionalities of good governance. The stress in general was on the reorganisation of government's role in market regulation and urban development as essential to ensure more effective urban economies as the 'engine for development' with 'associated increasing incomes'. The argument was that governments had for too long been dealing with the symptoms of urban housing problems, not the basic causes. An important factor influencing this approach was the change of emphasis from 'development' philosophy to structural integration with the global economy, with structural adjustment basically geared to remove the various forms of economic insulation between developing countries and the world markets (Pugh 1995). In practice, however, the effect of Structural Adjustment Programmes in actually reducing disposable incomes for lower-income groups has been in direct conflict with the self-help housing approaches of the previous period.

The Urban Management Program developed by the World Bank, UNCHS (Habitat) and UNDP in the 1980s (see Chapters 6 and 8) linked housing to the wider urban economy, arguing that local government was more responsive to electorates and citizens than national governments had been, and thus more open to guidance. In the 1990s the World Bank thus increasingly turned to focus on promoting municipal development and institutional changes in urban management. These included promoting legislation on land (focused on development of transferable property rights) and entrepreneurial town planning; identifying key infrastructure improvements; developing partnerships for service provision; promoting better organisation and competition in the building industry; targeting limited anti-poverty subsidisation; and undertaking environmental protection/ management. The overall package however, is 'very demanding, requiring well developed public administration, effective coordination among participants, and complex systems of cooperation' (Pugh 1995: 70). As such, where basic thresholds of urban management capacity existed these were assisted, but where these had not developed – or had been negatively affected by structural adjustment – the effect was often negative rather than positive as weak local governments struggled to find their feet in severely restricted institutional and political contexts.

Analytical impasse

As noted above, the 'self-help housing debate' began in the late 1970s and carried on with a series of counter positions (mainly between Burgess and Turner) through to the early 1990s in various books and many articles. During the 1980s Turner's writing increasingly stressed the need for community control over decisions affecting neighbourhoods; however, he still saw the state as needing to provide access to basic resources (e.g. land) and intermediate agencies as necessary to provide components such as infrastructure. In Turner's opinion, the collapse of the state socialist economies accentuated the emphasis on the capitalist market system, which he saw as being relatively efficient. He thus promoted the need for a 'third alternative' based on community control, enabled by government and supported by the private sector. In this approach the private and community sectors (i.e. the 'Third Sector') would implement devolved public sector roles – the community sector mainly seen as acting for lower income groups.[14] Burgess on the other hand went on to expand his critique of self-help through an analysis of the role of neo-liberalism's impact on self-help housing, which this chapter has drawn on and expanded.

In the late 1980s a few writers tried to sum up the self-help housing debate,[15] reiterating a sense of theoretical impasse and concern with the need for new analytical development. Kosta Mathey, in what was essentially the last important contemporary text on the theoretical and empirical basis for housing in the 'developing world' at the beginning of the 1990s, stated that the '... magnitude of the housing problem world-wide, and the evident failure of both exclusively state and exclusively market provision approaches, leaves no alternative to self-help solutions or, in other words, subsistence production, at least as a complementary measure to other programmes' (Mathey 1992: 1). He argued that previous criticisms of self-help, such as double exploitation, are not as important in the current situation where only a privileged minority have access to formal employment, and thus the possibility of self-help as a means to empowerment at neighbourhood level is an 'entry point for the poor to enter the "negotiation" processes with the ruling classes' (ibid: 2). In addition he suggested that the growing body of evaluation and investigation of the application of self-help housing in the 1980s in a wide variety of forms had led to the possibility of assessing what specific configuration is appropriate in any given context. He advocated comparative analysis of the differing application and results of the wide variety of self-help housing policies and practices in the various configurations produced by this analysis, as the basis for new approaches.

Fiori and Ramirez (1992) agreed that greater research and analysis and a more nuanced analysis of contexts are needed. Their position was that the articulation theory critique of self-help housing needed re-assessment from various points of view, primarily that of the political and economic contexts which require different state responses and hence different housing and urban development policies. They pointed out ambiguities in the perceived relationship between pre-capitalist forms of housing production and the dominant capitalist mode, in some situations these being seen as essential to capitalist accumulation and in others as obstacles. In fact these different processes may co-exist in concrete situations and therefore need specific analysis, rather than generalisation. They thus criticised the Neo-Marxist analysis as tending to characterise the state as a monolithic entity whose exploitative policies are under direct control of the ruling classes.[16] They were also critical of the World Bank's neo-liberal approach, seeing as unlikely that its focus on increasing supply through removing institutional constraints, and consequent reductions in the costs of commodified land and housing, could be realised without continued subsidisation, which entails redistribution of resources and is often in direct conflict with political tendencies. They argued that frequently 'self-help' housing is the only available option for the majority, and it thus has importance in terms of social stability and state legitimacy, potentially influencing policy.

How this translates into political intervention, however, depends on the political context, but typically involves emphasis on popular 'participation', and housing is thus an arena of *de facto* negotiation concerning state re-distribution of resources. Fiori and Ramirez's position was therefore that while self-help housing policies tend to commodify housing, at a general level, they generate new conditions for social organisation and hence new possibilities for negotiation between state and residents, involving wider resource distribution and the opportunity for more democratic decision making. They argued for research that goes beyond '... isolated analyses of projects that do not take into account the wider context of the city and of the socio-economic and political factors surrounding...' these (Fiori and Ramirez 1992: 27), and highlighted a need for empirical research into the links between local negotiation and the wider process, and between project and policy level in specific political situations.

Marcussen (1990: 13) considered the debate was based on '... two epistemologies that failed to generate a common conceptual frame of scientific discourse', increasing the gap between theory and practice. He argued that at the root of the different positions were different conceptions of value, especially use-value of housing. He argued that Turner stressed the primacy of social and cultural attributes of the housing process, e.g. the 'sense of belonging', while Burgess, in the Neo-Marxist tradition, saw housing as a commodity and divided societal life into distinct spheres of economic production and social reproduction, using theoretical categories defined in 'traditional' political economic terms such as value, abstract labour, etc. As Marcussen points out, difficulties with this analysis arise with the question of how to define when housing actually acquires commodity status: when it is perceived as exchangeable or when it is actually exchanged. This led to definitions of differences between 'real commodity' and 'potential commodity' status and increasing convolution of argument.

In addition the Neo-Marxist view of the state as exclusively acting rationally to support the capitalist system was seen as simplistic. Turner's view was seen as more complex – the state is flexible and can act at times 'irrationally' against the capitalist system. The former view is based on class analysis, but there are limits to class formation, especially in Latin America, Asia and Africa, where this is often overlaid by socially based identity groupings and traversed by vertical patron–client relationships and pre-capitalist power structures. In reality the interests of the ruling classes are not necessarily tied to processes of capital accumulation, and they are not defenceless against the penetration of global capitalism, with bureaucracy performing a 'cushioning' role in many places. Ruling elites may also be constrained politically by strong civic organisations representing specific interest groups – for example 'slum dwellers' in Latin America. In general, however, usually it is the ruling elites' vested interests in low-income settlements that have political expression (and not those of the poor) – one of the reasons for the reluctance to accept sites and services and aided self-help housing, which ran counter to existing socio-political structures and competition in existing housing systems.

Marcussen (1990) saw both approaches as Euro-centric, the Neo-Marxist approach relying on theoretical constructs such as the working class, which cannot be applied globally, and the self-help approach promoting notions of 'local community' unrelated to traditional social and socio-political relationships.

Marcussen thus expressed the view that the role of traditional social relationships and pre-capitalist socio-political structures (indigenous or of early colonial origin), required more attention in housing studies than they received in the so-called 'self-help debate' – a position this book hopes to promote. He suggested that housing is not a 'noun' or a 'verb' (as popularised by Turner), but a 'struggle' that results in specific articulations of a housing system, albeit within certain overall parameters set by the dominant capitalist mode of production. Marcussen suggested that the way out of this theoretical impasse would be a programme of comparative research based on a model derived from the various theoretical and practical typologies developed to date, linking these in an analytical system which differentiated between different forms of integration within the dominant capitalist system. These forms (and how they have been facets of the previous analyses) are shown in Figure 7.7, and are defined as follows:

- The pre-formal housing system refers to systems for housing provision which pre-date the formal state control over housing developing from the end of the nineteenth century. In the developing world it refers to traditional, historical settlements, as well as those provided under colonialism (e.g. staff housing).
- The formal housing system refers to the housing system – market or state driven, or a combination – which is controlled by the state in terms of standards and control.
- The ad hoc projects/'normas minimas' housing system refers to land and housing provided by the state, including upgrading of informal housing areas. These are often ad hoc projects and use lower than normal standards. This typology also includes private sector provision of sites and services, where again standards can be lowered.

Self-help	Marxist		General use	Marcussen
"Heteronomous production"	Industrial production		"Conventional" housing	Pre-formal
				Formal
"Autonomous production"	Petty commodity production	Manufacturing form	"Informal" housing	Ad hoc / normas minimas
				Informal
		Self-help form		Marginal

7.7 Comparative typology of housing systems (Jenkins: 1998)

- The informal housing system refers to areas with permanent settlement formation on un-serviced land and extra-legal housing production, including rental. This would include most 'squatter' areas, as well as 'illegal' land sub-division. In these areas both social and economic patterns of shelter overlap and interact.
- The marginal housing system refers to the extra-economic system structured predominantly by social relationships. Spatially it tends to be organised in small colonies, each with its leadership, or aggregations of such colonies which (over time) create larger settlements. Inhabitants tend to be low income and more likely to be recent in-migrants to urban areas. Mobility is high. This typology can include the literally homeless (street-sleepers).

Marcussen then suggested a method whereby these were defined in terms of the mode of production as far as the three main activities of 'settling' (access to land), 'building' and 'redistribution' (or subsequent transfer) are concerned (see Table 7.1).[17]

Table 7.1 An analytical model of different modes of production within housing systems

Marcussen	Settling	Building	Redistributing
Preformal	Traditional, some now formalised	Traditional, some now formalised	Social relations predominate
Formal	State controlled system	Auto-construction, petty commodity and industrial production	Real estate market
Ad hoc / Normas minimas	Sites and services, upgrading	Auto-construction, petty commodity production	Social relations predominate
Informal	Pirate land subdivisions, land renting, land invasion	Auto-construction, petty commodity production	Social relations predominate
Marginal	Social relations predominate	Auto-construction	Social relations predominate

Source: Marcussen 1990

In practice none of these approaches to housing theory and analysis in the 'developing world' was developed to any notable extent (with the possible exception of doctoral research which has not been widely published).[18] This was probably due to two reasons: the lack of interest in funding housing *per se* in the 'developing world', as the next chapter will describe; and the fact that 'development' as a concept was also increasingly questioned, as has been outlined in Chapter 2. In addition, the swing in funding from housing to urban development, by donor agencies (except where financial institutions already were relatively strong), and the associated lack of interest in funding housing research, was compounded by structural changes in research institutions, which became increasingly dependent on 'directed' funding – usually applied research – as opposed to theoretical development. To some extent this book attempts to pick up these research trends and recommence the interrupted dialogues.

Chapter 8
Post-1990 issues in planning and housing

Introduction

This chapter provides an overview of the increasingly diverse themes in planning and housing policy and practice in the rapidly urbanising world in the last decade of the twentieth century and into the first decade of the twenty-first century. During this period there has been a swing of emphasis away from housing, which dominated discussion in the 1960–80 period, to a growing stress on planning and related themes, starting with urban management approaches in the 1990s. The focus on shelter in human settlements – in what are still often termed 'developing countries' – also moved into wider conceptual areas, before more recently returning to focus again on responses within the built environment. These wider conceptual areas focused on *sustainability* and its implications for urban development in terms of both 'green' and 'brown' agendas and the emergence of the *Habitat Agenda*, with a subsequent focus on *urban poverty* and eventually a more recent international emphasis on *slum eradication*. In parallel, the focus on urban management which began in the 1980s evolved through the 1990s and converged with a focus on 'sustainable cities', including an emphasis on *good governance* and *security of tenure*. The enabling markets approach of the 1980s was widened to include public–private partnerships as a favoured model for providing urban services, with an alternative approach promoting the role of civil society, and an overall *alliance-building* approach. More recently the focus on planning as such has come to the fore again, closely allied to converging tendencies in addressing what is the 'public interest' in urban areas, an example being a growing focus on *metropolitanisation*.

The emerging global normative agenda

An important theme running through the above conceptual developments is the creation of global policy platforms through a series of international conferences, generally organised by the United Nations, which set normative agendas. Such conferences had been held before, but their frequency was curtailed in the so-called 'lost development decade' of the 1980s when the Cold War was coming to an end, and influential neo-liberal Northern governments were pushing structural adjustment through international agencies (see Chapter 2). The re-emergence of global conferences in the 1990s reflected the changing global political and economic context, including the growing perception of the inter-connected nature of world systems: mainly seen as economic and environmental links, but also inter-connected social movements and eventually political decision-making. Another crucial factor was the growing perception that 'development' was an issue for all countries, North and South, a perception that the growing penetration of global information and communication technologies facilitated. The two principal emerging themes of this normative agenda at the turn of the millennium were a renewed focus on alleviating poverty and the role of establishing human rights, including in the human settlements sector.

The series of international conferences arguably began in 1988 with the adoption of the Global Strategy for Shelter for the Year 2000 by the UN General Assembly. This underlined the findings of the previous decades that project-based ad hoc solutions to shelter problems were inadequate, and promoted the 'enabling strategies' described in the previous chapter, starting with policy-oriented lending to improve housing markets, linked to wider macro-economic adjustment. The target of enabling adequate shelter for all by 2000 adopted by the conference was extremely ambitious, but seen as important to encourage immediate action. This conference was followed by a series of summits addressing a range of issues that had direct implications for human settlements: the 1990 World Summit for Children in New York; the 1992 UN Conference on Environment and Development in Rio de Janeiro, which adopted Agenda 21 as its blueprint for action to achieve sustainable development (see below); the 1993 World Conference on Human Rights in Vienna; the 1994 International Conference on Population and Development in Cairo; the 1995 Fourth World Conference on Women in Beijing; and the 1995 World Summit for Social Development in Copenhagen, which had a high participation rate from the non-governmental community, a growing aspect of the global conferences of the period.

The themes of the UN conferences and the related trends all fed into the 1996 Conference on Human Settlements, the last of this series in the period, also known as Habitat II, which was held in Istanbul in 1996. The conference and a parallel NGO Forum were well attended by representatives of central and local governments, NGOs, business, research and professional institutions and labour unions.[1] There was wide discussion and consultation between these various groups in the preparation of the resulting Istanbul Declaration and Habitat Agenda. One key approach promoted in the conference and thereafter was the showcasing of 'best practices' as a means to accumulate and disseminate experience. In the declaration the important role of urban areas in social, economic and cultural advancement was stressed and governments signed up to a series of priorities for action which drew together many of the themes of the previous conferences concerning sustainability, economic inequality, rights to basic services and shelter, and protection from violence and other forms of vulnerability. Governments were asked to undertake concerted actions, in partnership with private and non-governmental partners, as well as civil society, and alliance-building was the over-arching approach. The Habitat Agenda fleshed this declaration out as a plan of action with over 200 commitments (see below).

This series of conferences paved the way for an attempt to form a broad co-ordinated alliance between governments and other partners in development around specific goals as the world entered the new millennium. At a world summit in September 2000, world leaders defined eight broad Millennium Development Goals (MDGs), with a series of related targets to be met by 2005 or 2015, using 1990 as the benchmark (see Appendix C). These MDGs have, however, been seen as ambitious at the same time as they have been criticised for being: too narrow in scope, leading to reducing support for other important anti-poverty action; overly determined by 'external' experts; too concerned with measurable outcomes in top-down targeted interventions and reliant on indicators that are conceptually flawed (e.g. the $1/day measure of poverty) and for which data are notoriously inaccurate; overly focused on the action of international agencies and national governments (Satterthwaite 2003). Despite these concerns, most international and national development agencies are focusing on the MDGs in their global programmes.

The agency UN-Habitat has published two recent reports on how it interprets the MDGs in relation to shelter and human settlements (UN-Habitat 2003a, 2004), following a tradition of such overviews since the mid-1980s, and these represent important summaries of current dominant approaches to planning and housing (as well as many other human settlements issues) from the international perspective, as is summarised below.

The evolution of key issues in shelter and human settlements in the 1990s and the new millennium

In 1986 UNCHS published the first *Global Report on Human Settlements*, underpinning its 1987 launch of the Global Strategy for Shelter for the Year 2000. This broad overview of both UN normative proposals and current analysis of shelter worldwide was followed up ten years later with the UNCHS publication *An Urbanising World: Global Report on Human Settlements* (UNCHS 1996), which characterised cities as places of opportunity and 'engines of growth', and was closely tied to the Habitat II conference of that year, and the subsequent Habitat Agenda. The next sections of this chapter look in more detail at the Habitat Agenda and how key development themes which have been highlighted by this – sustainable development, urban poverty, good governance, alliance-building, secure tenure and metropolitanisation – are reflected in shelter policy for the rapidly urbanising world.

The Habitat Agenda

As mentioned above, alliance-building was built into the organisation of the Habitat II conference, with the participation of a wide range of stakeholders including from civil society. The aim of the conference was explicitly stated as 'reaffirming existing and forging new partnerships for action at the international, national and local levels to improve our living environment' (UNCHS 1996: 5). The goals of the Habitat Agenda were adequate shelter for all and sustainable human settlements development in the urbanising world. The Habitat Agenda indicated that the definition of 'adequate' shelter needs to be undertaken at a local level, but saw the role of governments as formulating housing policies that were integrated with overall macro-economic, environmental and social policies, through frameworks that enabled markets to work, as well as facilitating community-based production of housing. In order to do so, governments were expected to ensure access to land, as well as to basic infrastructure and social services, and to mobilise sources of finance. In terms of regulation, governments were to eliminate regulatory barriers whilst, on the other hand, developing whole new regulatory frameworks; this was to go hand in hand with decentralisation. With regard to sustainable human settlements development, the document recognised in its diagnosis the problems arising in urban areas due to rapid urbanisation and declared there was a need for co-operative action among interested parties, among which it highlighted the role to be played by local authorities. In more specific environmental terms, the importance of rural–urban linkages, carrying-capacity of urban areas, and environmental sustainability of economic activities was stated. In addition, there was a call for the mitigation of unbalanced geographical development of human settlements, not explicitly through national and/or regional planning but through partnerships and management.

As a response to these issues, desirable action was spelt out in relation to a long list of fields ranging from sustainable land use to disaster prevention and post-disaster rehabilitation.[2] Crucial to addressing these issues was to be capacity-building and institutional development for the planning and management of human settlements, metropolitan areas being seen as in particular need of institutional strengthening. Essentially, the Habitat Agenda, in its comprehensiveness, is a *collaborative approach* that combines elements from the UN's original statement of enablement in 1986 and the World Bank's more market-based enabling policies (see Chapter 7). It has been suggested, however, that this comprehensiveness and inclusiveness was a reflection of the conflict avoidance strategy adopted during the running of the conference itself. As Strassmann (1997: 1730) put it: 'In Habitat

Agenda, one finds the usual liturgy about establishing, promoting, supporting, enhancing, facilitating, encouraging, strengthening, mobilising and harnessing everything that is good, appropriate and sustainable "at all levels".'. Importantly, the expression of collaborative management of human settlements did not analyse the political-economic background with regard to the problems it sought to address, assuming a neutral, interest-free and willing attitude in 'stakeholders' that is in fact far removed from reality. It also, among other omissions, avoided the more radical – and therefore politically controversial – interpretations of sustainability (Strassmann 1997).

The quinquennial review of the Habitat Agenda was also documented in 2001 by a new global report: *Cities in a Globalising World* (UNCHS 2001). This analysed urbanisation trends and the effects of information and communication technology (ICT) on human settlements as the basis for a review of the impact of globalisation on shelter. Key arguments included the tendency for polarisation between wealthy and poor, no longer primarily geographically expressed, and the growing urbanisation of poverty. It also focused on the importance of urban governance and politics, highlighting the challenge to democracy and some of the new trends within this in Latin America. In terms of shelter it reviewed housing finance and shelter delivery systems and looked at a number of themes in urban areas: health, environment, transport, energy, infrastructure, as well as institutional capacity building and post-disaster reconstruction. It continued the normative orientation with its conclusions concerning providing adequate shelter for all, mainly through stressing housing rights, land tenure reform and good governance. Overall the report focused on the uneven effect of globalisation on and in cities, but the important role of urban areas as agents of change.

The Millennium Development Goals

The Millennium Development Goals are arguably the peak of the trend in global normative approach to development, and these include issues related to shelter and human settlements. This was made explicit in the global report on human settlements published in 2003, entitled *The Challenge of Slums*, referring to MDG Target 11 of Goal 7, which calls for 'significant improvement in the lives of at least 100 million slum dwellers by the year 2020'. Slums were defined as places without access to adequate drinking water, sanitation, quality of housing and security of tenure, and seen as being the product of two main processes: rapid urbanisation and urbanisation of poverty. This report estimated that in 2001 32 per cent of the total world urban population (some 924 million people) lived in these slums, with a higher incidence in 'developing regions' (43 per cent) and 'least developed countries' (78 per cent). This MDG was therefore targeted at around 11 per cent of this current estimated global slum-dweller population, and even less in the light of projections that the slum population can possibly grow to

2,000 million by 2030 if no significant changes take place (UN-Habitat 2003). As this report stressed, this MDG is thus a minimal approach to the growing problems of shelter across the world, especially in urban areas, although it is itself an ambitious target.

While focusing on ways to improve life within slums, the report recognised that such areas also provide important forms of affordable shelter, especially for the growing proportion of urban informal sector workers. They also were seen as being the basis for positive social and cultural movements. The report stressed that efforts to resolve living conditions in such areas had declined since the 1980s when they were a major development focus, and that slum upgrading or eradication programmes had failed to address underlying causes of the existence of these areas, mainly poverty. It thus stressed the importance of income generation promotion and the integration of shelter improvement actions in wider poverty-reduction policies. It also reiterated the focus on security of tenure in land and housing for the urban poor as a means to socially and economically include the urban poor, stressing the need for appropriate policies to underpin sustained financial commitment to scaling-up slum upgrading at city-wide, regional and national level. This report thus re-emphasised the global trends in urbanisation, inequality and urban poverty and the role of links between local and national governments in addressing urban shelter problems.

The increasingly frequent publication of UN normative overview reports continued in 2004 with the publication of *The State of the World's Cities*, this time as a contribution to the Universal Forum of Cultures in Barcelona (2004). This report focused on the cultural impact of globalisation on cities. Cities were again characterised as often facing growing poverty, deepening inequality and polarisation, widespread corruption, high rates of urban crime and violence and deteriorating living conditions for many. Urban culture is increasingly diverse and differentiated, often with high levels of discrimination and even segregation. The report stressed the importance of creating cities open to all, while planning for difference, thus building on the benefits of multi-cultural existence, especially the role of innovation. Again focused on the Millennium Development Goals, and seen as the second in a series of reports on progress in implementation of these (UN-Habitat 2003a being the first), the report highlighted the importance of cultural factors to build citizenship rights in peaceful ways despite the trends in globalisation and growth of poverty within cities, and how culture-driven strategies can assist cities to market themselves globally. In this it stressed the role of urban planning, not only focusing on land use, but addressing wider social, economic and environmental concerns, and as proactive activity in promoting social inclusion. In general, thus, this report expanded on the issues and themes of the previous three reports published within the period 1996–2004, especially on the uneven impact of globalisation, without much new in terms of response, except the return to stressing the importance of urban planning.

A critical view of the normative global agenda

All of the above reports since 1996 have explicitly linked globalisation, increasing economic volatility and forms of social inequality and exclusion, with growing urban poverty and challenges to forms of urban governance. They have analysed trends in urbanisation and urban poverty from a wide spectrum, including political, economic, social and cultural issues. However, this has all been within the context of normative exhortation to such concepts as 'good governance' and 'best practice', which fundamentally assumes that clear understanding of the situation based on empirical evidence, together with analysis of the sectoral causes, and examples of what are seen as successful experiences, should lead to improved policies and action. In other words, forms of knowledge exchange hold the potential for positive development. While this may be true, this position ignores a realpolitik where individuals, institutions and governments tend to act for their own perceived benefit first, and perhaps are prepared to act in more voluntarist and wider beneficial ways secondly, if at all.

According to the new international political economy analysis outlined previously, this position also ignores the fundamental underlying trends in late capitalism's global re-structuring, as described in Chapter 3, which will undermine the possibility of widespread application of the proposed solutions. The position also skims over any deeper analysis of the actual political and economic – and at times social and cultural – context which so-called best practices have happened within, and thus of the possible transfer of this experience, while acknowledging the need for adaptation. This approach thus correctly links globalisation to increasing social and economic polarisation worldwide, but it assumes that 'fair play' can exist, as long as information is clear, analysis correct and dialogue possible. In this it is very similar in approach to that of 'collaborative' or 'communicative planning', which aspires to create 'level playing fields' for all possible and interested stakeholders to discuss and arrive at consensual decisions (see Chapter 6). On the contrary, the reality is that power relations, whether at a local or global level, will tend to reproduce themselves to their own benefit, albeit being prepared, in the name of 'good governance' to discuss and even adopt the rhetoric of a global 'public good'. As such there is no guarantee of fair play or dialogue, and in fact the way that knowledge is selectively produced also conditions the form of analysis – whoever sets the rules and agenda dominates the action and dialogue.

This theme will be returned to in the conclusions to the book, as it fundamentally underpins the nature of the approach to planning and housing that the book promotes – one that is politically aware, applies critical analysis and is proactive. The remainder of this chapter focuses rather on some of the recent key development themes that have had an impact on shelter and urban development policy in the rapidly urbanising world.

Key issues in human settlements

Sustainable urban development

The much quoted Brundtland Commission definition of sustainable development as 'development which meets the needs of the current generation without jeopardising the needs of future generations' (WCED 1987) is only one link in a long debate over the interaction between environment and development. In the 1970s the focus of debate was the ecological limits to economic growth mainly through natural resource exhaustion, shifting in the late 1970s and 1980s to the impact that economic development has on the environment through pollution and global environmental change. These issues were addressed by the Brundtland Report in 1987 and in the United Nations Conference on Environment and Development (UNCED) in Rio de Janeiro in 1992, which in turn resulted in a series of international conventions and declarations related to environmental issues, and their relationship with development.

The disagreement at the UNCED summit between 'northern' and 'southern' countries over the conceptualisation of sustainable development and the setting of priorities for achieving this illustrates the highly contested nature of this concept. The former advocated steps to protect the 'natural' environment, particularly at the global level, which required curbing polluting development processes, seen as threatening world eco-systems. The latter saw this approach as denying them the opportunity to undergo development processes already embarked on by the 'developed world', thus denying their societies the possibility of reaching comparable living standards. This polemic mirrors other intellectual arguments which in the early days of the debate could be summarised as:

- the environmentalist view: development and nature must be linked, and sustainable development can be achieved through regenerative settlements, renewable resources and recycling;
- the economist view: decision making should combine environment and economics, achieving sustainable development through the market system (using principles such as 'polluter pays');
- the political economy view: the root of environmental problems lies in capitalism, through consumerism, the pursuit of profit and the generation on inequality in wealth distribution.

These arguments and debates have become increasingly diverse and complex. Although initially seen to be the remit of economics and environmental sciences, the concept of 'sustainable development' has also been tackled by the social sciences, which have highlighted its inherent social, political, institutional and cultural aspects.

A key debate of direct relevance to human settlements and urban development is that between urban environmental issues related to environmental health (the 'brown' agenda – see Figure 8.1) and those linked to ecological sustainability (the 'green' agenda). Conflicts arise over the priority each of these agendas should be given, particularly in urban areas in the rapidly urbanising world. For example, the 'green' perspective would question the impact that city-based consumption would have on rural resources and ecosystems. Conversely, the 'brown' agenda approach would raise the question of the needs and priorities of the poor. Pugh (2000) notes the correlation between the level of national income and the type of environmental priority (see Figure 8.2). He also highlights that in many large cities the different agendas are equally present, though these may be differentially prioritised by different income groups.

8.1 The brown agenda – hazardous solid waste by an open-air market in Luanda, Angola (Harry Smith)

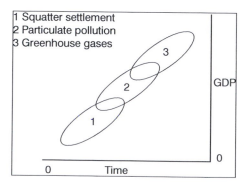

8.2 National income and type of environmental priority (Pugh 2000: Figure 2.1)

McGranahan and Satterthwaite (2000) set out the stereotypical features of the 'brown' and 'green' agendas (see Table 8.1). According to these authors, although there are conflicts between the proponents of these agendas in relation

Table 8.1 Stereotypical features of the 'brown' and 'green' agendas

	The 'brown' environmental health agenda	The 'green' sustainability agenda
Characteristic features of problems high on the agenda:		
Key impact	Human health	Ecosystem health
Timing	Immediate	Delayed
Scale	Local	Regional and global
Worst affected	Lower income groups	Future generations
Characteristic attitude to:		
Nature	Manipulate to serve human needs	Protect and work with
People	Work with	Educate
Environmental services	Provide more	Use less
Aspects emphasised in relation to:		
Water	Inadequate access and poor quality	Overuse; need to protect water sources
Air	High human exposure to hazardous pollutants	Acid precipitation and greenhouse emissions
Solid waste	Inadequate provision for collection and removal	Excessive generation
Land	Inadequate access for low income groups to housing	Loss of natural habitats and agricultural land to urban development
Human wastes	Inadequate provision for safely removing faecal material (and waste water) from living environment	Loss of nutrients in sewage and damage to water bodies from the release of sewage into waterways
Typical proponent:	Urbanist	Environmentalist

Source: McGranahan and Satterthwaite 2000: Table 4.1

to priorities, and some approaches based on one agenda may adversely affect issues important to the other, it is important not to create a false dichotomy (see Figure 8.3). They point out that a concern for greater equity is central to both, and suggest environmental improvements that serve both agendas. For example, land use management linked to high-quality public transport, good traffic management, and other controls on private car use can address brown agenda concerns over low income groups' needs for health, air quality and good public transport, as well as green agenda concerns to reduce fossil fuel use and ecologically damaging air pollution. They suggest that reconciling the brown and green agendas in urban development requires institutions and processes that: 'reduce the inequities that are of concern to both the brown and green agendas; enable collective and democratic responses to the public aspects of both green and environmental problems; and provide a better understanding of the environmental issues that different cities face' (McGranahan and Satterthwaite 2000: 85). This links the issues of sustainable development into governance issues, an aspect that has become increasingly acknowledged in international approaches to poverty, as is seen below.

8.3 Brown vs. green agendas – streets flooded by the monsoon in India. Sea level rise and increased flooding are expected to increase health risks in affected areas (Catherine Smithson)

Urban poverty

Our understanding of poverty is becoming more sophisticated through recent research (see below). However, in most countries official measurements of poverty rely on the following typical measures: absolute poverty, usually defined as comprising those who cannot afford to buy a 'minimum basket' of goods; and relative poverty, comprising the proportion of people below some threshold, often a percentage of local median income. Recently the World Bank has promoted the use of a simple 'extreme poverty' measure based on having a daily income below US$1 (adjusted for purchase price parity). This is a very blunt and contested instrument to measure poverty, but is currently used extensively by international agencies. According to this measure half the world (nearly 3 billion people) lives on less than US$2 a day, and while the proportion of people living in extreme poverty of less than US$1 a day declined from 29 per cent in 1990 to 23 per cent in 1999, the total number of people in extreme poverty had increased up to 1988, and was back at 1988 levels in 1998, a decade later.

Extreme poverty and its trends are also not geographically homogenous, as Table 8.2 shows. Thus while proportions of the extremely poor have fallen in Asia and the Middle East/North Africa, they have remained stable in Latin America and Africa, increasing in Eastern Europe. This however translates into increasing

Table 8.2 Geographic distribution of poverty

	Percent living in extreme poverty (below US$1/day)		Millions living in extreme poverty (below US$1/day)	
	1987	1998	1987	1998
East Asia	26.6	15.3	417.5	278.3
(excluding China)	23.9	11.3	114.1	65.2
Eastern Europe	0.2	5.1	1.1	24.0
Latin America	15.3	15.6	63.7	78.2
Middle East and North Africa	4.3	2.0	9.3	5.6
South Asia	44.9	40.0	474.4	522.0
Africa	46.6	46.3	217.2	290.9
Total	28.3	24.0	1,183.2	1,198.9

Source: UN-Habitat 2003a: Table 2.2.

numbers in extreme poverty in these latter macro-regions, particularly in urban areas, which are increasingly the locus of poverty in both absolute and relative terms (UN-Habitat 2003a). As for the main causes of continuing poverty levels, UN-Habitat points to insufficient economic growth in many of the poorest countries, and inequalities that inhibit the poor from participating in growth when it does occur. The reduction of poverty is now the prime objective of development policy (see Appendix D). Millennium Development Goal 1 is to halve the proportion of people living in extreme poverty by 2015, in relation to the figures for 1990.

During the 1990s, research and policy developed an increasingly direct focus on poverty. The concept of poverty was analysed and new conceptualisations emerged. These recognised that poverty is not just about income or expenditure levels but is multifaceted, covering a wide range of aspects: prospects for earning a living; deprivation and exclusion; basic needs; social aspects; psychological aspects, etc. New approaches to the study and assessment of poverty have developed the following concepts:

- Vulnerability: a dynamic concept referring to negative outcomes on the well-being of individuals, households, or communities from environmental changes (Moser 1996).
- Asset ownership: (see Appendix E) individuals', households' and communities' ability to resist negative impacts relates to their ability to mobilise assets in the face of hardship (Moser 1996).
- Livelihood: comprises the 'capabilities, assets (stores, resources, claims and access) and activities required for a means of living: a livelihood is sustainable which can cope with and recover from stress and shock, maintain or enhance its capabilities and assets, and provide sustainable livelihood opportunities for the next generation'. (Chambers and Conway 1992: 6)

While there are new dynamic conceptualisations of poverty which can be applied to urban areas, this is still not widespread as much of the above needs to be assessed qualitatively and is subject to contextual differences. It has thus less influence on broad statistical descriptions of poverty, but can be more influential at a programme or project level with definition of poverty levels made in relation to other socio-economic groups. There is as yet no clear way that this context-dependent work on more flexible understandings of urban poverty can become more established in terms of planning and housing policies, although attempts to relate these approaches to shelter issues include Moser (1996), Satterthwaite (1998, 2002a), Rakodi and Lloyd-Jones (2002), and Van der Schueren *et al.* (1996).

Good governance and sustainable cities

Increasingly, approaches to eradicating poverty, and urban poverty in particular, have been linked to good governance agendas. Although there is no generally accepted definition, governance is generally seen as involving a wider spectrum of actors other than the state in decision-making and actions in the public sphere, including the private sector, voluntary sector and civil society (Smith 2004; UNCHS 2001). The UN-Habitat Global Campaign on Urban Governance, for example, aims to contribute to the eradication of poverty through improved urban governance, on the stated basis that the quality of urban governance is increasingly seen as the most important factor for the eradication of poverty and to foster prosperity.[3]

The UN's approach to good urban governance focuses on ways in which the state, particularly local government, relates to other actors. UNCHS (2001: 59) thus identifies the 'emerging elements of governance' as decentralisation and formal government reforms, participation of civil society, multi-level governance, and process-oriented and territorially based policies. Similarly, the World Bank sees improved urban governance from the perspective of reformed local government which allows greater accountability, transparency and public participation (see Table 8.3) and, at a more macro level, is increasingly tying international lending to 'good governance' conditions.

This is a growing area of research, a good example being a project funded by the UK Department for International Development (DFID) on urban governance and poverty (Devas 2001). This comparative study of 10 cities focused on how urban governance influences the conditions for urban economic growth; the ways in which urban governance institutions seek to distribute the benefits of that growth and who benefits from such distribution processes; and how the poor influence the agenda of the institutions of city governance in their interests.

The research findings showed both the potential and limitations of actors involved in the case study cities. They suggested that the multi-dimensional nature of poverty means that there are also multiple opportunities for intervention, and in this respect, 'bad governance' undermines the position of the poor. City governments were identified as potentially having a great effect on poverty reduction through direct provision of infrastructure and services, and ensuring access to land. Various elements of civil society were shown to play a vital part in relation to poverty reduction, but their limitations also need to be recognised. In general, political relationships at city level are complex and often opaque, informal as well as formal, but they can, and often do, deliver some benefits for the poor, and, as such, democratisation at the local level can widen the scope for the urban poor to make their claims, and for urban politics to move beyond clientelism towards more open political bargaining (Devas 2001).

Table 8.3 Comparison of World Bank urban policy statements in the 1990s and 2000

World Bank Urban Policy and Economic Development Agenda for the 1990s – Objectives (World Bank, 1991)	World Bank Urban and Local Government Strategy – Dimensions of Sustainable Cities (World Bank, 2000a)
Improving urban productivity: • strengthen urban infrastructure management; • improve the regulatory framework to increase market efficiency and private sector participation; • improve municipal institutions' financial and technical capacity; • improve financial services for urban development.	Livability: ensuring a decent quality of life and equitable opportunity for all residents including the poorest. The World Bank would provide support for: • clients to establish appropriate policies at national and local levels, involving many sectors and disciplines, e.g. for neighbourhood upgrading; • facilitating participatory urban environmental management and the assessment and reduction of cities' vulnerability to natural disasters.
Alleviating urban poverty: • increasing labour productivity; • investing in the human capital and basic needs of the poor; • targeting 'safety net' assistance to the poor.	Competitiveness: building livable cities requires buoyant, broad-based growth of employment, incomes and investment. The World Bank would provide support for: • facilitation of city-wide economic analysis and strategy development with urban clients through participatory processes involving a wide range of stakeholders; • local economic development approaches that promote diversified growth strategies, serving domestic as well as international markets, and developing the potential of both formal and informal sectors; • development and dissemination of urban regulatory assessments and policy-relevant urban performance indicators.

Table 8.3 continued

World Bank Urban Policy and Economic Development Agenda for the 1990s – Objectives (World Bank, 1991)	World Bank Urban and Local Government Strategy – Dimensions of Sustainable Cities (World Bank, 2000a)
Developing effective responses to the growing urban environmental crisis: <ul><li>increase awareness of the urban environmental crisis;</li><li>develop an information base and understanding of the dynamics of urban environmental deterioration;</li><li>develop city-specific strategies for environmental management;</li><li>identify high-priority curative actions;</li><li>establish preventive policies and incentives;</li><li>regulation and enforcement.</li></ul>	Good governance and management: implies inclusion and representation of all groups in urban society; accountability, integrity, and transparency of local government actions; a capacity to fulfil public responsibilities, with knowledge, skills, resources, and procedures that draw on partnerships. The World Bank would support: <ul><li>regular and formal interaction between local government and residents;</li><li>fiscal decentralisation;</li><li>public–private partnerships for service delivery, ensuring the poor do benefit;</li><li>metropolitan-level management approaches;</li><li>capacity building and training of municipal staff in urban development projects.</li></ul>
Increase urban research.	Bankability: financial soundness in the treatment of revenue sources and expenditures and, for some cities, a level of creditworthiness permitting access to the capital market. The World Bank promotes: <ul><li>clear and internally consistent systems of local revenues and expenditures;</li><li>a commercial approach to many of the service and administrative functions of cities, while keeping social concerns in view;</li><li>specialised financial intermediaries such as municipal development funds;</li><li>a transition to market-based municipal credit systems;</li><li>access of credit-worthy cities to the capital market;</li><li>appropriate national policy frameworks for financing local public expenditure.</li></ul>

Sources: World Bank 1991, 2000a

This research also showed that the design of the city-level political system is of great importance, periodic elections alone not being a sufficient mechanism of local accountability and participation but needing to be accompanied by effective and accessible mechanisms for holding elected representatives and officials accountable. Government decentralisation in many countries has focused attention on city government, but most city governments face severe constraints and need to be strengthened, rather than assigning important functions to other agencies over which there is little or no democratic control, such as parastatals or higher level government agencies. The personal qualities of civic leadership can also make a difference and civic education is important. Finally, for larger cities, the research showed that there is a strong case for a two-tier system of government, i.e. the need for a metropolitan level (Devas 2001).

The above findings assist in breaking down in practical terms the general exhortations and specific requirements from multi-lateral and bi-lateral development agencies for good governance in situations of rapid urbanisation. This has increasingly been a condition for assistance programmes, focusing mainly on the creation or reinforcement of (representational) forms of democratic governance, decentralisation of government to local levels, and transparency and accountability in government actions. While seemingly reasonable as requirements, if not at least to ensure appropriate use of assistance funds, the interpretation of these 'conditionalities' in any specific context is usually predominantly that of the development agencies, and this is reflected in the definition of measures seen as appropriate as well as subsequent evaluation and monitoring. While accepting the need for improvements in governance systems, and the need for international assistance, many governments see these conditions as impositions in this format.

From urban management to Cities Alliances

The World Bank's 'Agenda for the 1990s' (see Chapter 7) has been spearheaded by the Urban Management Programme (UMP), among other initiatives. The UMP was established as a technical co-operation programme involving the United Nations Development Programme (UNDP), the United Nations Centre for Human Settlements (Habitat) and the World Bank, and assisted cities in implementing innovative programmes in five areas: urban land management; infrastructure management; municipal finance and administration; urban environmental management; and urban poverty alleviation (UNCHS 1996). The programme developed in three phases:

- 1986–92: development of policy framework and discussion papers on municipal finance, infrastructure management, urban land management and the urban environment.

- 1992–6: centred on raising awareness levels and promoting the quality of urban research and the orientation to more practicable policy alternatives. The UMP was not funded to undertake projects but to contribute to setting up regional networks of institutions involved in urban management.
- 1997–9: completion of the process of 'institutionally anchoring the regional assistance networks' (Wegelin 1994: 135) and securing long-term structural funding (from programme clients rather than from donors).

The UMP had a predominantly policy focus and was seen as part of an effort to increase local capacity to address needs in the urban sector more generally, rather than to implement specific programmes. It shared the same ethos of supporting the exchange of information, capacity building and partnerships on a programme basis evident in UN activities of the 1990s, but adopted the market-oriented focus of the World Bank. This approach was also closely allied to the stress on good governance and smaller, more responsive, government which had increasingly become a feature of structural adjustment programmes, including strong encouragement for government decentralisation. Decentralisation processes are still very much under way in many countries, and some have just begun to address urban management problems very recently. In general the resources and skills available at local level, however, are often insufficient for the increasingly complex tasks associated with urban management, especially in the partnership form envisaged. Again, vested interests do not adapt easily to such new forms of operation, and the objectives of efficiency, transparency and accountability are often not shared by either local politicians or civil servants (see Chapter 6 for a discussion of the limitations of the urban management approach).

Jones and Ward (1994: 46–7) reviewed the assumptions on which the UMP was based and concluded that the motive for the World Bank's adoption of the UMP included the perception that urban poverty 'will become the most significant and politically explosive problem in the next century'; and that the attempt in the UMP to shift policy application away from serving explicit social groups towards other less identifiable targets was in tune with a need for a broad understanding of political reality, though this may lead to more dangerous and volatile situations in cities where the UMP requires local government to do more but resources and subsidies are reduced. They also considered that the UMP appears to blame poverty and inequality on the poor management of cities and especially of their 'distorted' land and housing markets; however, the market-led nature of the UMP discourages the state from acquiring land for large-scale distribution schemes, and thus could undermine action to alleviate poverty. While they considered the focus on productivity and efficiency as useful, addressing the structural limits to poverty, it did so by ignoring the moral issues of justice, equity and access, and as such they argued that in effect the UMP is less of a programme and more an ideology: a 'beefed-up' version of neo-classical economics.

In 2000 the World Bank published its new urban strategy, *Cities in Transition: A Strategic View of Urban and Local Government Issues*. The aim of this strategy was stated as '...to promote sustainable cities and towns that fulfil the promise of development for their inhabitants – in particular, by improving the lives of the poor and promoting equity – while contributing to the progress of the country as a whole' (World Bank 2000a: 6). The strategy is based on a 'guiding vision' of sustainable cities, which comprises liveability, competitiveness, good governance and management, as well as bankability. A comparison of the key aspects of this new strategy with that of 1991 is shown in Table 8.3.

This new urban strategy is to be implemented through placing emphasis on four main activities within the World Bank's renewed programme of urban support:

- formulating national urban strategies;
- supporting city development strategies;
- scaling-up services for the poor, including upgrading low-income urban neighbourhoods; and
- expanding assistance for capacity building.

Further partnership approaches to urban poverty based on the above include the Cities Alliance (see www.citiesalliance.org). The Alliance was established in 1999 as a follow up to the Habitat Agenda, and comprises a coalition of cities and their development partners with the objective of addressing urban poverty reduction, supported by multilateral and bilateral development agencies and international development banks. The priorities of the Alliance are:

- City Development Strategies (CDS), which link the process of how local stakeholders define their vision for their city with clear priorities for action and investments;
- City-wide and nation-wide slum upgrading to improve the living conditions of at least 100 million slum dwellers by 2020 (see Box 8.1). Crucially, this plan acknowledges that upgrading needs to be complemented by other measures to reduce urban poverty.

Box 8.1 The 'Cities without Slums' action plan

The Cities without Slums action plan was launched at the inaugural meeting of the Cities Alliance's Consultative Group in Berlin in 1999, and was endorsed at the UN Millennium Summit. The plan called for donors, governments and slum communities to get involved in improving the lives of 5–10 million slum dwellers by 2005 and 100 million by 2020; increasing World Bank investments supporting the provision of basic services for the urban poor; moving from pilot projects to upgrading city-wide and nation-wide; and investing in knowledge and capacity in slum upgrading and the reduction of new slum growth (Cities Alliance n.d.).

Six key actions were identified as being necessary to meet the Millennium Goal:

1. Strengthening in-country capacity – through a range of actions from restructuring policy to strengthening learning and training.
2. Preparing national city/upgrading programmes – helping countries to design such programmes.
3. Supporting regional and global knowledge and learning – to support better outcomes and scaling-up.
4. Investing in slums – i.e. in appropriate basic infrastructure and municipal services, to be identified, implemented and operated with the community.
5. Strengthening partner capacity – focusing on the resources, knowledge and tools required by governments and communities.
6. Leadership and political buy-in by the partners in the Alliance.

The action plan was to be implemented in an incremental way, expecting to achieve the launching of 20 city-wide and or nation-wide programmes in five regions in 2001–5, and of 50 nation-wide programmes with slum improvements as a central element of urban development strategies in most countries in 2006–20. To this effect, budget allocations were made to provide grants for country capacity-building and programme preparation, to increase the World Bank's urban budget to strengthen upgrading capacity, and to support the actual costs of upgrading, to which the World Bank would contribute 25 per cent of the total, with the remainder being expected to come from governments, private sources and the upgraded community.

Sources: Cities Alliance n.d., 2001

Secure tenure

While good governance is a theme running through the above key issues, another is that of achieving secure tenure. This was established as a UN-Habitat Global Campaign (the Global Campaign on Urban Governance is the other), as 'an advocacy instrument designed to promote security of tenure for the poorest populations, especially those living in informal settlements and slums, with the goal of making a significant impact on the living and working conditions of the world's urban poor'.[4] The focus of the campaign is information collection, publications and support of negotiations on secure land and housing tenure for low-income populations. This draws on the Urban Management Programme, Cities Alliance, and other recent research activities in tenure options, which have focused on the impossibility of providing secure tenure through formal, relatively sophisticated mechanisms such as used in more wealthy countries or countries which urbanised a considerable time ago. Recent research has in particular focused on how informal settlements in fact manage land in urban areas, and how these mechanisms can perhaps be the means for improving land rights and management in more realistic ways given the often scarce resources (Payne 1999, 2002; Durand-Lasserve 2002).

The problems of urban land access, occupation/registration, and transfer – both in terms of rights and processes – are exacerbated in many rapidly urbanising situations due to the fast spread of these areas. This leads to many different forms of authorities being involved, over and above the private sector, NGOs and communities themselves. Many urban areas now straddle several different forms of local government (e.g. urban and rural, or large-scale and small-scale urban), as well as traditional and 'modern' forms of administration and land management. There are at times maybe various different systems of land management in operation: a 'customary' form of allocation (linked to rural traditions usually); a 'modern' form of allocation or registration (linked to local authorities in urban centres usually), which may or may not include formal private sector activities; de facto allocation/activities by other government actors, such as central government and international agencies entities; and informal activities, which can be community-based and/or private sector oriented. Each of these may establish a set of claims to rights on land and operate through different, and even overlapping, mechanisms. The effects of this are: reduced efficiency of the urban land system, with negative economic consequences; inequity in access to urban land, with social implications; and political impacts as different socio-economic groups vie for rights.

Metropolitanisation

In this usage of the term, metropolitan urban forms are essentially those which have expanded beyond their territorial boundaries, and one of the observations is that these are increasing with globalisation as economic growth has become more concentrated and any form of state-led regional re-distribution of this is tempered by the perceived economic opportunities of agglomeration (e.g. Gugler 2004). In parallel with this, in countries where rapid urbanisation is taking place, this economic concentration has provided a spill-over effect in the informal economy which thus continues to attract immigrants or reduce emigration. In some semi-peripheral countries this process may now be changing as, similar to the core global economic countries, populations seek better social environmental conditions and new forms of production permit decentralisation, encouraged by civic boosterism (e.g. Brazil – see Figure 8.4). In East Asia and Latin America the initial rapid growth of metropolitan areas started in the 1960s, continuing through the 1980s, although it is now slowing.

One of the ways for such cities to avoid the loss of populations and jobs is to expand their territories to catch up with the demographic and physical expansion, and this is also often driven by the need to co-ordinate strategic issues such as transport and service supply. This is also expressed in the creation of distinct sub-centres distant from the main urban centre, which often come to dominate with

8.4 View of Curitiba, Brazil – a rare example of controlled land use and development density, which has led to the metropolitanisation of poverty through concentration of low-income settlements outwith the city boundaries (Harry Smith)

decay in the older centre – which may then be subject to urban regeneration. Metropolitanisation has a number of important dimensions (UN-Habitat 2004): spatial, economic, social structure and institutional. While there are positive features such as economies of scale, these can become self-defeating and other negative features such as fragmentation, polarisation and spatial mismatch can be dominant. Studies of metropolitanisation trends focus on re-structuring of the economy; the effects of globalisation on urban space and regeneration and associated re-structuring of urban form; the investigation of diversity and conflict; and forms of urban interpretation (e.g. Soja 2000). As yet no clear normative agendas have been identified, and these issues are examined in the following chapters focusing on macro-regions.

A new role for urban planning and housing

The increasing diversity of urban areas worldwide, in political, economic, social and cultural terms, has been a factor in a revised role for urban planning. Modern urban planning arose originally from the rapid urbanisation process in Europe, associated with industrialisation but also the changing nature of land rights, and evolved mainly in the post-war settlement of the welfare state systems of Europe, or more free-market oriented North America. Planning continued to evolve as there were changes to forms of government in the light of the growing crisis of these political and economic systems. As noted in Chapter 6, following the development of a focus on systems, with more flexible strategic planning, there was a period of significantly reduced state engagement, and latterly a re-statement of the role of planning as a decision-making system on land and environmental resource use with wide economic, social and cultural interests. Generally speaking these trends in planning in the core global economic regions have been mirrored in the semi-periphery, and to a limited extent in the periphery. In these contexts the systems have tended to reflect the often elite-oriented governance systems and thus have had a socially exclusive impact, which has increasingly been seen as being the case also in the core regions through the macroeconomic re-structuring of globalisation (described in Chapters 1 and 3). Urban planning in these regions is thus evolving yet again to address growing social inequality and cultural diversity as well as global economic competitiveness, within political contexts of widening governance.

In these situations, as well as 'technical' skills in areas of activity such as law, environmental issues, and design, planners are increasingly called on to develop forms of understanding of ranges of values – in other words, there is no one 'public good' as previously defined. There have been two broad approaches to this in the past, one embedded within the planning systems created in the post-war settlement and existing legislation of (limited) public consultation, and another of creating wider joint decision-making arenas, based on structured forms of communication. As noted above, this latter approach has been criticised for being voluntarist and ignoring power structures and their tendencies. However, a new form of planning – which has existed in subordinate ways since the 1960s – is emerging, where the planner is seen not as a neutral agent but as a proponent, whether on behalf of government, the private and non-governmental sectors, or civil society (for more detail see Appendix F).[5] These participatory planning roles vary enormously from engaging more proactively with broad population groups on strategic and local planning issues (such as Local Agenda 21 and City Development Strategies), re-assessing the land rights of indigenous groups or informal urban settlement residents, re-defining the design and management of 'public space', to researching how ICT can be used proactively in these processes.

While planning as it developed in the past century was more about control and regulation of private interests in the built environment in the light of public interests, new forms of planning are both wider and more integrated in scope, and less regulatory and more proactive and dynamic. This entails a certain degree of entrepreneurialism within governments, but also growing regulation within the private sector as public sector capacity to regulate has diminished. The scope of planning has not only widened in sectoral terms (e.g. including wider forms of knowledge and new techniques such as ICT), but also in scale – with planning happening at many different levels from macro-regional to site level. Perhaps most importantly, what is the 'public interest' is now seen to be more open to negotiation as opposed to expert, or elected representative, definition. This has led to planning being less about 'plan-making' as an activity fixed in time, followed by strict regulatory control, to forms of action-planning which can respond to change and are open to negotiation. Not all of these tendencies are necessarily positive however, as without regulation the prevalent power structures tend to plan as suits them (Hague and Jenkins 2004).

While some of these tendencies have become evident and are promoted in the core regions, many also are identified in the south – particularly issues concerning planning as a form of governance and entrepreneurial planning. Thus rather than adapting techniques from the already largely urbanised world to produce a specific form of planning for the 'developing world' as was previously proposed, planning has the challenge of evolving across multiple locations in very different contexts. However, the spread of such innovation in planning is slow in most places, and the weak institutional capacity and opportunity for building even basic planning systems in some countries mean these tend to lag even further in innovation. This, however, does not have to be the case. Such new forms of planning – and the same can be applied to housing – require ongoing critical analysis of contexts and objectives in which the 'planner' and the 'public' as well as other stakeholders engage interactively and negotiate for their interests. This can at times be conflictive and consensus cannot always be reached, so the rules of 'engagement' and the nature of the 'agenda' for negotiation as well as the locale and language for this (the 'arena') are also objects of negotiation. Planners in this context cannot feign neutrality, although they can (but may not always actually) aspire to be as objective as possible (see Appendix F for more detail). Fundamentally, this form of planning and housing development is embedded within existing political, economic, social and cultural contexts as explicitly as possible. While planning may focus on the best strategy for economic development within a new global economy, it equally has a strong role representing the social and cultural needs of existing populations. Thus importing planning systems, plans, capacity and techniques is not the answer, but negotiating what is possible and desirable within the actual context and realpolitik can be – i.e. a form of endogenous planning and housing. This concept is further discussed in Chapter 12.

As can be seen from the above, a very wide range of key issues in shelter and human settlements have evolved in the 1990s and into the new millennium, going far beyond the more sectorally distinct issues of housing and planning that characterised earlier decades. This has widened the scope of action for planners and housing professionals enormously in principle, although many continue to work in quite narrow professional areas. One of the challenges is how these wider concepts can become embedded within the professions, as teaching and training in planning and housing generally follow quite traditional trends. This issue is also returned to in the concluding chapter. Of equal importance is to consider where the broad normative agendas have come from and who is promoting them, and reflect on this in relation to policy and practice in real contexts.

As noted above, recent dominant literature has been produced by multi-lateral and bi-lateral agencies (closely associated with internationally oriented institutions such as universities and related consultants). The United Nations and the World Bank continue to dominate with the normative agendas on which they broadly agree. Most bi-lateral international agencies follow suit, although some push forward the agendas on their own. They are joined by international non-governmental organisations, and to a less obvious extent, by international private sector agencies. Not all of these agree, but the ongoing series of international (and macro-regional) conferences provide the platform for negotiation on these agendas.

The main aspect stressed in this chapter (and the book as a whole) is that these are normative agendas, full of exhortation, as well as based on certain forms of analysis which are often not that clearly identified. Not only does the key literature exhort all and sundry to understand and act more rationally for the greater good, but these exhortations are illustrated with 'best practices'. As noted above, the contextual basis for these (as well as any form of objectivity in analysis) is often missing. Thus, not only is there a danger that the normative agenda often focuses on actions without clarifying how these have happened, but also that agendas assume rational decision-making based on the presented information. This is not the real context in which shelter issues get addressed in the world, but an idealised view of this. In fact the key underlying issues concerning shelter, human settlements and poverty in urban areas are often glossed over in this approach, as being too political or economically unsuitable. In this respect the trends of understanding and discussing these issues which were developed in the 1970s and 1980s have not been continued, and an ever widening set of analytical foci have distracted analysts and decision-makers from addressing these. Again this theme will be returned to in the concluding chapter.

Finally, the previous chapters argued that there has been a close relationship between the evolution of housing and planning policies and practices in the face of rapid urbanisation, and those of development theory and practice. The crisis 'development' thinking entered in the early 1990s, emerging with a much broader set of agendas which often now run in parallel, is also evident in the shelter sector, as this chapter has shown. The continuing dominant hold on the definition of agendas by international and national development agencies does not mean that all actors within these are dependent and subservient to these agendas, but the growing need for analysis and agenda-setting in the core countries, as these re-structure, has tended to absorb most of the initiative. There is, however, evidence that this is changing as increasingly other 'non-core' countries begin to set and influence new agendas in this sector (as in others). This is examined next in the following macro-regional chapters.

Part Three:
Case Studies

Chapter 9
Urban development and housing in Sub-Saharan Africa

Introduction to the region

The physical and historic context for urban development

Africa is a vast continent, with more than 30 million square kilometres,[1] many different socio-cultural groups and great environmental diversity. To deal with this as one macro-region therefore entails a certain amount of generalisation. However, there are distinctive issues in urban development and housing, and a distinctive political economy, that differentiate the macro-region from other regions. This chapter deals with Sub-Saharan Africa, as the Sahara has effectively been a barrier for human activity – albeit traversed for long periods – and North Africa's climate and cultures are closer to the Mediterranean and the Middle East. Tropical Sub-Saharan Africa has been at the centre of mankind's and the world's physical development yet remains a region with some of the most pressing human and environmental challenges today, including rapid urbanisation. The following text provides a basis to understand how this has evolved historically.

The land mass of Africa is the core of the super-continent Gondwanaland which split up 200 million years ago to create Latin America, South Asia, Australia and Antarctica. This is considered to be the reason why the continent has a comparatively compact shape, and this – together with its open ocean location – has provided few safe sea harbour opportunities. The geology is made up of very old rocks, considerably shaped over time, which has contributed to the relatively poor soils over much of the macro-region, especially on the higher inland plateaux. Other geological features of note are large river basins (the Congo being the greatest, but also the Niger, Nile and the Zambezi); rift valleys running from north to south, creating high mountain chains; and coastal plains. The soil quality is also affected by the long-term effects of climate, and around half of the continental land area is affected by desertification and erosion. Only a few areas are continuously watered, in the extreme southeast and in the low-lying equatorial central west. The seasonal rain cycle has thus had great importance for the development of human activities, which continue to be affected by global climate change.

Paleontology has identified the first human beings as emerging in the region some 200,000 years ago. Early mankind is thought to have developed at the margins of different ecological systems, thus permitting access to a diversity of natural resources. Different vegetation systems are linked to soil types, water availability and other local factors such as altitude, and in Sub-Saharan Africa include rain forest, woodland-grassland mosaic, grassland savannah, desert steppe and desert vegetation. While earlier human societies were hunting-gathering societies, these developed through time to specialise in pastoralism and agriculture, the latter in areas with better soils and water availability, with the dominant form being 'slash and burn' agriculture which migrated over time as soil fertility dropped. In time the development of metal-working – drawing on the rich continental mineral deposits – brought changes in agriculture and also social and political structures, and population growth, technological changes and conflict all led to large-scale migratory trends across the continent.

These migratory trends are evidenced in the language structure of the macro-region, with four major language groups, split into more than 1,000 language groups, some large, many small and disappearing. One of the largest language groups – the Bantu – stretches across the southern third of the continent from the Gabon rain forest in the west to the highlands of Kenya in the east and to the southeast coast in South Africa.[2] The wide spread of this language is associated with the long-term migratory tendency from the core south-central West Africa region to the east and south between 500 BC and 300 AD. To the south the Bantu-speaking migrants encountered the Khoisan peoples, who eventually became restricted to the desert regions of the Kalahari and who represent a totally different language group. Another major language group stretches across the whole Sahelian belt south of the Sahara, from west to east. This broad range of language groups is reflected in other cultural manifestations and social organisation, and their consolidation is linked to larger more hierarchical socio-political forms such as states. Although not all of the hundreds of different ethnic groups were amalgamated into such states, these are known to have existed before the fourteenth century (e.g. Mali), and include the Songhay empire (in what is now Sudan) and Kongo kingdom (fifteenth/sixteenth centuries), with state formation – and disintegration – continuing into the nineteenth century (e.g. in Ghana with the Ashanti empire, and the South-east African Zulu kingdoms).

While the long-term migration noted above is tied to the socio-economic forms of agricultural production and pastoralism, this was slow and gradual. In fact there was often limited contact between different groups as the terrain made this difficult and animal transport was limited. Rivers and lakes were the main transport routes, but rivers were often un-navigable due to rapids and large differences in seasonal flows. External transport links did, however, exist across the Sahara and along the coast – especially the East African coast where Arab and Asian traders used the monsoon winds. Longer distance maritime transport was generally dominated by such outsiders, but created new opportunities for trade which affected the economic, social and political structures of those peoples with which this came into contact. Early empires, kingdoms and states were generally organised around trade and its control – in natural products (salt, ivory and skins), minerals (gold and copper and iron metalwork), and slaves. This trade gave rise to early coastal settlements, often temporary, but consolidated over time. In the late fifteenth century maritime developments permitted wider European exploration, which concentrated on finding sea trading routes to the Far East, but led to increased trade with Sub-Saharan Africa. This trading contact was often temporary, but created a series of small settlements for supplying the shipping routes, and links between existing African trading networks and growing European economies, and then through this to the European economic expansion into North and South America.

This European contact had a marked socio-economic impact which affected political structures. Higher levels of trade and new products, with changes in military possibilities through new weaponry, often led to centralisation of power in indigenous military states. This was compounded by growing populations and internal political friction, and had quite marked impacts in some parts of the macro-region, perhaps the greatest being de-population and social disruption through slavery – with an estimated 19 million slaves being exported (Rakodi 1997: 21). Overall the changing social, economic and political contexts led to different forms of human settlement, however urban settlements were relatively limited in scope and still not permanent in most of the macro-region throughout the pre-colonial period (see below). The colonial period *per se* was sparked off by the realisation by (generally) Northern European powers that they should ensure continued, and preferential, access to raw materials and markets in the region as they industrialised. The potential for this had been mapped throughout the nineteenth century by a succession of explorers, and the 'Scramble for Africa' began towards the end of this period when European states claimed rights to large areas where they had been active in trade, competing for general control. Between the Berlin Conference in 1884–85 and the outbreak of the First World War in 1914 the region was effectively divided up by six colonial powers[3] who then established control over the indigenous economies and political systems through a series of military campaigns. Colonial occupation led to different forms of exploitation – ranging from controlling indigenous economies (mainly West Africa), through granting exploitation (and associated subordinate governing) rights to private consortia (Central and South-east Africa), to direct exploitation by settlers and companies (Eastern and Southern Africa). Colonisation had a massive effect on human settlements patterns which is still of great importance today, as the next section describes.

The evolution of urban settlements in Sub-Saharan Africa

Most human settlements in Sub-Saharan Africa were of a rural and/or temporary character prior to European engagement – but not all. As noted above, various societies had evolved quite structured forms of states, and these often had larger settlements with economic, political and ceremonial functions, as well as extensive residential populations – examples include Axum in the highlands of what is now Ethiopia, Great Zimbabwe, Djenne in what is now Mali, Ife and Benin in Nigeria and various settlements around the Great Lakes (Anderson and Rathbone 2000). However, while arguably urban by the nature of their density and function, these were still closely linked to rural hinterlands and many residents still practised agriculture. Exceptions to this pattern were the trading settlements for the trans-Saharan trade routes (such as Timbouctou, Kano and Sokoto), and coastal trading settlements created by Arabian/Asian traders (e.g. Kilwa on the East) and the early European traders (e.g. Luanda on the West). Many of these settlements date back to the fifteenth century and a few were as large as 100,000 residents. The most developed urban settlement forms were, however, in what is now southwest Nigeria, where the Yoruba people established trading towns with administrative and military roles from as early as the tenth century. By the nineteenth century, some 34 such urban areas were in existence, the largest probably having also about 100,000 people (Ibadan). Settlements created by Northern Europeans came later – Cape Town being the oldest, founded by the Dutch in 1652 – the majority being associated with the colonial period.

Urbanisation began to increase with colonisation. This required settlement of administrators and military to rule the colonies, and transport centres for colonial exports and imports. Most pre-colonial urban settlements were nodes on trade routes, although they usually also had administrative and military functions, and the colonial interests in increasing external trade led to the consolidation of some of these, usually ports, with the slow deterioration of others (e.g. interior trading posts). Colonial activity also led to the establishment of completely new settlements, for instance railway nodes and mining towns, and some new military and administrative centres. The overall urban system which developed was highly influenced by the transport infrastructure which was developed in the early phases of colonial rule, as well as the nature of colonial exploitation. Thus in West Africa more indigenous urban nuclei survived as these still had an economic function in the export of produce, whereas in Eastern and Southern Africa whole new urban nuclei were built to service the new colonial settler population. In both, ports were the main nodes of the urban system, but important new mining settlements were also created – especially in Central and Southern Africa. While the colonial state supervised urban development in general terms, in many areas private investment determined the way urban areas grew. Large plantations and mining settlements, for instance, were usually dominated by private sector companies and had limited other functions, and residential provision was often temporary in nature (in barracks and compounds).[4] This temporary nature was assumed for much of the labour force in urban areas in the predominant settler colonies of East, Central and South Africa, but this attitude to indigenous residents was not a strong feature in West Africa, where many new colonial urban settlements were based on the traditional towns, although physical segregation was the general rule.

O'Connor (1983) identified six different types of African city that developed historically, including:

- the indigenous city of West Africa, most clearly identified with Yoruba culture in southwest Nigeria;
- the Islamic city, dominant in the northern Sahel region, but also with characteristic traits on the Eastern seaboard;
- the colonial city, as noted above, based on colonial political and economic domination;
- the 'European city', as a special case of the colonial city, with little indigenous influence;
- the 'dual city', where colonial and indigenous influences remain separate; and
- the 'hybrid city', increasingly prevalent.

As noted above, *indigenous cities* were sometimes of significantly ancient origin, and grew in number and size throughout the period when external trade developed, with considerable impact on political instability in the immediate pre-colonial period. Defence led to more concentrated urban growth in walled towns, and despite growing numbers of refugees most urban areas remained quite small, with strong rural links. The physical form was often concentric around the palace and market with land being allocated through kinship systems in quarters divided by radial routes. There were limited functional distinctions and a relatively high density, but low rise, form of land use, many buildings being in mud brick. When colonial governments later settled these towns, this was generally outside the old contained walled area. The *Islamic city type* is similar in form and origin, however more influenced by Middle Eastern urban traditions (see Figure 9.1). These urban areas were mainly located on the trade routes across the Sahara, some being capitals of pre-colonial states and important religious centres. Some of this type of settlement also grew up along the East African coast with Arabian and Indian influence. These urban areas are typically centred on a palace, mosque and market with similar forms of development to the indigenous cities.

Colonial urban forms were imported, sometimes implanted over or alongside indigenous urban areas, sometimes completely new settlements. Most urban areas

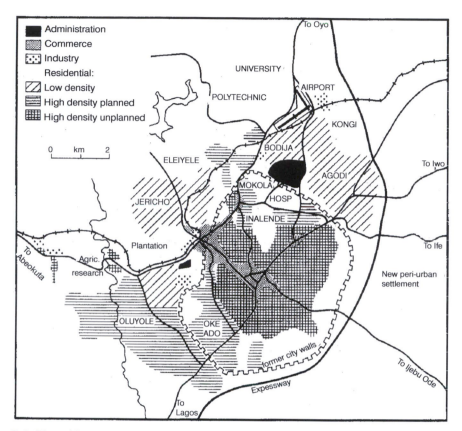

9.1 Plan of Ibadan, Nigeria (O'Connor 1983: 197)

which exist today were created or substantially re-structured in the colonial period, although the impact of this has now declined in importance. While some were based on much older ports, most of these were developed in the late nineteenth century through to the middle twentieth century when decolonisation started. The colonial urban type – as distinct from the European type below – was characterised by physical segregation of class and race, although with varying degrees of assimilation of the indigenous people. This form was more prevalent in West Africa, with higher levels of assimilation in Francophone Africa, albeit distinguishing the modern and the indigenous. This at times gave rise to a *'dual' city typology* where the pre-existing indigenous city remained alongside the modern colonial plantation – an example is Kano in Northern Nigeria (see Figure 9.2). This distinction was not only physical and historical, but the two different urban areas operated to a great extent in different ways and with different functions, reflected even in different dominant cultural traits such as dress and language.

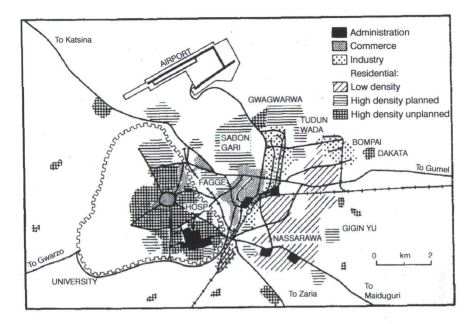

9.2 Plan of Kano, Nigeria (O'Connor 1983: 201)

Where colonisation led to completely new urban areas, or extensive new expansion areas, these often drew on European norms and new planning and building techniques – and indeed echoed the form of other colonial cities created in the same period in Australia and Canada, etc. (see Chapter 5). These *European cities* were more typical of new settler colonies, where indigenous settlement and labour were more strictly controlled, and more typical of (generally Anglophone) colonies in Eastern, Central and Southern Africa. This was evidenced in limited provision for indigenous urban living (mostly temporary) and marked physical segregation of races, classes and land uses. Nairobi and Lusaka, which were originally railway nodes, are typical of these. As can be seen in Figure 9.3 these cities were much lower density and occupied larger areas, following the then prevalent garden cities planning concepts.

All the above urban types were identifiable in the 1960s when O'Connor undertook his research, but are less so today, as rapid urban growth engulfs the original urban forms in large, generally unplanned, expansion areas. The last typology identified by O'Connor – the *'hybrid' city* – has become by far the predominant type, and as such is of limited use as a general type for contemporary analysis. This process of 'hybrid' urban expansion generally started after the later colonial period as managed decolonisation was implemented, associated with new development policies and growing economies during the World War period when import substitution was important. As noted in Chapter 2, modernisation policies

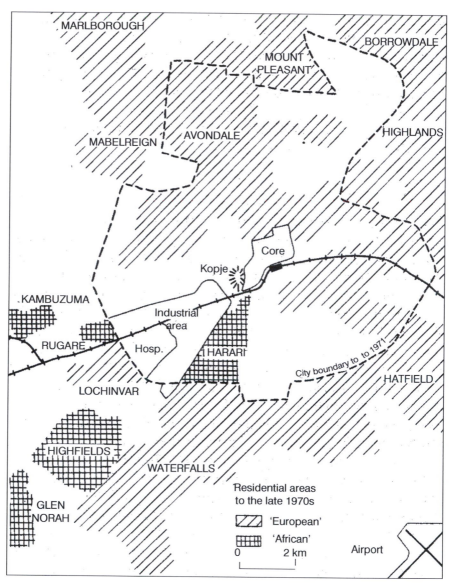

9.3 Plan of Harare, Zimbabwe (O'Connor 1983: 36)

assumed that cities would establish their own size automatically, however in many colonies there was still control of inward urban migration, especially in settler colonies. Independence for most Sub-Saharan African states came generally in the 1950s and 1960s, and this removed most or all such controls. This coincided with the impact of improved social services and continued economic improvements, albeit dominated by the legacy of colonial rule and neo-colonialism. In this period the new independent governments aspired to modern urban areas with new housing, and their increasing involvement in their economies through forms of Keynesian development policies – yet neo-colonial reliance – was manifested in grandiose urban plans, urban system analysis and growth pole development, and even completely new urban areas, such as capital cities.[5] These in fact largely followed European city types, negating the indigenous city forms, albeit with class segregation instead of race and ethnic segregation.

The world economic downturn of the 1970s was a massive shock to Sub-Saharan Africa, highly dependent as it was on the 'developed' world economies for markets and imports (especially oil). While there was no immediate change of focus for urban development plans in many states, the grandiose urban planning and housing schemes which continued to be prepared (mainly by foreign consultants) became increasingly obsolete and few were implemented. The countries which achieved independence in this period often still tried to emulate these forms of modern development, although many reacted to longer and more violent forms of decolonisation through isolationist ('self-reliant') and socialist development policies.[6] However, there was no bucking the economic trend and soon the capacities for states to plan urban development and housing, and for the private sector to find bankable clients, diminished in the face of continued urban influx as rural economies also stagnated and urban areas were seen as offering better prospects. The increase in political and military instability which this period was associated with also fuelled this trend in many countries, the result being high rates of urban growth with very limited capacities to provide for these in any formal housing or planned urban development, leading to the *de facto* 'informalisation' of most cities, with the formal areas (usually the cores) being overwhelmed with their surrounding informal areas.

Urbanisation trends

By the time Sub-Saharan Africa was fully colonised (at the end of the First World War), only some 5 per cent of the African population lived in urban areas of more than 20,000 inhabitants. This proportion rose slowly through to 1960, when some 16 per cent were in such areas. However, while still relatively sparsely populated in 1960 (some 140 million people), increasing general demographic growth meant this represented a five-fold increase in urban population, rising from seven to 36 million. These initially low urbanisation rates changed quite dramatically in the 1950s and 1960s as most countries achieved independence. From a globally low existing threshold, urban growth rates rose quickly to some of the highest recorded worldwide, reaching 8 per cent or more in many countries in the 1960s and 1970s. These have fallen to some extent since then,[7] but remained comparatively high as other macro-regions in the rapidly urbanising world began to stabilise their demographic pattern, and Sub-Saharan Africa is expected to overtake, for instance, the Latin American urban population by 2015.

The initial trend in urbanisation was marked by concentration in a few large urban areas in each country which grew much more quickly than other urban areas. The most urbanised countries were South Africa and Nigeria, reflecting the historical evolution discussed above, although some smaller countries also have high urbanisation rates (e.g. Gabon and Namibia). The balance between rural and urban populations changed throughout this period as rural to urban migration continued and urban populations continued with high birth rates but lower mortality rates. This balance also varied by region, again reflecting historical development, West and East Africa generally having lower urbanisation levels than Southern and Central Africa.

More recent estimates of urbanisation rates published by the UN (2001) now show a degree of demographic stabilisation with the overall population growth rate down to some 2.2 per cent per year. These estimates indicated that by the new millennium 37 per cent of the total African population was in urban areas, which entailed a growth from some 102 million in 1970 to 295 million in 2000. The largest urban areas – Lagos at 8.7 million (2000), Kinshasa at 5.1 million and the Greater Johannesburg Region (a conurbation) at 7.3 million – still exhibit primate city characteristics. This is changing however, as by 2000 there were another 40 cities with populations of between one and 5 million, and another 40 or so with between 0.5 and 1 million (see Figure 9.4). On top of that more than 60 per cent of African urban residents lived in cities of less than 0.5 million. The structure of urban systems is thus changing, with small and medium urban areas becoming more important. This is likely to be where a significant proportion of new urban growth takes place, with annual growth rates projected at some 3.3 per cent. While lower than the peaks mentioned above, the much larger urban population base leads to various estimates of the urban population in the macro-region at between 750–790 million in 2030. This represents two-and-a-half times the urban population of 2000, and thus is in itself a major challenge. What compounds this is growing urban poverty, as Sub-Saharan Africa slides out of economic development as indicated in Chapter 3. In 2000 the World Bank assessed that in the period 1987–98 the number of people living in absolute poverty (on less than $1 a day) in the macro-region rose from 217 million to 291 million, with a high proportion of the poor in urban areas – some 47 per cent overall. This trend is expected to continue as the urban population continues to rise, and this creates an enormous challenge for urban development and housing policy and practice.

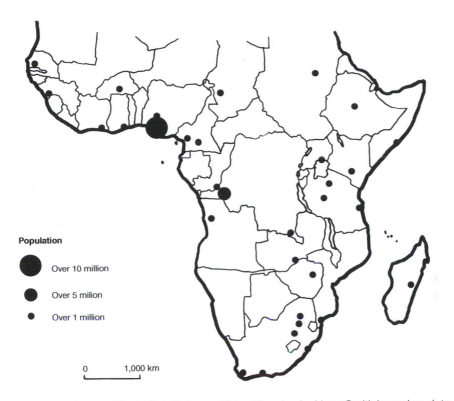

9.4 Map of large cities in Sub-Saharan Africa (Drawing by Harry Smith based on data in UNCHS 2001)

A short introduction to contemporary urban Africa

Currently Sub-Saharan Africa is divided into some 50 countries,[8] most of these being the legacy of the colonial period. Independence generally came in the period 1955–75, with democratic regimes only being introduced in some countries later than this (e.g. South Africa in 1994). The post-colonial nation states have suffered considerable political and military instability since independence, which has been seen as a result of the decolonisation process, with its transfer of power to elite groups, compounded by the declining global economic situation from the mid-1970s as various elites contested power. While there has been a wide range of different political positions, ranging from capitalist through to Marxist-Leninist, in general the tendency for a strong state role in the economy in the colonial period continued through to the mid-1980s, when external economic and political pressure led to major adjustments in macro-economic and political structures. In the above context the relationship between wider society and the government and the formal economy is weak, with large proportions of the population working and living in so-called 'informal' conditions. The often weak nature, however, of civil society institutions, especially in urban areas, is partly due to historic legacies of control by colonial and post-independent governments, but also abrupt social change as macro-level changes impact on society, such as urbanisation (see below). This has been an element of the poor engagement with political processes, which has tended to continue even after transition from elite power regimes to potentially more open democratic regimes.[9]

There has been a strong neo-colonial legacy in Sub-Saharan Africa, embedded within the economic system as well as cultural attributes such as language, with French, English and Portuguese remaining the main languages. This was to some extent adjusted, but also partially reinforced, in the Cold War period when the the United States and the Soviet Union had some involvement in the region – at times direct, but often indirect through the 'proxy' governments they supported. These influences waned in the late 1980s and disappeared in the 1990s, at a time of forced macro-economic structural adjustment, and as a result political change also took place with a transition to constitutional multi-party democracies. Political change was also evidenced within government structures as international agencies supported decentralisation policies. The result is a much changed constitutional political structure as countries entered the new millennium, however the extent to which multi-party representative democracy and local-level decision-making is in fact in operation is still questionable.

This continues to be dogged by economic factors, as most Sub-Saharan African economies have suffered continued disinvestments from the mid-1970s high point of neo-colonialist and Cold War related activity. The 1980s and 1990s were generally negative in economic terms and economic outlooks remain weak in many countries despite the adherence to international agency prescriptions of structural adjustment, open borders for economic activity, export-oriented development, constitutional change and good governance. The most recent international prescriptions focus on poverty alleviation strategies, allied to Millennium Development Goals, with Africa seen as the main focus for development aid in the new millennium.

Development policies and strategies in the past were focused on modernisation in the post-independence period, shifting at times to self-reliant import-substitution policies in some countries in an interim period (1960s and 1970s), when achievement of basic needs was also considered a regional national goal. This was followed by the trend to state-withdrawal and privatisation, led by Structural Adjustment (1980s and 1990s), with a growing focus on poverty alleviation. Development policies are still focused on poverty alleviation, but economic development is now seen as requiring fine-tuning of management through state–business partnerships – forms of state developmentalism (see Chapter 3) in the face of globalisation.[10]

Sub-Saharan Africa thus has experienced economic decline since the 1970s. At the beginning of the new millennium, real GDP per capita in 2001 in 24 African countries was less than in 1975, with 12 countries experiencing levels even lower than those of the 1960s (UN-Habitat 2003a). One of the main features of this decline has been the reducing capacity for export as raw materials and agricultural exports decline in volume, but also through declining terms of trade, a form of 'resource bondage' (see Chapter 3). This is partly due to widening global competition, but also international negotiation over trade barriers and incentives. The shift from food production – partly domestically oriented – to exports has led to food security problems in various countries, compounded also by decline in infrastructure for distribution as well as management capacity. Economic mismanagement has been seen as a major problem in many economies, but the reduction of the state's role in the economy and privatisation in the 1980s and 1990s has not necessarily led to improved management. In general the low level of skills, exacerbated by pandemics such as HIV-AIDs and an exodus of the better skilled, has led to higher 'technological rents' (see Chapter 3). It has also reduced the attractiveness for inward investment, which has fallen to very low levels from its high of some 20 per cent of all world foreign direct investment (FDI) in 1972.[11]

In 1997, eight countries in Sub-Saharan Africa experienced net outflows and another 22 countries only had inflows amounting to $1–2 per capita (UN Habitat 2003a). These investments are usually related to mining and cash crops, depending on foreign technology, expertise and markets, with limited knock-on effects for the local economy. The tendencies in the 1970s to accumulate debt as a means to cope with declining development, led to relatively low global levels of indebtedness (in $ terms), but cripplingly high levels in terms of the economic capacity to service this, and thus debt led to greater indebtedness in a vicious spiral of 'debt peonage' (see Chapter 3). Total export revenue increased by 6 per cent in 1997 but the region only accounted for less than 2 per cent of world trade that year. Arguably only those countries with small and/or relatively skilled populations and substantial natural resources (such as South Africa) have any real hope of longer-term economic growth in an unrestrained global market. Even where there has been economic growth, however, often the majority do not benefit. This is related to the slow growth in formal sector employment, with formal minimum wages also falling by between 50–70 per cent since the 1980s. Informal sector employment accounts for more than 70 per cent of all non-agricultural employment in the macro-region, and the vast majority of new jobs are expected to be created in this sector in the next decade.

Near to 50 per cent of the total Sub-Saharan population are estimated to be living with less than $1 per day and 74 per cent under $2 per day. Using Purchasing Power Parity, the Gross National Income per capita for 20 countries is below the UN average for 'Least Developed Countries' and only six countries are above the

'Less Developed Regions' (UN-Habitat 2004).[12] While extreme poverty remained proportionally stable in the region at 46–47 per cent between 1987 and 1998, absolute numbers affected rose from some 217 million to some 291 million and are expected to reach 404 million by 2015 (46 per cent) (UN-Habitat 2004). International assistance is now primarily concentrated on the need to produce National Poverty Reduction Policies, linked to other forms of macro-economic assistance by bi-lateral and multi-lateral agencies (e.g. World Bank and IMF), with a sectoral stress on Good Governance and Secure Tenure (led by UN agencies).

Sub-Saharan Africa is still the least urbanised macro-region of the world, but is only starting its demographic transition, and experiences continued high birth rates with lowering death rates, as well as high urbanisation rates. The region is expected to grow from some 650 million in 2000 to 1,041 million in 2020, with an average 2.4 per cent annual growth – the highest regional growth worldwide. However, the urban proportion of this population is expected to grow from between 34 to 37 per cent in 2000 to 46 per cent in 2020, more than doubling from between 220–295 million to 476 million. Urbanisation in the region is considered 'exceptional in the sense it is occurring largely without industrial and economic growth' (UN-Habitat 2004: 69). The largest proportion of urban dwellers is expected to be in slums, as these grew by 4.5 per cent between 1990 and 2001, 2 per cent faster than general population growth, reaching 166 million (nearly 72 per cent of the urban population).[13] By 2015 the slum population could be 332 million – not taking into account HIV-AIDS, which is difficult to predict, although an estimated 30 million people are infected in the region (Un-Habitat 2004).

Despite these rapid urbanisation trends, the majority of international agencies still focus on rural development and agricultural as the mainstay for development options. This is partly due to the need to stabilise secure food production, but is also based on the assumptions concerning commodity export. There is often a restricted global market for many of these products, however, as the core countries of the North export a significant proportion of their agricultural production – traditionally heavily subsidised. Sub-Saharan Africa thus suffers from a range of forms of structural disadvantage identified in Chapter 3 above: resource bondage, technological rents and debt peonage. The result is many countries facing severe problems of widespread poverty, sickness and disease, unstable food security and low skills levels, as well as declining terms of trade, access to export markets, deteriorating (colonial) infrastructure and continually dropping investment (internal and external). This has led some more 'developed countries' to campaign for debt relief and a 'Marshall Aid' plan for the macro-region as the only way to create the opportunity for this to realise its potential. Whether this will be successful or not remains to be seen, but what is certain is that Sub-Saharan Africa will continue to rapidly urbanise and poverty will continue to increase in urban areas, providing arguably unique challenges for urban planning and housing.

Current planning and housing issues in Sub-Saharan Africa

Urban investment

A major issue for cities in Sub-Saharan Africa is their role in the fast-changing world economy. The nature of the world economy has changed significantly since the colonial period, where industrialisation in the core countries was the driving force, through the period of the Cold War when a wide range of development options were attempted, to the fragmented situation today with fast-growing economies in some macro-regions, and stagnation, or economic decline in others (see Chapter 3). While urban areas still have local and national social and economic roles, there are growing gaps between those which achieve world status, those with regional or national status and those which have only local importance. The main manifestation of this tendency is the fast growth of the economy in world cities and some regional cities, with some regional and national cities maintaining a viable economic basis, others losing this, and many local urban areas becoming redundant in terms of the wider globalising economy. Sub-Saharan African cities are mainly in the latter categories – few have any claim to world status, and this is often only partial (see Simon 1992, 1997) – and while various cities have regional or national importance, the projected growth in urbanisation noted above is also expected to be largely in small and medium-sized urban areas.[14]

One way that urban areas are trying to adapt to increase their opportunities for benefiting from increasingly competitive global economic activity is through developing their linkages – for example the development corridors initiatives, one of the first being that linking the Gauteng conurbations (led by Johannesburg) with the nearest port in Maputo, Mozambique (see Soderbaum and Taylor 2003).[15] How this will affect inward foreign investment is not as yet clear. Another option is offering tax incentives – these can be direct incentives (e.g. tax exemption) as well as indirect (relaxed regulatory environment such as labour and environmental laws). However, as noted previously, the tendency in foreign direct investment to the region is to increasingly focus on raw commodity exploitation, such as minerals, energy, environmental resources, and much of this type of involvement does not stimulate wider employment of linkages with other parts of the economy.

Decentralisation

Decentralisation is a key feature of the 'good governance' campaigns promoted by multi-lateral and bi-lateral development agencies. This normally focuses on local government development, although improved provincial/sub-regional government is also a focus. While many decentralisation efforts have been started in Sub-Saharan countries, few have led to any significant devolution, with decentralisation being more a sharing of responsibility without powers and access to resources.[16] Urban areas thus remain highly subordinated to central governments in real terms, with decreasing budgets in many cases as central government withdraws its financial support. As many urban areas are becoming *de facto* poorer, the alternative for them to rely on their own fiscal base is also diminishing. The net result is a reduction in resources available at city level for urban development. Thus, while new forms of more democratically elected governments are becoming more common in urban areas, their room for action is extremely limited. This leads to conflict over the limited resources and competition with other urban areas, when in fact collaboration might be more relevant. It also can lead to short-term horizons for decision making, such as concerning environmental impacts, as any investment is seen as better than none. The result is rapidly growing urban areas without the essential services and environmental controls which the levels of population require and hence a proliferation of what are currently seen as 'slums'.

Urban economic basis

Cities were created in the pre-colonial and colonial periods as centres for trade and political control, albeit in the colonial period this was oriented to foreign exploitation. However, in the colonial period there was significant investment in infrastructure, including in urban areas. This legacy was retained after independence, with limited expansion of infrastructure as various forms of neo-colonial or non-dependent development were attempted, with cities consolidating their economic role, especially where import-substitution was developed. Urban-based elites are seen to have consolidated their control of countries in this period, and this, associated to increased urban influx, has been seen as the basis for urban-biased development policies. While these are now queried, the development literature and policies and practices of the main international agencies became heavily oriented to rural development from this time forward. Structural adjustment, with its associated cut-back on subsidies such as urban food, were seen as a means to re-structure economies to their globally competitive potential. However, as noted elsewhere, other factors such as open markets were not in place and hence while these policies had an effect on urban growth (see Simon 1997; Bryceson and Potts 2006) they did not significantly alter the overall economic basis for development. In fact they significantly undercut urban-based development options through massive loss of formal sector jobs as state-based employment was reduced and privatisation led to rapid economic re-structuring with limited social safety nets. The result has been the growth of informal sector economies and the reversion to forms of urban-rural circular migration and subsistence survival for many urban dwellers.

Although the evidence suggests that urban areas have slowed their growth, the existing demographic structure of urban areas is such that these will continue to grow even if there is limited further in-migration or a degree of outward migration. An increasingly large proportion of the urban population cannot find a place within the formal economy as this re-structures in line with global capitalist trends (see Chapter 3). However, the opportunities in rural areas are also declining in many regions. In this context, the dominant tendency of continued urbanisation for the majority is implicitly based on a rejection of labour by the global economic system and radically different from forms of urbanisation in other regions, whether historically, or more recently – as in Latin America and Asia (see following chapters) (Jenkins 2003). The undercutting of rural development opportunities – through for instance the focus on export-led growth in highly controlled world markets – drives this process as much global dependency has eroded urban opportunities. However, even if less attractive than those of the past, current urban opportunities are marginally better than the alternatives, although more so in smaller urban areas where subsistence can be improved by 'straddling' urban and rural-based economies.

Urban policies and planning

Few countries in the region have developed urban policies, with these usually being implicit in national, rural and industrial development policies, or in land laws (although generally focused on rural land) as well as in physical planning laws (where these exist). There is thus little overall link between broader development policies – economic, social and environmental – and urban development strategies. While many countries do prepare urban plans, these still tend to be of the master planning variety, with a focus on land use control – i.e. the regulatory aspect of planning. Some countries also promote more strategic urban plans such as structure plans, which may include city regions, however metropolitanisation is less an issue for most urban areas in the region than elsewhere, although of growing importance and already essential for the mega-cities which exist. In practice, master planning has had very limited impact as governments have decreasing capacity to control or direct land use and market and informal processes dominate land use with minimal controls. In some cases these master plans have become nothing more than the vehicle for claiming land rights for a dominant class, or defining major infrastructure investment programmes. Infrastructure planning has been suggested as the most important role for urban planning (Watson 2005), as land use tends to follow infrastructure. However, the main decisions about infrastructure are often taken from a general economic viewpoint and by a range of sectoral institutions, with little attention being paid to the master plan. Thus, while some 'overview' land use planning may take place, this is not effective or equitable in practice and most master plans – still often prepared with external private sector assistance – are impossible to implement.

In many cities, planning is a matter of dealing with localised land use, either through responding to individual land demarcation and sub-division requests or through limited land development projects, at times with international agency support (Figure 9.5). In some countries, broader national programmes of such projects have been developed, but generally with limited overall effect in relation to the demand for urban land (e.g. Tanzania). In some situations the local planning capacity has been mainly directed to dealing with emergency land use – i.e. removing populations from unsuitable areas (often forcefully) and re-locating populations from areas which have suffered disasters or are proposed for major development projects. In more recent times, as local governments take over more funding responsibilities, however, land development has become a means for self-funding, with state-owned lands being developed commercially – often with fairly low service infrastructure. This process also takes place informally: through allocation by city officials and elected members, by informal sector land and housing developers, and through collective action such as organised invasion. The weak institutional and technical capacities in local governments to undertake planning are thus swamped by *de facto* informal land systems, and the local realpolitik and

9.5 Plots demarcated and occupied with shacks in peri-urban Luanda, Angola (Paul Jenkins)

withdrawal of national support has led to open entrepreneurialism in land use, with or without planning (Rakodi and Leduka 2005).

In many situations, land use planning is not well linked into the wider scheme of government and hence there are competing claims on who controls land – agricultural, defence, fishery ministries all have claims, and national government roles *vis-à-vis* local government responsibilities may be unclear. This is compounded by the proliferation of special project units, often set up to deal with specific situations or projects, and often supported by external agencies who shy away from tackling sector-wide problems, due to their scope. This is further compounded in metropolitan situations where territorial and functional divisions may not be clear. Apart from this lack of clarity within government on land use planning, there is limited linkage between physical planning and other forms of development planning, with physical planning often being seen as a subsidiary activity. The need for land use planning to be part of cross-sectoral development planning is, however, becoming increasingly recognised, and in some countries local land use planning is subordinated to integrated city or municipal development plans, which focus on economic, social and environmental issues as much as land use. While this is a positive move in terms of cross-sectoral planning, the opportunity for land use planning to play a key role here is often undermined by capacity and attitudes – from planners and other actors – in these development plan processes. Therefore, in general, city planners work with extremely limited resources and poorly defined mandates and responsibilities, which further erodes initiative.

Finally, as planning requires decisions about land-based resources, there is a need for engaging with the wider population in terms of what is acceptable and beneficial. While the specialist master planners assumed they can define this for the public good, and subsequent system planners have done little to change this approach, in fact there has often been a limited sense of accountable decision-making for plans and land use control. This reinforces the sense of irrelevance of plans and land use decisions for the majority, whether community or private sector. Planning in this form is usually a top-down exercise, often carried out with national or private sector involvement due to limited technical capacities at local government level. The results are often not seen as relevant or legitimate by the main actors in terms of *de facto* land use, and hence are largely ignored. The defensive attitude of local authorities to existing plans and emerging entrepreneurial attitude to state land use exacerbates this situation. In general, therefore, land use planning suffers from the more general structural problems of governance in many countries.[17]

The above snapshot is not applicable to all situations, and probably errs on the negative side, but is realistic given the projections of urban growth, trends in decentralisation, and the implications of continued under-investment in the urban planning sector by governments. Governments need to understand the role of planning in a different way, and target their action at what is practical, equitable and efficient, and not be tied to what has been traditional in planning and land use control. This suggests a different form of planning which would be more participatory in order to focus and guide broader private sector and community activity, as opposed to attempting to control and block this. These forms of broader 'participatory planning' have been promoted by international agencies in 'City Development Strategies (CDS)' in various pilot situations (see www.unhabitat. org/programmes/ump/cds.asp), but their impact still needs to be understood more specifically in context. The CDS approach has tended to be quite normative and assume the possibility of open discussion and 'level playing fields', which is usually far from the case, hence a more nuanced approach based on analysis of the realpolitik in each situation is required to create the likely parameters for planning activities and decision-making on urban land. Such a form of planning can make it more relevant to a greater number, but also recognises that consensus may not be reached and therefore targets forms of negotiated settlement.

Key to land use planning is establishing land use control, without which there can be no planning. Hence, while planning can be participatory as outlined above, this has to be based on realistic, pragmatic and popularly acceptable land use control mechanisms. There is no way that city authorities in large or small cities in the region can control land use across their territory with existing trends using typical traditional allocation or modern cadastral-based methods. The highly technical and costly modern land use management mechanisms (land survey and registry) which were imported with colonial powers from the North are not relevant for the majority of land use – with the exception of city centre, economic development and higher income areas. By far the largest land areas in Sub-Saharan African cities are residential, and many of these already manifest high degrees of informality in land occupation/registry and development. To 'clean up' this situation through planning, land rights adjudication, titling and establishing or working regulatory land use controls is in most contexts impossible, even with modern technology such as GPS and GIS.

The recognition of this, and the tendency for 'formal' land use management and planning systems to exclude the majority from land rights, has led to recent research across the region into different forms of actual informal land management processes and how these can be recognised and strengthened to provide mutual benefit for the majority of residents and the state and private sector (CEHS-DW 2005; Rakodi and Leduka 2005; Home and Lim 2005). This research has focused on how informal systems work in practice – including traditional, social, and devolved administrative systems which often underpin these – and what can be done to recognise and strengthen these practices systematically. This approach is thus different from that which seeks to formally regularise all informal land rights and occupation as a means to 'kick-start' economic growth (de Soto 2000) which have been attempted since the 1970s in upgrading projects. The approach recognises, first, that land rights need to be separated from the modern mechanism of recognising these through formal titles, which are costly to create, and seeks to develop locally effective and legitimate ways to underpin various rights, tied to social responsibilities. Second, these approaches recognise that even with titles many may not want, or be able, to use these for their economic value (e.g. through mortgaging land) as their social value is much higher and thus land markets as traditionally proposed do not automatically work.[18]

Again in this approach there is a need for realistic assessment of the realpolitik of the situation. There may be strong interests in the private sector and government who may not want to accept wider land use rights and who may see the restriction of these as a means to increase speculation in land by privileged elites. More often, however, there is an attitude that the only mechanisms which can be used are the formal modern ones for land use management and planning that have been developed in the 'North' and a lack of self-confidence in developing context-appropriate solutions. This position is being overcome in some middle-income countries which are still experiencing rapid urbanisation – such as in Latin America – but is not widespread in Sub-Saharan Africa as yet. A key theme emerging with reference to urban planning and land use management in Sub-Saharan Africa, is the need to draw on real social, economic, cultural and political resources to promote solutions which are appropriate to the context. While 'best practices' from other countries may serve as inspiration, these need to be de-contextualised from the contexts where they have been implemented and re-contextualised for the actual situation. If not, they run the risk of not being any more applicable than the previous imported systems. This process is best achieved through direct analysis of the context with a clear objective based on the basic needs for land use planning and management and not the blind importation of mechanisms, or 'best practices', from elsewhere.

In general, therefore, land use planning and management faces severe challenges as the region experiences ever higher levels of urbanisation, yet decreasing capacities – and often high-level interests – to confront urban problems. The key is to change the problems into solutions, and start with existing resources. Often what is most difficult in this is changing attitudes which have been embedded for long periods, and underpin general attitudes to urban areas, as unsuitable for the majority and 'parasitic', for instance. To confront these challenges and turn problems into solutions needs not only an entrepreneurial spirit but a clear definition of public rights, with rights to decision-making on urban land use seen as an integral part of governance and development, and an openness to innovate and self-confidence to develop appropriate solutions.

Housing policies and strategies

It has been argued above that land use planning and management are facing immense challenges of rapid urbanisation with general economic decline and fast-growing urban poverty, with diminishing actual and relative capacities for government, compounded by poor governance structures in general, and limited cross-sectoral co-ordination. The situation for housing policies and practice is the same basic context, and thus similar approaches need to be taken in maximising collaboration of state and local governments with individual and non-state effort. This section briefly reviews how housing activities have changed in the region in the period since Independence, and the current tendencies.

In the colonial period, housing was often used as a means for population control in urban areas, through either limited supply or legal and administrative controls. The most extreme form of this was in South Africa during the apartheid period; however, even there, growing urbanisation trends and declining economic growth led to changing approaches. The main approaches to housing in the post-Independence periods have mapped fairly closely to international trends described in the previous chapters: (a) initial limited state and private sector provision; (b) Keynesian forms of increasing housing demand and supply (e.g. prefabrication); (c) growing reliance on 'self-help' forms of supply (adapting colonial forms for this), linked to serviced land supply ('sites and services'), and then later to upgrading of 'squatter' areas, eventually with community development and participation; (d) a growing focus on policy change and national programmes; and finally (e) a concentration on housing finance.[19]

The main difference between Sub-Saharan Africa and other regions in the above phases (a) to (d) has been the scale of activity. Governments have been limited in their financial capacity and political interest in developing urban areas and hence international agencies have had a major role in funding and determining these approaches, but this has nearly always been at a scale which is far from that needed. The result has been informal settlements having a long and consolidated history in urban areas of most countries of the region, with limited state involvement. There has been a major change in the last phase of policy/practice, narrowing the focus to housing finance, but the general weakness of housing finance systems in the region has led to much of the international focus on this having limited effect on the majority, unlike in other regions with more middle-income countries and greater opportunities for market-based solutions. In this sense the 'enabling markets' approach has not been successful and formal housing markets still only respond to a small fraction of the upper-income elite needs in many countries. This process has been exacerbated by economic decline, and only in a few of the middle-income countries (e.g. South Africa and Botswana) have housing finance systems been a focus for pro-poor activities, and even here this has been very limited in impact.[20]

Decreasing state engagement in low-income housing of any form in most countries has resulted in increasing informalisation of housing provision for the majority of urban dwellers, while a small minority benefit from increased formal housing market activity (see Figures 9.6 and 9.7). The nature of informal access to housing is, however, changing as this sector grows. Initially, informal access to housing was often through getting informal access to land and 'self-managed' building (usually without government assistance). However, while this may still be possible in smaller urban areas, there is a much greater commodification of land and housing now which means that getting access to land costs more, making rental more likely, although land purchase is still predominant in most countries. Rental housing can be in many forms, but much of it is still in small-scale format, i.e. rented by a landlord who has several properties, many being on the landlord's plot or nearby. However, as rental housing becomes more established as an important form of housing provision, this small-scale landlord structure is likely to change and this may lead to greater insecurity and exploitation.

The impact of structural adjustment in the region has spurred on this process of informalisation, as many more people drop out of formal employment and find formal housing too expensive. This has led to increased 'downward raiding' of housing projects which the government and international agencies have targeted at lower-income groups, as those selling out in the formal market have higher

9.6 Informal house-building in Maputo, Mozambique (Paul Jenkins)

9.7 Simonstown – flats provided by the formal market in South Africa (Paul Jenkins)

purchasing power. While this overall trend to commodification of land and housing can be seen as 'enabling a market' it was not what was intended by the international agencies which promoted this approach. However, there is still an assumption that, with a return to economic growth, these informal housing markets can be regularised. The projected trends of massive urbanisation and likely continued growth of urban poverty, however, work against this and there is arguably a need for greater state involvement in the housing system. The international literature has recently been concerned with housing rights, which – as with land rights – are tied into a 'rights-based' approach to development. As above, there is a need for caution as to what rights can be realised in the still fairly precarious legal systems of many Sub-Saharan African countries, especially as these systems tend to be dominated by the elite, and the nature of governance systems in general are hardly likely to change this in the shorter term.

In general, therefore, the main issue concerning housing for the majority is again a contextual understanding of the housing systems that operate in any particular country and urban area, and an approach which focuses on establishing rights to decent housing where possible, in parallel with promotion of new forms of partnership and recognition of the importance of the informal sector by the government. Whether this is politically possible or not depends more on the political and social structures than on the housing demand *per se*. Again, much can be learned from comparing with Asian and Latin American experiences – where informal housing commodification has been much more prevalent for longer. However, again as noted above, there is a need for caution as to what is transferable from the experience or 'best practice' from another context – and indeed as to whether this is sustainable in the Sub-Saharan African context which is somewhat different as argued above.

Urban environmental issues

The rapid urbanisation and collapse of urban planning, with increased informalisation of land use and massive expansion of generally low-rise informal housing, have been a major factor in negative impacts on urban environments. However, these trends are paralleled by critical forms of use of land and environmental resources promoted by government, such as permitting inward foreign direct investment to operate virtually free of environmental controls, and to prioritise forms of environmental improvements to higher-income groups, using up limited available budgets in the process. The result is that many urban environmental problems that have been inherited from the colonial period are growing to very serious proportions and impact on not only the growing urban population but other populations such as those downstream or in the wider environmental footprint of a city or urban region. Many colonial locations for urban areas were determined by strategic transport and defence factors and are not well sited to begin with (e.g. swampy areas near river mouths or hillsides around natural ports). As urban populations and densities rise these locations become environmentally dangerous and land erosion and pollution become major problems. This is all exacerbated by the ongoing deforestation for solid fuel, uncontrolled use of natural resources for other purposes (such as building material) and poorly designed land use and infrastructure.

Over and above this, urban environments extend much further than their territorial or physical limits (in the sense of density and type of land use), as cities consume natural resources and produce waste that affect much larger areas – the ecological footprint of the city. As land use controls decrease in impact and city governments become more entrepreneurial to be able to undertake any development, the impact of such situations often worsens and the natural habitat as well as public health suffers. These have been characterised as the green and brown agendas (see Chapter 8), but in many African cities the green agenda has limited importance as natural habitats have long since been obliterated, and the brown agenda is what is most important.[21] However, natural habitats are still seen as important where there is tourism, and here the conflict between national and local development needs may clash. The most severe urban environmental problems may arise in smaller and intermediate urban areas, which are the location of continuing urbanisation, with virtually no capacity to invest in responding to brown or green agenda issues – a problem once again related to governance.

The challenge for planning and housing in Sub-Saharan Africa

The above sections have laid out some of the major challenges facing planning and housing in the region in the face of rising urbanisation and growing urban poverty, with decreasing government capacity and increasing informalisation. The principal focus has been on the need for planning and housing to be seen within a governance context, as this is what largely determines access to resources and the definition of what is accepted as 'formal' and state-supported and what is not. The main argument is that continuing to consider the majority of land occupation and housing as 'informal' and exclude this from state support – or insist in formalising this without adequate resources, political will or popular agreement/legitimacy – will only increase social and economic exclusion and prevent the public sector from playing its essential role of protecting and furthering collectively agreed action. This is not a naïve political position which assumes consensus will be achieved, but one where hard negotiation has to take place. Currently, the majority in urban areas in the region use the political 'exit' strategy as opposed to the 'voice' strategy – i.e. they opt out of political engagement, or do not have adequate possibilities to so engage. This may change, or alternatively there may be rising unrest as social groups who are excluded either support violent change or turn to such measures in ad hoc ways when issues 'boil over'.

How does this approach compare with the normative agenda which the last chapter described? The normative agenda is predominantly determined outside of the region, by the core countries, but the severe dependence of most countries in the region on international assistance since the 1980s places most governments in invidious positions in terms of developing their own 'agendas', policies and programmes. However, the governance issues focused on above might well mean that such agendas continue to be focused on the elite and preferential position of this group *vis-à-vis* international opportunity as opposed to broader socially oriented development – this certainly seems to be the trend even after constitutional change in many countries. Nevertheless, planning and housing actors can develop alternatives within the context of a realistic appraisal of the governance systems they work within, and can be actors in change in relation to these – in other words, agency can work in the face of structural factors. So the fact that these agendas are to some extent imposed is an issue which can be challenged as long as alternatives have been investigated – challenging the relevance of the normative agenda with no clear basis other than a sense of sovereign grievance will not produce any significant impact. The Millennium Development Goals (MDGs) are arguably one such normative agenda which is little criticised to date, yet the practical impact of these will not necessarily achieve much in this most needy region.

The Millennium Development Goals

There already exists a critique of the MDGs which derives from close partnership between Northern and Southern institutions (Satterthwaite 2003), much of which is particularly pertinent for Sub-Saharan Africa. In this region the challenges to the MDGs are enormous, and the goals – even if achievable – would do little to change the basic situation. This can be demonstrated by examining the key MDG of relevance to planning and housing, that of improving the lives of 100 million slum dwellers by 2020. In the region, the UN estimates that urban slum dwellers may rise from 166 million to 332 million by 2015, i.e. an increase of 100 per cent and the increase in itself of 146 million – i.e. more than the worldwide targeted reduction. As the above critique stresses, the lack of clear definition of this target, and the indicators to achieve this, means that it will be difficult to measure success in this MDG in general, but it in itself could only begin a much needed wider process for beginning to include excluded 'slum' populations in urban areas, which hopefully it may stimulate.

Sustainable urban development

As noted above, urban environmental problems are growing as fast as, if not faster than, the urban areas of the region, as previous basic infrastructure breaks down and is overwhelmed with the rising demand. Increasingly new 'not urban, not rural' urban forms are appearing which are based on lifestyles that straddle urban-rural contexts, which the people of the region increasingly have to adopt to survive, with a mix of subsistence agriculture and informal sector trade/production, including maximising chances of social benefit. These new 'not urban, not rural' areas have virtually no infrastructure and no urban governments, and the rural authorities they fall under will probably find them hard to deal with. As such this is a new challenge to sustainable urban development beyond the existing challenges of existing urban area growth and spreading metropolitanisation. While green agendas may feature in some countries' development strategies as key for economic resources use (e.g. tourism, water for hydropower, etc.), the brown agendas are inevitably the most pressing, although as McGranahan and Satterthwaite (2000) argue, these are not necessarily conflicting agendas. Dealing with brown agendas with virtually no governance infrastructure will be extremely difficult and the issues around managing urban environments in such extremes of poverty and weak governance are just now being investigated. Public decision-making mechanisms need to be created even if there is no adequate state structure to undertake this, and here what remains of traditions of rural self-government, albeit limited, can perhaps be the basis for local community-level organisation, if politically these can be accepted.

Urban poverty

This chapter has documented the trends towards macro-economic stagnation and urbanisation of poverty in Sub-Saharan Africa. Urban poverty is a fact and will remain so for the majority of urban dwellers in the region for the foreseeable future, despite the Poverty Reduction Strategies that international agencies and foreign governments currently promote. The core issues are those of the changing global economy as discussed in Chapter 3, and hence there is a need to prepare for new forms of urban management in the face of such poverty – whether in planning, housing, environment or other areas of local development. There is no point in assuming the urban populations will go back to rural areas *en masse* – some may do so, and many may establish new rural linkages such as circular migration and split household economies or inhabit the emerging 'not urban, not rural' settlement forms. Even with accelerated rural development programmes – and the possible use of forced relocation which has a negative history in the region – the urban areas will continue to grow. Projections may not be accurate, as they are after all estimates – but all the pointers show that urbanisation is a major issue for the future. There needs to be a greater realisation of this by governments and international agencies, and a more realistic planning for this in urban policies. Key issues will be stabilising food security, and here urban and rural development policies need to be better co-ordinated. Equally there needs to be a better understanding of how the poor cope in urban areas – what are their survival strategies?; what are the likely trends for them to slip into, or pull out of, poverty?; and what are the key areas of vulnerability? – using a more nuanced approach to the definition of poverty. In responding to this there is a need to work with the poor to establish what their priorities and proposals are and how the government or other actors can assist. There is a danger, however, that these efforts focus on 'containing' poverty – i.e. making it more bearable and not seeking ways for it to be overcome. This should not detract from the need to challenge the structural ways in which the whole macro-region is being impoverished through debt peonage, technological rents and resource bondage, and to push for change in these areas which are dominated by the core countries. However, as this book argues more generally, despite structural constraints, action is possible, but needs to be based on real possibilities and not normative agendas and imported policies and practices.

Chapter 10
Urban development and housing in Latin America

Introduction to the region

The physical and historic context for urban development

Latin America comprises most of the land mass of South America, Central America and Mexico, as well as several islands in the Caribbean and the Atlantic and Pacific Oceans – i.e. a land area of approximately 20 million square kilometres.[1] Though a current approach is to study the Americas as a whole (see e.g. Fernandez-Armesto 2003), this chapter focuses on Latin America because it has particular features in its history, cultural legacy and 'development' which set it apart from 'core' countries in North America (the United States and Canada).

South America is predominantly a vast plain with the Andean ridge running along its western edge, and a high plateau in what is currently Bolivia. The eastwards drift of the continent makes the western coast prone to seismic and volcanic activity. This seaboard is dry, with small rivers and liable to mudslides. The eastern plain contains the basins of the rivers Amazon and Paraná, among the largest in the world. Central America is a seismically active isthmus, with high mountains extending into Mexico, most of which is a high plateau. Central America and the Caribbean coast are also prone to flash floods, while in Mexico water again becomes scarce on the arid plateau.

Latin America is rich in oil deposits and various mineral resources; although its gold lodes are now practically exhausted, there is still some silver, and precious stones are abundant. Mining has been a key driver of foreign interest in the area from Spanish colonisation to present-day trans-nationals. Three main soil regimes in South America support different types of agriculture: cereal production and cattle-grazing on the eastern temperate plains; grazing and a variety of crops in the subtropical to temperate parts of the Andes; and coffee, cacao and sugar cane in eastern and south-eastern Brazil. However, only 10 per cent of the surface of South America is covered with fertile soils, and erosion is a major problem. There is a wide variety of climates, from cold mountain conditions in the Andes to subtropical and tropical climates at lower altitudes. The Caribbean periodically suffers tropical storms, including hurricanes. Variety in topography and climate is reflected in the vegetation, ranging from deserts and steppes on the plateaux and along the eastern coast of South America, to tropical and subtropical forest and savannah in much of the rest. Rainforest is abundant, the Amazon basin being the largest in the world. However, the rate of deforestation is alarmingly high.

It is thought that humans crossed to the Americas from Asia via the Bering Strait, probably between 25,000 and 40,000 years ago, reaching Tierra del Fuego by 9000 BC – human settlement therefore took place later than in other parts of the world. The present population is the result of five centuries of ethnic mixture among the indigenous population, Iberians, Africans, and other overseas immigrants. Three ethnic regions can be defined:

- Indo-American: the western highlands, which were the most densely settled when the Spanish conquest began, now home to the highest ratio of indigenous population;
- Mestizo-American: the tropical and subtropical lowlands, characterised by European groups as well as Africans and mulattos;
- Euro-American: the temperate zone, with an overwhelming majority of European population, comprising the 'southern cone'.

As a result of colonisation, Spanish is the official language in most of Latin America except Brazil, where Portuguese is spoken. Indigenous languages still survive throughout, particularly in areas where strong civilisations had developed prior to European colonisation and where colonisation did not penetrate deeply. In Mesoamerica the most widespread is Nahua (Mexicano), and in South America there are circa 350 indigenous languages, with the most widely spoken being Quechua and Aymará (along the Andean ridge) and Guaraní (official in Paraguay, though also spoken in neighbouring countries).

The earliest settlements of hunter-gatherers were established in the Mexican plateaux and the Andes. Lowland savannahs and tropical forests were occupied later, from about 8000 BC, because of lower food resources in these habitats. Crop cultivation began between 8500 and 2000 BC, and herding and pastoral economies developed in the Andes. Advanced urban civilisations developed mainly in two foci: Mesoamerica and the central Andes.

In Mesoamerica the first concentrations of human populations took the form of small compact villages or denser rural settlements around a temple-pyramid nucleus. The Olmec culture, with its small governing and religious elite and its complex ceremonial centres, reached its zenith at the time of the Roman Empire and set the pattern in terms of urban layout for later urban civilisations in the region. Its capital city Teotihuacán was laid out on a cruciform plan, its structure reflecting functional hierarchies (ceremonial, commercial, etc.). The Toltecs later developed an economy based on agriculture which was irrigated by dikes and dams, with a network of cities of considerable size,[2] but disappeared in the twelfth century possibly largely due to the continual inflow of migrants. The Aztec empire began in central Mexico in the early fifteenth century. Economically it depended on military conquest and payment of tribute by defeated city states, leading to concentration of wealth and power in the capital city, Tenochtitlán (currently Mexico City), one of the largest cities in the world at the time.[3] Tenochtitlán was the centre of a highly urbanised society, with social institutions and classes, and an economy based on trade, tribute and specialised crafts – it was the most advanced example of urban life in pre-Columbian America (Hardoy 1967). The Mayan civilisation, which flourished in southeast Mexico and Guatemala from 1500 BC to the early 1500s AD, was rural, though it developed hundreds of settlements which followed a common pattern, including a central complex with ceremonial and possibly residential functions.

In the Andean region, pre-Inca cultures predominantly lived in small villages, but urban centres appeared towards the end of the first millennium (Figure 10.1). During the struggles between city states from 1000 AD to 1400 AD urbanisation intensified along the Pacific coast, with some large cities evolving such as Cajamarquilla and Chan Chan.[4] A single empire was established from 1440 to 1532, extending along the Pacific coast for about 2,500 miles, and reaching an estimated population of 6 million. This was an urban culture with a stone-paved road network, and terraced and irrigated agriculture. The political and administrative power of the Inca Empire was centred on the capital city of Cuzco. Like the rest of Inca cities, this was unfortified, with a large and regular-shaped central square which was used for a variety of functions and was traversed by the road connecting to other cities (Hardoy 1967). Hence, unlike Sub-Saharan Africa, in Latin America a wide variety of urban cultures and forms preceded European colonisation and conquest.

The arrival in 1492 of an expedition sponsored by the Spanish Crown marked the beginning of rapid European invasion of the Americas, with the world being divided between the two European colonial powers of the time only two years later,[5] effectively allocating the western part of Latin America to Spain, and the east to Portugal. Spanish *conquistadores* quickly penetrated their 'allocated' land, thanks to their military superiority. Diseases previously unknown to the American continent spread rapidly and decimated the native population. The more impenetrable land on the east was colonised more slowly by the Portuguese, initially keeping to the coast. Their initial approach was colonisation rather than conquest, trading with the indigenous populations. The overall impact of conquest and colonisation – through war, disease and a form of slavery – was devastating. It has been estimated that the population fell to about one-twentieth of its pre-conquest level.

10.1 Sunken courtyard in the pre-Inca city of Tiahuanaco, Bolivia (Harry Smith)

The Spanish Crown controlled the colonisation of its new territories by building a civil service and dividing the land into viceroyalties. Spain was primarily interested in the extraction of precious metals, underpinning its position as a world power. This initially focused on placer gold, shifting from the mid-sixteenth century to silver extraction from underground ores, i.e. to fixed locations where urban development took place, thus focusing Spain's colonial rule on the silver-producing regions (Mexico and Bolivia – Figure 10.2). The new Spanish mining towns used indigenous labour, either forced or drafted as free labour, sometimes resulting in the loss of agricultural land through either abandonment or direct destruction. However, the Spanish gradually developed agriculture in certain areas by establishing the *encomienda* system, whereby Spanish settlers were allocated land by the Crown and became responsible for the indigenous people living on it. Though not strictly a form of land ownership initially, this semi-feudal system did

10.2 Potosí and the silver mines of Cerro Rico in the background, Bolivia (Harry Smith)

mark the beginning of concentration of land ownership, which is endemic to Latin America.[6] Mining in Brazil started later, the supply routes to the mines forging links within Brazil which survived independence, and the profits from mining later helping to finance the country's early coffee economy. However, rather than mining, Portugal initially used its colony in Brazil to grow sugar, leading to importation of slaves from Africa due to the high death rate of indigenous labour, the establishment of landowners who received huge extensions of land from the Portuguese Crown for exploitation, and widespread environmental destruction along the northeast of Brazil, turning tropical forest into barren savannahs. Sugar production in Brazil crashed at the end of the seventeenth century through increased competition from the Caribbean – it was thus the first example of cash crop production on which many parts of Latin America were to depend later, within the increasingly unequal international division of labour.

By the late seventeenth and the eighteenth centuries, in Spanish Latin America there was an established landed class descended from Spanish settlers which began to reclaim power from the metropole. Decentralisation and other political reforms in Spanish Latin America during the eighteenth century led to administrative subdivision into smaller viceroyalties, the merchant classes of which began to compete against each other. By then Latin America was probably retaining large parts of the profits from mining, allowing for the importation of consumer goods. At this time Brazil became a destination for Portuguese emigrants as well as for African slaves.[7] The period of Spanish and Portuguese rule highly influenced Latin America's later development. According to Gilbert (1990: 1): 'Some of Latin America's most enduring characteristics, language, religious beliefs, pattern of land holding, export orientation and social inequality, were firmly established during that period'.

The Enlightenment in Europe precipitated the independence of Latin America, with all the mainland colonies becoming independent in the 1810–29 period.[8] The newly independent countries engaged in various wars and split into smaller units during the nineteenth century, reaching the current political configuration by 1903. Independence was brokered by the upper classes, and meant little in terms of improved living conditions for the poor. In Mexico, for example, after independence large *haciendas* persisted, effectively preserving the concentration of land ownership and forcing the indigenous population to become waged labourers.[9]

Britain, the new dominant European colonial power, and later the United States, used politically independent Latin America to obtain raw materials and to export their growing industrial production, and played key roles in the development of major productive sectors and transport infrastructure within the Latin American economies, always geared towards export – thus establishing a neo-colonial relationship without colonisation. Mining was revitalised due to growing industrial demand in Western Europe and the United States, lower transport costs, and the openness of Latin American countries to overseas capital and technology (i.e. openness to a situation generating 'technological rent' – see Chapter 3). In addition, cash crops played an increasing role in the export economies of Latin American countries during the nineteenth century, remaining so during the twentieth and thus making these economies highly vulnerable to changes in world markets. Crop production was mainly in the hands of national oligarchies and foreign companies, while export and distribution was usually under the control of large trans-nationals, thus continuing the 'resource bondage' initiated by the 'conquest' in the sixteenth century. The demand for export products from Western Europe and the United States generated different levels of economic development among Latin American countries,[10] and the type of export product the economy was based on also had an impact on wealth distribution and social structure.[11]

During the first half of the twentieth century the Latin American economy slowly grew, except during the Great Depression in the 1930s and the Second World War, which highlighted the dependence of the export economy on Western consumer markets and manufactures, thus prompting several governments to encourage industrial development. After the Second World War Latin America adopted import-substitution policies, with national governments increasingly involved in the national economy, improving transport systems and power generation, giving incentives to industry, and adopting protectionist measures against foreign manufactures. These policies succeeded in increasing Latin American industrial production, but were faced with the limitations of import-substitution, which the home-grown *dependencia* school of thought sought to explain through its conceptualisation of the world as consisting of a developed 'centre' and an underdeveloped 'periphery' (see Chapters 2 and 3). The Latin American state tried to address these limitations, through (a) attempts to create economies of scale by establishing a division of labour within agreed economic regions, i.e. signing free-trade agreements which established two short-lived common markets, and (b) returning to export economies, with incentives being created for exports and direct state involvement in production through nationalisation.

The above historical evolution of Latin America's social, economic and political structures has had a huge impact on the development of urban settlements and on the generation of an urban pattern in this macro-region. The next section focuses on urban development against this historical background.

The evolution of urban settlements in Latin America

The history of urban civilisation in this macro-region goes back to Aztec and Inca (and earlier) cultures, as seen in the previous section. However, the Spaniards destroyed most of the cities and towns they came upon in Latin America. While old capitals such as Tenochtitlan and Cuzco were transformed practically obliterating their original form,[12] other settlements were razed to the ground, their inhabitants being forced to move to new cities. These new settlements followed a chequerboard plan with (usually) square blocks and a square in the centre containing the main buildings (Figures 10.3 and 10.4) – a plan which was designed in Spain and applied throughout Spanish Latin America through the 'Laws of the Indies'. Architectural historian Leonardo Benevolo (1980: 624–6) described this as 'the first town-planning model of the modern era', which he saw as a combination of European medieval tradition and Renaissance culture, with the following characteristics:

- The model was based on the initial establishment of a two-dimensional regulatory plan which allowed building plot allocation to owners who built when and how they saw fit, rather than determining the erection of buildings in a set period of time.

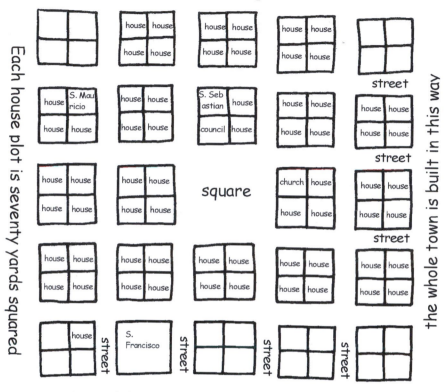

10.3 Plan of the original layout of Santiago de Leon, currently Caracas, Venezuela (Redrawn by Harry Smith from Benevolo 1980: Fig. 915)

- It allowed expansion in all directions when needed. The external boundaries of cities were always temporary, and thus there was no sharp contrast between the city and the countryside.
- The chequerboard plan was extremely uniform. Often being planned in the metropole with no direct knowledge of its location, the city was prevented from adapting to its natural environment. However, the original layout has continued to be used even to date.

Portuguese colonisation of Brazil was less systematic. Ports were established along the coast during the 1530s, and what would become Brazil's largest urban centres in this century (São Paulo and Rio de Janeiro) were established in the 1550s. Portugal had no codified urban planning method comparable to the

10.4 Main square in Villa de Leyva, Colombia (Harry Smith)

Spanish 'Laws of the Indies'. However, new cities in Brazil were usually also based on grid plans.

   Spanish colonisation established an urban pattern focused on the mines and the routes for transportation of mineral to the metropole, as well as provision of supplies to the mining towns.[13] This first phase of Spanish colonisation, based on achieving control over concentrations of Indian labour and mineral extraction, was centred on the areas where the most advanced American civilisations had flourished (Mexico and Perú). A comprehensive urban system was created in these areas to secure military and administrative control. Although the rest of Spanish Latin America, reliant on agricultural production, was comparatively neglected until the eighteenth century, cities were established in these areas using the same principles.[14] However, growth of some of these cities was thwarted by the strict controls the Spanish Crown imposed on trade.[15] Only in the late eighteenth century did some of these cities start to develop more, as a result of decentralisation of the Spanish empire. The protectionist mercantile policies of the Spanish Crown therefore directly influenced the establishment and growth of the urban settlement pattern in Spanish Latin America until the nineteenth century. This urban system has persisted to this day, with 15 of the 20 most populous cities in Latin America in 1970 having been founded during 1520–80.

   The roots of some of the major problems faced by Latin American cities in the twentieth century can be found in this imperial period. The establishment of cities as centres for the control of colonial territories with few internal communication links other than those with the capital, created the conditions for rural-urban migration later on, as well as for strong primacy of capital cities. Construction of new cities also established racial segregation, with a planned central city for those of European descent, and neighbourhoods (*barrios*) and separate townships for the Indian labour force. Despite the amount of planning that went into building cities and creating the infrastructure linking them to their hinterland, by the end of the colonial period Spanish cities in Latin America were on average small and modest (Morris 1994), a situation which was similar in Brazil, where at independence the largest city, Rio de Janeiro, had a population of about 30,000 (Morris 1994).

Rapid urban change occurred in certain areas during the 1800s through European investment in infrastructure and economic activities, and a new influx of European migration, particularly in areas that had been less developed under Spanish and Portuguese rule, such as the 'southern cone'. Rather than the establishment of new cities, this phase saw a different distribution of population emerge throughout the continent, with some cities reaching exceptional growth rates towards the end of the nineteenth century.[16] With rapid growth, sanitary and housing conditions in many cities worsened, leading to temporary population decline in some cases. Cities rapidly grew beyond their colonial gridiron cores, through affluent suburban expansion imitative of English and currently US models, as well as extensive low-income self-help neighbourhoods.

Towards the end of the 1800s and beginning of the 1900s, a transport and services infrastructure was built using European models and capital. New transport infrastructure allowed the development of housing districts for the growing middle classes, and the development of docks and industry led to the development of high density workers' districts, which rapidly became slums (Hardoy 1982). Inspiration in European approaches to planning led to the preparation of master plans by French, German and Austrian consultant architects and engineers, and by the first local planners who were trained in Paris, Berlin and Vienna. According to Hardoy (1982), these master plans were city-wide and showed a concern for transport problems and sanitary conditions, but focused on the design of new avenues, the improvement of central districts, the designation of open spaces, the establishment of building codes and zoning regulations, and the control of urban expansion and land use, while ignoring social segregation, the urban economy, city finance and the conditions of the poor. Although this approach did not have an important impact on urban development, it was followed by a new wave of master-planning based on the principles of Modernism, with master plans being prepared, for example, for Buenos Aires and Rio de Janeiro in the 1930s by Le Corbusier, and Modernism being embraced by architects throughout Latin America and incorporated into planning approaches (Figure 10.5).

10.5 Rio de Janeiro, Brazil – nineteenth-century middle-class neighbourhood of Urca in the foreground, mid-twentieth-century modernist layout of the seafront across the bay and informal settlements on the hillsides in the background (Harry Smith)

From the 1930s to the 1950s planning departments were established in many Latin American cities. This happened, however, during a period in which local government lost much of its power to higher levels (national or provincial). According to Healey (1974) these urban planning offices, which were derived from prior models either from core countries or from earlier experiences within the country, had led to some changes in spatial structure and administrative behaviour, but were not in a position to induce directed changes. Healey (1974) argued that this was due to planning institutions being established under conditions of structural change, and not under the conditions of structural stability prevalent in European and North American societies when planning had developed. In addition, it has been noted that in Latin America planning as a form of urban resource distribution has had to compete with the strong tradition of patronage. Thus procedures such as public land allocation, planning permission and contract allocation have a highly political content, rather than merely administrative. However, planning institutions created in Latin America in this period have continued to operate, and new ones have been created, as is seen later in this chapter.

Rapid urbanisation led in the 1960s and 1970s to concern in academic and government circles about 'over-urbanisation', i.e. the notion that cities were growing too quickly. This view was linked to two other perceived problems: tertiarisation, whereby too many people in urban areas were seen to be working in services; and the theory of marginality, according to which low-paid people did not participate 'properly' in the city and led ways of life that were 'marginal' (Gilbert 1998) (see Chapter 7). The implication for many social scientists and decision makers was that cities should not be allowed to grow so large and so fast. This conclusion led to policies and actions aimed at either stemming the flow of migrants from rural areas or returning migrants who had already settled in cities. The major strategies adopted to achieve these goals in Latin America were:

- Incentives to keep population in the rural sector, for example the agrarian reform programmes implemented in many countries.[17] Most of these did not provide lasting benefits, because of either expropriated land being returned by subsequent governments or the effects of reform being undermined by later events. Currently, concentration of land ownership is continuing throughout Latin America, eroding many gains achieved through land reform and other programmes.

- The development of alternative urban centres, which took the form of growth poles and new cities. New cities were created as part of a programme for mineral resource development (e.g. Ciudad Guayana in Venezuela) or to create a new capital (e.g. Brasilia).[18] It is hard to gauge the impact of these new urban centres on existing ones for which demographic pressure was supposed to be relieved, but evidence shows that these new cities have developed the same problems.

Urbanisation trends

Although there is a long-established urban tradition, general urbanisation is really a twentieth-century phenomenon in Latin America. In 1900 the population was mostly rural, but by 1940 about 33 per cent lived in towns or cities. Whereas in 1900 only three cities had more than half-a-million inhabitants, by 1950 six had over one million inhabitants. In the second half of the twentieth century urbanisation accelerated, with the proportion of urban population rising to 75.4 per cent by 2000 (UN-Habitat 2004). Reasons for such rapid urbanisation were falling mortality rates, rapid internal migration, economic development and changing technology. Rapid urbanisation has been linked to overall demographic growth in Latin America, from 100 million inhabitants in 1930 to 425 million in 1990, with average national population growth rates reaching 2.7 and 2.9 per cent in 1950–5 and 1960–5 respectively (Gilbert 1998). Urbanisation is not uniform throughout Latin America, with South America's being the highest (77.2 per cent) and slowing, while in Central America and the Caribbean it is still growing, with urbanisation levels of 68.2 and 63.1 per cent respectively in 2000 (UN-Habitat 2004).

City growth rates in the above context were spectacular – reaching annual growth rates of 8 per cent during the 1940s for example – particularly in the case of large cities, with Mexico City increasing its population by 5.1 million and São Paulo by 4 million during the 1970s (Gilbert 1998). Urban primacy, already incipient in the colonial urban system due to political and administrative centralisation, was further encouraged by the port location of many capital cities after independence. Such predominance of capital cities in the total population intensified dramatically in the twentieth century, with several capital cities becoming megacities: in 2000 Mexico City had a population of 18.1 million, and São Paulo 17.9 million. Out of the 20 cities with over 10 million inhabitants in the world in 2000, four were in Latin America (UN-Habitat 2004) (see Figure 10.6).

Long-standing rural–urban migration dramatically intensified during the twentieth century, especially since the 1940s. Recently the rural population in Latin America has begun to decline in absolute terms as well as in relative terms. The main driving force of this exodus is poverty, accentuated in some places by natural disasters and political violence. Although projections indicate that over the 1950–2010 period there will have been a consistent trend of declining average annual urban growth rates, this applies to increasingly larger absolute urban populations, and does not necessarily translate into slowed absolute urban growth rates. By 2000, 31.6 per cent of this macro-region's total population lived in the 50 cities exceeding one million inhabitants, while 15.1 per cent lived in cities exceeding 5 million inhabitants. Over the past few decades the nature of urbanisation in Latin America has been changing, with regional forms of urbanisation becoming prevalent over city-centred urbanisation, thus leading to new forms of polycentric, multi-nodal urban regional systems. Growth seems to be highest in medium and small municipalities located in the commuter belt of metropolitan areas and along their radial transport corridors, thus forming extended metropolitan areas (UN-Habitat 2004), leading to increasing focus on metropolitanisation (see Chapter 8).

A short introduction to contemporary urban Latin America

Latin America is divided into 20 countries,[19] all of which resulted either from independence from Spain and Portugal, or from subsequent wars and secessions

Population

● Over 10 million

● Over 5 milion

• Over 1 million

0 ____ 1,000 km

10.6 Map of Latin American large cities (Drawing by Harry Smith based on data in UNCHS 2001)

during the nineteenth century. All Latin American countries are currently nominally republics with democratically elected governments.[20] This political constitution was originally the result of the wars of independence, inspired by the US and French revolutions in the eighteenth century, with the exception of Brazil, which remained a monarchy until 1889. However, the colonial legacy of authoritarian elites linked to military power led to a history of revolutions and military take-overs during the nineteenth and twentieth centuries, with most recently the 1970s and 1980s being a period of war in Central America and undemocratic and repressive authoritarian regimes in South America. Politically, the 1990s saw a general transition from military rule to democracy throughout Latin America, as well as the consolidation of peace in Central America after decades of civil and international war. Whether during dictatorship or during revolutionary periods, the state has had a strong interventionist role in the Latin American economy and society, for example through nationalisation of major means of production at the macro-economic level, and the operation of clientelistic links with the private sector and communities on the political level. Recently there has also been a move towards devolving power to local government in countries which heretofore had been highly centralised, and the re-establishment of democracy has been accompanied by the rise of the debate on participatory versus representative democracy.[21] However, the consequences of increasing privatisation and deregulation, as well as of central governments' inability to provide sustainable solutions to the economic situation since the 1980s crisis, have weakened the state in favour mainly of the private sector – both foreign and national. Civil society is also relatively strong, with a history of organised action and increasing social and NGO activity in response to economic crisis and the need to provide for basic needs, in the light of government decisions (e.g. privatisation of basic services) and political events.

Since their independence, and besides a strong British influence in the nineteenth century, Latin American countries have been generally under the dominant sphere of influence of the United States, both politically and economically.[22] The United States both openly and covertly supported authoritarian regimes in Latin America during the twentieth century, and had a direct impact on housing and community development initiatives in the region through USAID financing of projects, with the aim of staving off revolution on its doorstep. More recently, the United States has promoted the signing of free trade agreements: the Central America Free Trade Area (CAFTA) and the Free Trade Area of the Americas (FTAA) (see Chapter 3).

The weakness of Latin American states in the face of international pressures to liberalise and privatise owes much to the financial crisis they underwent in the 1980s. Prior to the 1980s, twentieth-century Latin American economies – based on primary product export and some degree of industrialisation through import-substitution – were growing steadily. However, heavy borrowing from foreign banks during the 1970s led to high levels of indebtedness, leading to a severe crisis in the early 1980s. Debt repayment was rescheduled on condition that IMF adjustment programmes be implemented by the national governments, their main objective being to ensure that Latin America earned enough foreign currency to service its debt, and a key mechanism chosen to achieve this being a drastic reduction in imports. Latin America thus became a major net exporter of capital to developed countries, and the 1980s came to be known as 'the lost decade', and perhaps the most extreme case of 'debt peonage' (Chapter 3).

Latin America could not afford, however, to disconnect itself from the world's financial markets, and by 1990 all Latin American governments (except Cuba) had accepted the need for restructuring in the direction advocated by the United States and international organisations, i.e. through privatisation, deregulation and cutting back of the state. The implementation of the IMF policy recommendations initially meant recession, a drop in real wages, massive unemployment, rapid inflation and a reduction in investment in the private and public sectors. These policies, though highly unpopular and leading to widespread social unrest during the 1980s, intensified during the 1990s. Growth has, however, been achieved again in many Latin American countries since the beginning of the 1990s, though subject to great fluctuations such as due to the Asian crisis (see Chapter 11). The recent economic crisis in Argentina in 2001 has affected the economy of the entire region, and it can be said that, at the time of writing, Latin America's economy faces its greatest crisis since the Great Depression of the 1930s (UN-Habitat 2004).

Although social indicators have improved and poverty has decreased from its mid-1980s peak, in most countries in the region the levels of social welfare attained before the crisis have not been regained. Progress in reducing poverty has stopped since 1997, with poverty and extreme poverty rates remaining stable, but total numbers rising. In 2002 the number of poor were 220 million (43.4 per cent of the population), of which 95 million (18.8 per cent) were extremely poor (UN-Habitat 2004). Levels of poverty are expected to rise due to the lack of growth in GDP, particularly in urban areas. Urban poverty tripled between 1970 (44 million) and 2000 (138 million), while the number of rural poor remained stable (UN-Habitat 2004). Inequality is severe, with levels that are among the most extreme in the world,[23] and linked to ethnicity (UN-Habitat 2004).

Latin America represents the most urbanised macro-region in the rapidly urbanising world, due to a growth process that has already passed its peak. Falling rates of fertility and economic recession slowed the pace of urban expansion during the 1980s and 1990s. Natural population growth in the city, as well as demographic pressure in rural areas, are both expected to continue to slow down in the future. In addition, primate cities are losing their advantage over smaller cities due to new production trends and to the environmental and economic problems created by their sheer size. On the other hand, in some parts of Latin America city-ward migration has actually increased due to political instability and rural violence (Colombia, Peru). In addition, Central America is still under-urbanised in relation to Mexico and South America, and urbanisation here is likely to continue. Of this stabilising urban population in Latin America, 32 per cent (128 million people) were living in slums in 2001, thus representing 14 per cent of the world's slum population. This proportion is variable, with an average 35.5 per cent of the South American population living in slums, rising to 42.4 per cent in Central America[24] (UN-Habitat 2004). Thus, while rapid urbanisation continues to dominate some parts of the region, structural urban change is more important in most countries of Latin America – all with still relatively high poverty and growing socio-economic polarisation.

Housing issues in Latin America

Latin American housing

Traditional forms of housing developed in different parts of Latin America under the various social, economic, cultural and environmental influences as described in Chapter 4. Paul Oliver (1997) divides Latin America into eight regions with their distinctive housing forms, some of which continue to exist in rural areas, others having been adapted in self-built homes in informal settlements in urban areas (see Appendix G). Although there was some degree of continuity in housing form in some areas, colonisation drastically affected the lives and traditions of the indigenous population, including the provision of housing. In many rural areas traditional housing forms and processes disappeared, whilst in others they have survived. Urban civilisations saw their cities destroyed and replaced with new town layouts which were the physical framework for urban housing, which was largely self-built. The indigenous population, however, normally had to live in segregated areas, or in settlements of their own close to the new urban centres, with lower standards such as smaller blocks and narrower streets.

Urban growth in the nineteenth and early twentieth centuries led to provision for lower-income population by private landlords, often around communal courtyards with shared facilities, which adopted different forms throughout Latin America. This was insufficient to meet demand, and many provided themselves with shelter by building shacks on the outskirts of the growing urban areas. Housing provision was therefore already an issue in the early days of rapid urbanisation in Latin America, becoming acute in recent decades. According to Salas (1993), Latin America is characterised by an overwhelming and growing need for house building, informal sector predominance in providing shelter and a high urbanisation rate, comparable to that of core countries, with limited prospects of finding a solution to these problems.

Although housing deficit figures are controversial, they can give an approximate idea of the magnitude of the housing problem in Latin America. On the basis of defining a dwelling as a separate space with independent access that can be used as a living space, the Economic Commission for Latin America (CEPAL) estimated housing deficit in Latin America to be as much as 35 million units, whilst more pessimistic estimations cite 50 million (Salas 1993). It has been estimated that about 60 per cent of housing provision is met by the informal sector, very often in vulnerable areas,[25] with few services and overcrowding. Levels of service provision diverge widely from extremely low levels in the poorest countries (e.g. Haiti and Bolivia), through to much higher levels in other countries (e.g. Argentina) (UNCHS 1996: Table 16). The high urbanisation rate makes the housing shortfall a more pressing problem in urban areas but, on the other hand, it is in these areas where the levels of service provision are higher.

Salas (1993) estimated that 35 per cent of Latin American households would be unable to meet the costs of a house built to minimum standards (such as those developed by international aid agencies) even if they devoted their entire income during six years. Estimations of the number of houses built annually in Latin America are difficult to make, especially due to the large and usually unregistered contribution of the informal sector. However, the perception is that housing deficit is growing. In order to trace the responses to housing problems in Latin America, this section now looks at how the role of four actors – the state, the private sector, NGOs and the community – has evolved during the twentieth century. It ends with a look at rental housing.

The state

The state began to adopt a proactive role in providing housing in Latin America during the 1940s, following Western models, when a series of short-lived socialist experiments (Brazil, Mexico, Venezuela) developed European-type public housing for rent, associated with the modern movement in architecture. These imaginative and highly visible projects were, however, of little quantitative significance. This approach was discontinued during the 1950s, when housing was seen as a consumption good or as social overhead capital, and governments focused on national development plans as a way to provide the economic growth that was thought to be needed to 'modernise'. However, rapid urban growth and the proliferation of slums and informal settlements became a cause for concern during the late 1950s and early 1960s. The assumed relationship between slums, social problems and political subversion led to political pressures for improved housing, tending to override the economists' argument. In addition, at the height of the Cold War, the US government established the 'Alliance for Progress' in Latin America, with a major emphasis on US funding for housing.

Again, experience in the core countries was drawn on for: (a) housing solutions, especially European solutions then enjoying high prestige; and (b) a body of social theory, developed especially in the United States (see Box 7.1). The European model was based on direct provision by the public sector of subsidised mass 'public housing', i.e. normally completed housing units in often large-scale 'schemes' built to 'modern minimum standards'.[26] Owner-occupation through mortgages was favoured over the European solution of housing for rent, thus reflecting growing US influence in the 1950s. Predominant urban policies in Latin America in this period were provision of public housing for a state-linked labour force, and slum clearance and transfer of slum dwellers to public housing.

Housing agencies were normally new central government ministries of housing or semi-autonomous agencies. Financing was heavily dependent on foreign funds at subsidised interest rates. These public housing approaches tended to fail for the same reasons as elsewhere in the rapidly urbanising world: remote un-serviced locations, inadequate dwelling space, lack of opportunities for income generation, high costs and lack of accessibility to the lowest income brackets.[27] The failure of public housing provision to meet the growing demand for housing in the low-income sector of the population led the state to concentrate on the provision of land and finance.

In quantitative terms, state land allocation in Latin America has more often taken the form of allowing or recognising the illegal occupation of public land. Experience has been varied, ranging from allowing or encouraging 'illegal' land occupation to opposition and evictions. However, in general the state has tolerated the establishment of informal low-income settlements on 'illegally' occupied land, an approach that Gilbert and Ward (1985) considered effective in maintaining existing social and economic systems. This approach has been seen as favouring the interests of various actors in Latin America:

- the elites, through safeguarding private property and land values by segregating land (see below);
- industrial and commercial interests, gaining from a cheaply housed low-wage labour force;
- politicians, increasing constituencies and patronage in informal settlements;
- the state bureaucracy, increasing its fiscal base and opportunities for bureaucratic expansion.

The latter, however, is also the most threatened by informal settlements, because it is usually legally responsible for the provision of infrastructure and services, a responsibility that is often difficult to meet and leads to pressures from different sources.

Whatever the motivations, in recent years Latin American state agencies have experimented with both supply and demand instruments to stimulate production of formal housing. A key supply-side instrument is land banking and development. A demand-side instrument used in several Latin American countries is direct subsidies to households,[28] which are predicated on economic growth to finance such subsidies, have generally provided expensive complete housing units, and have had little impact on the housing needs of the low–moderate income majority, though more recent programmes are diversifying in the type of housing investment they support and in the range of subsidies (Ferguson and Navarrete 2003).

The private sector

Private entrepreneurs developed tenements in many Latin American cities in response to the development of docks and industry in the late nineteenth and early twentieth centuries and the resulting housing need. These often consisted of dozens of rooms built on both sides of narrow patios or a central corridor with common privies and wash basins (Hardoy 1982). Following rent freezes in the early 1900s, private developers later switched their attention to land speculation, and to the provision of serviced plots for the middle classes.

Privileged sectors of society have been able to benefit from informal settlements. When invasions have been confined to public land and illegal subdivisions to clearly demarcated areas, this has served to reinforce the value of middle and high income areas. In addition, landowners participate in the sale of land to the poor, sometimes through the state as an intermediary after the invasion of private land, other times through the illegal subdivision of land in which property developers do not have any interest. Squatter settlements also offer a consumer body to the producers of building materials, produced predominantly in the private sector.

The private sector is also increasingly becoming involved in housing finance through the provision of microfinance, which was initially set up to support micro-enterprise, but has been taken up by low- to moderate-income households mainly for home improvement and expansion. This type of finance is attractive to such households because it supports an incremental building process and avoids the long-term and large-scale commitments a mortgage entails. In addition, it addresses the fact that most of the mortgage systems that had been established in Latin America in the 1960s and 1970s, which reached middle-income groups though not low- and moderate-income households, collapsed during the 1980s' crisis (Ferguson and Navarrete 2003).

Non-Governmental Organisations

Latin America has a long tradition of Non-Governmental Organisations (NGOs) working in low-income settlements in programmes to improve housing conditions or improve basic services, often as a result of initial engagement in community development. The role of NGOs increased during the 1980s, as a result of the withdrawal of the state. Sánchez (1994) suggests that NGOs in Latin America have gone through three stages: (a) as philanthropic institutions led mainly by the local oligarchy, and with no alternative political agenda (1940s to 1960s); (b) benefiting from international donations and focusing on social assistance, emphasising longer-term strategies and based on a variety of development styles (1960s to 1980s); and (c) increasingly supporting communities in engaging with market-oriented development, often contesting the dominant context of neo-liberalism (1990s).

In relation to housing, in recent years NGOs in Latin America have been involved mainly with facilitating access to finance, especially in countries where new housing finance systems based on one-off grants and subsidised loans have been introduced (see above).[29] Although NGO activity in housing in Latin America has provided useful lessons, especially in relation to housing finance, the scale of housing construction achieved by or through these organisations is very low in relation to the overall need for housing in the region and they serve perhaps as pioneers in new solutions as well as advocacy organisations.

Self-help housing

Housing, traditionally built by its occupants in rural areas, was increasingly provided this way in urban areas too. Whereas at the end of the nineteenth century few cities in Latin America had areas of self-help housing, by the beginning of the 1990s the percentage of people living in self-help settlements ranged from 26 per cent in Bogotá to 60 per cent in Mexico City (see Table 10.1). The growth of self-help took off after 1945, and during the second half of the twentieth century the majority of poor Latin American families provided themselves with shelter through their own efforts.

This reliance on self-help is mainly due to the inability of the formal sector (state and market) to meet the housing needs of the poor. However, this does not explain fully why the level of self-help is so high in Latin American cities in comparison with cities in other rapidly urbanising countries. Gilbert (1998) suggests three further factors have contributed to the rise of self-help housing in Latin America: improvements in mass transport permitting urban expansion; the benign attitude of the state, not only tolerating but in some cases even encouraging self-help housing; and the growing ability of most governments to provide services and infrastructure to new urban areas.

Table 10.1 Trends in self-help housing in selected Latin American cities

City	Year	Per cent of population in self-help settlements
Mexico City	1952	14
	1966	46
	1970	47
	1976	50
	1990	60
Lima	1956	8
	1961	17
	1972	24
	1981	32
	1989	38
Caracas	1961	21
	1964	35
	1971	39
	1985	61
	1991	42
Bogota	1955	40
	1965	43
	1975	30
	1985	31
	1991	26

Source: Gilbert, 1998: 82

The prominence of self-help in Latin America is reflected in the relative abundance of research into the phenomenon in this region, including Mangin and Turner's influential writings (see Chapter 7), which were based mainly on the self-help strategies followed by poor households in the *barriadas* of Lima. These writings later provided the basis for the debate on self-help housing that dominated the literature on housing in the 'developing world' during the 1970s and 1980s.

How land is occupied depends on local circumstances, but generally much land occupation in Latin America is undertaken by organised groups of households. These community organisations usually plan land invasions to minimise the chances of eviction by targeting certain types of land (publicly owned or belonging to foreigners or members of the political opposition), choosing certain dates, negotiating with public authorities, etc. Their main objective is to avoid eviction; this does not necessarily mean owning title deeds, but rather the certainty that they will be allowed to remain on the land. Once land has been claimed, the process of consolidation of individual homes and communal services and infrastructure commences, gradually leading to the consolidation and improvement of the settlement (see Figure 10.7). While building one's home tends to be a household issue, obtaining services and infrastructure tends to keep community organisation together, with community leaders and authorities entering negotiations which tend to rely on deals often related to party politics.

Rental housing

The growth of informal settlements has led to a marked increase of owner-occupiers in Latin American cities, who do not necessarily have legal titles to the land, but do exercise *de facto* tenure rights. However, although renting tenants have fallen in relative terms, in absolute terms they have increased – for example Gilbert (1998) cites the case of Mexico City, where tenant households increased from 484,000 in 1950 to 1.2 million in 1980. Renting among the urban poor in Latin America was virtually ignored by the academic community during the 1970s and 1980s, when the debate was dominated by issues related to self-help housing. However, some research during the 1990s has addressed this form of housing and re-assessed its importance (UN-Habitat 2003b).

The typical tenant location is still the central city, as it was before the massive growth of peripheral informal settlements. Older informal settlements, with a well-developed infrastructure and services, provide rental accommodation which has to an extent replaced that lost in city centres through tenement demolition. This has led to a shift from landlords owning large numbers of properties in tenement slums to landlords with only a few tenants in consolidated informal settlements. Research has shown that tenant–landlord relationships are different in the two types of location. The former tend to be conflictive, with often organised tenants and landlords who, due to rent controls, might not be interested in maintaining properties and want to sell. Relations in informal settlements tend to be less confrontational, and evictions uncommon. Tenure length tends to be long,[30] especially in central areas (Gilbert 1998).

The predominant ideal in Latin America is home ownership. Tenants who do not eventually move to owner-occupation are constrained sometimes by high costs, other times by the inconvenience of what is available – distant and poorly serviced settlements. Where incomes are low and rents are rising, poor families have no other choice but to take part in a land invasion or to buy a cheap plot in a distant settlement. Another alternative to home rental is sharing, which

10.7 Informal settlement in San José, Costa Rica (Harry Smith)

is common in cities where rents are high and plots expensive (see e.g. Gilbert 1983, 1998).

In conclusion, it is clear that in Latin America, in general, despite the huge growth in owner-occupation, home rental is still an alternative for a large number of the population. For poor households, this alternative has increasingly been provided by small landlords in self-help settlements, rather than by the state or the formal market.

Urban development and planning in Latin America

Changes in the urban economy

Deregulation of production processes and labour markets has become dominant throughout the continent. Tax-free zones and assembly plants have been set up for international markets, and new types of urban services have been expanding. However, manufacturing jobs have been lost in order to increase productivity and competitiveness in the world market. The public sector, a large employer in Latin America, has also shed jobs. Job creation has therefore not kept up with job demand due to urban population growth, and unemployment levels have increased, with growing reliance on the informal economy, sometimes through dramatic changes.[31]

These changes are having an effect on the territorial distribution of the population, with a reduction in the levels of urban primacy and city growth in the most economically active regions, and increasing growth of middle and small sized urban areas, though linked to metropolitanisation. The increasingly competitive environment of the global economy is seeing higher competition between cities and city regions rather than between nation states, often hinging on prestige developments that seek to attract large service and financial sector international firms and wealthy residents, such as waterfront developments. However, these developments are increasingly removed from the social and economic reality of the majority of the population, reinforcing the pattern of increasing segregation and polarisation outlined in Chapter 3.[32]

Somewhat counter to increasing inter-city competition are the efforts to provide economies of scale, returning to the ideas of regional economic integration of the 1960s, through a revitalisation of economic blocs modelled on the European Union, such as Mercosur, which was established in the early 1990s. Central to these strategies of economic integration is the provision of a major transport infrastructure to link up the major cities in the region; however, such initiatives have been difficult to implement due to the predominance of competition, as well as to changes in national governments which affect international relations and therefore the continuity of major cross-border projects.

Urban governance: decentralisation, democratisation and governance of metropolitan areas

Since the late 1980s there has been a generalised reform of local government throughout Latin America, in parallel with the return to democracy. Local government reform has two components: devolution of power from the centre to sub-national governments (decentralisation); and the increased inclusion of civil society in decision-making at a local level (democratisation).

Decentralisation has been implemented in most Latin American countries in different forms, devolving power to regional governments in some cases and to municipal governments in others, depending on the administrative structure of each country. In this, Portuguese and Spanish legacies have had an impact. Portuguese local authorities traditionally had more power, making Brazilian municipalities the most autonomous in the region and with one of the highest shares of public sector expenditure, especially after decentralisation programmes in 1988. Brazilian municipalities are thus now not only responsible for a range of services including land-use control, but also share responsibilities with state governments in other areas. Despite sweeping reform throughout Spanish-speaking Latin America, municipal government spending and responsibilities have not generally reached the same levels as in Brazil. However, there has been a uniformly upward trend in local authorities' share of tax revenue expenditure, though it is still modest. The experience of decentralisation has ranged from full devolution, through de-concentration, to privatisation. This variety has been linked to the diversity of reasons for decentralisation throughout this macro-region, ranging from central government responding to debt problems by passing functions down the line, to political purposes related to certain interest groups, and aiming for increased transparency and accountability in order to increase legitimacy (Manor 1999, in Stren 2000). Another explanation argues that many governments (encouraged by international agencies) were led to decentralise because of the generalised fiscal crisis, combined with continuing urban growth, unmet demand for local services and pressure from new social movements (Nickson 1995, in Stren 2000). Whatever the reasons, decentralisation has shifted towards municipalities an increasing share of public sector activity, though this is still well below that prevailing in core Northern countries.

Another aspect of the change in urban governance in Latin America is democratisation. Significant trends have been direct local elections and increasing participation of civil society in decision-making and service delivery. There has been a growing recognition of the importance of civil society in various aspects of urban development, particularly land development and housing, and this is currently a much debated issue, with great emphasis on participatory democracy versus representative democracy in local government. A case in point is the

Central American countries that emerged from years of armed conflict and started using open consultations (*cabildos*) and other mechanisms during post-war reconstruction. Another example is participatory municipal budgeting, as practised in a considerable proportion of large Brazilian municipalities, where neighbourhood and higher level committees, directly involving citizens, periodically make decisions on allocations of a proportion of the city's capital budget. These processes have been strongly linked to the rise of left-wing political parties – long-standing authoritarian traditions and traditions of alternation between largely conservative political parties are being broken, with alternatives such as parties representing indigenous peoples or broad left-wing coalitions rising to power. In addition, local governments are increasingly experimenting with participatory processes. This is still a process in the making, and the ways in which civil society can participate in local government are still subject to debate and conflict.

Finally, urban governance is becoming increasingly complex in the growing poly-nuclear metropolitan areas, which invariably fall within the jurisdiction of several authorities, sometimes a collection of municipal authorities, other times a combination of local and higher level administrative bodies. Urban issues increasingly tend to have impacts across these metropolitan areas, but institutional arrangements capable of dealing with these at a strategic level and of addressing the growing geographic distribution of inequality within metropolitan areas, are usually lacking.

Urban planning and management

Generally urban planning in Latin America is based on the use of zoning and urban codes specifying land use, densities and various physical parameters, usually embodied in city-wide master plans. Such plans may have an impact on physical development of some areas, but are irrelevant in the large informally developed areas of which urban growth increasingly consists. Although there are examples of planned cities (Brasilia, Ciudad Guayana – as seen above) and of cities where planning has had a strong guiding role in urban development (Curitiba – see Figures 6.3 and 8.4), provision of planning frameworks is patchy throughout Latin American cities, largely due to the traditional weakness of local government (at least in Spanish Latin America) and therefore its lack of capacity, with smaller cities often having to depend on plans being produced by central government agencies. Cunningham (1980) noted that constraints on planning in much of Latin America included poor planning facilities, few planners, administrative and financial constraints, and narrowness in the concept of urban planning and its objectives. The narrow physical remit of these plans is compounded by the lack of co-ordination between urban planning agencies and agencies for other sectors, for example housing and transport (Ward 1996). Other authors (Gilbert

1996; Rolnik 2000) have noted the lack of impact of urban regulations on the increasing process of spatial segregation – and even its underpinning of this (Lungo and Baires 2001). In fact, market forces have often been stronger than regulatory forces, with elite areas being protected by high land values and high costs of land servicing, and with government agencies following such market forces through providing services in the first instance to those areas that could pay (Gilbert 1996).

Nevertheless, it has also been argued that Latin American urban governments have managed to cope relatively well in providing infrastructure and services during a period of extraordinary urban growth and general lack of resources, with levels of provision of water, sewerage and electricity to urban populations generally improving over the last few decades despite economic stagnation (Gilbert 1998). Such provision was increasingly in the hands of state agencies until the 1970s, though this tended to politicise their delivery through clientelism, and also to underpin top-down decision making. Structural adjustment in the 1980s led to the reduction or elimination of subsidies to some of these services, causing public unrest and riots, a reaction that has continued to date in response to the ongoing drive for privatisation of public utilities.

In contrast to relative state withdrawal from direct subsidised infrastructure and services delivery, there is an increasing trend to recognise the informal city and to try to redress its low levels of servicing. Whereas in the 1950s and 1960s the state engaged in massive slum and informal settlement removals, there is now a widespread – though not universal – acceptance in many Latin American government agencies that the way forward for informal settlements is their improvement. Some local governments are therefore attempting to scale up slum improvement, as called for in the Cities Alliance's 'Cities Without Slums' action plan (see Chapter 8). Notable examples are the Favela-Bairro programme in Rio de Janeiro and the Plano Resolo in São Paulo (see Riley *et al.* 2001). There are limitations, however, to what such programmes can do to address spatial segregation, the intensification of which can be seen in the gentrification of historic city centres that have benefited from government funding, the concentration of investment on high-profile projects targeting international investors, and the proliferation of high-income gated communities served by nearby shopping malls.

The growth of participatory approaches to local government has also affected planning, with citizens increasingly being invited to participate in planning processes either within wider participatory budgeting frameworks such as in Porto Alegre, Brazil (Baiocchi 2004) or directly in plan preparation. A particular type of planning that has been experimented with in Latin America in recent years, with participation as one of its key tenets, is strategic planning. According to Steinberg (2005), this is characterised by its adaptable methodology, its focus on local development and strategic interventions, its use to promote progressive forms of governance involving public and private urban stakeholders, its participatory and democratic nature, and its facilitation of urban management during times of frequent and substantial change. Steinberg's comparative analysis of strategic planning in nine cities in five Latin American countries led him to conclude that the success of this approach depends on political will, the institutional framework, thematic focus, participatory and technical processes used and technical capacity. Indeed, what Latin American experience in planning generally shows is the key importance of political aspects, which in the case of strategic planning is clearly manifest for example in the instances of discontinuation of such plans due to changes in political leadership.[33] Although varying in success, strategic planning is a positive move away from the traditional spatial 'grand planning', towards more flexible and participatory forms of urban planning and management.

Urban environmental issues

The massive expansion of Latin American cities has created problems related to both the brown and green agendas. Some of the problems related to health and safety issues in the low- and moderate-income informal settlements can be addressed through improvement of infrastructure and services, which can come about as a result of negotiation between community organisations and the relevant authorities and agencies or through upgrading programmes and projects. However, it is more difficult to address the risk generated by informal settlements being in vulnerable locations – a factor that can lead services agencies and local authorities to refuse to provide services that might consolidate the settlement, but leads to prolonged situations of poor environmental standards if alternative land is not immediately available. Latin American cities also suffer environmental problems because of relative wealth, particularly through pollution. In the larger mega-cities, air pollution caused by both growing car use and unregulated industry has become a major source of concern. In some cities, measures to control car use have been introduced with varying results, and there have been some attempts to improve public transport as a way to induce modal shift. Water pollution is also severe, as sewage treatment is often non-existent, and effluent is discharged raw into water courses.

In terms of the green agenda, some cities are beginning to suffer the direct consequences on their ecological footprint, with water tables being depleted and even causing subsidence (Mexico City), increasing contamination of agricultural land by sewage, or logging in the surrounding hills increasing the frequency and severity of flash floods (San José, Costa Rica), etc. (Rowland and Gordon 1996).

Finally, there are many areas in this macro-region where human settlements are exposed to climatic and geological hazards. Hurricane Mitch was described as having set back development by a couple of decades in the Central American countries it affected in 1998. Earthquakes regularly hit cities along the Andean ridge and in Central America and Mexico, causing much devastation. The effects of such occurrences could be much reduced through careful location of settlements and use of more appropriate building standards, but these are unlikely given the lack of resources and capacity.

Prospects for the future

There is a considerable range of diversity in levels of 'development' throughout Latin America, from low-income countries to countries that decades ago appeared to be developing along the lines of European countries. Within this diversity, Latin American countries generally had attempted to follow developmentalist paths and had achieved some level of diversification in their economies, including industrial production, though constrained by 'resource bondage' and 'technological rents'. The crisis in the 1980s – leading to 'debt peonage' – and subsequent economic policies have taken this macro-region back to relying on exports, though this is no longer only based on minerals and agricultural products. However, production that complements these traditional exports tends to be in low-paid industries (such as the *maquilas* – assembly plants which receive materials and parts from a foreign market to which the finished product is returned, particularly in Mexico), the future of which is uncertain in the face of growing competition from, for example, China. In addition, evidence shows that this macro-region faces persistent and worsening poverty, as well as widening income inequality. Thus although the form of urbanisation is changing, the nature of the impact of rapid urbanisation, and the fragile nature of economic development in global contexts, provide continuing challenges for the macro-region in planning and housing responses.

However, also in this context, more open and inclusive forms of local governance and planning approaches are beginning to be experimented with, potentially providing means to address income inequality, if perhaps not overall levels of poverty. Although not necessarily restricted to left-wing governments (whether local or central), such more participatory approaches are generally associated with the political ascendancy of the left, which looks set to continue in the immediate future. This trend can be seen in recent electoral results in various Latin American countries where long-established and traditional 'conservative' parties are being ousted from power. In local government, therefore, and in urban planning as part of this, there appears to be an opening up of spaces for negotiation where civil society is finding an opportunity to engage in debates over priorities in public spending and urban management. It remains to be seen how far these spaces for negotiation will allow redressing of inequality in terms of service provision and spatial segregation, and what boundaries the political and economic elites will seek to protect. It is clear that such boundaries are under pressure from a civil society that started to organise with the growth of urban social movements in the 1960s and 1970s, and is continuing to find innovative means to engage with the state or to self-organise. Some of these innovations are responses from long-suppressed ethnic groups (the rising *indigenista* movements), others are responses to severe economic crisis within societies that had achieved relatively high levels of 'development'. The latter responses could hold valuable lessons for those sectors of urban society in the core countries that are increasingly segregated from core capitalism, while the new participatory approaches to local government and planning could be relevant to both core and rapidly urbanising countries, though only through appropriate contextual political economy analysis.

Chapter 11
Urban development and housing in East Asia

Introduction to the region

The physical and historic context for urban development

Although the term East Asia has been used widely over the recent years, there is no common definition of what constitutes this region. *United Nations World Urbanisation Prospects (the 2003 Revision)* used the terms 'Eastern Asia' and 'South-eastern Asia'. Eastern Asia consists of China (including Hong Kong and Macao), Democratic People's Republic of Korea, Republic of Korea, Japan, and Mongolia. South-eastern Asia includes Brunei Darussalam, Cambodia, Democratic Republic of Timor-Leste, Indonesia, Lao People's Democratic Republic, Malaysia, Myanmar, Philippines, Singapore, Thailand, and Vietnam. In other UN documents, the same region of 'Eastern Asia' is referred to as 'North and East Asia'. In academic publications, the region normally referred to as East Asia also varies. Besides China, Japan, Korea and Mongolia, academic definitions of East Asia may include some countries listed in the UN's South-eastern Asia group. This chapter aims to examine urban planning and housing changes and discuss some of the distinctive features in the rapidly urbanising countries in East Asia, adopting a loose definition of the region and focusing mainly on China (including Hong Kong) and Singapore, with some references to South Korea and Vietnam.

Although the number of countries included is small, the region covers a very large territory. China is the largest country in the region (about 5,000 kilometres from north to south and from east to west) with many different geographical features. The hills, mountains and plateaus in the west which cover two-thirds of the country's total land area are only inhabited by one-third of its population. This landscape provides favourable conditions for developing a diversified economy. Plains are mainly located in the east, though the southeast is mainly hills. Because the hills, mountains and plateaux are very high, only about 10 per cent of the total land area is cultivated for agricultural production. Population and economic activities are concentrated in the much more limited areas of great plains, valleys between mountains and hills, and river deltas. Singapore is a small tropical island country between Malaysia and Indonesia, with a total land area of 692.7 square kilometres. Despite its small size, Singapore is a focal point for South-east Asian sea routes. The majority of its population is of Chinese origin.

East Asian countries have a very long history of civilisation and development. Traditional government in the region was essentially shaped by complete supremacy of the monarch and Confucianism. Divine rights of the rulers and Confucianism were based on the tradition that all power and authority flowed from the emperor or ruler, whose interests were considered paramount. The tradition of public service was very weak, as often governors or local officials were appointed from above and were removed not because of their poor record of service to the people, but because they displeased the Emperor or the rulers.

China (about one-fifth of the world's population) is one of the world's oldest civilisations, with about 4,000 years of written history. Since the First Emperor (Qin Shi Huang) of the Qin Dynasty – who is often associated with the building of the Great Wall – established the first centralised, unified feudal state in 221 BC, through dynasty after dynasty, China has experienced about 2,000 years of the feudal system.

> The centre established law and a mechanism of rational administration, where office holders were recruited by examination, and the economic base of the system revolved around peasant agriculture. The society was ordered around family, kin network, clan group and language group. The culture celebrated family and ancestors and had religious expression in the traditions of Confucianism, Buddhism and Islam.
>
> (Preston 1998: 25)

One of the outstanding features of Chinese civilisation is its age and its continuity. China today is remarkably homogeneous in language, culture and tradition. The Han people, the main nationality of China, who have a common written language with several distinct dialects, make up approximately 92 per cent of the total population. The other 8 per cent of the population is made up by over 50 ethnic minority groups who mainly live in the mountainous and hilly regions.

China's economy grew substantially between the fourteenth and twentieth centuries. However, two features distinguish this growth from the modern economic growth in the Western countries following the Industrial Revolution. First, since the fourteenth century, the level of technological change was in no way comparable to that of the industrial revolution in the West. Economic growth in the five centuries before 1840 was accompanied by few major changes in technology and thus it was characterised by an increasingly complete exploitation of available land resources instead. Second, economic growth was accompanied by a substantial growth of population, which, although the evidence is inconclusive, probably prevented a long-term rise in per capita income and possibly caused it to fall. China's huge size and its legacy of political and cultural unity had both favourable and unfavourable implications for modern economic growth. A comparison of pre-industrial Europe with China by the World Bank suggests that it may have been the diversity of Europe rather than the homogeneity of China that was conducive to industrialisation and modern economic growth. Europe's pluralistic institutional structure stimulated dynamic and individualistic innovation, as well as the introduction and diffusion of new technologies and ideas. Effective control and the preservation of unity seem to require strong restraint on independent centres of initiative in thought and economic action, but economic progress demands the mobilisation of popular enthusiasm, energies and talents (World Bank 1984).

The Chinese system had a wide influence in the historical development of East Asia. It played a role of central power and exercised its influence over many tributary states over different periods, such as Korea and Vietnam. Early Japanese civilisation was also modelled on the Chinese system. However, Chinese influence in East Asia was weakened by the Emperor's decision in the mid-sixteenth century to withdraw from trade and turn inwards. 'This decision … coincided with the start of the expansion of Europe so that when the traders arrived in East Asia they found the region without major established competitors' (Preston 1998: 25).

Colonial development in East Asia was essentially based on trade, and modern forms of economic production were not initiated on a large scale. Western powers and the Japanese established their own areas of influence. The British colonised Singapore and the Malay Peninsula and some other islands; the French took control of Vietnam, Laos and Cambodia; the United States controlled the Philippines; and the modernised Japan occupied a large part of North-east Asia including Taiwan and Korea. China was not colonised entirely, but because of the gradual collapse of the Qing dynasty and the succession of weak and incompetent governments that followed, the major imperial powers established trading concessions in various parts of the country. The Second World War swept away the established colonial/ imperial system in East Asia, and a nation-building phase began with independent states emerging. China, Mongolia, North Korea, Vietnam and other Indo-China countries became socialist following the Soviet model. During the Cold War period, the region was divided into two interlinked groups: Japan, the Newly Industrialised Countries (NICs) and South-east Asia on one hand; and China with Indo-China on the other (Preston 1998).

East Asia is one of the fastest urbanising regions after the Second World War, where many countries have also experienced dramatic economic growth. Cities on the forefront of global economic restructuring (see Chapter 3), such as Hong Kong, Singapore, Seoul, and Taipei, enjoyed unprecedented growth rates of more than 10 per cent per annum throughout the 1970s and the early 1980s. All of these cities now rank among the top trading cities in the world, with the level of gross national product per capita in Hong Kong and Singapore exceeding that of many European countries. Similarly, rapid urban transformation is now being seen in the 'new' newly industrialising economies of Malaysia, Thailand, and Indonesia (Montgomery *et al.* 2004). At the national level, however, some countries in the region remain predominantly rural. China, for example, has a GNP per capita that places it in the lower middle-income range, but some large cities in the country resemble the rapidly developing patterns observed in other parts of East Asia. Its coastal region in particular has witnessed very rapid urban and industrial development since 1978. The Pearl River Delta region, the Yangtze River Delta region, and the areas surrounding the national capital Beijing are some of the most dynamically developing urban regions in the world today.

The evolution of urban settlements in East Asia

Although East Asia had a relatively low rate of urbanisation until very recently, urban settlement, large and small, is not a new phenomenon. The urban system has roots that stretch deep into the region's long history. China, for example, was a pre-industrial society with many cities, including some of incredible scale. Changan, Keifeng, Hangzhou, Nanjing and Beijing have each at one time been the largest cities in the world, with populations as large as one million as long as a thousand years ago (Murphey 1980). China's feudal town system was determined by the socio-economic structure of that time. With centralised state power as the main ruling style, and a relatively large territory, a hierarchical system of administrative towns was established as early as the Qin Dynasty (221–207 BC). By the Tang Dynasty (618–906 AD), feudal centralised power reached its peak. The feudal town system developed into a mature stage with the national capital city (Changan – Xi'an today), provincial capitals and other local administrative seats as local administrative, economic and cultural centres. In the Ming (1368–1644) and the Qing (1644–1911) dynasties, for instance, beside Beijing as the national capital, cities like Chengdu, Nanjing, Fuzhou, Xian and Hangzhou were for the most part strongholds of feudal rule in the region. The *fu* (prefecture), *zhou* (sub-prefecture) and *xian* (county) cities were centres of feudal rule at the sub-province level and also centres for local handicrafts and commerce and the trade of local agricultural products (Wu 1986).

Tang Changan city serves as a good example of feudal town planning practice in China. When Tang Emperor came to power in 618, the city experienced major development for more than half a century. The city walls of rammed earth were 9.7 kilometres long from east to west and 8.7 kilometres wide from south to north, enclosing some 84 square kilometres of land. Taking account of the external palaces and gardens, Tang Changan city occupied 250 square kilometres of land, with an estimated population of nearly one million (Tongji University 1985) thus making it the largest city not only in China but in the world. Inside the walls, the city comprised three major functional areas: the palaces, the markets and the wards (neighbourhoods). The major palace areas were separated from the residential wards of the townspeople, of which there were 108. In the palace areas the Emperor's palaces were separated from the Administration area by the palace wall. Two main market places – the West Market and the East Market – were located symmetrically on both sides of the north–south axis, containing the city's major commercial activities. There were nine main streets from south to north and 14 from east to west in the city, with the 150-metre-wide central north–south street being the main axis (Figure 11.1).

Tang Changan is only one example of city development and planning in Chinese history. In Beijing, the national capital under the rule of the last two feudal dynasties, city planning and design reached another level (see Hou 1986; Wu 1986), but the main characteristics of Chinese city planning remained. The plan of the city not only had a great influence on later Chinese city development in the feudal society, but also affected city planning in other parts of Asia, with several Japanese historical cities following these patterns.

With the coming of Western imperial powers, the urbanisation process in East Asia changed in some of the coastal cities. Commercial functions gradually superseded some of the old administrative roles, and the traditional feudal control of these cities declined, Shanghai being a typical example. This city was a traditional local administrative and commercial centre for over a thousand years and by 1840 it was a compact town surrounded by a wall with about 500,000 people. The Treaty of Nanjing, signed in 1842, ended the Opium War between Britain and China and established British rights to trade at Shanghai and to station a consul there (White 1982). By 1845 the number of foreigners had increased considerably and foreign power-controlled 'concessions' were soon established. By 1915 over 46 square kilometres had become concessions for British, American, French, Japanese and those from other imperial powers. With the influence of Western technology, Chinese quarters developed rapidly as well, as did newly established industries, such as ship-building. By 1880 Shanghai had developed from a county town to a city with one million people but only 50 years later, in 1930, its population was over 3 million. After the Second World War the city recorded over 6 million people and became the largest city in the Far East.

There was no regulation or plan for this large-scale urban development. The Chinese feudal government had neither the power to make any regulation, nor the administrative skill to do so. The Shanghai Municipal Council was founded in 1854 – possibly the first local authority independent from feudal control – but it was established by foreigners and no Chinese sat on the Council until 1928. Unified Chinese administrative control only came after the Japanese Surrender in 1945 (White 1982). In the foreign concessions, foreigners built their own houses, parks, churches, schools, colleges and hospitals. They brought in their missions,

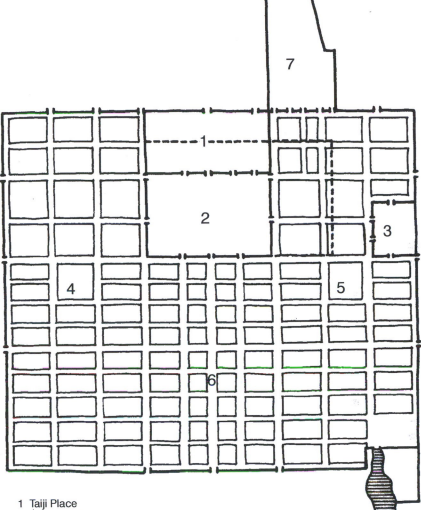

1 Taiji Place
2 Imperial City
3 Xingqing Palace
4 West Market
5 East Market
6 Wards
7 Garden

11.1 Plan of Tang Changan, China (Drawing by Harry Smith)

sporting and cultural clubs, charitable organisations and societies; and opened their bars, cafes and big hotels. In the different concessions, the roads, water, and electricity supply were separate systems.

Shanghai entered the stage of modern commercial and industrial development in the second half of the nineteenth century (Wu and Yusuf 2004). Banking, education and other services also began to develop. By the 1920s, the city had become a meeting ground for people from all countries (Figure 11.2). Ranked as the seventh largest city in the world in 1936, no modern Asian city from that period could 'match Shanghai's cosmopolitan and sophisticated reputation' (Yeung 1996: 2). However, such dramatic urban growth only happened in a small number of places in China along the coast and big rivers with significant Western influence, and the majority of inland cities retained their traditional structure and lifestyle. The lives of the vast majority of farmers in rural areas were not dramatically changed. Murphey (1970) and Chang (1976) viewed the late nineteenth- and early twentieth-century Chinese urban system as dichotomous, a system in which coastal and riverside foreign-influenced treaty ports were distinct from the great indigenous corpus of Chinese cities. The latter were interior in location and were based on local commercial and administrative functions, while the coastal ones were composed of commercial and industrial centres associated through external contacts with the world's modern economic systems.

Early and colonial urban development in other parts of East Asia resembles the Chinese experience. Traditional towns were small in scale and for local

11.2 Nineteenth- and early twentieth-century buildings on the Shanghai waterfront (Ya Ping Wang)

administration and trade purposes. National capital seats were normally well developed and there was a weak integration at regional and national levels. The arrival of colonial powers also brought rapid urban growth along the coastal areas and there was usually segregation between the local residents and colonial rulers. Singapore and Hong Kong, for example, as British colonial trading posts, were cities that consisted of foreigner quarters with surrounding largely low-rise and congested slums and squatter areas.

Urbanisation trends

According to statistics published by the UN, Eastern and South-eastern Asia had a total population of 849 million at the end of the First World War (Table 11.1). The region had a relatively low level of urbanisation, with only about 16 per cent of the population (135 million) living in urban areas. Apart from Singapore, Hong Kong and Japan, most countries in the region had less then 20 per cent of the population classified as urban residents. Urban residents in China and Vietnam were only around 12 per cent. Since then, there have been fast growth rates in both total and urban populations. In 2000, the total population in Eastern and South-eastern Asia has reached 2,001 million, of which about 40 per cent (804 million) were classified as urban (Table 11.2).

Inside the region, currently there are important variations in urbanisation levels. In the city state of Singapore and Hong Kong all residents are classified as urban. China and Vietnam saw a slow increase in urban population during the socialist period of the 1950s, 1960s and the 1970s but – while both have experienced fast growth rates over recent years – the proportion of urban population is still relatively low in comparison to the NICs in East Asia and West European countries. Because of this, the projected trend in East Asia is a very high urban population growth rate. The UN has estimated that, by 2030, the total population in Eastern and South-eastern Asia will reach 2,370 million, of which 1,471 million (60 per cent) will be urban.

East Asian urbanisation in the last five decades has been dominated by the growth of large cities (see Figure 11.3). In 1950, only five East Asian cities were among the top 30 largest urban agglomerations (ranked by population size), two in Japan and three in China. By 1960 this had increased to eight. In 2000, nine East Asian cities were in this group: Tokyo (1), Shanghai (7), Osaka-Kobe (11), Jakarta (12), Beijing (13), Metro Manila (19), Seoul (20), Tianjin (22), and Hong Kong (29). In China, urbanisation in the past five decades likewise shows a clear sign of increasing dominance by large cities. In the early 1950s, there were only five cities with over one million inhabitants, with a total population of 10 million, about 25 per cent of the total urban population. By the end of 1987 there were 23 cities with over 1 million inhabitants, accounting for a total population of 29.8 million,

Table 11.1 Population in Asia (thousands)

	1950	1960	1970	1980	1990	2000	2010	2020	2030
Urban population									
Asia	232,185	337,572	485,751	692,783	1,011,737	1,369,980	770,494	2,214,364	2,664,282
Eastern Asia	108,012	160,431	225,113	302,981	445,086	598,413	766,054	921,854	1,039,087
South-eastern Asia	27,482	41,140	61,008	91,609	138,937	206,228	282,547	359,842	432,014
Total population									
Asia	1,398,488	1,701,336	2,143,118	2,632,335	3,167,807	3,679,737	4,148,948	4,570,131	4,886,647
Eastern Asia	670,985	792,228	986,777	1,177,958	1,349,961	1,481,110	1,576,112	1,641,260	1,659,389
South-eastern Asia	178,073	222,804	285,871	358,038	439,926	520,355	594,191	659,826	711,236

Source: United Nations Department of Economic and Social Affairs, Population Division 2004

Notes: 1950–2000: estimates. 2010–30: projections

Table 11.2 Percentage of population residing in urban areas

	1950	1960	1970	1980	1990	2000	2010	2020	2030
Asia	16.6	19.8	22.7	26.3	31.9	37.1	42.7	48.5	54.5
Eastern Asia	16.1	20.3	22.8	25.7	33.0	40.4	48.6	56.2	62.6
South-eastern Asia	15.4	18.5	21.3	25.6	31.6	39.6	47.6	54.5	60.7
China	12.5	16.0	17.4	19.6	27.4	35.8	45.1	53.6	60.5
China, Hong Kong	82.6	85.0	87.7	91.5	99.5	100.0	100.0	100.0	100.0
Dem. People's Republic of Korea	31.0	40.2	54.2	56.9	58.4	60.2	63.6	68.2	72.8
Republic of Korea	21.4	27.7	40.7	56.9	73.8	79.6	81.9	84.1	86.2
Mongolia	19.0	35.7	45.1	52.1	57.0	56.6	58.0	61.7	66.9
Japan	34.9	43.1	53.2	59.6	63.1	65.2	66.5	69.2	73.1
Singapore	100.0	100.0	100.0	100.0	100.0	100.0	100.0	100.0	100.0
Philippines	27.1	30.3	33.0	37.5	48.8	58.5	66.1	71.8	76.1
Vietnam	11.6	14.7	18.3	19.4	20.3	24.3	29.4	35.8	43.2
Malaysia	20.4	26.6	33.5	42.0	49.8	61.8	68.2	73.5	77.6
Indonesia	12.4	14.6	17.1	22.1	30.6	42.0	53.2	61.6	67.7

Source: United Nations Department of Economic and Social Affairs, Population Division 2004

Note: 2010, 2020, 2030 are projections

thus increasing their share to 40.3 per cent of the total urban population. These cities are now the major administrative and industrial centres in the country. In 2001, 13 cities had an urban population (non-agricultural population only) of over 2 million; 28 cities had a non-agricultural population of between 1 and 2 million; and 61 cities had an urban population of between 500,000 and one million (State Statistics Bureau of China, Urban Social and Economic Survey Team 2003).

A short introduction to contemporary urban East Asia

Contemporary East Asian urban development has followed different routes in different geopolitical blocks. Japan, as an advanced industrial country, experienced very different urban development from the rest. China, Vietnam (and other Indo-China countries), Mongolia, and North Korea embarked on a socialist route after the Second World War, and urban development from the 1950s to the 1970s was influenced by a planned economic development approach and was isolated from the world economy. From the 1980s onward, some of these countries began to reform their economies and entered a transitional phase towards market economies. The NICs, particularly the four 'Tiger' economies, experienced fast economic and urban growth by active participation and integration with the world economic system. Living standards in cities in the NICs is very different from that in the former socialist bloc. Cities that developed under different ideologies showed very different characteristics between the 1950s and 1970s. More recently, socialist economic reform brought East Asian economies closer to each other and urban development has shown some converging features over the last 25 years, such as large-scale development of private houses and other properties, general improvement of the urban living environment, increasing numbers of cars and traffic congestion, and integration with the global economy and the use of foreign investment.

China, as the largest socialist country in the region, underwent some interesting experiences in urban development during the early years of Communism. The establishment of the new government in 1949 brought colonial control to an end. Since then urban development largely responded to industrial development, but also went through many radical transformations. The large-scale industrialisation process started with the implementation of the First Five Year Plan (1953–7), which intended to change the traditional concentration of industry in the eastern coast areas, particularly the treaty port cities. New investment, supported by the Soviet Union, was mainly directed to the inland cities (Wang and Hague 1992). These first generation industrial projects were mainly in the traditional manufacturing sectors such as iron and steel, trucks, textiles and so on.

As national development priorities shifted several times between urban-based industrialisation and rural-based agricultural growth, urban development ebbed and flowed in response to the national policy changes (Kwok 1982). In 1958 there was

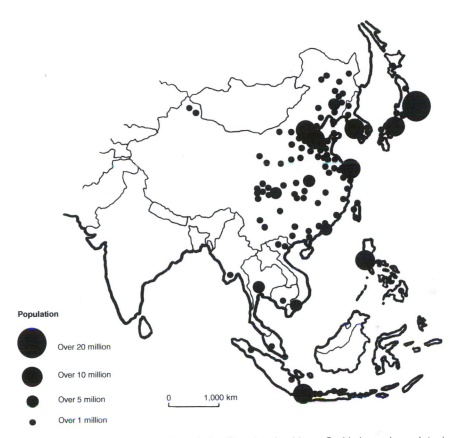

Population

Over 20 million

Over 10 million

Over 5 milion

Over 1 million

0   1,000 km

11.3 Map of large cities in East Asia (Drawing by Harry Smith based on data in UNCHS 2001)

a change with the national policy towards decentralisation and a new emphasis on the countryside, however this coincided with the withdrawal of help from the Soviet Union and a natural disaster in agricultural production. With a brief adjustment during 1963–5, urban-based industry started to again increase in strength, but the Cultural Revolution (1966–76) soon disrupted this effort and led to another process of decentralisation. Many second generation industries, such as electronics, were directed to remote areas away from major cities for defence reasons. Post-1949 Chinese urban growth was not primarily orientated to overseas trade, and thus not dominated by world markets. It was largely an attempt to create an indigenous industrial infrastructure, and to meet demands for home consumption at a time of rapid demographic change and rising consumer expectations.

Chinese city population growth during the socialist period was fuelled by both rural–urban migration and natural increase. The proportion of migration to cities changed from time to time. During 1952–60, with rapid industrial development, the average annual urban population increase was 7.8 per cent. This was considered too fast by the government, which reacted with a massive programme that relocated about 20 million people to rural areas in the following years. The Cultural Revolution period then saw a stagnation of urban population, with slow development of urban-based industry, and during 1971–8 urban population increase was controlled at about 2 per cent a year. The government considered this to be a reasonable rate which could be supported by agricultural development. Since economic reform, government control on migration has been relaxed, and temporary stays in urban areas have become possible, with now many millions of farmers moving around the country to seek employment in sectors such as building and service industries.

Economic reform has brought significant changes to China over the last 25 years. The old style of socialist economic planning has gradually given way to a so-called 'Chinese style socialist market economy'. The speed of economic growth and transformation of Chinese society has been remarkable. Throughout the reform period, China's GDP growth was maintained at around 10 per cent. Even during the late 1990s, while most Asian countries were in an economic crisis, China still achieved an annual growth of more than 7 per cent. Between 1996 and 2002, China's GDP per capita increased by 69 per cent from US$585 to 986 (State Statistics Bureau of China 2003). Fast economic growth brought a large-scale increase in personal and household incomes. Between 1978 and 1995, per capita disposable incomes more than tripled in Chinese cities. During the Ninth Five Year Plan period (1996–2000) average annual disposable income per person in urban areas increased by 47 per cent from US$516 to 757. By the end of 2002, it had reached US$928 (an increase of 23 per cent over the two-year period) (State Statistics Bureau 2003). Because of this remarkable economic growth, China has been hailed as the most successful transitional economy.

Economic growth has been accompanied by accelerated urbanisation. Between 1979 and 1999, the number of cities (administratively recognised status) in China increased from 193 to 663 (State Statistics Bureau of China 2000) and officially registered urban population has increased from 18 per cent in 1978 to 39 per cent in 2002 (State Statistics Bureau of China 2003), although this does not include the estimated 100 million rural labourers working in urban areas. Changes in the urban landscape in many cities are also striking. Old industrial facilities of the socialist period and poor quality traditional houses have been replaced by high-rise office blocks and new residential estates and the built-up areas in most cities have expanded rapidly (Figure 11.4). Beijing's built-up area has more than doubled over the last 25 years. This city's expansion towards suburban areas can be measured by the layers of new ring roads constructed, with four rings of such roads being built between 1980 and 2000, and another two under construction. Some coastal cities and towns have in fact turned into little more than huge construction sites (Figure 11.5).

11.4 Central business district of Guangzhou, China (Ya Ping Wang)

11.5 Model plan for central area of Shenzhen City (Ya Ping Wang)

Urban economies have also been transformed. There has been a steady decline of the state and collective industrial sectors, and an expansion of private sector and joint venture businesses. In 1978 almost all urban residents were employed in either the state or the collective sectors, but by the end of 2002, over 33 per cent of urban employment was in the private or 'other' sectors, including the self-employed (Ministry of Labour and Social Security and the State Statistics Bureau of China 2002). Government is by far no longer the sole job provider, and urban residents have more freedom in choosing their jobs and careers (Ma 2002). This diversification of employment and increased household income has been a factor in a significant improvement of the general living conditions in cities and towns. For 30 years after the Communists came to power, housing conditions remained very poor. Average housing floor space stagnated at merely three square metres per person and much of the housing stock was of poor quality and simple construction. The majority of urban residents had no exclusive access to a toilet or kitchen. However, reform in the housing provision system and the construction industry has revolutionised urban living. Thousands of new residential estates have been built each year and average housing floor space in urban areas had reached 20 square metres by 2001. Many families have moved into purpose-built apartments and over 80 per cent of official urban residents now own their homes (Liu 2003; Wang 2004).

In the NICs, economic and urban development went through three different phases: an international trading-based economy phase in the immediate post-war period; an industrial manufacturing and processing economy phase of the 1970s and the 1980s; and an industrial restructuring phase of moving towards a high-tech, information-based economy since the 1990s. Singapore is a good example of these shifts in urban development. Singapore is a small state, roughly 20 miles across and 15 miles wide. Apart from its geographical advantage of being located on the intersection of international air and sea routes, it has no other natural resources. When the fishing island of Singapore was bought by the British in 1819, it became a main trading post in the Malacca Straits between the Indian and Pacific oceans. Even when Singapore became independent in 1965, port-related trading was the mainstay of its economy. By then, it had had nearly 150 years of trading experience on an international basis and had become an integral part of a vast network of traders around the world. However, such business was confined to a small community in the colony and the post-colonial government recognised the need for rapid and large-scale expansion of the job market, and thus took the opportunities created by the emerging trans-national corporations to kick-start its industrialisation programme. Trans-national corporations (TNCs) were looking for cheap land and labour, Singapore having plenty of unemployed labour and being willing to trade its swampland for factories. Over the next 20–25 years, this industrialisation led to the kind of economic development of

Singapore that many outsiders have called an 'economic miracle'. Towards the latter half of the 1980s, Singapore's economic planners began to emphasise the need for the development of the services sector in addition to the manufacturing and trading of goods. It was becoming increasingly evident that Singapore's competitive edge in producing and trading in low tech, low skill and low margin products was being eroded by a number of other emerging economies in the region. If Singapore were to maintain its economic lead over its competition, there was thus little choice but to up-scale in technology and know-how, and particularly into areas which required information, knowledge and creativity (Mahishnan 1999).

Hong Kong resembles Singapore in some aspects, but it had a different development path. In Singapore, independence took place before development, and it was the independent city state that elevated Singapore to its global city status. In Hong Kong, development took place before decolonisation. It was under the colonial government that Hong Kong achieved global city status in the 1980s and the 1990s (So 2004). Singapore acts as a regional centre for South-east Asia, and it has developed extensive economic networks with the South-east Asian states. Hong Kong acts as a regional centre for East Asia, and it is deeply embedded in the production and trading networks of the East Asian states. The Cold War in Asia transformed Hong Kong from an entrepot to an industrial city in the 1970s, changing further into a service centre in the early 1990s with the Chinese national reunification project. The recent Asian financial crisis and the competition for a global metropolis have provided the impetus to transform Hong Kong into a high-tech centre in the twenty-first century (So 2004).

Current planning and housing issues in East Asia

Major themes of East Asian urbanisation

Lin (1994) investigated the urbanisation process in Asia and identified several major themes. The first one concerns the role of cities in regional economic growth. Two opposing views were identified: the first saw cities as centres of modernisation which act as catalysts for economic growth and social change. Officials and planners who supported this view suggested that planning for future development should be centred on an efficient approach to large cities. The other view saw cities as 'enclaves' surrounded by a hostile peasantry, and as parasitic institutions that permit the accumulation of capital for, and/or siphoning off of resources to, the metropolitan centres of 'developed' countries. This latter view was often related to the discussion about dualism: the co-existence of an advanced or modern sector with a backward or traditional sector – despite increases in industrial production, the number of jobs has not increased at a fast enough rate to absorb all the available labour force (McGee

1971). The study of East Asian urban development also has a strong relationship with the examination of the impacts of trans-national capital on urbanisation and spatial implications of the globalisation of production and investment. Early studies also emphasised the impacts of socialism and focused on the debates about anti-urbanism or pro-urbanism. More recently the study of metropolitan regions has been seen as a new research theme with region-based urbanisation as an alternative to that of the conventional city-based model (Laquian 2005).

While this discussion has focused on some of the early features of East Asian urban development, new features have emerged since the 1990s. Early debates about the role of cities in regional economic growth were mainly related to the socialist experiences and associated with the discussion about anti- or pro-urban development. With the progress in economic reform in socialist countries, the important role of cities in regional development has been recognised by most researchers and government officials. Throughout East Asia, urban-based economic development has been established as the main government development policy, with policy makers abandoning the anti-urban ideology.

This change in development strategy has arguably helped bring about a general increase in family income and improvement in living in major cities. However, this approach did not resolve the problems of dualism. Urban and rural differences have substantially increased in some countries, such as in China. In urban areas a well-off middle class is emerging, while quality of life in rural areas, particularly in remote rural areas, has improved very slowly. Urban-based economic activities created many job opportunities and have attracted a large number of people to cities, this large-scale rural–urban migration giving new meaning to dualism. Differences are now not only apparent between urban and rural areas, but also between different groups in cities. Government officials, professionals, enterprise owners and managers on the one hand have formed a new middle class that enjoys substantially increased incomes, quality of life and property ownership. Industrial workers and other urban low-income groups, on the other hand, have formed the new working class, facing the prospect of job insecurity, and poor pay and employment conditions, with most of the latter working in the informal sector and/or for small family-based businesses (Wang 2004).

Apart from the difference between middle and working classes, urban social structure in East Asian countries shows some other characteristics. There are large numbers of rural migrants in all major cities who are normally not counted as formal urban residents. Local governments treat them as temporary or seasonal workers, and they are engaged in the least desirable jobs on very low wages. Being temporary visitors, they are not entitled to any social and economic benefits offered to formal urban residents. However, such migrant workers in industrial factories in the Pearl River Delta, as well as in Beijing, Shanghai and other large coastal cities in China, are in the millions. In Hong Kong and Singapore most domestic workers come from other poor countries, and are also treated as temporary workers. This exclusion in citizenship discourages the gradual integration of migrants with local communities and represses labour, but is key to keeping wages for manual and non-skilled workers low and maintaining the competitiveness of the local economy in the international market.

Another feature of East Asian urban development is related to the particular regional culture through the influence of Confucianism. Literature on Hong Kong refers to the Neo-Confucian spirit of Chinese entrepreneurs and it is argued that the Confucian familism has facilitated the pooling of capital among kin, the reliance on unpaid family labour and the avoidance of bureaucratic rules among family members. The small family firm has been described as highly dynamic and able to adjust to work with the fluctuation of the business cycle, and Confucian education is said to have generated an educated workforce highly committed to work and the firm (Wong 1988).

As the Singapore experience demonstrated, East Asian NICs' successful pursuit of the goal of economic development over the post-Second World War period owed much to the strong role played by the state. Preston (1998) characterised this form of development guided by the state, as 'developmental capitalism'. The particular experiences of these countries are quite different from the models provided by the classic European and also American traditions of social science. Hong Kong, South Korea and Taiwan to some extent also owed their fast growth to strong government planning and directions, often under strong military control. The Chinese development process over the last 25 years again followed this approach. The success of economic reform owes much to the strong control exercised by the Communist government, which provided a stable social and administrative environment in which the urban-based economy has flourished.

East Asian urban development also benefited from the strong control over the urban land by municipal government. In the socialist bloc, urban land is owned by the government, which made the planning and development process simple and straightforward. Large-scale development of new housing estates, road and other infrastructure can be approved easily and constructed quickly. In Hong Kong the development right of land rests with the government, which owns practically all land and leases plots out competitively at auction for development. By adjusting the amount of land released, therefore, it can directly influence land values and, indirectly, general property prices. In Singapore much of the land development rights also rest with the government. The important tool in land assembly in Singapore is the Land Acquisition Act, which enabled the state and its agencies to compulsorily acquire any land and building for public purposes or national development, stipulating the procedure to be followed, the rules for assessment of compensation and the rate of compensation. The Act has allowed the government and its agencies to assemble fragmented land to carry out their various programmes

– between 1959 and 1985 the government acquired a total of 17,690 hectares of land, or about one-third of the total land area of Singapore (Yuen 2004: 66).

Urban economic basis

As explained previously, East Asian cities were built as regional centres in the agricultural society before the arrival of colonial powers. Most of the traditional cities were located in fertile agricultural areas away from the coast. During the colonial period, cities along the coast and major rivers began to flourish, with places such as Shanghai, Hong Kong and Singapore becoming the trading ports for the colonial powers. After the Second World War, and in combination with a nation-building process, both traditional and modern cities expanded as local and regional industrial bases during the 1960s and the 1970s. Early industrial development concentrated on the manufacturing and textile sectors (cloth, toys and other related textile products) for export. Along with international and national industrial restructuring, major cities gradually moved towards high-tech and electronic production during the 1980s and the 1990s. Household white goods gradually replaced soft toys and cloth. Older generation industrial establishments moved away from major cities and relocated to poorer countries in the region or inland rural areas. Hong Kong, Singapore, Taipei, Seoul, and more recently Shanghai and Beijing, are aiming to develop an information technology based economy (Wu 2001) and international finance and banking is increasing in importance (UNESCAP 1998).

Hong Kong, for example, has experienced a major transition from a manufacturing industrial city to a service-based economy. In the early 1980s, manufacturing was the major contributor to the total economic output, however, manufacturing at the beginning of the twenty-first century declined to only 5.9 per cent of GDP and, like in most 'developed' countries, Hong Kong's economy is now firmly based on services, representing 85.6 per cent of GDP and accounting for 83.4 per cent of the workforce in 2000 (Cullinane and Cullinane 2003: 279–88). The city possesses the busiest container port in the world. It is the world's tenth largest banking centre in terms of external banking transactions and is Asia's second largest stock market in terms of market capitalisation (GIS 2002). The major reason for the reducing significance of manufacturing in Hong Kong has been its migration over the border to the Guangdong province in mainland China. Hong Kong's direct investment in Guangdong province amounted to US$50 billion at the end of 2000, equivalent to about 40 per cent of its total direct investment in mainland China.

The large territory, population and the shared cultural and historical values in East Asia have all contributed to the development process of the whole region over time. Economic and technological development waves were pushed by the advance of capitalism from more 'advanced' locations to 'backward' areas. Because of the strong territorial and cultural connections, industrial projects could be shifted between countries and cities to take advantage of cheap labour and other resources. Taking textile and the clothing industry as an example, the four 'Tiger' economies provided the world market with a lot of cheap products during the 1960s and the 1970s. When these economies upgraded to electronic products, manufacturing and textile factories moved into mainland China which, along with Vietnam, Indonesia and Thailand, then became the main supplier of textile products to the world market. Over recent years, there is a trend towards another wave of moving manufacturing away from large Chinese coastal cities towards the inland regions to the west.

This development pattern extended the normal life of enterprises in East Asia. Rather than being closed off and stopping production entirely, factory owners can move their workshops and machinery around between countries to take advantage of the cheap labour in the backward regions. This continuity has also allowed for technology upgrading and product improvements. The overall advance and enlargement of the urban economic base has resulted in a continuous increase of the importance of the East Asian economies in the global market system. The fast circulation of investment and export across the borders is a key part of the East Asian market. The 'Tiger' economies also put a lot of emphasis on exports and tight control of imports, particularly during the early stages of development.

Urban policies and planning

Town planning has a long history in East Asia. Many historical cities, particularly capital cities such as Changan (see earlier discussion), Nanjing and Beijing, were built according to some sort of plans. These plans usually reflected the political and social organisations of the urban society at the time, including the absolute control of the Emperors and the feudal administrative system. Town planning in its modern form was only practised in some cities by colonial powers in more recent times, the two earliest modern town plans in China being those produced in 1900 by the German occupiers for the city Qingdao in Shandong province (a master plan) and by Tsarist Russia for Dalian in Liaoning province. Both plans were short lived because the plan-makers were soon replaced by the Japanese, who had a great influence over urban industrial development in China in the north-eastern part of the country. Plans for foreign occupied cities clearly showed an aggressive colonial nature, with obvious racial separation – in 'local' quarters density was higher, housing quality poor and roads narrow. Architecture in the foreign-occupied areas was in the style of the metropole.

The earliest town planning projects carried out by a non-colonial government in China were started in 1927 by the then Guomingdang Government (Republic of China). Town planning was first introduced in the capital city, Nanjing, and then other large political and economic centres. The plan of Nanjing in 1929 was a relatively comprehensive land development plan, which zoned out different functional areas such as the Central Government District, City Administration District, Industrial Districts, Shopping Districts, Cultural and Educational District and Residential Districts. This zoning experience showed clear influences from both the Chinese tradition and western practice. The Chinese style of architecture was emphasised, but the whole distribution of land use could not avoid the pattern developed in Western countries to meet industrial development. Plan implementation was interrupted by the Japanese invasion in 1937.

Urban planning during the communist period in China after 1949 followed the principles of the socialist industrial city. New planning policies were first introduced in the economic sphere, based on the Russian model of industrialisation. The first national Five Year Plan (1953–7) envisaged more than 10,000 new industrial projects, of which 921 were large and medium ones with national importance, and 156 key projects supported and designed by the Soviet Union. Those industrial projects were mainly heavy industries such as steel and iron, car and truck manufacture, airplanes and machinery (Zhou 1984). They were directed to inland urban centres such as Xian, Baotou, Lanzhou and so on, where city construction was planned around the development of these key national industrial projects. By the end of 1956 about 150 cities had some kind of plan, among them 39 new towns with extensive expansion planned in 54 others. The 1950s was thus a period of strong urban development and planning in China prior to the economic reform programme.

Urban development and planning in China experienced a period of stagnation from the late 1950s until the late 1970s, when national economic development priorities shifted from urban to rural areas. After the Cultural Revolution, however, cities became the focus again and most cities started to make urban plans or revise their old ones. Central government also started to increase capital investments in urban public facility developments. At the same time, central government permitted 41 large cities of over 500,000 people, and six other historical medium-size cities, to use 5 per cent of local total production income for urban maintenance and construction purposes. Besides industrial development, the human living environment also came onto the agenda (Wang and Murie 1999).

Unlike the previous period, lack of urbanisation at this time was seen as backwardness. Cities, as 'advanced' economic centres, were seen as means to stimulate the development of surrounding rural areas, to seek integration of the organisation of production and circulation, and to progressively establish various types of economic regions based on urban nodes. Initial emphasis of urban development policies focused on the development of small cities to avoid the problems of large industrial cities observed in the West. This approach was soon found not to be practical, however. Economic arguments in favour of high speed development also advocated the 'universality' of the urbanisation process, and cast doubt upon the idea of a lower stage of industrial development within an advanced urban system (Kirkby 1985). Subsequent policies thus favoured the development of larger and well-located cities and this led to the designation of four Special Economic Zones (SEZs) along the south-east coastal region in the early 1980s and the opening up of another 14 major cities for international co-operation. These SEZs and open cities all played a very important role in economic reform and urbanisation in the country.

As well as China, all other countries in the region also developed comprehensive urban planning systems. Singapore, for example, experienced rapid urban growth and associated economic, environmental and social problems in the 1960s: high population growth rate, poor housing conditions, stagnant economy and increasingly high unemployment (Yuen 1996). Rather than continue with the colonial *laissez-faire* attitude, the new government decided to intervene and implement proactive development policies. It played a dominant and entrepreneurial role in urban development, proactively engaging in economic development, urban redevelopment and public housing (Yuen 2004) and the government became the largest entrepreneur and developer. Two statutory boards, the Economic Development Board and the Housing Development Board were established to translate such vision and plans into concrete form.

> Singapore is one of the few countries to have at an early stage of its growth prepared and implemented a comprehensive plan for the control of urban development and growth. Following the British planning system of develop-ment plan and development control, its development plans – the statutory Master Plan and the long-range Concept Plan – have variously provided an important channel for the coordination of development activities in support of the growth of key economic and social sectors. In setting out the likely directions of future land development, the Plans demonstrate a conscientious attempt to direct urbanisation pressures towards a planned and preferred development pattern to ensure a more appropriate spatial arrangement for urban activities.
>
> (Yuen 2004: 58)

In Hong Kong, due to limitation of land, developments have always been carefully planned. Various land use plans were produced to guide the development process (Staley 1994; Ng 1999; Hamer 1997; Yeung 1997). A Metroplan, for example, was produced in 1989 to create a land-use–transport–environmental planning framework for restructuring the main urban areas. This plan set out broad land use patterns and purpose guidelines with regard to the type, form and density of different kinds of development. The overall pattern of land use was formulated within a network of highways and railways to provide for the safe and convenient movement of goods and passengers. Different from a programme of public works, Metroplan forms a conceptual strategy which could guide the selection of projects. The concepts were translated into action plans through development statements for each of the seven metro districts (Hong Kong Government 1996).

Apart from planning in the central city, Hong Kong also planned and developed several new towns in the New Territories (Lai and Ho 2001) through a programme that started in the early 1970s with the aim of reducing overcrowding in Kowloon and Hong Kong Island. From 1971 to 1991 the population of the New Territories rose by 250 per cent, from 680,000 to 2.3 million. By 2001 there were nine new towns at various stages of development which accommodated over 3 million people. Shatin New Town, located in the mid-east New Territories, has a population of 623,000 people in a development area of around 2,000 hectares. Sixty-eight per cent of these people live in public rental and subsidised housing developments, all of which are high-rise (Figure 11.6).

Similar to Hong Kong, much of the new housing in Singapore was built in new towns (Eng 1996). These new towns, identified under the long-range Concept Plan, have played an important part in redistributing urban growth to different parts of the main island. New towns are primarily planned according to the principles of neighbourhood and hierarchy of service provision, in which the distribution of activity nodes such as the town centre, neighbourhood centre and sub-centres is clearly defined. They are also different from similar developments in Europe and the United States in its high-rise, high-density form (Yuen 2004).

Urban housing policies and provisions

East Asian countries share many common features in housing policy and provision. Despite the difference in political systems, the built environment in East Asian cities has become more and more similar. The first and most important characteristic of East Asian housing provision is public sector involvement. Apart from the socialist public ownership of urban houses in China and Vietnam, Hong Kong, Singapore and South Korea all have very powerful housing authorities which have built, distributed and managed urban housing stock (Ramesh 2004).

Similar to other parts of the world, post-war reconstruction in East Asian cities led the initial development of public housing. In Singapore, housing conditions were very poor in the 1950s. New immigrants from China and India moved to the fringe of the city area and formed slums of wood, corrugated iron and scrap materials. In 1959, when the Singapore government took office, one of their most urgent tasks was to provide homes for those who needed them. A year later, the Housing and Development Board (HDB) was established to tackle the

11.6 Hong Kong Housing Authority high-rise housing in Shatin New Town, Hong Kong (Hong Kong Housing Authority)

housing shortage problem by providing basic shelter in a high-rise, high-density environment. The main emphasis was on quantity and speed of production. The flats built were predominately one-room to three-room designs until the mid-1970s. In 1984 for example, the rate of construction of the HDB housing units was one new flat built per year per nine families, or a completion rate of one unit per eight minutes. However, by contrast, the birth rate in the year was one baby every 13 minutes (Yuen 2004).

Initially, the HDB rented their units to residents, but in February 1964, an important scheme was introduced to help occupants own the flat in which they resided. This scheme was known as the 'Home Ownership for the People' scheme. Subsequently, this scheme was boosted by the introduction of the Central Provident Fund (CPF), a kind of social security fund. By 1979, the housing shortage problem had gradually become less dominant and, since then, HDB has been continually upgrading and building better quality flats. Their goal has evolved from providing basic shelter to providing affordable high quality housing. Throughout the 1970s and the 1980s, HDB continued to increase not only the number of flats, but also the number of educational, communal and recreational facilities to provide for the overall residential needs. By the mid-1980s, HDB alone was managing over half-a-million residential units throughout the island. To make management more efficient, town councils were formed to help HDB manage these housing estates. Since then, some of HDB's major functions have been handed over to town councils, especially in the areas of estate management and community development, while HDB continued handling all administrative work such as allocation, sale and rental of flats. High-rise and high-density buildings are always a main feature of all public housing estates in Singapore, with housing estates usually including predominantly 10- to 13-storey slab blocks, several 4-storey blocks and several 20- to 25-storey point blocks. Accompanying them are facilities that are relevant to meeting the needs of local residents such as car parks, hawker stalls, vegetable markets, provision shops and community centres, etc.

Although initially and principally concerned with meeting the housing needs of the urban poor, HDB's housing activities have evolved over time to include both lower- and middle-income groups. It has also extended to embrace the promotion of home ownership to virtually all residents who cannot afford private housing. Because of the high level of government involvement and the Home Ownership for the People scheme, Singapore has achieved a very high rate of home ownership (93 per cent) – 94 per cent of the HDB flats are owner-occupied units while the remaining 6 per cent being rental units. About 84 per cent of the resident population live in HDB built flats, and of the total of 1.1 million housing units in 2003, 80 per cent were HDB apartments (Wong and Yap 2003; Yuen 2004).

Hong Kong's public housing programme is also widely admired and is one of the largest in the world (Chiu 2000). There was only a minor programme of public housing for many years and a policy to support this programme came into being in 1972. Since then, public housing development has played a key role in housing development and provision. In 2003, nearly half of the population (49.6 per cent) lived in public housing in Hong Kong; 31 per cent of the population lived in rental public housing and another 18.6 per cent in owner-occupied flats sold at publicly subsidised prices. In addition, 1,074,000 permanent flats (out of a total of 2,332,000) were built by the public sector (Hong Kong Housing Authority 2003). As opposed to the poor image of public housing in Western societies, public housing in Hong Kong (and Singapore) is still one of the popular options. About 92,000 families were waiting for the allocation of public housing in 2003/4, and the average waiting time for allocation of public rental flats was 2.3 years.

Apart from active involvement in housing development by the public sector, most East Asian governments also developed innovative policies to promote home ownership. Special financial arrangements such as housing provident funds were set up to help urban families to purchase their homes. As the Singapore case shows, much so-called public housing was actually sold to residents with a subsidy rather than rented to them. Policies were also formulated to enable families to return older and smaller houses to the housing authority and exchange for a bigger one to accommodate their expanding families. Hong Kong has also actively promoted the sale of public housing. Probably the most striking housing changes have been in the socialist countries such as China and Vietnam, however. Under the traditional socialist system, most urban housing was owned by the public sector, with private property ownership kept at a very low level. In China, about 80 per cent of urban houses were owned by the public sector (municipal or work unit ownership) in 1981 (Wang and Murie 1996, 1999). After over two decades of urban housing system reform, however, most of the purpose-built public housing has now been privatised. In 2003, over 80 per cent of urban families owned their homes, most of these through buying the houses allocated to them in the past by municipal housing authorities or their public sector employers (Li 2000; Wang 2004; Wu 1996).

Much East Asian urban housing is in high-rise blocks of flats with extraordinarily high densities (Lai 1993; Chan *et al.* 2002; Yuen 2005). There seems to be an unquestioned belief that these countries' limited land area determines that public housing must be high-rise and high-density, a belief that has been propagated by planners and government officials, and is strongly supported by construction firms that profit from high-rise building. Singapore and Hong Kong adopted the overseas town planning ideology of high-rise building in the early 1960s and have strongly resisted change since. The current tallest public housing in Singapore is a 30-storey building, with plans to construct more high-rise housing (40 to 50-storey) in both the public and private sectors as the population continues to grow (Yuen 2005). Hong Kong's housing style is very similar to that in Singapore. In mainland China, most large housing estates built recently by the private house builders are also high-rise buildings.

The challenge for planning and housing in East Asia

The above sections have outlined some of the key features of East Asian urban planning and housing systems, with a focus on China, Hong Kong and Singapore. The discussion shows that international linkages and trade are an important factor in the urban development process, and export oriented industrial development was the engine of early economic and physical development in coastal cities such as Hong Kong, Singapore and Shanghai. The continuous expansion in international trade ensured a sustained growth of the Asian economies, during the post-war period. This growth, as we have indicated in Chapter 3, has also relied on high degrees of state intervention in the promotion of rapid industrialisation. The developmental states (often undemocratic) used their control of public sector investment, land and other resources to promote participation in the global market. The use of urban planning also helped to direct the desired development into favourable locations. In some sense, this integration with the global market happened on relatively less unequal terms, though the products contributed by these economies usually involved low level technologies and machinery. This national state-controlled participation in the globalisation process has helped to limit some of the negative effects of unfair trading and exploitation of the East Asian cities by the core and enable them to develop into regional economic centres in the global economic system. This feature could be one of the main differences between East Asia and some other developing countries located in Latin America or Sub-Saharan Africa. This successful integration with the world market, however, did not apply to everywhere in East Asia and is highly concentrated in major coastal cities. The development of these cities has also relied on the particular geographical and historical characteristics of individual cities or regions. As we have indicated in Chapter 3, this approach was unique in the geo-political context of the Cold War as well as the economic opportunity afforded by the seeking of lower wage options by core region manufacturing freed from regulation.

Another feature of the East Asia development is the inter-regional integration and co-ordination. Investments, technologies and resources could be transferred between different cities and countries, which enabled development waves to pass through different areas, for example from 'advanced' countries to poor ones, and from 'advanced' coastal cities to inland cities. The shared social, cultural and historical background and values helped this regional integration. This could be another difference between East Asia and other parts of the developing world. This regional integration, however, created *a core and peripheral relation within the region* (Smith 1996), which has reinforced the traditional dualism of development. Middle-class residents living in the cities at the regional core such as Hong Kong, Singapore, Shanghai and Beijing, enjoy a lifestyle which is comparable to those in the 'advanced' industrial countries, while the rest of the population live a life which is typical in 'developing' countries. Undemocratic governments have often helped to suppress the labour force and maintain the huge gap between the rich and the poor.

These characteristics have contributed to the economic success of East Asian countries. They are also the underlying reasons for many problems which challenge the policy makers in the region. Fast economic and urban development has caused a lot of concerns about environmental problems in cities. Increased wealth of the middle class has created huge demands for quality houses which, in turn, consume large quantities of agricultural land. Land shortage problems in Hong Kong and Singapore are a long-standing problem. Inside China, urban development had turned several traditional good quality agricultural areas into conurbations.

Cities in the Pearl River Delta, Yangtzi River Delta and Bohai Bay (Beijing and Tianjin region) are beginning to merge. This large-scale loss of agricultural land has posed serious questions about the sustainability of the urbanisation process. Inside each city, increased car ownership has created serious traffic congestion and environmental pollution, leading to further expansion of suburban housing estates. Dramatic increases in housing stock over a short period, particularly in the number of housing units in high-rise blocks could create more social, economic and physical problems for the future. The replacement of traditional houses with modern blocks also leads to the loss of East Asian cultural heritage.

On the social and economic side, the main challenge will be the increased gap between the rich and the poor and the urbanisation of poverty, particularly in large countries such as China. A continuous supply of cheap labour has helped the fast growth of East Asian economies and maintained the region's competitiveness in the global market. This, however, has created a large army of urban poor in many cities, including the most prosperous ones such as Hong Kong and Shanghai. In China, poverty used to be a rural issue in the past, but recent industrial restructuring has resulted in huge numbers of former state-owned enterprise workers becoming unemployed. In addition, about 100 million rural migrants are working in cities, where they are not treated equally as the local residents. This number is expected to rise in the future because the urbanisation level in China is still low. Resolving the problems of both urban and rural poverty is a long way off.

Part Four:
Conclusions

Chapter 12
Conclusions

Development discourse, planning and housing –
a continuing relationship?

This book has argued that there have been broad trends in development theory and praxis which have affected the nature of urban development itself, as well as policy and practice in planning and housing. This situation is of course continuing and current issues in planning and housing continue to be linked to current development discourse. However, the concept of 'development' – as discussed in Chapter 2 – assumes some form of deliberate and 'progressive' direction, usually as defined by national and local government (and increasingly also by supra-national institutions and non-governmental organisations) – i.e. development policy makers and practitioners – as well as the development theorists that emerged in the past 50 years. Part of the crisis of 'development' in the so-called 'developing world' is that much of what happens in reality is in fact <u>not</u> consciously directed by these actors. This is certainly the case for urban development, which is much more directly affected by broader political, economic, social and cultural trends than normative development discourse. The book has thus argued that in situations of rapid urbanisation the mismatch between normative policy, related deliberative practice and actual reality has become particularly acute.

Does this have to be so? We believe that it does not, as policy and practice should be based more clearly on actual reality. However, current actual global trends are making the discrepancies between development policy and practice and what happens in reality more acute rather than fundamentally alleviating these, and this is likely to continue unless there is a different approach. Thus, while reviewing the impact of development theory and practice on urban planning and housing in various parts of the rapidly urbanising world during the past 50 years in some detail, the book has also investigated the major political and social effects of economic globalisation on urban development trends and argued for a contextual analysis which takes the impact of this into account realistically in different contexts, and has sketched this out for some regions in a general way.

As has been seen in Chapter 2, the discourse around 'development' has become highly contested, not only within the 'developing world', but in the 'developed world'. This is reflected in the impasse in theoretical development and the proliferation of approaches to development policy and practice across the world. The book has followed a 'post-development' position, with a strong adherence to a new international political economy approach – arguably one of a number, but the one we as authors feel is most critical and relevant. In this we have argued that there is equally a proliferation of planning and housing policies and practices which can be drawn on in the rapidly urbanising world, and that a clear analysis of the political economy of the context, as well as the social and cultural context, is essential to select what is appropriate and possible in any specific context. We thus take a very 'context-dependent' approach to the subject matter.[1]

Planning and housing in the rapidly urbanising world

Approaches to planning and housing in situations of current rapid urbanisation need to be different from those in situations where urbanisation took place closely linked to economic expansion, as in the core regions from the mid-nineteenth to mid-twentieth centuries, although it is acknowledged that in these areas urban re-structuring is taking place and new forms of planning and housing provision are also emerging. The main issues that need to be faced concerning planning and housing in situations of rapid urbanisation, are:

(a)   How do the contextual trends and histories of urban development condition the realities of urbanisation, urban land occupation and forms of shelter?

(b)   What forms of investment are likely to be available in urban areas for public and private interventions, this being affected by: overall economic possibilities; governance structures which can guide and distribute economic surplus; and the socio-cultural forms of need and demand?

(c)   What are the current (formal and informal) processes for planning and housing and who benefits and how – with a particular focus on how can rising values of property in urban areas benefit the majority?

Areas which underwent rapid urbanisation in the core regions of capitalist development, with associated massive immigration to, and exploitation of, other regions of the world, have largely stabilised in terms of proportion of population in urban areas (and overall population rates); the structure of urban networks is largely in place (although subject to change as demographic changes lead to new forms of demand); and there is capacity to provide adequate shelter and public urban services for the majority. The main challenge here is the changing nature of global economic domination, with this becoming increasingly restricted to financial, high technological and knowledge sectors, with less geographic grounding in these countries, and less absorption of the working population. As such, not only are demographics changing, but also social and economic structures, and this affects the planning and housing sector. This is evidenced, for example, through the problems in providing affordable housing for key service sectors (such as nursing and teaching) in key global economic nodes such as London.

This book has argued that areas which have been undergoing rapid urbanisation in the second half of the twentieth century face a very different situation. We have distinguished three broad categories, to some extent related to macro-regional differences: regions where rapid urbanisation started in the 1980s and are in an 'urban explosion' phase (e.g. most of Sub-Saharan Africa, although not exclusively so); regions where rapid urbanisation started in the 1970s and which are now emerging from the 'urban explosion' phase, but still experience rapid growth in secondary urban areas with major urban structure changes (e.g. Latin America); and areas where rapid urbanisation began also in the 1970s, but which have reached relative stabilisation of urban populations and restructuring of urban networks, but where this still needs to consolidate in terms of service delivery and shelter and environmental quality (e.g. parts of East Asia). Not only are the trends in urbanisation different, but the (related) integration into the new global economy is different, with different opportunities for continued economic development as outlined in Chapter 3, these two factors of course being inter-related.

The main difference between these regions is to do with the gap between social needs for land, urban services and housing, the economic (and institutional) capacity to provide this – whether public, private or public–private partnerships – and the political will to use resources in this way. This in turn is related to: (a) possibilities and mechanisms for wealth creation and its distribution; and (b) the nature of state taxation and public investment. Within the global political economic parameters that the book has outlined, factors of both wealth creation and taxation are closely related to political systems and nature of governance. As we argue that the responses to rapid urbanisation – including those of planning and housing – need to be based within the parameters permitted by the global, regional and local context, the nature of the governance systems that these operate within are of crucial importance and largely condition the nature of the response.

Globalisation, urbanisation and the impact on planning and housing

Globalisation in its current phase will have a distinctive impact on urbanisation and urban development, with continued rapid spread and consolidation of the former. The three main issues are likely to be as follows:

• Increasing contestation of power based in urban areas, partly through decentralisation and partly through the growing dominance of urban economic elites, with local decision-making strongly contested as different forms of development options are pitted against one another – including endogenous and exogenous. In some contexts, while local land use decision-making may develop innovative mechanisms to engage wider groups with the intention of widening social and economic inclusion, this will be contrary to the interests of the elite and more easily avoided where states are strong in relation to civil society and social groups.

- Fragility of formal land and housing markets as these are increasingly linked to global financial flows, with tendencies for 'booms' benefiting upper income groups (who can protect themselves better) and hence the impact of 'busts' being passed on to lower income groups. This affects much wider groups where market mechanisms have penetrated more deeply and non-capitalist systems have been significantly undermined through articulation with the increasingly global capitalist system, but the commodification of land and other components of housing (e.g. materials and finance) as well as the rise of rental housing, affects a very wide range of urban populations who are only marginally linked into the economic system.

- This process drives the development of 'informal' markets in land and housing, which are less articulated to the 'formal' local or global systems, but which are affected by these as well as previous forms of socio-economic interchange (e.g. social and traditional systems). Informal forms of provision and use of land and housing are often the most utilised form in many urban areas at the periphery and in the semi-periphery, but are beginning to be of importance in the core regions also as state-mediated forms of planning and housing begin to break down as global economic trends continue.

The essential fact is that the new global economy will not expand geographically for the foreseeable future in any significant way, as argued in Chapter 3. It will in fact move geographically as finance capital seeks comparative advantages in the 'semi-periphery', but much of this investment will be short term and will avoid investment in longer-term costs such as infrastructure. As a result the local elites will be expected to provide more of this as they compete for inward investment, and this will probably be achieved largely by further exploitation of the wider urban and rural poor. Where political engagement has deepened within modern organisational forms, this process can be contested by political parties, organisations within civil society (e.g. trade unions, religious organisations and urban social movements), as well as economic groups that have lesser benefit, and this can lead to forms of negotiation such as corporatist interest groups within representative democracy, or more participatory democracy. Where modern political organisational forms are poorly developed, there is less opportunity for this form of negotiation and any negotiation will probably tend to clientelism.

In this context we argue that there is a need to develop urban development policies that reflect the real political, economic, social and cultural contexts of countries, which will vary enormously but still display features of similarity across the range. Hence there are no special planning or housing techniques for the 'developing world', but a range of actions of more or less relevance in planning and housing for different situations. These cannot be classified as 'developed' or 'developing', any more than they fit closely to the macro-regional categorisation we have suggested above. However, certain trends can be seen, and certain key issues can guide approaches to action across the range. For instance the division between urban and rural is becoming blurred in a wide range of countries, whether urbanised generally a long time ago, undergoing re-structuring of more recent urbanisation, or in the early stages of widespread urbanisation – however, the forms this urban-rural situation takes in each context will be very different (e.g. polycentric urban development in the countryside in the North and ribbon 'not urban, not rural' sprawl in parts of the South).

Again, the tools for the professional planner need to be applied differently in different situations – detailed land use planning in situations of rapid urbanisation, weak institutions and high poverty is not relevant in the way it might be in inner city re-development in older or more recently urbanised regions. However, the role of the planner to investigate what is the appropriate land use management mechanism for the actual context is essentially the same. The nature of housing demand, both quantitative and qualitative, will also vary enormously across the range of countries, as will the mechanisms to deliver this; however, the need for housing providers to analyse the nature of this demand and to understand what forms of delivery are possible and more appropriate will be not dissimilar, although the outcomes will be in different contexts.

Where urbanisation is widespread and consolidation is the main focus, the key social needs/demands in urban areas are likely to be more appropriate environmental controls and improvements to basic services for the majority, whereas the key economic focus may be enhancing infrastructure for inward investment. Both of these have strategic as well as local implications on land use. The relatively established middle classes will be in a stronger position to influence decision-making in their favour unless there are mechanisms for organisations representing the poorer minority to also negotiate. Decentralisation can be a key factor, as long as power is also decentralised. In these situations there is more opportunity for local engagement in decision-making on land, but also more opportunity for dominance of decision-making by local elites. Strategic planning is likely to conflict with local plans, and this can provide wider spaces for negotiation on both strategic and local issues. Housing is likely to be significantly provided by the market, but the differential between how this benefits the upper end through rising values, and the lower end of the market is likely to be significant, and thus there is a need for market intervention to ensure wider benefit, including specific assistance to groups which are not able to access housing through the market. Here an 'enabling market approach' is likely to have more success as market mechanisms are well established, governance regimes are relatively stable and more open to societal pressure and there is more wealth overall to be invested and/or taxed.

Where urban growth is still relatively rapid but has existed for some time, and urban systems are re-structuring, there is an important role for regional as well as urban planning, as well as continued significant needs/demands for urban services. Here the conflict over different uses or access to limited investment is likely to be more intense, yet governance systems are less likely to be open to direct societal pressure. Housing provision is likely to be partly through formal markets, mainly for upper socio-economic strata, but also skilled working and middle classes, which may be growing as the economy grows, or may be shrinking as it declines. Significant majorities may rely wholly or partially on informal housing solutions, but these will be predominantly market-based, and articulated with the formal market. There is likely to be significant conflict over resources and decision-making in this context, with strong corporatist interest groups having considerable influence on government, including the social and economic elite. An 'enabling market' approach will have limited effect in this context as the overall capacity of the market to provide for the still-growing urban population will have limits related to the comparative success (or not) of economic growth. Here there will be a need from innovative solutions to allow the formal land/planning and housing systems to be accessed by and articulated with the informal systems, and hence less focus on the 'traditional' formal roles of planning and housing provision.

In the context of rapid initial urbanisation and the commencement of re-structuring of urban systems, the capacity of the formal planning and housing systems to provide even basic public services for the majority will be limited and the benefit from these formal systems will accrue predominantly to the elite. There will be limited political will to do anything else, and limited effective political demand for this also. As such, the urban majority, mainly poor, will continue to provide for themselves on the margins of the formal system, with limited articulation with this, and a wide variety of pre-capitalist forms of provision will co-exist with capitalist forms. That said, it is in these situations that forms of land planning and management as well as housing provision can have most impact on creating wealth and reducing poverty, as well as promoting social, economic and political inclusion. However, the state and the private sector will not prioritise this as they may opt for more immediate gains through continued exploitation of the urban poor.

What are appropriate approaches for planning and housing in the rapidly urbanising world?

What form of planning can develop in these contexts? To answer this we need to de-construct what we mean by planning. The function of planning is closely linked to land rights and these have evolved from pre-capitalist systems of land rights and the systems of land use management, many of which continue to exist today in parallel with 'modern' systems developed by and for capitalism. The earliest forms of land rights are generally collective rights linked to reciprocal socio-economic systems (hunting and gathering, fishing, pastoral and basic agricultural social economies). These generally existed where natural resources were not highly contested and socio-political structures were often 'horizontal' and non-hierarchical. These societies are sometimes seen to have exhibited less exploitation but there were significant gender and age differences within them. These were slowly superseded by both collective and individual rights linked to social and political re-distributive systems associated with pastoralism, agriculture and trading societies. As populations grew in relation to resources there was also more competition within societies and polities and between these. The result was usually more hierarchical societies with higher degrees of division of labour and exploitation and more direct conflict between societies as well as differential development of classes within societies. Collective land rights came to depend on allocation by elites and also became much more complex – often constituting a bundle of rights – as were the systems of management and governance of which they were part. Re-distributive land rights underpin long periods of historically recorded development in many societies and polities across the world, such as in feudal systems. Land rights in these derived from the ultimate authority. The rise of capitalism and the development of nation states are associated with the development of exclusive individual land rights from the seventeenth century onwards. Individual land rights have, however, been mitigated by the increasing role of the state throughout the past three centuries in different forms and with different levels.

Land use allocation and forms of management have been a feature of all of the above systems, whereas 'land use planning' as 'rational' decision-making on the future use of land has developed in relation to individual land rights and state-market relations from less than a century ago, and is closely allied to the growing dominance of scientific forms of knowledge. Planning as such essentially represents the control by the state over individual land use – arguably largely to compensate for the reduction of controls which had been embedded in previous socio-political formations. Planning developed initially as mainly a local function but increasingly became a higher level strategic function as states increased their power and complexity of action. This has been to a great extent also related to the increasing complexity of human settlement – their density, proximity, diversity, nature of change, etc. – and the relations between human settlement forms and broader political, economic and social contexts. In broad terms, planning is a structured way to take decisions on (future and actual) land use, through projecting these in the future as the basis for on-going decision-making. As this form of decision-making becomes more and more complex, linked to the more pervasive role of the state in all spheres of economic and social life as well as more complex forms of land use such as growing urbanisation, plans are increasingly seen as a mechanism to provide the opportunity for broader engagement in this form of decision-making and hence the basis for legitimacy to ensure compliance. Planning is therefore essentially a form of governance.

In the past 100 years in the core countries in the North there has been a pendulum swing between stronger individual land rights and stronger collective rights (as managed by the state in modern societies), and this has been reflected in a swing between stronger and weaker roles for planning – the peak of collective rights can be seen after the Second World War, with the peak of individual rights being in the neo-liberalist doctrines of the 1980s and 1990s. The current phase of this pendulum swing is one of middle range negotiation and jointly managed action: state–market partnership (the Third Way). However, there is also a crisis in governance, represented by a dilution of the power of the nation state in relation to other levels of government and forms of authority (vertical issues), as well as the diminishing capacity of the state and hence its relations with other economic and social actors (horizontal issues). In this context, various recent approaches to land use planning and land rights have tended to stress wider social interests arguing that this has been subordinated to private (market-dominated) and public (bureaucracy-dominated) interests. This has led to more emphasis on how wider society can become involved in the decision-making process on land use.

At the same time, there has been a trend to more strategic levels of planning, including supra-national planning and supra-national foci for planning, as globalisation and trans-national activity increase in importance. Planning is thus tending to separate between, on the one hand, macro-level strategic planning and land use decision guidance, with limited structured forms of representative decision-making dominated by state interests in the face of global economic pressures, and micro-level planning on the other hand, which is more open to participatory decision-making as a means to build legitimacy and broad acceptance – and therefore implementation – of plans in local spaces. Land use decisions in both are, however, subject to a hierarchy of responsibilities, with micro-level planning being conditioned by intermediate meso-level planning (e.g. city/region), in turn largely conditioned by macro-level planning and guidance. In many ways it is the link between these that is the critical point – how local 'bottom-up' initiatives can fit with 'top-down' national and supra-national pressures.

In the rapidly urbanising world, there are different dynamics for changing governance – partly also dealing with vastly different human settlement structures, but higher degrees of social, economic and cultural change. The impact of urbanisation is enormous and unprecedented, especially as in some regions there is urbanisation without economic growth and hence exacerbation of poverty at wider levels than previously experienced in urban areas worldwide. Overall, however, the nature of the reconstruction of governance has been to question and reconstruct previously imposed state structures – often repressive due to their illegitimacy – and the themes of participatory planning are more about new construction of participatory governance systems than reconstruction of out-of-date ones. Planning is thus arguably at an important moment when it can change its structure to both better balance social interests *vis-à-vis* state and market interests, through widening participatory decision-making, as well as contributing to better refined mechanisms for wider governance of increasingly complex human settlement patterns. The issue is inclusion – and some of the mechanisms can be shared, although they are sited in different dynamics. However, at the same time, while greater legitimacy in governance is developing, there are increasing pressures for strategic decision-making by governments who seldom have the resources (including time), even if they have the will, to broaden decision-making at this level, and hence there are also conflicts where 'top-down planning meets bottom-up planning'.

How do we conceive of housing in this context? There is again a major difference between providing new and reasonable standards of shelter for societies in rapid urban growth and those which are reconstructing. There are massive demands for housing in the North, but this is due more to socio-cultural change in the form of household structure – permitted by the continually increasing degrees of economic individualism – than population growth *per se*. Thus housing stock needs expanding but also restructuring for smaller units and in different places as global economic capitalism continues to concentrate wealth in core regions. The pressures this leads to raises issues of definition of urban areas – the past enforced distinctions between urban and rural being challenged for instance. Equally, the concentration of economic growth in certain regions has a direct knock-on effect on the market, with rising demand pushing up prices and values in nodal areas and undermining these in more peripheral areas. As economic distribution becomes more concentrated this leads to higher levels of socio-economic exclusion of groups within urban areas who are trapped in unsuitable housing (in size, location or standard) or who stand to lose significant investment. While core regions of the world still contain significant proportions of global wealth, the problem here is thus not so much how this wealth can be created but how it can continue to be distributed in (relatively) equitable ways. There are thus calls for forms of state intervention in housing markets, or changes of state intervention such as through planning controls.

In the rapidly urbanising world the demand is more basic – for adequate quantity and quality of housing for many of the new urban residents, and that which will continue to arise due to the medium-term effect of demographic processes presently underway. However, as we have argued in the book, there are big differences in macro-regional contexts across the rapidly urbanising world, with some regions already tailing off demographically, and thus entering the stable phase of demographic stability (or decline) of the 'developed' world. In these countries the issue is more of catching up in quantity and quality with the existing demand, with quantity and quality being locally defined. The urban structures in these areas are changing in that the major metropolises created in the initial surge of urbanisation and population growth are now decentralising and new urban structures and regions are developing. In areas which are only now beginning to urbanise rapidly (such as Africa) the issue is much more acute; although most get some form of shelter, this is highly inadequate in quantity and quality, and the backlogs of adequate shelter are increasing rapidly, especially in urban areas. However, the form of urbanisation without economic growth that is being experienced leads to different forms of urbanisation – rural urbanisation such as linear villages and rural peripheral growth of urban areas as well as circular migration. The traditions of housing provision through pre-capitalist forms remain important in many situations within the urbanising world, although where economies are stronger and urbanisation more established the housing stock becomes more permanent and more likely to be rented. In countries at the beginning of the urbanisation process, direct access to land is still an option (but disappearing fast). In countries which have been urbanising for some time, land access is more complex as the rights have been grabbed by previous residents. Here the development of mechanisms for access to finance are as important as land rights *per se*.

In the rapidly urbanising world the mechanisms for housing provision are more complex than those in the already urbanised world, as 'traditional' forms of housing provision – i.e. those incorporating a high degree of social and individual engagement – co-exist side by side with market-provided and state-provided forms, or combinations of these. The solutions for housing provision need to recognise this complexity and housing policy needs to be more closely associated with actual practice – there has been a tendency in the past to assume that either the state or the market can prevail in provision. This is now generally seen as not possible, and negotiated state–market mechanisms are the main focus of housing policy and practice. However, in situations where socially based provision remains important this represents a third part of the equation which is not often factored in, except through initiatives such as aided self-help and slum upgrading.

Final considerations

While we have written this book primarily as a textbook, we do not advocate that the book act as a 'manual' for different approaches in future in planning and housing in the 'developing world', as has been the case in much of the preceding literature. The lapse in the literature, as we have argued in the Introduction, has largely reflected the redundancy of this approach. Rather we advocate for development of ability to analyse the context for planning and housing in political, economic, social and cultural terms, and then draw from the range of mechanisms available, and invent new mechanisms, to address this. Whereas in the past many planning and housing professionals have been trained either in institutions in the so-called 'developed' world or in institutions in the so-called 'developing world' with a syllabus dominated by theory and practice from the 'developed' world, there is a need for a recognition that theory and practice can and should develop in all contexts, based on clear principles and contextual analysis. In addition, the assumption in the 'developed world' that it cannot learn from the 'developing world' is also false and arrogant. While we recognise the power of global capitalism, we have investigated pre-capitalist forms of planning and housing deliberately to illustrate that this is not how things always have been, or necessarily always will be. In fact the new international political economy perspective argues that global capitalism is retracting in many ways and the main challenge in some parts of the rapidly urbanising world is what to do at the retreating edges of the capitalist system, which has destroyed (and continued to subordinate) other forms of social and economic activity. This requires new and innovative practice and theory which derives from the unique context that is appearing.

This book hopes to contribute to the furtherance of the above objectives. It is based on the position that there is much to be learnt across the spectrum from various political, economic, social and cultural situations in different countries. It is also based, however, on the concept that where rapid urbanisation is either recent or ongoing, the activities of planning and housing have to be significantly different from what has been developed in the past. The objectives, basic concepts and approach, however, can be similar. In terms of approaches, we argue for an analytical approach in planning and housing which takes into account the political, economic, social and cultural realities, and also creates spaces for negotiation on objectives and permits open monitoring. This in itself may be idealistic, as planning and housing professionals will have their own interests to defend, and planning and housing activities will take place in real political contexts. However, if a wide range of professional positions are developed there will be the possibility for debate on these. There are key roles for professional and academic institutions in promoting this, however the authors acknowledge that resources can constrain this area of 'development' as much as any other area of activity, and countries undergoing rapid urbanisation often have fewer resources to invest in the area of professional training, as well as more polarised social, economic and political positions with which to deal. Nevertheless, we hope this book can contribute as a stimulus to the development of such an analytical approach to the objectives, processes and options for planning and housing in a wide variety of situations of rapid urbanisation. There is no 'textbook solution', only a 'textbook question' – how do we approach the situation and for what end?

Appendices

Appendix A

Different approaches to the study of traditional building

As noted in the introduction to Chapter 4, approaches to the study of traditional building have been undertaken in diverse fields. These include architecture, ethnology, history, geography, social anthropology, sociology and psychology, to name the most important. Underlying the various approaches to the subject is a wide range of concepts and assumptions developed during at least the past century. According to Lawrence (1987) the main approaches are in the English and French traditions and include:

- the aesthetic/formalist approach
- the typological approach
- evolutionary theory
- social and geographical diffusion
- physical determinants (construction technology, materials, site and climate)
- social determinants (defence, economy and household structure)
- socio-cultural determinants (religion and collective spatial images).

Lawrence summarised these as follows.

The aesthetic/formalist approach

The history of architecture has been written, during the last century or more, in terms of historical periods, with buildings classified according to aesthetic or functional qualities. Initially this was with the objective of providing formal models, with catalogues drawn up to disseminate styles. Later the study of history for the sake of theoretical appreciation has dominated, with histories being written based on functional uses within defined historical periods. These have almost exclusively focused on an aesthetic definition of architecture and the expression of this in monumental buildings. As a result the vast majority of built form – notably domestic, commercial and industrial – has been ignored (e.g. Pevsner 1976). From the mid-twentieth century architectural and art historians became increasingly interested in vernacular architecture and began to document many previously overlooked buildings, nonetheless the dominant approach has continued to be aesthetic, describing the formal characteristics of facades and decoration (e.g. Rudofsky 1964, 1977). The concern in this approach with formalism rather than the socio-cultural influences for construction has been criticised and alternative approaches which have studied socio-cultural aspects have included the study of social and psychological meanings of decorative and functional elements of vernacular houses (e.g. Oliver 1975).

The typological approach

During the late eighteenth and early nineteenth centuries architectural theorists advocated a formal typological classification of architectural space, looking for a universal theory of the formal composition of architecture. This approach differed from the catalogues of model types mentioned above, as what was advocated was not explicit copying but implicit absorption of forms. In these typologies a type of vernacular building is seen as specific to certain regions and periods, whereas a model refers to a specific building at a precise date. Thus an architectural type could be deduced from historical experience, but had no definite prescribed form. Rapoport 1969 implicitly accepts that vernacular types can be identified, although does not develop such a typology. However, some specific studies did take up this approach (e.g. Glassie 1975).

Evolutionary theory

The concept of evolution in built form has been present in architectural history since the eighteenth century. This approach has been applied to specific studies in vernacular architecture as well as more generally (Mercer 1975; Smith 1975).

Social and geographical diffusion

These approaches are closely related to the evolutionary approach and argue that the spread of ideas, practices and customs from the gentry to the peasant classes was a form of social diffusion (e.g. Raglan 1965; Braun 1940). Diffusionism between different socio-economic groups in society has, however, been challenged within anthropology. Concerning geographical diffusion, new ideas, etc. (such as construction techniques) are introduced by foreigners or spread across regions by imitation. This approach has been applied to colonial architecture for instance (King 1984).

Physical determinants

This has been one of the most common approaches in the study of vernacular building, starting at the end of the nineteenth century (e.g. Addy 1898; Innocent 1916). Rapoport (1969) leads the criticism that this approach is simplistic and ignores evidence that built form does not only rely on physical determinants. This criticism, however, does not mean that classifications according to physical determinants are not valid, albeit limited (e.g. Brunskill 1971).

Social determinants

While a number of specific local studies have focused on the importance of defence and economics, others – particularly for non-European studies – have also focused on social norms such as kinship and marriage rites (see Rapoport 1969: 31–40 for examples).

Socio-cultural determinants

Apart from studies in social anthropology, a few studies have focused on the relationship between vernacular buildings and religion and other socio-cultural beliefs (e.g Oliver 1975; Hayden 1976). However, Rapoport (1969, 1976) has been the leading proponent that socio-cultural factors have a primary (but not deterministic) influence on the design of vernacular buildings. Lawrence, however, criticises Rapoport for his use of general terms for 'socio-cultural' factors and his reliance on secondary sources. He also does not investigate language and terminology and gives a low priority to differentiation of use of space, or changes and variation in such use. Lawson also criticises Rapoport for his generalisations of relations between social and spatial factors, without adequate investigation of political, economic or other factors. Again, while Rapoport stresses that vernacular building is fundamentally dated and transformed throughout time, he avoids the development of any temporal analysis.

Appendix B

Socio-cultural housing functions

Rapoport (1969) attempts to break down the *socio-cultural functions* of the dwelling to cover:

- Basic needs
  This includes attitudes to fresh air/smells; light/darkness; temperature levels

and comfort; attitudes to cooking and eating; purity and cleanliness; ways of resting (sitting/sleeping); and clothing rules (e.g. shoes on/off inside).

• Family
While the family unit is basic in primitive and pre-industrial societies, its structure varies considerably – for example the extended family group, monogamous and polygamous relationships, attitudes to elders and children (and unmarried); even separation of male and female after marriage.

• Position of women
While this is an aspect of the family structure, attitudes to the role of women in public as found particularly in Muslim societies are very strong determinants on dwelling form. In many African cultures, the relationship between generations and non-blood relatives is also of great importance (e.g. role of mother-in-law). This is also related to privacy.

• Privacy
Attitudes to physical and visual privacy are highly affected by socio-cultural attitudes. In some cultures close proximity does not affect privacy in the same way as in others, due to cultural definition of roles and relationships. Attitudes to privacy not only affect the dwelling, but the relationships between dwelling and public/private space concepts.

• Social intercourse
Also related to public/private concepts, however social intercourse is seen as a basic human need. The ways in which people meet and where this takes place varies enormously, however, with much social intercourse taking place outside the home (e.g. the street corner, cafe, square, well, shop, bar, etc.).

Appendix C

The Millennium Development Goals

The Millennium Development Goals include:

• Eradicating extreme poverty and hunger: halve the proportion of people living on less than $1 per day and those who suffer from hunger by 2015.
• Achieving universal primary education: ensure all boys and girls complete primary school by 2015.
• Promoting gender equality and empowering women: eliminate gender disparities in primary and secondary education preferably by 2005, and at all levels by 2015.
• Reducing child mortality: by two-thirds among children under five by 2015.

- Improving maternal health: reduce by three-quarters the ratio of mothers dying in childbirth by 2015.
- Combating HIV-Aids, malaria and other diseases: halt and begin the reversal of spread of HIV-Aids and the incidence of malaria and other major diseases by 2015.
- Ensuring environmental sustainability: integrate the principles of sustainable development into national policies and programmes and reverse the loss of environmental resources, reduce by half the proportion of people without access to safe drinking water by 2015, and achieve significant improvement in the lives of 100 million slum dwellers by 2020.
- Developing a global partnership for development: develop further an open trading and financial system that includes a commitment to good governance, development and poverty reduction (nationally and internationally), address least developed countries' special needs, including those of landlocked and small island developing states, deal comprehensively with developing countries' debt problems, develop decent and productive work for youth, provide access to affordable essential drugs in developing countries (in co-operation with pharmaceutical companies), and make available the benefits of new technologies – especially information and communication – in co-operation with the private sector.

Appendix D

International and donor agencies' strategies to tackle poverty

Two examples of these are briefly outlined here, The World Bank (*World Development Report 2000/2001: Attacking Poverty* (2000)) proposed a strategy for 'attacking' poverty in three ways: promoting opportunity, facilitating empowerment and enhancing security. The UK Government's Department for International Development (DFID) in *Meeting the Challenge of Poverty in Urban Areas* (2001) proposed placing a crucial emphasis on poverty reduction and growing urbanisation, and therefore on the need for direct engagement with the interests and priorities of poor people in the projects it supports. DFID's contribution would be set within its increasing support for agreed poverty reduction strategies in the countries it engages with (mainly the Asian Sub-Continent and Sub-Saharan Africa, and to a lesser extent Latin America).

Appendix E

Main assets focused on in the livelihoods approach

Financial assets	income and savings (usually fragile for the poor); debt and credit.
Human assets	quantity (e.g. number who can work in a household); quality (e.g. health, education and skill levels) availability (number of hours, distance to work factors).
Physical assets	social and economic infrastructure (e.g. access to education and health facilities, water, electricity, sanitation and transport); housing (nature, size and location of housing as well as security and suitability are important factors); access to the environment (for productive or recreational requirements).
Socio-cultural assets	household relations (e.g. life-cycle issues and gender/age differentials); reciprocal and redistributive networks/structures (e.g. kinship, good neighbourliness and community/religious organisations); mutual trust and socio-cultural norms.
Political assets	effective right to influence the structures of power that affect life in various ways either through representation or participation.

Appendix F

Sandercock (1998) identifies the following contextual evolution for the roles planners have played, focusing on the 'North'. These are also relevant to the 'South'.

The rational comprehensive model – *dominant role up to mid-1960s*

Based on a belief in rationality in comprehensive public policy decision-making and faith in technology and social science, planning was seen as a scientific tool for social progress. The planner drew on his/her 'knowledge' of what is in the public interest and assumed a benign and neutral status – paralleling the economists' view of rational economic man and resource allocation.

The advocacy planning model – *emerged in the mid-1960s (mainly North America)*

Based on the occurrence of major urban riots and the national civil rights movement, this stressed the role of politics in planning, arguing that determining public interest is politics not science. It thus stressed the need for planners to act in the political arena and to unpack embedded values and interests inherent in plans. This role of the planner was, however, largely conceived as complementing the rational model above by expanding the scope of planning in a plural democracy. However experience demonstrated that it was not technical assistance through advocacy that was needed, but political power. Some advocates of the model later found it manipulative with the planner being seen as an agent of social control.

The radical political economy model – *which was prevalent in early/mid-1970s for about a decade*

This drew on radical geographers such as Harvey (1973) and Castells (1977) – Marxist analysts who saw planning as a function of the capitalist state: rationalising and legitimising capitalism and negotiating and mediating between different fractions of capital, as well as regulating pressures and protest of the dominated classes. This primarily theoretical position of urban political economy was based in academic departments of geography, sociology and urban studies, and its lasting value is at the level of critique as opposed to planning practice, which is its weakness.

The equity planning model – the mid-1970s on

Equity planners worked within the political system in what they saw as a progressive way, taking on board some of the radical political economy analysis, however, with the objective of redistributing power and resources from local elites to the poor. These planners also do not see the state as one monolithic entity, but a terrain of political struggle. In this the planner still had a specialist role, mainly focused on communication, but also as researcher (gathering and analysis of information) and formulator of issues. While still arguably top-down it is much more inclusionary.

The social learning and communicative planning model – mid-1970s on

A different reaction to the radical model was called 'communicative action'. This recognised the validity of personal experiential knowledge as well as processed 'expert' knowledge, and stressed the growing distance between experts such as planners and their 'clients'. This led to a 'transactive' style of planning where both were seen to be involved in mutual learning through communication, which required skills of resolving conflicts as well as recognising non-verbal forms of communication. The concept of 'communicative action' also had a strand which entitled itself 'critical planning', which attempted to see beyond the expressed communication to perceive the relations of power which were embedded in situations. However, while perceiving these it did not essentially lead to changing these in practice.

The radical planning model – mid-1980s on

Planners who espouse this model have arrived at this via various routes, including the post-advocacy planners, anti-racist and feminist analysts, and those who have worked with other 'excluded' groups, including in international development. Their critique focuses on existing unequal relations and distribution of power, opportunity and resources, and their goal is to work towards structural transformation of these systemic inequalities through empowerment. In this they do not assume the simplistic structural class analysis of the Marxists of the late 1970s and early 1980s, perceiving many other forms of oppression and disempowerment. Most have focused on social transformation through community organisation and urban social movements as opposed to working with the state (or corporate economy), and work in and with these institutions. There are two main positions: those who insist that the planner has to 'cross over' into the community, shedding their professional status – i.e. the community is not a client and the community initiates action, not the planner – and others who insist that some form of autonomy for the planner who works with communities needs to be retained. For both, a strategic objective is to change the structure of how the state operates, as otherwise the impact of planning is at best localised and limited.

Appendix G

Indigenous housing form in Latin America

The eight areas of housing form identified by Paul Oliver (1997) are:

1   *Amazonia*: Indigenous peoples in this region range from sedentary to more mobile, building settlements that range correspondingly from large towns on river banks to temporary shelters deep in the forest. Although the indigenous population has drastically declined in this region and the influence of white people is constantly increasing, traditional forms of settlement layout and construction are still followed.

2   *Andes and the West Coast*: Inca methods of farming and patterns of social organisation continue to survive in rural areas, including a system of reciprocal aid in work among kin and friends, which encompasses mutual participation in the building of houses. There is a rich and expanding rural tradition in these countries, which is now finding expression in the squatter settlements in urban areas on the Andean west coast.

3   *Argentina*: Three major groups can be differentiated in this area: the sparse hunter-gatherer Guaraní-speaking population on the flat grasslands of the pampas, who built transient and scattered timber settlements; the Quechuas in the northeast, who came from the Inca civilisation, led a more settled lifestyle and built in stone; and the Araucarians, who lived in the Andes and occupied the pampas in the mid-seventeenth century, first living in tents, and then settling and erecting long rectangular dwellings housing several families under one roof.

4   *South Brazil*: The original population in this area was either reduced to slavery or exterminated during European colonisation, and their traditions of building and use of space were virtually annihilated. Under colonial rule, a new form of land occupation arose, based on tightly clustered settlements with irregular layouts. Construction techniques drew on the traditions of different European and African migration influxes.

5   *Caribbean Islands*: The population of the Caribbean was devastated by European settlement, leaving only a few pockets of American Indians. Their buildings were similar throughout the region, a typical example being the *ajoupa*, a usually circular hut, with timber supports, open sides and a

thatched roof. These were replaced by a great diversity of housing types and construction techniques brought by European and African influence.

6   *Colombia and North Coast*: A densely populated area when the Spanish settlers arrived, with highly developed socio-political structures in parts. Most pre-Columbian architecture in this part of the continent used earth, wood and palm trees, and has left no material traces but stone terraces and paths. However, this type of construction has survived in some of the current four types of vernacular architecture in the area: Amerindian; African tradition blended with Indian and Spanish; a blend of Indian and Spanish traditions; Caribbean cultures combining Anglo-African heritages.

7   *Mexico*: When the Spanish settlers arrived, Mexico harboured much cultural diversity, including the Aztec empire. An overall analysis of the area is difficult to provide due to its heterogeneity. Indian housing prototypes tended to disappear as Indian ethnic groups disappeared. The current vernacular architecture of the area can be classified according to its three main components: the Indian culture; the Spanish culture; and the *mestizo* culture.

8   *Yucatán and Central America*: Much of this region corresponds with the territory of the Maya, whose advanced culture developed over 1,000 years. Social structure was hierarchical, with a highly organised state. This civilisation depended particularly on the cultivation of maize corn, for which a plot of land was allocated by the chief to each family. Mayan farmers' houses were built on a stone plinth, sometimes shared with two or three others, and had palm thatch roofs. Current Mayan farmers' houses differ very little from that model.

Glossary

This glossary is compiled using definitions from various sources including internet-based materials and dictionaries. We focused on the meanings which are most relevant to the subject of our book.

Age structure   Age structure refers to the relative proportion of individuals in each age group in a population. The age structure affects a nation's or a city's key socio-economic issues. Places with a large proportion of young people, for example, need to invest more in schools, while places with a large proportion of elderly people need to invest more in the health sector.

Agency   While the more general use means an administrative unit of government or international organisation, or a business that serves other businesses, in social studies it refers to individual or collective action and is usually seen in reference to 'structure', which refers to the political and economic forces which shape activity.

Aided self-help   Refers to the housing provision in which individual families are encouraged to build or acquire their own houses with some public support.

Beaux Arts tradition   The term applied to art and architectural schools in the late nineteenth and early twentieth centuries, which originated at the French Ecole des Beaux-Arts, whose courses stressed the study and imitation of design ideas from the past, historic forms, rich decorative detail, and a tendency to monumentality and symmetry.

Blueprint approach   Blueprint is a plan of a building in such detail as to enable workmen to construct it from the print. The name comes from the photographic process which produces the plan in white on a blue background. The blueprint approach in planning refers to detailed prescriptive master plans which set out the future city or area as it was to be built.

Capitalist hegemony   Hegemony is the dominance of one group over other groups, with or without the threat of force, to the extent that, for instance, the dominant party can dictate the terms of trade to its advantage; more broadly, cultural perspectives become skewed to favour the dominant group. Since the end of the Cold War, analysts have used the term 'hegemony' to describe the United States' role as the sole superpower in the modern world. Capitalist hegemony refers to the dominance of world trade by Western capitalist systems.

Clientelism Personal relationships that link patrons and clients together in a system in which jobs, favours, and protection are exchanged for labour, support, and loyalty. Political clientelism is an unofficial system of political organisation based on patronage, 'behind-the-scenes' control, and longstanding political ties within the structure of a representative democracy.

Collaborative planning Collaborative planning differentiates from conventional planning approaches by promoting the togetherness of and communication between various stakeholders and fostering collaborative action. It draws on a wide range of new thinking in social, political and spatial theories for the establishment of a new framework for planning which is rooted in institutionally fragmented societies.

Colonialism The establishment of government/sovereign rule in a foreign territory over an alien people; the political, social, economic, and cultural domination of a territory and its people by a foreign power for an extended time. It was practised by European states such as Britain, France, the Netherlands, Spain and Portugal in Africa, Asia, the Americas and Australasia/Oceania. It also refers to the forced change in which one culture, society, or nation dominates another.

Commodification The process by which an object, service or person becomes a commodity. It is the transformation of what is normally a non-commodity into a commodity, to assign economic value to something that traditionally would not be considered in economic terms, for example, an idea, identity, gender.

Comprador capitalism Comprador capitalism refers to foreign commercial and/or political establishments in a country undertaken by local people who serve these foreign interests.

Conditionalities A special term in international development. Conditionalities are extra requirements other than repayment demanded by the lender before new loans are granted. They are conditions attached to a loan or to debt relief, typically by the International Monetary Fund or World Bank. Conditionalities may involve relatively uncontroversial requirements to enhance aid effectiveness, such as anti-corruption measures, but they may involve highly controversial ones, such as the privatisation of key public services, which may provoke strong political opposition in the recipient country.

Core-periphery The structural relation between centralised core, often an urban area, and communities on the periphery, usually tribal or rural, resource-based communities. Dependency theorists also use this term to refer to the dominant trading relationship imposed on the poor countries by the advanced Western countries.

Decentralisation The spread of power away from the centre to local branches or governments to bring it closer to the point of service or action.

Demographic transition The slow parallel decline in the crude birth and death rates that historically appears to be a consequence of improving health and prosperity.

The decline in death rates precedes the decline in births by a generation or more, resulting in a dramatic increase in the population size during the transition. The change that typically takes place, as a country develops, in the birth and death rates of its population, both of which tend eventually to fall as per capita income rises.

Dependency Dependency theory posits that the low levels of development in less economically developed countries (LEDCs) are caused by their reliance and dependence on more economically developed countries (MEDCs). Some proponents of dependency theory assert that LEDCs will remain less developed because the surplus that they produce will be siphoned off by MEDCs – under the guise of multinational corporations. There is, as such, no profit left for reinvestment and development.

Détente Détente is French for relaxation. Generally, it may be applied to any international situation where previously hostile nations not involved in an open war 'warm up' to each other and threats de-escalate. However, today it has come primarily to refer to a general reduction in the tension between the former Soviet Union and the United States and a weakening of the Cold War, occurring from the late 1960s until the start of the 1980s.

Development It could mean evolution, growth, expansion, enlargement, advance, progress, improvement, etc. A narrower meaning refers to the advancement of the management and use of natural resources to satisfy human needs and improve the quality of human life. In the British planning system, it means 'the carrying out of building, engineering, mining or other operation in, on, over or under land, or the making of any material change in the use of any building or other land'.

Discourse A discourse is a system of ideas or knowledge, inscribed in a specific vocabulary; a conversation; the act or result of making a formal written or spoken presentation on a subject.

Economic inclusion Economic inclusion is a response to concerns about economic isolation and community disconnectedness experienced by less privileged people in society, for example youth and seniors. It promotes the employment of groups marginalised by society and extending financial services to these groups of people.

Epistemology The branch of philosophy that investigates the possibility, origins, nature, and extent of human knowledge.

Exchange value Instantaneous parity of a thing at the time of the exchange. In Marxist political economy, exchange value refers to one of three major aspects of a commodity: use value, value and exchange value, which is created – usually as a monetary price – when traded in a market.

Fordist The social institutions of mass production. It began to emerge in the United States early in the twentieth century and extended into the immediate post-Second World War. Cold War ideology played a crucial role in the political stabilisation of Fordist institutions in the United States. Institutionalised Fordism, in turn, enabled the United States to contribute almost half of world's industrial production in the immediate post-Second World War years, and thus provided the economic dynamism necessary to spark reconstruction of the major capitalist countries after the War, and to support the emergence of both the consumer society and the military-industrial complex in the post-war United States.

Globalisation The growing interdependence of countries world-wide through the increasing volume and variety of cross-border transactions in goods and services, and also through the more rapid and widespread diffusion of technology. It describes the changes in societies and the world economy that result from dramatically increased international trade and cultural exchange due to the falling of barriers and the interdependence of countries. In specifically economic contexts, the term refers almost exclusively to the effects of trade, particularly trade liberalisation or 'free trade'. More broadly, the term refers to the overall integration, and resulting increase in interdependence, among global actors (be they political, economic, social, cultural or otherwise).

Good governance Governance: 'the act or manner of governing', of a country, organisation etc. This is linked to the process of decision-making and the process by which decisions are implemented (or not implemented). It thus refers to the processes of interaction between actors in their roles and relationships – formal and informal – and thus can be used as a wider concept than government, referring to the sphere of relations between government and other actors in civil society or non-governmental sectors as well as the private sector. The term can be used in several contexts such as corporate governance, international governance, national governance and local governance. Good governance may have some of these characteristics: participatory, consensus oriented, accountable, transparent, responsive, effective and efficient, equitable and inclusive and follows the rule of law. 'Good governance' is increasingly used as a conditionality (see above) and is meant to ensure that corruption is minimised, the views of minorities are taken into account and that the voices of the most vulnerable in society are heard in decision-making. It is also responsive to the present and future needs of society.

Gross National Product (GNP) The value of a country's final output of goods and services in a year. The value of GNP can be calculated by adding up the amount of money spent on a country's final output of goods and services, or by totalling the income of all citizens of a country including the income from factors of production used abroad. GNP per capita is used to reflect the average income of a country's citizens. Knowing a country's GNP per capita is a good first step towards understanding the country's economic strengths and needs. Since 2001, the World Bank refers to the GNP as the GNI, gross national income.

Imperialism   The practice of one country extending its control over the territory, political system, or economic life of another country. Political opposition to this foreign domination is called 'anti-imperialism'.

Indigenous   Natural to a country or region; native; originating where it is found.

Indirect rule   Indirect rule involved the use of local chiefs to implement colonial policies. Chiefs appointed as Native Authorities were empowered to collect tax revenue within their jurisdictions for expenditure by the colonial Administrators or on their advice. Indirect rule was a key policy on which British colonial control was based; its purpose was to incorporate the local power structure into the British administrative structure. A British governor and council of advisers made laws for each colony, but local rulers loyal to the governor kept some of their traditional authority.

Industrialisation   The development of industry on an extensive scale; a process of social and economic change whereby a human society is transformed from a pre-industrial to an industrial state. This social and economic change is closely intertwined with technological innovation, particularly the development of large-scale energy production and metallurgy.

Informal settlement   Informal settlements (often referred to as squatter settlements, shanty towns or slums) are settlements comprising communities housed in self-produced shelters under conditions of informal or traditional land tenure. They are common features of developing countries and are typically the product of an urgent need for shelter by the urban poor.

Informalisation   Informal sector refers to the portion of a country's economy that lies outside of any formal regulatory environment, for example by labour or taxation laws. Informal sector activities are rarely reflected in official statistics on economic activity (e.g. gross domestic product). Informalisation indicates an expansion of this sector through changes in the formal sectors or privatisation. What is 'informal' generally refers to what is unauthorised in some form, but in many instances what is informal (and possibly also illegal) can also be seen as legitimate by the majority, which queries the negative use of the term and any authority action against such informal action.

Keynesianism   The economic theories of John Maynard Keynes, who advocated government monetary and fiscal programmes intended to stimulate business activity and increase employment.

Kinship network   A network based on kinship which refers to membership in a family and the relationship between members of that family (blood or marriage or adoption), including imagined descent or (sometimes) marriage.

Landed oligarchy   The word oligarchy is from the Greek for 'few' and 'rule'. Oligarchy is a political system governed by a few people; a form of government in which power is centralised in the hands of an organised elite (typically the most powerful, whether by wealth, land ownership, military strength, ruthlessness, or political influence) and where this power is used for the elite's social and/or economic benefit. Landed oligarchy is a political system dominated by large land owners.

Market enablement   Enablement means giving (a person, etc.) the means or authority to do something. Market enablement characterises local economies and their relationship with the central government according to neo-liberal policy. Market enablement requires the state's role in production, marketing, and regulation to be 'rolled back', and use of market solutions. It requires government to relinquish the ability to control prices, exchange rates, interest, and credit. NGOs can also enable the market by providing advice on standards and specifications as well as economic consultation.

Market exchange   The anonymous price-based exchange of commodities through formalised markets. In terms of cultural anthropology, market exchange is seen as a third, more recent, form of socio-economic exchange, in relation to reciprocity and redistribution (see below).

Master plan   Document that describes, in narrative and with maps, an overall development concept including both present property uses as well as future land development plans. The term master plan is used synonymously by many to refer to the comprehensive plan.

Mercantilism   Mercantilism was the dominant school of economics from the sixteenth to the eighteenth centuries, which roughly corresponded to the emergence of the nation state. It held the view that money was the only form of wealth, and that the prosperity of a nation depends upon its supply of capital. Mercantilism suggests that the government should play an active, protectionist role in the economy, by encouraging exports and discouraging imports, especially through the use of tariffs.

Modernisation   The process of changing the conditions of a society according to modern technology or modern knowledge. It involves an interlocking set of social, economic, political and cultural processes and relationships that emerged in the past from the European view of modern life that we see developing from the seventeenth-century Enlightenment. Modernisation is closely linked to classical liberalism. The concept of modernisation comes from a view of societies as having a standard evolutionary pattern, as described in the social evolutionism theories. According to this, each society would evolve inexorably from barbarism to ever greater levels of development and civilisation. The more modern states would be wealthier and more powerful, and their citizens freer and having a higher standard of living. This theory stressed the importance of societies being open to change, and maintaining tradition for tradition's sake was thought to be harmful to progress and development. This approach has been heavily criticised, mainly because it conflated modernisation with Westernisation.

Modes of production   Economic systems that are a society's dominant way of providing for people's material needs. In the writings of Karl Marx and the Marxist theory of historical materialism, a mode of production is a specific combination of productive forces (these include human labour-power, tools, equipment, buildings and technologies, materials, and improved land) and social and technical relations of production (these include the property, power and control relations governing society's productive assets, often codified in law, co-operative work relations and forms of association, relations between people and the objects of their work, and the relations between social classes).

Monetarism An economic doctrine that stressed the importance of the money supply as an instrument of economic policy. Monetarists believed that if governments simply left the economy alone and instructed the central bank to control the money supply, inflation would be banished, entrepreneurial activity would thrive, economic growth would take off and unemployment would disappear. Although monetarism is commonly associated with conservative economics and economists, not all conservatives are monetarists, and not all monetarists are conservatives.

Neo-colonialism Informal dominance of some nations over others by means of unequal conditions of economic exchange, usually based on prior colonial dominance. It used to describe certain economic operations at the international level which have alleged similarities to the traditional colonialism of the sixteenth to the nineteenth centuries. The contention is that governments have aimed to control and dominate less powerful countries through indirect means such as economic, financial and trade policies.

Neo-liberalism It is widely used as a description of the revived form of economic liberalism that became increasingly important in international economic policy discussions from the 1970s onwards. It refers to a political-economic philosophy that de-emphasises or rejects government intervention in the domestic economy (i.e. the opposite of Keynesianism). It focuses on free-market methods, fewer restrictions on business operations, and property rights. It opposes socialism, protectionism and environmentalism, and is often at odds with fair trade and other movements that argue that labour rights and social justice should have a greater priority in international relations and economics.

Normative agendas A normative value or principle is one that says how things should be and why they should be like that, for example 'people should be substantively equal' is a normative value because it is a statement of how things should be. Normative agendas usually promote equality in society. Normative ideas are difficult to prove or disprove.

Paradigm A 'view' of how things work in the world or a model used to explain a concept or theory. The term paradigm was introduced into science and philosophy by Thomas Kuhn in his landmark book *The Structure of Scientific Revolutions* (1962). A *paradigm* is the predominant worldview in the realm of human thought. A *paradigm shift* occurs when cultures transform their way of thinking from one thought system to another.

Patrimonial state   This refers to a traditional political system in which government is highly personalised, and government administration is effectively an extension of the pre-eminent ruler's personal power. This ruler personally controls the political and economic life of the country, and relationships with him or her are the mechanism for the rise or decline of the political or economic elite.

Petty-commodity   The production of commodities for sale based on individual and/or household means of production and labour, although temporary or seasonal wage labour may also be employed.

Political economy   The study of how political factors influence the functioning of an economic system. A theoretical approach which emphasises the importance of combining political and economic analysis in understanding a society. An approach to social study that emphasises the political/social construction and consequences of economic activity.

Post-colonial   Refers to those countries which had some colonial history in the past, but colonial control has ended. Post-colonial also refers to the study of the interactions between European nations and the societies they colonised in the modern period.

Primate cities   A primate city is a major city that works as the financial, political and population centre of a country and is not rivaled in any of these aspects by any other city in that country. Normally, a primate city must be at least twice as populous as the second largest city in the country. Not all countries have primate cities, but in those that do, the city is typically depended upon by the rest of the country for cultural, economic, political and major transportation needs.

Reciprocity   Reciprocity, in term of international relations, refers to a principle whereby favours, benefits, or penalties that are granted by one state to the citizens or legal entities of another, should be returned in kind. In terms of cultural anthropology, reciprocity has been defined as movement between correlative points of symmetrical groupings, such as obligatory gift giving between kin and friends, and is seen in relation to redistribution and market exchange.

Redistribution   A mechanism whereby a politically or economically powerful individual (or group) collects goods and services from the members of society and reallocates them among the society's members; the process of reallocating wealth and income to achieve an economic or social objective. In terms of cultural anthropology, redistribution has been defined as appropriational movements towards a centre and out again, such as obligatory payments to central, political, social or religious authorities, and is seen in relation to redistribution and market exchange.

Sites-and-services   Under a wide variety of types and variations, 'Sites-and-Services' schemes are the provision (by a government or other public agency) of plots of land, either on ownership or land lease tenure, along with a bare minimum of essential infrastructure needed for habitation. The actual house building is left to the beneficiaries themselves to use their own resources and at their own phase.

Slum A heavily populated urban area characterised by substandard and poor housing and squalor. Lack of infrastructure and crowded conditions mean they are often characterised by disease, disaster and crime. Slums can be found in most large cities around the world and are at times seen as more inner city phenomena and thus different from peri-urban shanty towns.

Slum clearance and redevelopment Slum clearance and redevelopment is a conventional approach to slum problems. It may involve demolition and removal of slum buildings and structures and making the land available for development or redevelopment by private enterprise or public agencies. The alternative approach to clearance and redevelopment is upgrading and improvement which preserves the existing community.

Social reproduction The concept that over time groups of people, notably social classes, reproduce their social structure and patterns.

Squatter settlement Definition of a squatter settlement varies widely from country to country and depends on a variety of defining parameters. In general, it is considered as a residential area in an urban locality inhabited by the very poor who have no access to tenured land of their own, and hence 'squat' on vacant land, either private or public. As a result of their illegal or semi-legal status, infrastructure and services are usually inadequate.

State developmentalism State developmentalism or developmental state is one that determined to influence the direction and pace of economic development by directly intervening in the development process rather than relying on the unco-ordinated influence of the market to allocate economic recourses. It took upon itself the task of establishing substantive social and economic goals with which to guide the development process and social mobilisation. Developmental states rely on a highly competent bureaucracy dedicated to devising and implementing a planned economic development process.

Structural adjustment It is a term used by the International Monetary Fund (IMF) for a package of 'free market' reforms it recommends for developing countries to create economic growth and generate income to pay off accumulated debt. These reforms may include cutting social expenditures, focusing economic output on direct export and resource extraction, devaluing currencies, lifting import and export restrictions, encouraging foreign direct investment and opening of domestic stock markets, balancing budgets and not overspending, removing price controls and state subsidies, privatisation, or divestiture of all or part of state-owned enterprises, etc. Imposition of structural adjustment programmes has been tied to getting new loans from the IMF and the World Bank for many countries in the South. The term 'structural adjustment' has been somewhat replaced since the late 1990s by an emphasis on 'poverty reduction'; the content of this is often quite similar to Structural Adjustment Programmes.

Structuralism A theory of international relations stressing the impact of world economic structures on the political, social, cultural and economic life of countries.

Structure The structure of a thing is how the parts of it relate to each other, how it is 'put together'. This contrasts with process, which is how the thing works; but process requires a viable structure. In political and economic terms structure usually refers to the large-scale forces which often create parameters for action – hence 'structure' is opposed to 'agency' (see above).

Subaltern A junior grade; inferior in rank or status; a subordinate functionary; a British commissioned army officer below the rank of captain. In post-colonial studies this refers to people who were considered inferior in the colonial society and whose history, etc. was consequently down-graded – for example the **subaltern** underclass of workers and peasants

Trans-national firms Business firms with branches located in two or more countries, more usually referring to major international firms (also called multi-nationals) which operate across national boundaries and/or at global scale. Their operations raise a number of issues concerning how these firms relate to government control and taxation.

Trickle-down Refers to the economic theory believing that *laissez-faire* will benefit not just those well-placed in the market (the rich) but also the poorest. Because the wealthy spend lavishly and employ others, the process will not only benefit the rich, but gradually the poor as well.

Urbanisation The process by which a country's population changes from primarily rural to urban. It is caused by the migration of people from the countryside to the city in search of better jobs and living conditions and natural population growth rates. It can represent a level of urban population relative to total population of the area, or the rate at which the urban proportion is increasing. Both can be expressed in percentage terms.

Use value Use value is the qualitative aspect of value, i.e. the concrete way in which a thing meets human needs. In Karl Marx's political economy, any labour-product has a value and a use value, and if it is traded as a commodity in markets, it additionally has an exchange value, most often expressed as a money-price.

Vernacular architecture The traditional architecture of an area, used typically for houses, cottages and farm buildings and constructed of the locally available materials.

Voluntarist In social and political studies this refers to individual choice in decision-making, in contrast to determinist approaches to analysis.

Notes

Chapter 2

1 There are a number of good overview texts on development, this section drawing extensively on: Hettne 1990 and Martinussen 1997.

2 In 1944, with the Second World War coming to an end, 44 countries sent representatives to a meeting hosted by the United States in the small New England town of Bretton Woods. The deliberations of this meeting – termed the 'Bretton Woods agreements' – included the creation of the International Monetary Fund, and the International Bank for Reconstruction and Development, which started operations in 1947 and 1946 respectively.

3 The term 'Third World' is claimed to have been coined in 1952, when, after the Second World War, the world had become polarised into two opposing geopolitical camps – the capitalist and socialist, i.e. the First and Second Worlds. Although coined in the 1950s, it was only in the late 1960s that the term developed any widespread use (Hoogvelt 1985). By the end of the 1970s the term had considerably diminished in importance, as increasing emphasis was placed on actual differentiation of the 'Third World', as particularly the early 1970s oil crisis led to some previously 'developing countries' (oil-exporters) to become richer than the so-called 'developed countries' (as measured by income per capita). This led to a debate concerning the 'end of the Third World' as a concept (see Harris 1990). This in turn led to further definitions, including 'industrialised', 'middle income', 'centrally planned' and 'developing' countries, as well as 'capital-surplus oil economies'; or alternatively, 'developed market', 'developing market', 'less developed', 'centrally planned' and 'OPEC' countries. Later still the concepts of 'North' and 'South' have been used, stemming from the demands for a New International Economic Order (NIEO) in the mid-1970s and the formalisation of 'North–South' dialogue in the 1980s. The term 'Fourth World' appeared during the 1970s, as part of this redefinition process, and developed in relation to the fading concept of the 'Third World' – it was used to refer to the poorest of the poor countries, also known as 'most needy countries' and more widely, 'least developed countries' (LDCs). This latter term was officially adopted as a category by the UN General Assembly in October of 1970, and special measures

were destined to this group of countries during the Second UN Development Decade (1970–80). The UN changed the terminology after the oil crisis of 1974 to 'most needy countries' or 'most seriously affected nations'.

4 E.g. Chile under Allende, Jamaica under Manley, Tanzania under Nyerere, as well as Cuba and China.

5 One fundamental problem with this approach was the definition of what are 'basic needs' – whether these can be defined objectively or only subjectively. With reference to objective definition this focused on what is necessary in any society for basic physical reproduction (and therefore is essentially quantifiable). However, subjective issues concerning cultural values and what makes life worth living in any specific culture are much more qualitative and relative. The World Bank usage of the concept stressed the former with attention oriented to targeting the poor, using measures of 'absolute poverty' and 'relative poverty'. The absolute poor were identified as that part of the population living below an international poverty line of $50 per capita per annum in rural areas and $75 per capita per annum in urban areas (1971 prices). The relative poor were identified as all those whose incomes were less than one-third of the national average per capita income.

6 The concept of informality was developed in relation to employment in Ghana in the early 1970s (Hansen and Vaa 2004) and then adopted by the International Labour Office, subsequently being applied to other areas, including human settlements. Although often used quite loosely, the key criterion for definition in relation to human settlements is regulation, and the concept of informality fundamentally refers to activities without authorisation by government, whether through laws or other forms of regulation.

7 In South Korea alone this exceeded all aid to Sub-Saharan Africa between 1951 and 1978 (Dixon *et al.* 1995).

8 This is manifested in: redistributive strategies, starting with improved income and wealth distribution and high mobilisation of domestic resources in the development process; industrialisation strategies, emphasising the manufacturing sector as the lead in growth (for domestic or foreign markets); and green revolution strategies, focusing on increasing agricultural productivity through technological change as a means to foster growth.

9 The phrase 'Washington Consensus' was coined in 1990 to refer to the lowest common denominator of policy advice being addressed by Washington-based institutions – including IMF, the World Bank, etc. Williamson (1990) listed 10 propositions: fiscal discipline; redirection of public expenditure priorities towards fields offering both high economic returns and the potential to improve income distribution; tax reform; interest rate liberalisation; competitive exchange rate; trade liberalisation; liberalisation of inflows of foreign direct investment; privatisation; deregulation of market entry and competition; and secure property

rights. The term, however, is often used more losely to refer to 'neo-liberalism' or 'market fundamentalism'.

Chapter 3

1   The term 'core countries' is used here for countries which are at the core of world capitalism. Initially Western Europe, this later included North America and Japan.
2   With some notable exceptions, for example San Luis de Potosí (Bolivia) which in the early seventeenth century was the wealthiest and most populous city in Latin America, with a population of 160,000 – not far from London's population at the time of 220,000.
3   At the time Northern European colonialism was developing, Southern European colonialism was deteriorating, especially in Latin America and the Caribbean. However, these areas became increasingly 'semi-colonies' of the Northern European core, and later North America, and hence their development was not dissimilar from the parts of the world colonised in the late nineteenth to mid-twentieth centuries. They were in effect the first areas to suffer neo-colonialism.
4   In fact colonial trade was only a relatively small fraction of overall international trade for the main colonial powers until the inter-war period.
5   'Resource bondage' refers to the situation where most productive and service sectors remained in the control of metropolitan-based companies – including increasingly the United States – or previously settled colonial populations, which permitted continued control over economic growth and natural resources by the 'core' countries even where direct political control had been relinquished. An example of this is the declining price for oil between 1950 and 1970, from over $4 per barrel to $1.60 at 1974 prices (Hoogvelt 2001).
6   'Technological rent' refers to the costs of not having technologies that existed in the core countries, and thus the extra costs of technical dependence on these. This kept production focused on simple transformative techniques, and permitted the rise in costs of higher order technical production, and thus decreasing terms of trade between these. An example would be the rising amount of a raw or basically processed commodity (e.g. cotton, sugar) needed to import manufactured goods such as a tractor.
7   There is no clear agreement on what 'post-colonial' refers to, but the term is used here to avoid the geographical definition of 'developing world', which we argue now has little relevance, and as a term which focuses on the processes of engagement of previously colonially dominated societies and economies in the changing context of the global political economy – which is different from the 'neo-colonial'.

8 This crisis was sparked by the Organisation of Oil-Producing Countries (OPEC) unilaterally quadrupling the export price of oil, with a massive knock-on effect on the global economy, both in terms of costs to non oil-producing economies and income for oil-producing economies, as well as in the amount of capital injected into world markets by the latter and the easy availability of this for loans to the former.

9 Debt peonage' refers to the escalating levels of debt in peripheral countries, whereby (by the early 1980s) total outflows of capital began to exceed total capital inflows for the first time since the 1950s. The levels of debt were so high in many cases that there was no projected possibility for repayment, and re-structuring and servicing the debt led to vicious circles of further indebtedness, with debt increasingly passing from private institutions to multi-lateral and bi-lateral public institutions.

10 Other East Asian countries had growth rates of less than 3 per cent per annum.

Chapter 4

1 Paul Oliver in his introduction to *Dwellings: the house across the world* (2003) estimates that there may exist some one billion dwellings across the world, of which only a minuscule proportion have been designed by architects or fully produced by professional builders – probably less than 1 per cent.

2 These rules often were more to do with expressions of socio-cultural values and political hierarchy than with functional issues – for example in Latin America under the Spanish rule the Laws of the Indies (see following chapter), although they also developed functional attributes (e.g. the prescription of narrow streets for shade and uniformity of facades, etc.). The functional attributes often were initially to do with public safety and then in time with issues related to public health.

3 Oliver (2003) has a good overview organised by construction process.

4 The exception which survived is the monastic form, which carried on the courtyard tradition through the unsettled medieval period.

5 Larsson has produced a separate report on the impact of modernisation in housing on gender in Botswana: Larsson, A. (1989) 'Women householders and housing strategies. The case of Gaberone, Botawna', Research report SB:25 (National Swedish Institute for Building Research, Gavle).

6 Polanyi initially (in *The Great Transformation*) included a third: the Greek concept of 'householding' – i.e. production for one's individual or group's use. However, he later considered this as subordinate to redistribution.

7 Emergency support came from kin, friends, leaders and rulers, but this was not to assume that adequate material and psychological security was thus provided – i.e.

Polanyi did not subscribe to any myth of the noble savage or harbour nostalgia for primitive ways. He recognised that 'poverty' and disease were common but stressed that social relationships were crucial to one's well-being.

8   Polanyi argued that redistribution occurs for different reasons in different times and places (regional differences in soil and climate, differences in time between harvest and consumption, division of labour, etc.) and on all civilisation levels (from primitive hunting tribes to the vast storage systems of the ancient urban civilisations of Egypt, Sumeria, Babylonia and Peru). It can also occur within a group smaller than society in general – for example the Central African kraal, the Hebrew and Roman patriarchal household, the Greek estate, mediaeval manor, etc. Central power institutions include the tribe, city state, despot and feudal lord – with social relations expressed through kin (e.g. family), locality (e.g. settlement) and political-military position (e.g. manor). Examples of central regimes include Babylonian, Egyptian, Chinese, Indian and Inca kingdoms and states. Polanyi recognised that central power institutions tend to increase their political power through the redistribution process and hence this form of socio-economic integration can cover a measure of exploitation.

9   Polanyi considered that the commodification of land (land price = rent), labour (labour price = wage) and money (money price = interest), was actually 'fictitious' as these 'commodities' were not as such 'produced' but 'used'.

Chapter 5

1   This approach views the history of urban development in the rapidly urbanising world in a linear fashion (based on such periodisation as pre-colonial, colonial, neo-colonial and post-colonial), which gives the history of the North a central place in explaining that of the 'periphery' – an approach that has been much debated and criticised in relation to 'colonial studies', which have been seen as perpetuating colonialism through control over production of knowledge in western institutions and through the application of western constructs to explain phenomena in other societies (King 1992). The authors are aware of the limitations inherent in this linear approach to the analysis of the development of human settlements and shelter. However, the authors believe the analytical framework used in this book has strong explanatory powers. It is used here in a certain historiographical way, which is inherently offered as a tool to be adapted and applied in local contexts by local analysts and practitioners around the world, and thus can challenge these concepts. In the concluding chapter the authors argue that such local analysis is indeed essential in order to address the increasingly complex issues in urban development and housing in the rapidly urbanising world. As such the use of this periodisation, and the model of 'development discourse' to which this is linked, is a device to bridge between past forms of analysis and possible new forms.

2   Other parts of the world – North America, Australia, New Zealand, etc. – were also colonised by Western powers, but do not form part of what is now referred to as the rapidly urbanising world. These are the 'European settlement' type of colonisation identified by Christopher (1988, in King 1990), the other being the exploitation of indigenous societies. Furthermore, some of these former 'European settlement' colonies became 'neo-colonial' powers in the twentieth century, particularly the United States, which exerted an influence on urban development and housing elsewhere, both directly (in the Caribbean and the Pacific) and through international agencies.

3   For a more detailed overview of the geographic and historic scope of colonialism see King 1990: 2–7.

4   A classic case is that of Nigeria, where the Town and Country Planning Ordinance of 1946 was directly based on the British Act of 1932.

5   From pavilion and veranda type timber barracks for the indentured labour system in the Caribbean and in ports such as Singapore and Hong Kong, to rows of concrete-built rooms with corrugated-iron roofs in West Africa, and rental barracks or single sex hostels in South Africa (Home 1997: 93–8).

6   Similar types of housing evolved in other parts of the rapidly urbanising world, such as the corral (similar to the chawl) in parts of Latin America.

7   In recent decades 'informal settlements' has been the term used for what was once referred to as 'squatter settlements'. These have been considered as a phenomenon that is different to 'slums', the latter term being applied to areas within towns and cities, often 'formally' built, characterised by substandard conditions and overcrowding. However, since the United Nations' adoption of the Millennium Development Goals in 2000, which included achieving a significant improvement in the lives of at least 100 million *slum* dwellers by 2020, recent literature uses the term 'slum' in a rather general and undefined way, apparently including informal settlements as well as substandard and overcrowded areas of formal housing.

8   Harris (1998b) goes further back, however, tracing aided self-help practices to many European nations and cities, as well as the Soviet Union and the United States, particularly following the First World War and during the Depression. This position is supported by Harms (1982).

Chapter 6

1   This chapter focuses on developments in planning in the non-socialist core countries and their implications for planning in non-socialist 'developing countries'.

2   The first French law on '*urbanisme*', adopted in 1919, required that all towns with a population of over 10,000 prepare a master plan to regulate growth and enable 'beautification' (Çelik 1997).

3   Landmark examples of this kind of plan include regional plans for New York (1929–31), Greater London (1929–33 and 1944) and Moscow (1935), which adopted the master plan approach (Cherry 1980).
4   An illustrative example is the emergence in Germany of a new regional identity around the industrial 'Rhine-Main' area in the 1890s, which was followed by attempts to co-ordinate data collection and planning for the region starting in the 1920s (Rebentisch 1980).
5   This section draws extensively on Devas (1993).
6   The arguments for and against encouraging and supporting the informal sector are similar to those around aided self-help housing – see Chapter 7.
7   This concept includes the ecological impact of provision of water, fuel, food, as well as the disposal of solid and water-borne wastes and other run-offs, much of which relies on, or affects, a much larger area than the city's physical land occupation, or even its economic sphere of influence.
8   For example the Community Management Programme and the Training Programme in Community Participation, which together constituted UNCHS's Community Development Programme.
9   Stone (1993: 18–22; cited in Taylor 1998: 142) identifies four regime types: 'maintenance regimes', focused on maintaining a status quo; 'development regimes', seeking to promote economic growth; 'middle class progressive regimes', focusing on issues such as environmental protection and conservation; and 'regimes devoted to lower-class opportunity expansion', which seek social improvements.

Chapter 7

1   Accordingly, in the 1960s, financial support for savings and loans (and also industrialised housing production) was provided through foreign financed investment guarantees such as the United States Housing Investment Guaranty Program created in 1963 and still active four decades later in much the same way as it was when formed.
2   Chile, Brazil, Peru, Colombia, Guatemala, Costa Rica, El Salvador and the Dominican Republic.
3   These include: the initial establishment of industrial capitalism in Europe in the nineteenth century; the Great Depression in the 1930s; and disjuncture between the housing market and lower income group affordability in northern countries in the 1960s, due in part to reductions in state subsidisation (Harms 1982: 46).
4   Abrams, together with another key figure, Otto Koenigsberger, acted as an advisor for the United Nations from 1952 and also advised the United States government on housing programmes. Both were influential in the development of international agency policies (Wakely 1998).

5   His arguments were initially set out in a paper at the 1966 UN seminar on Uncontrolled Urban Settlements, requested by the (then) UN Centre for Housing, Building and Planning, and later published in Turner (1968). The two key books that popularised his arguments were:

  •   Turner and Fichter (1972), where it is argued that the same principles applied to North America (in 1964 Turner had moved from Peru to North America, where he taught at Massachusetts Institute of Technology as well as undertaking consultancy for United States and international housing and urban development agencies). The book was the result of a symposium on User-Controlled Housing at the 135th meeting of the American Association for the Advancement of Science, organised by Anthony Leeds, a professor of anthropology who has written extensively on informal settlements ('favelas') in Brazil (e.g. Leeds 1969).
  •   Turner (1976), where he generalised about the approach – this being very influential in the 1976 UN conference. He returned to the United Kingdom in 1973 and subsequently joined the staff at the Development Planning Unit (DPU), University College London in 1976.

6   Turner was active in the NGO Forum associated with the conference, which was also heavily influenced by Otto Koenigsberger and Nigel Harris, who both taught at the DPU, as they were commissioned to write background papers (Wakely 1998).

7   'Sites and services' are planned land subdivisions with basic services provision such as water, sanitation and road access.

8   'Upgrading' is the provision of basic services to existing informal housing areas, usually with land regularisation.

9   Community participation mainly related to the land, services and housing provision process, and also small local enterprise development. In this phase also, in certain countries, World Bank lending became directed to housing finance institutions rather than to governments for direct project implementation.

10   It has been estimated that perhaps only 9 million people in 'least developed countries' were affected during the 1970s by such programmes, at a time when it was estimated that nearly 9 million units were necessary per annum to address urban housing deficits (Burgess 1992).

11   Between 1972 and 1990 the Bank had been involved in financing a total of 116 sites and services projects with complementary slum upgrading programmes in 55 different countries, with an average loan of $211 million (Mayo, cited in Pugh 1995: 63). This represented around a third of all World Bank urban lending (although only 1.8 per cent of total lending). Slum upgrading was generally more successful than sites and services in reaching the poor, mainly as this was directed

to areas where the poor lived as opposed to green-field sites and services. World Bank evaluations showed that the anti-poverty thrust of sites and services was also undermined by the trading of housing rights to higher income groups and cost recovery objectives were often undermined by hidden subsidies in low rates of interest and written down land values.

12 In 1972–5 the average housing loan size was $19 million, but rose to $211 million in 1985–90.

13 The DPU worked with the Sri Lankan National Housing Authority between 1983 and 1990 developing this approach at a policy and programme level. According to Wakely (1998) this initiative, together with those of the Sri Lankan Prime Minister, were instrumental in both the declaration of the International Year for Shelter for the Homeless in 1987, but also the adoption of the UN of the Global Shelter Strategy.

14 The private sector is understood as dealing with the housing demand from all other income groups.

15 See also Gilbert (1986) and Nientied and van der Linden (1983).

16 This economistic and mechanistic approach has also been criticised by others, e.g. Gilbert 1986.

17 Marcussen proposed that the research based on this model should be applied at city and 'nested' lower levels, and should be undertaken on a wide comparative basis and focusing on specific subjects – e.g. bureaucracy – which cut across Marxist and non-Marxist positions. In his opinion this would permit theoretical reformulation, thus narrowing the '...widening gap between theory and practice, which inhibits mutual understanding and interaction between academia and workers in the field. Bridging the gap is beyond the capability of any individual, project or institution. By its very nature it is a long term, collective task and to some extent a political one ...' (Marcussen 1990: 7).

18 Both Jenkins and Smith undertook doctoral study in this area: Jenkins, P. (1998) 'National and International shelter policy initiatives in Mozambique: housing the urban poor at the periphery', PhD thesis, Edinburgh College of Art/Heriot-Watt University; Smith, H. (1999) 'Networks and spaces of negotiation in low-income housing: the case of Costa Rica', PhD thesis, Edinburgh College of Art/Heriot-Watt University.

Chapter 8

1 Apart from 171 governments and 2,400 NGOs attending the conference, a further 8,000 people were active in a parallel NGO Forum.

2 These fields were: sustainable land use; social development, encompassing the eradication of poverty, the creation of productive employment and social integration; demographic issues; health and environment; sustainable energy use;

sustainable transport and communication systems; conservation and rehabilitation of the historical and cultural heritage; the improvement of urban economies; balanced development of settlements in rural regions; and disaster prevention, mitigation and preparedness, and post-disaster rehabilitation capabilities.

3   www.unhabitat.org/campaigns/governance/campaign_overview.asp.
4   www.unhabitat.org/campaigns/tenure/Background.asp.
5   'Urban planners are inescapably caught up in this dynamic. The new planning is less codified and technical, more innovative and entrepreneurial. It is also more participatory and concerned with projects rather than whole urban systems. Planning expertise is increasingly sought not only by the state, but also by the corporate sector and civil society. Planners seek to forge agreements through negotiation and mediation among contesting parties. Planning is no longer lodged solely in urban government as a font of privileged knowledge about 'the public interest'. What is controversial is not urban planning *per se*, but its goal: whether it should be directed chiefly at efficiency, reinforcing the current distribution of wealth and power, or whether it should play a distributive role to help create minimum standards of urban liveability' (UNCHS 2001: xxxiv).

Chapter 9

1   Only the Asian macro-region is larger – the African continent is three times the size of Europe and four times the size of the United States.
2   Bantu languages, which form the greatest sub-classification, include Kongo, Zulu, Lengala, Bamba, Shona, Ganda, Kikuyu and many others.
3   Britain, France, Portugal, Germany, Belgium and Italy. Spain had only one minor territory south of the Sahara – Equatorial Guinea.
4   Particularly in Northern and Southern Rhodesian (now Zambia and Zimbabwe) settlements as well as in South Africa, but also in other countries where plantation production was developed (e.g. central Mozambique).
5   Examples being Dodoma in Tanzania, Abuja in Nigeria and Lilongwe in Malawi.
6   For example the previous Portuguese colonies.
7   See Rakodi (1997: 33) for sub-regional differences and Bryceson and Potts (2006) for more up-to-date analysis based on census figures.
8   Including island states. Excluding island states the total is 42.
9   For an analysis of relations between civil society and the government across the region, see Swilling (1997).
10 A good general overview of the effect of globalisation on the region is Simon (1997).
11 This was principally in primary (extractive) sectors of the economy (Rakodi 1997).

12   The six countries above the 'Less Developed Regions' are: Botswana, Gabon, Mauritius, Namibia, South Africa and Swaziland (UN-Habitat 2004).

13   The next highest region in slum dwellers as proportion of urban residents is South-central Asia (58 per cent). The global average was 32 per cent, the average for 'developing regions' was 43 per cent and for Least Developed Countries 78 per cent. Sub-Saharan Africa has the third highest population of slum dwellers, after South-central Asia (262 million) and Eastern Asia (194 million) and higher than Latin America and the Caribbean (128 million).

14   In Sub-Saharan Africa the candidates for 'world city' status are really only in South Africa, especially Johannesburg and possibly Cape Town, as other major urban areas, such as Lagos and Kinshasa, are not in any sense active in the formal global economy.

15   This type of initiative is a key feature of the New Partnership for Africa's Development (NEPAD).

16   UN-Habitat 2003 reports that only 20 cities in the region could set local government taxes and 32 cities could set service charge levels.

17   A partial survey of 56 cities in 33 Sub-Saharan African countries (mostly capital cities) shows that civil society was involved in some form in decisions about new major roads, land use zoning changes or major public projects in under 60 per cent of the cases (UN-Habitat 2004).

18   Recent research from Peru contests the de Soto thesis that titling will lead to economic change, with most families not only reluctant to mortgage land, but also few mortgage lenders interested to lend on this basis, and much land being peripheral and hard to develop anyway (Ramírez Corzo and Riofrío 2005).

19   See Rakodi (1997: 55–60) for more details.

20   The experience of South Africa's housing subsidy policy shows that in only a small percentage of the subsidised cases did households get access to additional housing finance from the formal system, leading to a change in emphasis in the policy to higher subsidisation (and thus narrower scope of action as housing budgets did not increase).

21   This does not mean 'green agenda' issues are of less importance, as in fact these may be the underpinning of the wider possibilities of the ecological footprint, but in terms of specific urban environmental management, they tend to be lower priority in most cities.

Chapter 10

1   It is twice the size of Europe, and 2.2 times that of the United States.

2   Chichén-Itzá, Tula, Xochicalco, El Tajín and MonteAlbán.

3   It is estimated Tenochtitlán had a population of between 150,000 and 300,000.

4 This city covered an area of some 20 square kilometres.

5 The Treaty of Tordesillas, which was sanctioned by the Pope.

6 The system imposed obligations on the 'entrusted' natives to provide personal services and payment to their *encomendador*, and on the Spanish *encomendador* to contribute one-fifth of his income from the *encomienda* to the Crown, as well as to 'educate' the natives in Catholicism. This system was initially hereditary for only one generation, and was not a form of land ownership because what was granted to the settler was only the natives' labour. However, as land became increasingly valuable because of the growing value of its products, settlers strove to own land through for example Crown grants, conquest, and expulsion of indigenous population from communal lands and later of white and *mestizo* homesteaders from private lands, creating large properties known as *haciendas*.

7 It has been estimated that between five and six million African slaves were taken to Brazil up to the nineteenth century (Galeano 1973: 80).

8 Brazil became nominally independent in 1822, but was home to the Portuguese Crown following the Napoleonic invasion of Portugal and was declared a republic only in 1889. Caribbean island colonies gained independence later.

9 In 1856 corporate land holding was abolished, thus leading to church and community lands being converted to freehold property and contributing to the extension of the *haciendas*, as well as depriving Indians of their last independent means of subsistence, thus becoming waged labourers.

10 For example, by the end of the nineteenth century Argentina, with an economy based on livestock and cereal export, had reached levels of economic development which were comparable to those of northern countries, whilst Bolivia, reliant on tin mining, remained poor.

11 Banana growing, for example, is based on a plantation economy, usually owned by foreign and trans-national companies. Coffee production, on the other hand, is more likely to give rise to small-scale land holding, usually linked to more equitable wealth distribution.

12 Tenochtitlán became the new capital of the Spanish administration in Mexico; Cuzco was replaced by Lima, a new city on the coast, as capital city of the viceroyalty of Peru.

13 The impact of the changes in the economic base of the colonies on urban development is clearly illustrated by the case of the Bolivian mining town of Potosí, which between 1570 and 1620 produced half of the world's silver. It developed into the richest and most populous city in the Americas at the time and became the home of the Spanish empire's Royal Mint (see Figure 10.2), but after silver production fell, its population dwindled. From 14,000 inhabitants in 1545, Potosí grew to around 160,000 by 1650, at the peak of silver production. By 1825, however, only 8,000 people lived in this town (Davis 1974).

14 Caracas, Bogotá, Asunción, Buenos Aires.

15 Spain forbade the colonies to trade not only with other European nations, but also between themselves. Buenos Aires, for example, was a port that was closed to all international trade, thus forcing produce from the pampa region of Argentina to be transported across the Andes and up to Panama before being shipped to Europe (Davis 1974).

16 Buenos Aires grew annually at 5.2 per cent between 1895 and 1900, Rosario at 7.2 per cent between 1887 and 1895, São Paulo at 12.5 per cent between 1886 and 1890 and Bogotá at 5.7 per cent between 1870 and 1884 (Hardoy 1982: 29).

17 Bolivia, Chile, Cuba, Guatemala, Mexico, Nicaragua and Peru.

18 The latter approach has continued. In 1965 Belize moved its capital to Belmopán, in 1987 Argentina approved the transfer of its capital to Viedma-Carmen de Patagones, 1,000 kilometres south of Buenos Aires, and Peru has considered moving its capital from Lima to the eastern slopes of the Andes (Gilbert and Gugler 1992: 254–5).

19 Including the island states of Cuba, Dominican Republic and Puerto Rico (though this is an associated state of the USA), and excluding non-Spanish or Portuguese-speaking countries (Caribbean islands and Surinam, Guyana and French Guiana on the mainland).

20 An exception to the political regime prevailing in Latin America is Cuba, where the socialist regime installed by the revolution in 1959 was, at the time of writing, under great external pressure under a US embargo. Cuba is also the exception to the prevailing economic system in Latin America, which is capitalist.

21 A few examples of the former have been implemented, such as the People's Participation Law in Bolivia, open community councils (*cabildos*) in some Central American countries, and participatory local government budgeting in some Brazilian municipalities.

22 When the Spanish colonies started to break away from Spain in the early 1800s, the possibility of alliances between European powers to fight the risings prompted the then US President James Monroe to declare in 1823 that his country would not tolerate further European colonisation in the Americas, and in exchange would not interfere in internal European affairs. This came to be known as the Monroe Doctrine.

23 In 1999 the Gini coefficients for all Latin American countries were higher than the world average of 0.4.

24 Also to extremely high levels in particular countries such Haiti and Nicaragua.

25 UN-Habitat (2004: 111), for example, reports that 49.3 per cent of São Paulo's informal settlements are located on river banks, 32.2 per cent on periodically flooded land; 29.3 per cent on steep slopes; 24.2 per cent on land being eroded; and 9 per cent on waste tips or landfill sites.

26 Referring both to 'off-plot' space, infrastructure and service standards and to 'on-plot' standards of dwelling space, equipment, materials, etc.

27 Two extreme examples of this approach, due to their sheer scale, were the 'Superblocks' programme in Caracas, Venezuela, and the CHISAM projects in Rio de Janeiro, Brazil (Dwyer 1975; Perlman 1976).

28 Starting in Chile, the use of these direct demand subsidies has spread to many Latin American countries including Costa Rica, Venezuela, Paraguay, Uruguay, Colombia, El Salvador, Ecuador, Guatemala, Nicaragua and Panama (Ferguson and Navarrete 2003).

29 An illustrative example is FUPROVI, in Costa Rica (see Sevilla 1993).

30 Averages of six to nine years have been found in different cities.

31 Such as those brought about in Argentina's society by its economic crisis of 2001.

32 Puerto Madero, the regenerated waterfront of Buenos Aires, is a case in point in a country where levels of employment and income have plummeted while this exclusive development using designers of worldwide renown has created a pocket of ostentatious wealth.

33 The issue of changes in political power affecting planning processes has affected all forms of planning, including traditional planning (e.g. the Curitiba master plan was momentarily abandoned during 1985–9 while the opposition party was in power in local government). Often a key concern when introducing new forms of urban planning and management has been to establish these as a system beyond alternation in political power, as in the case of Brazil's participatory budgeting, or Costa Rica's Triangle of Solidarity (see Smith 2004).

Chapter 12

1 For anyone interested in a theoretical discussion of why 'context counts', see Flyvbjerg 2001, especially Chapter 4.

Bibliography

Abrams, C. (1964) *Housing in the Modern World*, London: Faber and Faber.

Addy, S. (1898) *The Evolution of the English House*, London: George Allen and Unwin.

Amis, P. and Lloyd P. (eds) (1990) *Housing Africa's Urban Poor*, Manchester: Manchester University Press.

Anderson, D.M. and Rathbone, R. (2000) *Africa's Urban Past*, Oxford: James Currey.

Auty, R. and Brown, K. (1997) 'An overview of approaches to sustainable development', in Auty, R. and Bron, K. (eds) *Approaches to Sustainable Development*, London and Washington, DC: Pinter.

Baiocchi, G. (2004) 'Porto Alegre: the dynamism of the unorganised', in Chavez, D. and Goldfrank, B. (eds) *The Left in the City: Participatory Local Governments in Latin America*, London: Latin America Bureau.

Benevolo, L. (1980) *The History of the City*, Cambridge, MA: The MIT Press.

Berry, B.J.L. (1981) *Comparative Urbanisation, Divergent Paths in the Twentieth Century*, London: Macmillan Press.

Braun, H. (1940) *The Story of the English House*, London: Batsford.

Brookfield, H. (1975) *Interdependent Development*, London: Methuen.

Brunskill, R.W. (1971) *Illustrated Handbook of Vernacular Architecture*, London: Faber and Faber.

Bryceson, D. and Potts, D. (eds) (2006) *African Urban Economies: Viability, Vitality or Vitiation?*, London: Palgrave.

Burgess, R. (1977) 'Self-help housing: a new imperialist strategy: a critique of the work of John F.C. Turner', *Antipode*, 9: 50–9.

Burgess, R. (1978) 'Petty commodity housing or dweller control?', *World Development*, 6(9): 1105–33.

Burgess, R. (1982) 'Self-help housing advocacy: a curious form of radicalism', in Ward, P.M. (ed.) *Self-help Housing: A Critique*, London: Mansell.

Burgess, R. (1985) 'The limits to state self-help housing programmes', *Development and Change*, 16: 271–31.

Burgess, R. (1987) 'A lot of noise and no nuts: a reply to Alan Gilbert and Jan van der Linden', *Development and Change*, 18(1): 137–46.

Burgess, R. (1992) 'Helping some to help themselves: third world housing policies and development strategies', in Mathey, K. (ed.) *Beyond Self-Help Housing*, London: Mansell.

Carter, H. (1995) *The Study of Urban Geography* (4th edn), London: Arnold.

Castells, M. (1977) *The Urban Question*, London: Edward Arnold.

Çelik, Z. (1997) *Urban Forms and Colonial Confrontations: Algiers under French Rule*, Berkeley, CA: University of California Press.

Centre for Environment and Human Settlements/Development Workshop (2005) 'TERRA. Urban Land reform in post-war Angola: research, advocacy and policy development', *Development Workshop, Occasional Paper*, No. 5.

Chambers, R. and Conway, G. (1992) 'Sustainable rural livelihoods: practical concepts for the 21st century', IDS discussion paper, No. 296, Brighton.

Champion, T. and Hugo, G. (2004) 'Introduction: moving beyond the urban–rural dichotomy', in Champion, T. and Hugo, G. (eds) *New Forms of Urbanization*, Aldershot: Ashgate.

Chan, E.H.W., Tang, B. and Wong, W. (2002) 'Density control and the quality of living space: a case study of private housing development in Hong Kong', *Habitat International*, 26: 159–75.

Chang, S. (1976) 'The changing system of Chinese cities', *Annals, Association of American Geographers*, 66: 398–415.

Cheema, G.S. (1987) *Urban Shelter and Services: Public Policies and Management Approaches*, Westport, CT: Praeger Publishers.

Cherry, G. (1980) 'Introduction: aspects of twentieth-century planning', in Cherry, G. (ed.) *Shaping an Urban World: Planning in the Twentieth Century*, London: Mansell.

Chiu, R.L.H. (2000) 'Environmental sustainability of Hong Kong's housing system and the housing process model', *International Planning Studies*, 5(1): 45–64.

Cities Alliance (no date) *Cities Alliance for Cities Without Slums: Action Plan for Moving Slum Upgrading to Scale*, New Delhi: UNDP/World Bank.

Cities Alliance (2001) *Cities Alliance 2001 Annual Report*, available at www. citiesalliance.org.

Cohen, B. (2004) 'Urban growth in developing countries: a review of current trends and a caution regarding existing forecasts', *World Development*, 32(1): 23–51.

Collier, S., Blakemore, H. and Skidmore, T.E. (eds) (1993) *The Cambridge Encyclopedia of Latin America and the Caribbean*, Cambridge: Cambridge University Press.

Connell, J.B., Dasgupta, B., Laishley, R. and Lipton, M. (1976) *Migration from Rural Areas: The Evidence from Village Studies*, Delhi: Oxford University Press.

Cullinane, S. and Cullinane, K. (2003) 'City profile: Hong Kong', *Cities*, 20(4): 279–88.

Cunningham, S.M. (1980) 'Brazilian cities old and new: growth and planning experiences', in Cherry, G.E. (ed.) *Shaping and Urban World*, London: Mansell.

Dalton, G. (ed.) (1971) *Primitive Archaic and Modern Economies: Essays of Karl Polanyi*, Boston, MA: Beacon Press.

Davis, K. (1965) 'The urbanization of the human population', *Scientific American*, 213(3): 40–53.

Davis, K. (1974) 'Colonial expansion and urban diffusion in the Americas', in Dwyer, D.J. (ed.) *The City in the Third World*, London and Basingstoke: Macmillan.

De Soto, H. (2001) *The Mystery of Capital: Why Capitalism Triumphs in the West and Fails Everywhere Else*, London: Black Swan.

Devas, N. (1993) 'Evolving approaches', in Devas, N. and Rakodi, C. (eds) *Managing Fast Growing Cities: New Approaches to Urban Planning and Management in the Developing World*, Harlow: Longman.

Devas, N. (2001) *Urban Governance and Poverty: Lessons from a Study of Ten Cities in the South*, Birmingham: University of Birmingham.

Devas, N. and Rakodi, C. (1993) *Managing Fast Growing Cities*, London: Longman.

DFID (2001) *Meeting the Challenge of Poverty in Urban Areas*, London: Department for International Development.

Dixon, C., Simon, D. and Narman, A. (1995) 'The nature of structural adjustment', in Simon, D., Van Spengen, W., Dixon, C. and Narman, A. (eds) *Structurally Adjusted Africa: Poverty, Debt and Basic Needs*, London: Pluto Press.

Drakakis-Smith, D. (2000) *Third World Cities* (2nd edn), London: Routledge.

Durand-Lasserve, A. and Royston, L. (eds) (2002) *Holding Their Ground – Secure Land Tenure for the Urban Poor in Developing Countries*, London: Earthscan.

Dwyer, D.J. (1974) 'Attitudes to spontaneous settlements in Third World cities', in Dwyer, D.J. (ed.), *The City in the Third World*, London: Macmillan.

Dwyer, D.J. (1975) *People and Housing in Third World Cities: Perspectives on the Problem of Spontaneous Settlements*, London: Longman.

Emerson, R. (1968) 'Colonialism', in *International Encyclopaedia of Social Sciences*, New York: Macmillan.

Eng, T.S. (1996) 'Character and identity in Singapore new towns: planner and resident perspectives', *Habitat International*, 20(2): 279–94.

Escobar, A. (1995) *Encountering Development: The Making and Unmaking of the Third World*, Princeton, NJ: Princeton University Press.

Ferguson, B. and Navarrete, J. (2003) 'New approaches to progressive housing in Latin America: a key to habitat programs and policy', *Habitat International*, 27: 309–23.

Fernandez-Armesto, F. (2003) *The Americas: A Hemispheric History*, New York: Random House.

Fieldhouse, D.K. (1965) *The Colonial Empires: A Comparative Survey from the Eighteenth Century* (2nd edn), Basingstoke and London: Macmillan.

Fiori, J. and Ramirez, R. (1992) 'Notes on the self-help housing critique', in Mathey, K. (ed.) *Beyond Self-Help Housing*, London: Mansell.

Flyvbjerg, B. (2001) *Making Social Science Matter: Why Social Inquiry Fails and How It Can Succeed Again*, Cambridge: Cambridge University Press.

Friedmann, J. and Wulff, R. (1975) *The Urban Transition: Comparative Studies of Newly Industrializing Societies*, London: Arnold.

Galeano, E. (1997, 1st edn 1973) *Open Veins of Latin America*, New York: Monthly Review Press.

Geddes, P. (1968, 1st edn 1915) *Cities in Evolution*, London: Ernest Benn Limited.

Gilbert, A. (1983) 'The tenants of self-help housing: choice and constraint in the housing markets of less developed countries', *Development and Change*, 14: 449–77.

Gilbert, A. (1986) 'Self-help housing and state intervention: illustrative reflections on the petty commodity production debate', in Drakakis-Smith, D.W. (ed.) *Urbanisation in the Developing World*, London: Croom Helm.

Gilbert, A. (1990) *Latin America*, London: Routledge.

Gilbert, A. (1996) 'Land, housing, and infrastructure in Latin America's major cities', in Gilbert, A. (ed.) *The Mega-city in Latin America*, Tokyo: United Nations University Press.

Gilbert, A. (1998, 1st edn 1994) *The Latin American City*, London: Latin America Bureau.

Gilbert, A. and Gugler, J. (1992) *Cities, Poverty and Development* (2nd edn), Oxford: Oxford University Press.

Gilbert, A. and van der Linden, J. (1987) 'The limits of a Marxist theoretical framework for explaining state self-help housing', *Development and Change*, 18(1): 129–36.

Gilbert, A. and Ward, P. (1984) 'Community participation in upgrading irregular settlements: the community response', *World Development*, 12(9): 913–22.

Gilbert, A. and Ward, P. (1985) *Housing, the State and the Poor: Policy and Practice in Three Latin American Cities*, Cambridge: Cambridge University Press.

GIS (2002) *Hong Kong Yearbook 2001*, Hong Kong: Hong Kong Special Administration Government.

Glassie, H. (1975) *Folk Housing in Middle Virginia*, Knoxville, TN: University of Tennessee Press.

Graham, S. and Marvin, S. (2001) *Splintering Urbanism*, London: Routledge.

Gugler, J. (2004) *World Cities Beyond the West: Globalisation, Development and Inequality*, Cambridge: Cambridge University Press.

Hague, C. (1984) *The Development of Planning Thought: A Critical Perspective*, London: Hutchinson.

Hague, C. and Jenkins, P. (2004) 'Reconceptualizing the narratives of place identity in planning', in Hague, C. and Jenkins, P. (eds) *Place Identity, Participation and Planning*, London: Routledge.

Hamdi, N. and Goethert, R. (1997) *Action Planning for Cities: A Guide to Community Practice*, Chichester: Wiley.

Hamer, A. M. (1997) 'Planning urban development with a change of sovereignty in mind: a Hong Kong case study', *Cities*, 14(5): 287–94.

Hansen, K.T. and Vaa, M. (2004) *Reconsidering Informality: Perspectives from Urban Africa*, Uppsala: Nordic Africa Institute.

Hardoy, J. (1967) *Urban Planning in Pre-Columbian America*, London: Studio Vista.

Hardoy, J. (1982) 'The building of Latin American cities', in Gilbert, A., Hardoy, J. and Ramírez, R. (eds) *Urbanization in Contemporary Latin America*, Chichester: John Wiley and Sons.

Hardoy, J., Mitlin, D. and Satterthwaite, D. (2001) *Environmental Problems in an Urbanizing World: Finding Solutions for Cities in Africa, Asia, and Latin America*, London: Earthscan.

Harms, H. (1982) 'Historical perspectives on the practice and purpose of self-help housing', in Ward, P.M. (ed.) *Self-help Housing: A Critique*, London: Mansell.

Harris, N. (1990) *The End of the Third World: Newly Industrializing Countries and the Decline of an Ecology*, London: Penguin.

Harris, R. (1998a) 'The silence of the experts: "aided self-help housing", 1939–1954', *Habitat International*, 22(2): 165–89.

Harris, R. (1998b) 'Slipping through the cracks: the origins of aided self-help housing, 1918–1953', *Housing Studies*, 14(3): 281–309.

Harris, R. and Giles, C. (2003) 'A mixed message: the agents and forms of international housing policy, 1945–1973', *Habitat International*, 27(2): 167–91.

Harvey, D. (1973) *Social Justice and the City*, London: Edward Arnold.

Hayden, D. (1976) *Seven American Utopias: The Architecture of Communitarian Socialism, 1790–1975*, Cambridge, MA: MIT Press.

Hayek, F.A. (1960) *The Constitution of Liberty*, London: Routledge and Kegan Paul.

Healey, P. (1974) 'Planning and change: an evaluation of some attempts at introducing urban planning into Latin America, and a discussion of the relevance and potential of planning in situations experiencing structural change', *Progress in Planning*, 2(3): 143–237.

Healey, P. (1997) *Collaborative Planning: Shaping Places in Fragmented Societies*, London: Macmillan.

Held, D. and McGrew, A. (2003) *The Global Transformations Reader: An Introduction to the Globalization Debate* (2nd edn), Cambridge: Polity Press.

Hettne, B. (1990) *Development Theory and the Three Worlds*, Harlow: Longman.

Home, R. (1997) *Of Planting and Planning: The Making of British Colonial Cities*, London: E. and F.N. Spon.

Home, R. and Lim, H. (2004) *Demystifying the Mystery of Capital: Land Tenure and Poverty in Africa and the Caribbean*, London: Cavendish Publishing.

Hong Kong Government (1996) *Hong Kong City of Tomorrow: An Exhibition about the Challenge of High Density Living*, Edinburgh: City Art Centre.

Hong Kong Housing Authority (2003) *Housing in Figures, 2003 Edition*, Hong Kong: Hong Kong Housing Authority.

Hoogvelt, A. (2001) *Globalization and the Post-colonial World: The New Political Economy of Development*, Basingstoke: Palgrave.

Hoogvelt, M.M. (1985) *The Third World in Global Development*, London: Macmillan.

Hou, R.Z. (1986) 'Evolution of the city planning of Beijing', *TWPR*, 8(1).

Huchzemeyer M. (2004) *Unlawful Occupation: Informal Settlements and Urban Policy in South Africa and Brazil*, Trenton, NJ: Africa World Press.

Innocent, C. (1916) *The Development of English Building Construction*, Cambridge: Cambridge University Press.

Jacobs, J. (1969) *The Economy of Cities*, New York: Vintage.

Jencks, C. (1969) 'History as myth', in Jencks, C. and Baird, G. (eds) *Meaning in Architecture*, London: Barrie and Rockcliff.

Jenkins, P. (1998) 'National and international shelter policy initiatives in Mozambique: housing the urban poor at the periphery', PhD thesis, Edinburgh College of Art/Heriot-Watt University, School of Planning and Housing, Edinburgh, UK.

Jenkins, P. (2003) 'In search of the urban–rural frontline in post-war Mozambique and Angola', *Environment and Urbanization*, 15(1): 121–34.

Jenkins, P. and Smith, H. (2001) 'The state, the market and community: an analytical framework for community self-development', in Carley, M., Jenkins, P. and Smith, H. (eds) *Urban Development and Civil Society: The Role of Communities in Sustainable Cities*, London: Earthscan.

Jenkins, P. and Smith, H. (2002) 'International agency shelter policy in the 1990s: experience from Mozambique and Costa Rica', in Zetter, R. and White, R. (eds) *Planning in Cities: Sustainability and Growth in the Developing World*, London: ITDG.

Jones, G.A. and Ward, P.M. (1994) 'The World Bank's "new" urban management programme: paradigm shift or policy continuity?', *Habitat International*, 18(3): 33–51.

Jyoti, H. (1992) 'City as Durbar: theater and power in imperial Delhi', in AlSayyad, N. (ed.) *Forms of Dominance: On the Architecture and Urbanism of the Colonial Enterprise*, Aldershot: Avebury.

King, A. (1992) 'Rethinking colonialism: an epilogue', in AlSayyad, N. (ed.) *Forms of Dominance: On the Architecture and Urbanism of the Colonial Enterprise*, Aldershot: Avebury.

King, A.D. (1980) 'Exporting planning: the colonial and neo-colonial experience', in Cherry, G.E. (ed.) *Shaping an Urban World: Planning in the Twentieth Century*, London: Mansell.

King, A.D. (1984) *The Bungalow: The Production of a Global Culture*, London: Routledge and Kegan Paul.

King, A.D. (1990) *Urbanism, Colonialism and the World-economy: Cultural and Spatial Foundations of the World Urban System*, London and New York: Routledge.

Kirkby, R.J.R. (1985) *Urbanization in China: Town and Country in a Developing Economy 1949–2000 AD*, London: Croom Helm.

Koenigsberger, O. (1964) 'Action planning', *Architectural Association Journal*, 74 (Feb.). Reproduced in Mumtaz, 1982, 2–9.

Kwok, R.Y.W. (1982) 'Trends of urban planning and development in China', in Ma, L.J.C. (ed.) *Urban Development in Modern China*, Boulder, Co: Westview, Special Studies on China and East Asia.

Lai, L.W.C. (1993) 'Hong Kong's density policy towards public housing, a theoretical and empirical review', *TWPR*, 15(1): 63–85.

Lai, L.W.C. and Ho, W.K.O. (2001) 'A probit analysis of development control: a Hong Kong case study of residential zones', *Urban Studies*, 38(13): 2425–37.

Lamprakos, M. (1992) 'Le Corbusier and Algiers: the Plan Obus as colonial urbanism', in AlSayyad, N. (ed.) *Forms of Dominance: On the Architecture and Urbanism of the Colonial Enterprise*, Aldershot: Avebury.

Laquian, A.A. (2005) *Beyond Metropolis: The Planning and Governance of Asia's Mega-Urban Regions*, Washington, DC: Woodrow Wilson Centre Press, and Baltimore, MD: The Johns Hopkins University Press.

Larsson, A. (1984) *Traditional Tswana Housing: A Study of Four Villages in Eastern Botswana*, Lund: University of Lund, report D7.

Larsson, A. (1988) *From Outdoor to Indoor Living: The Transition from Traditional to Modern Low-cost Housing in Botswana*, Lund: University of Lund, report R4.

Larsson, A. (1989) *Women Householders and Housing strategies: The Case of Gaberone, Botswana*, Lund: University of Lund, report SB:25.

Larsson, A. (1990) *Modern Houses for Modern Life: The Transformation of Housing in Botswana*, Lund: University of Lund, report R1.

Lawrence, R.J. (1987) *Housing, Dwellings and Homes*, Chichester: John Wiley.

Lawton, R. (1972) 'An age of great cities', *Town Planning Review*, 43: 199–224.

Leeds, A. (1969) *The Significant Variables Determining the Character of Squatter Settlements*, The University of Texas at Austin, Institute of Latin American Studies.

Leonard, J.B. (1985) 'City profile: Rangoon', *Cities*, 2(1): 2–13.

Lewis, O. (1961) *The Children of Sanchez*, New York: Random House.

Lewis, O. (1966) 'The culture of poverty', *Scientific American*, 215(4): 19–25

Leys, C. (1996) *The Rise and Fall of Development Theory*, London: James Currey.

Li, S.M. (2000) 'Housing consumption in urban China: a comparative study of Beijing and Guangzhou', *Environment and Planning A*, 32: 1115–34.

Lin, G.C. (1994) 'Changing theoretical perspectives on urbanisation in Asian developing countries', *TWPR*, 16(1): 1–23.

Linn, J.F. (1983) *Cities in the Developing World*, New York: Oxford University Press (World Bank).

Liu, Z.F. (2003) 'Promote healthy and sustained development of housing and real estate', Speech at the 2003 Annual Housing and Property Conference, Wuhan, 13 January 2003.

Lloyd, P. (1979) *Slums of Hope*, London: Penguin.

Lowder, S. (1986) *Inside Third World Cities*, London and Sydney: Croom Helm.

Lungo, M. and Baires, S. (2001) 'Socio-Spatial Segregation and Urban Land Regulation in Latin American Cities', paper presented to the seminar *Segregation in the City*, Lincoln Institute of Land Policy, Cambridge, Massachusetts, 25–28 July 2001.

Ma, L.J.C. (2002) 'Urban transformation in China, 1949–2000: a review and research agenda', *Environment and Planning A*, 34: 1545–69.

Mahishnan, A. (1999) 'Smart cities, the Singapore case', *Cities*, 16(1): 13–18.

Manor, J. (1999) 'The political economy of democratic decentralization', Washington: The World Bank, in Stren, R.E. (2000) 'New approaches to urban governance in Latin America', paper presented at the seminar *IDRC and management of sustainable urban development in Latin America: lessons learnt and demands for knowledge*, Montevideo, Uruguay, 6–7 April 2000. Available at http://web.idcr.ca/en/ev-22827-201-1-DO_TOPIC.html.

Marcussen, L. (1990) *Third World Housing in Social and Spatial Development*, Aldershot: Avebury.

Martinussen, J. (1997) *Society, State and Market: A Guide to Competing Theories of Development*, New York: Zed Books.

Mathey, K. (ed.) (1990) *Housing Policies in the Socialist Third World*, London: Mansell.

Mathey, K. (ed.) (1992) *Beyond Self-Help Housing*, London: Mansell.

Mayo, S. and Gross, D. (1987) *Sites and Services – and Subsidies: The Economics of Low-Cost Housing in Developing Countries*, Nairobi: Ford Foundation.

McAuslan, P. (1975) *Land, Law and Planning*, London: Weidenfeld and Nicolson.

McGee, T.G. (1971) *The Urbanization Process in the Third World: Explorations in Search of a Theory*, London: G. Bell.

McGee, T.G. (1979) 'Conservation and dissolution in the Third World city: the "shanty town" as an element of conservation', *Development and Change*, 10(1): 1–22.

McGee, T.G. (1991) 'The emergence of Desakota regions in Asia: expanding a hypothesis', in Ginsburg, N., Koppell, B. and McGee, T.G. (eds) *The Extended Metropolis: Settlement Transition in Asia*, Honolulu, HI: University of Hawaii Press.

McGee, T.G. and Robinson, I. (eds) (1995) *The Mega-Urban Regions of Southeast Asia*, Vancouver: UBC Press.

McGranahan, G. and Satterthwaite, D. (2000) 'Environmental health or ecological sustainability? Reconciling the brown and green agendas in urban development', in Pugh, C. (ed.) *Sustainable Cities in Developing Countries*, London: Earthscan.

Meadows, D. and Forrester, J. (1972) *The Limits to Growth: A Report for the Club of Rome's Project on the Predicament of Mankind*, New York: Universe.

Mera, K. (1978) 'On urban agglomeration and economic efficiency', in Bourne, L.S. and Simmons, J.W. (eds) *Systems of Cities*, New York: Oxford University Press.

Mera, K. (1981) 'City size distribution and income distribution in space', *Regional Development Dialogue*, 2(1): 105–20.

Mercer, E. (1975) *English Vernacular Houses: A Study of Traditional Farmhouses and Cottages*, London: HMSO.

Ministry of Labour and Social Security and the State Statistics Bureau of China (2002) *Statistics Report of the 2001*, Beijing: Labour and Social Security Development, http://www.stats.gov.cn/tjgb/qttjgb/qgqttjgb/200206110029.htm.

Montgomery, M.R., Stren, R., Cohen, B. and Reed, H.E. (2004) *Cities Transformed, Demographic Change and its Implications in the Developing World*, London: Earthscan.

Morris, A.E.J. (1994) *History of Urban Form Before the Industrial Revolutions* (3rd edn), Harlow: Longman Scientific and Technical.

Moser, C. (1996) *Confronting Crisis: A Comparative Study of Household Responses to Poverty and Vulnerability in Four Poor Urban Communities*, New York: World Bank. Available at http://www-wds.worldbank.org/servlet/WDS_IBank_Ser vlet?pcont=detailsandeid=000009265_3961219091815.

Moser C., Gatehouse, M. and Garcia, H. (1996) *Urban Poverty Research Sourcebook: Module II: Indicators of Urban Poverty*, UMP Working Paper Series 5, UNDP/UNCHS(Habitat)/World Bank, Washington, DC.

Moser, C.O.N. and Peake, L. (1987) *Women, Human Settlements and Housing*, London: Tavistock.

Mumtaz, B. (ed.) (1982) *Readings in Action Planning*, London: Development Planning Unit.

Murphey, R. (1970) *The Treaty Ports and China's Modernization: What Went Wrong?* Ann Arbor, MI: Michigan Papers in Chinese Studies, No. 7.

Murphey, R. (1980) *The Fading of the Maoist Vision: City and Country in China's Development*, New York: Methuen.

Ng, M.K. (1999) 'Political economy and urban planning: a comparative study of Hong Kong, Singapore and Taiwan', *Progress in Planning*, 51(1): 1–90.

Nickson, R.A. (1995) 'Local Government in Latin America', Boulder, CO: Lynne Rienner, in Stren, R.E. (2000) 'New approaches to urban governance in Latin America', paper presented at the seminar *IDRC and management of sustainable urban development in Latin America: lessons learnt and demands for knowledge*, Montevideo, Uruguay, 6–7 April 2000. Available at http://web.idcr.ca/en/ev-22827-201-1-DO_TOPIC.html.

Nientied, P. and van der Linden, J. (1983) 'The limits of Engel's "the housing question" for the explanation of Third World slum upgrading', *International Journal of Urban and Regional Research*, 7.

Nientied, P., Robben, P. and van der Linden, J. (1986) 'Some comparative evidence on displacement and income-housing policy', mimeoscript cited in Mathey, K. (ed) (1992) *Beyond Self-Help Housing*, London: Mansell.

Oberai, A.S. (1987) *Migration, Urbanisation and Development*, Geneva: UN-ILO.

O'Connor, A.M. (1983) *The African City*, London: Hutchison University Library.

Oliver, P. (ed.) (1969) *Shelter and Society*, London: Barrie and Jenkins.

Oliver, P. (ed.) (1971) *Shelter in Africa*, London: Barrie and Jenkins.

Oliver, P. (ed.) (1975) *Shelter, Sign and Symbol*, London: Barrie and Jenkins.

Oliver, P. (1997) *Encyclopaedia of Vernacular Architecture of the World. Vol. 3 Cultures and Habitats*, Cambridge: Cambridge University Press.

Oliver, P. (2003) *Dwellings: The Vernacular House World Wide*, London and New York: Phaidon.

Parr, J.B. (1999) 'Growth-pole strategies in regional economic planning: a retrospective view, Part 2, implementation and outcome', *Urban Studies*, 36(8): 1247–68.

Payne, G. (1984) *Low Income Housing in the Developing World*, Chichester: John Wiley.

Payne, G. (ed.) (1999) *Making Common Ground: Public–Private Partnerships in Land for Housing*, London: ITDG.

Payne, G. (ed.) (2002) *Land, Rights and Innovation: Improving Tenure Security for the Urban Poor*, London: ITDG.

Peattie, L. (1968) *A View from the Barrio*, Ann Arbor, MI: University of Michigan Press.

Peattie, L. (1983) 'Realistic planning and qualitative research', *Habitat International*, 7 (5/6): 227–34.

Peattie, L. (1987) *Planning: Rethinking Ciudad Guayana*, Ann Arbor, MI: University of Michigan Press.

Perlman, J.E. (1976) *The Myth of Marginality*, Berkeley, CA: University of California Press.

Perroux, F. (1955) 'Note sur la notion de pôle de croissance', *Économie appliquée*, January–June: 1–2.

Pevsner, N. (1976) *A History of Building Types*, London: Thames and Hudson.

Pickvance, C. (1977) 'Physical planning and market forces in urban development', *National Westminster Bank Quarterly Review*, August.

Pieterse, J.N. (2001) *Development Theory: Deconstructions/Reconstructions*, London: Sage.

Polanyi, K. (1944) *The Great Transformation*, New York: Reinhart and Co.

Polanyi, K. (1977) *The Livelihood of Man*, New York: Academic Press.

Polanyi, K., Arensberg, C.M. and Pearson, H.W. (1957) *Trade and Market in the Early Empires: Economies in History and Theory*, Glencoe, IL: The Free Press.

Potter, R.B., Binns, T., Elliott, J.A. and Smith, D. (2004) *Geographies of Development* (2nd edn), Harlow: Pearson Education Limited.

Preston, P.W. (1998) *Pacific Asia in the Global System*, Oxford: Blackwell.

Pugh, C. (1995) 'The role of the World Bank in housing', in Aldrich, B. and Sandhu, R. (eds) *Housing the Urban Poor: Policy and Practice in Developing Countries*, London: Zed Press.

Pugh, C. (1997) 'The changing roles of self-help in housing and urban policies 1950–1996: experience in developing countries', *Third World Planning Review*, 19(1): 91–109.

Pugh, C. (2000) 'Sustainable urban development: some millennial reflections on theory and application', in Pugh, C. (ed.) *Sustainable Cities in Developing Countries*, London: Earthscan.

Qadeer, M.A. (2000) 'Ruralopolises: the spatial organisation and residential land economy of high-density rural regions in South Asia', *Urban Studies*, 37(9): 1583–603.

Qadeer, M.A. (2004) 'Urbanization by implosion' (Guest Editorial), *Habitat International*, 28: 1–12.

Raglan, L. (1965) 'The origin of vernacular architecture', in Foster, I. and Alcock, L. (eds) *Culture and Environment: Essays in Honour of Sir Cyril Fox*, London: Routledge and Kegan Paul.

Rakodi, C. (1992) 'Housing markets in third world cities: research and policy in the 1990s', *World Development*, 20(1): 39–55.

Rakodi, C. (ed.) (1997) *The Urban Challenge in Africa: Growth and Management of its Large Cities*, Tokyo: United Nations University Press.

Rakodi, C. and Leduka, C.R. (2005) *Informal Land Delivery Processes and Access to Land for the Poor: A Comparative Study of Six African Cities*, Policy Brief 6, International Development Department, Birmingham University, available at www.idd.bham.ac.uk/researcg/researchprojs.htm.

Rakodi, C. and Lloyd-Jones, T. (2002) *Urban Livelihoods: A People-centred Approach to Reducing Poverty*, London: Earthscan.

Ramesh, M. (2004) *Social Policy in East and Southeast Asia, Education, health, housing, and income maintenance*, London and New York: RoutledgeCurzon.

Ramírez Corzo, D. and Riofrío, G. (2005) 'Land titling: a path to urban inclusion? Policy and practice of the Peruvian model', paper at the 6th Annual Conference of the Network-Association of European Researchers on Urbanisation in the South (N-AERUS), *Promoting Social Inclusion in Urban Areas: Policies and Practice*, Lund University Housing Development and Management, September 2005, available at http://www.naerus.net/sat/workshops/2005/papers/32.pdf.

Rapoport, A. (1969) *House Form and Culture*, Englewoood Cliffs, NJ: Prentice Hall.

Rapoport, A. (1976) *The Mutual Interaction of People and their Built Environment: A Cross Cultural Perspective*, The Hague: Mouton.

Rebentisch, D. (1980) 'Regional planning and its institutional framework: an illustration from the Rhine–Main area, 1890–1945', in Cherry, G. (ed.) *Shaping an Urban World: Planning in the Twentieth Century*, London: Mansell.

Renaud, B. (1981) *National Urbanization Policy in Developing Countries*, New York: Oxford University Press.

Rhoda, R.E. (1979) *Development Activities and Rural Urban Migration*, Washington DC: USAID (mimeo).

Richardson, H.W. (1987) 'Whither national urban policy in developing countries', *Urban Studies*, 24: 227–44.

Riley, E., Fiori, J. and Ramirez, R. (2001) 'Favela Bairro and a new generation of housing programmes for the urban poor', *Geoforum*, 32(4): 521–31.

Robertson, R. (2003) *The Three Waves of Globalization: A History of a Developing Global Consciousness*, London: Zed Press.

Rogers, A. and Williamson, G. (1982) 'Integration, urbanisation and Third World development: an overview', *Economic Development and Cultural Change*, 30: 463–82.

Rolnik, R. (2000) 'Impacto da aplicação de novos instrumentos urbanísticos em cidades do estado de São Paulo', *Revista Brasileira de Estudos Urbanos e Regionais 2*, ANPUR, Recife, in Lungo, M. and Baires, S. (2001) 'Socio-spatial segregation and urban land regulation in Latin American cities', paper presented to the seminar *Segregation in the City*, Lincoln Institute of Land Policy, Cambridge, Massachusetts, 25–28 July 2001.

Rowland, A. and Gordon, P. (1996) 'Mexico City: no longer a leviathan?', in Gilbert, A. (ed.) *The Mega-city in Latin America*, Tokyo: United Nations University Press.

Rudofsky, B. (1964) *Architecture Without Architects*, New York: Museum of Modern Art.

Rudofsky, B. (1977) *The Prodigious Builders*, London: Secker and Warburg.

Salas Serrano, J. (1993) 'El problema de la vivienda problema común de las "Américas Latinas"', *CyTET*, 637–65.

Sánchez, N. (1994) 'Community Development and the Role of the NGOs: A New Perspective for Latin America in the 1990s, *Community Development Journal*, 29: 307–319.

Sandercock, L. (1998) 'The death of modernist planning: radical praxis for a postmodern age', in Douglass, M. and Friedmann, J. (eds) *Cities for Citizens*, London: Wiley.

Sarin, M. (1982) *Urban Planning in the Third World: The Chandigarh Experience*, London: Mansell.

Sassen, S. (1993) *The Global City: New York, London, Tokyo*, Princeton, NJ: Princeton University Press.

Satterthwaite, D. (1998) *Urban Poverty: Reconsidering its Scale and Nature*, London: International Institute for Environment and Development.

Satterthwaite, D. (2002a) *Reducing Urban Poverty: Some Lessons from Experience*, London: International Institute for Environment and Development.

Satterthwaite, D. (2002b) *Coping with Rapid Urban Growth*, RICS Leading Edge Series, London: RICS.

Satterthwaite, D. (ed.) (2003) *The Millennium Development Goals and Local Processes: Hitting the Target or Missing the Point?*, London: Institute for Environment and Development.

Savitch, H.V. (2002) 'What is new about globalization and what does it portend for cities?', *International Social Science Journal*, 54(172): 179–89.

Schlyter, A. (1996) *A Place to Live: Gender Research on Housing in Africa*, Uppsala: Nordic Africa Institute.

Schoenauer, N. (2000) *6000 Years of Housing*, New York: Norton & Co.

Schuurman, F.J. (ed.) (1993) *Beyond the Impasse*, London: Zed Press.

Sevilla, M. (1993) 'New approaches for aid agencies: FUPROVI's community based shelter programme', *Environment and Urbanization*, 5(1): 111–21.

Simon, D. (1992) *Cities, Capital and Development: African Cities in the World Economy*, London: Belhaven.

Simon, D. (1997) 'Urbanization, globalization and economy in Africa', in Rakodi, C. (ed.) *The Urban Challenge in Africa: Growth and Management of its Large Cities*, Tokyo: United Nations University Press.

Sinclair, S.W. (1978) *Urbanisation and Labour Markets in Developing Countries*, London: Croom Helm.

Smith, D.A. (1996) *Third World Cities in Global Perspective: The Political Economy of Uneven Urbanisation*, Boulder, CO: Westview Press.

Smith, H. (1999) 'Networks and spaces of negotiation in low-income housing: the case of Costa Rica', PhD thesis, Edinburgh College of Art/Heriot-Watt University, School of Planning and Housing, Edinburgh, UK.

Smith, H. (2004) 'Costa Rica's triangle of solidarity: can government-led spaces for negotiation enhance the involvement of civil society in governance?', *Environment and Urbanization*, 16(1): 63–78.

Smith, P. (1975) *Houses in the Welsh Countryside: A Study of Historical Geography*, London: HMSO.

So, A.Y. (2004) 'Hong Kong's pathway to becoming a global city', in Gugler, J. (ed.) *World Cities Beyond the West: Globalisation, Development, and Inequality*, Cambridge: Cambridge University Press.

Soderbaum F. and Taylor I. (eds) (2003) *Regionalism and Uneven Development in Southern Africa*, Aldershot: Ashgate.

Soja, E. (2000) *Postmetropolis: Critical Studies of Cities and Regions*, Oxford: Blackwell.

Sorenson, A.D. and Day, R. (1981) 'Libertarian planning', *Town Planning Review*, 52(4): 390–402.

Spengler, J.J. (1967) 'Africa and the theory of optimum city size', in Miner H. (ed.) *The City in Modern Africa*, London: Pall Mall.

Staley, S.R. (1994) *Planning Rules and Urban Economic Performance: The Case of Hong Kong*, Hong Kong: The Chinese University Press.

State Statistics Bureau of China (2000) *China Statistical Yearbook 2000*, Beijing: China Statistics Press.

State Statistics Bureau of China (2002) *A Judgement and Analysis of Urban Poverty Situation in Our Country*. http://www.stats.gov.cn: 25 February 2002.

State Statistics Bureau of China (2003) *China Statistical Yearbook 2003*, Beijing: China Statistics Press.

State Statistics Bureau of China, Urban Social and Economic Survey Team (2003) *Urban Statistical Yearbook of China 2002*, Beijing: China Statistics Press.

Steinberg, F. (2005) 'Strategic urban planning in Latin America: experiences of building and managing the future', *Habitat International*, 29: 69–93.

Stone, C.N. (1993) 'Urban regimes and the capacity to govern: a political economy approach', *Journal of Urban Affairs*, 15(1): 1–28.

Strassmann, W.P. (1997) 'Avoiding conflict and bold enquiry – a recapitulation of Habitat II', *Urban Studies*, 34(10): 1729–38.

Stren, R.E. (1990) 'Urban housing in Africa: the changing role of government policy', in Amis, P. and Lloyd, P. (eds) *Housing Africa's Urban Poor*, Manchester: Manchester University Press.

Stren, R. (2000) 'New Approaches to Urban Governance in Latin America', paper presented at the seminar *IDRC and management of sustainable urban development in Latin America: lessons learnt and demands for knowledge*, Montevideo, Uruguay, 6–7 April 2000. Available at http://web.idcr.ca/en/ev-22827–201–1–DO_TOPIC.html.

Stren, R. and White, R.R. (eds) (1990) *African Cities in Crisis: Managing Rapid Urban Growth*, Boulder, CO: Westview.

Swilling, M. (1997) 'Building democratic local urban governance in Southern Africa', in Swilling, M. (ed.) *Governing Africa's Cities*, Johannesburg: Witwatersrand University Press.

Taylor, J.L. and Williams, D.G. (eds) (1982) *Urban Planning Practice in Developing Countries*, Oxford: Pergamon.

Taylor, N. (1998) *Urban Planning Theory Since 1945*, London: Sage.

Todaro, M.P. (1994) *Economic Development*, London: Longman.

Tolley, G. and Thomas, V. (1987) *The Economics of Urbanisation and Urban Policy*, Washington, DC: World Bank.

Tongji University, City Planning Group, (1985) *History of Chinese City Construction*, Beijing: China Architectural Publishing House.

Tostensen, A., Tvedten, I. and Vaa, M. (2001) 'The urban crisis, governance and associational life', in Tostensen, A., Tvedten, I. and Vaa, M. (eds) *Associational Life in African Cities: Popular Responses to the Urban Crisis*, Uppsala: Nordic Africa Institute.

Turner, J.F.C. (1967) 'Barriers and channels for housing development in modernising countries', *Journal of the American Institute of Planners*, 33(3): 167–81.

Turner, J.F.C. (1968) 'Housing priorities, settlement patterns and urban settlements in modernising countries', *Journal of the American Institute of Planners*, 34(Nov.): 354–63.

Turner, J.F.C. (1976) *Housing by People*, London: Marion Boyars.

Turner, J.F.C. (1978) 'Housing in three dimensions: terms of reference for the housing question redefined', *World Development*, 6(9/10): 1135–45.

Turner, J.F.C. (1982) 'Issues in self-help and self-managed housing', in Ward, P.M. *Self-help Housing: A Critique*, London: Mansell.

Turner, J.F.C. (1986) 'Future directions in housing policies', *Habitat International*, 10(3): 7–26.

Turner, J.F.C. (1988) 'Introduction', and 'Conclusions', in Turner, B. (ed.) *Building Community*, London: Building Community Books.

Turner, J.F.C. (1992) 'Beyond self-help housing: foreword', in Mathey, K. (ed.) *Beyond Self-Help Housing*, London: Mansell.

Turner, J.F.C. and Fichter, R. (eds) (1972) *Freedom to Build: Dweller Control of the Housing Process*, New York: Macmillan.

Tyrwhitt, J. (ed.) (1947) *Patrick Geddes in India*, London: Lund Humphries.

UNCHS (1987) *Global Report on Human Settlements 1986*, Oxford and New York: Oxford University Press.

UNCHS (1990) *The Global Strategy for Shelter to the Year 2000*, Nairobi: UNCHS (Habitat).

UNCHS (1996) *An Urbanizing World: Global Report on Human Settlements 1996*, Oxford and New York: Oxford University Press.

UNCHS (2001) *Cities in a Globalizing World: Global Report on Human Settlements 2001*, London: Earthscan.

UNESCAP, (1998) *Living in Asian Cities, Where We Come from: Historical Perspective and Major Trends*. Available at www.unescap.org.

UN-Habitat (2003a) *Global Report on Human Settlements 2003: The Challenge of Slums*, London: Earthscan.

UN-Habitat (2003b) *Rental Housing: An Essential Option for the Urban Poor in Developing Countries*, Nairobi: UN-Habitat.

UN-Habitat (2004) *The State of the World's Cities: Globalization and Urban Culture*, London: Earthscan.

United Nations (1979) 'Habitat Conference 1976: Declaration of Principles', in May, R. J. (ed.) *Third World Urbanization*, New York: Methuen.

United Nations, (2000) *World Population Prospects: The 1998 Revision, Volume III: Analytical Report*, New York: United Nations.

United Nations (2001) *World Urbanisation Prospects: The 1999 Revision*, New York: United Nations, Department of Economic and Social Affaires, Population Division.

United Nations, *Demographic Yearbook 2002*, Table 6.

United Nations Department of Economic and Social Affairs, Population Division (2004) World Urbanization Prospects: 2003 Revision, *New York: United Nations.*

United Nations Secretariat, Population Division, *World Urbanization Prospects: The 2001 Revision*, Data Tables and Highlights (ESA/P/WP.173, 20 March 2002).

Van der Schueren, F., Wegelin, E. and Wekwete, K. (1996) *Policy Programme Options for Urban Poverty Reduction*, UNDP/UNCHS (Habitat)/World Bank Urban Management Programme Paper 20. Available at http://www-wds.worldbank.org/servlet/WDS_IBank_Servlet?pcont=detailsandeid=000009265_3961219093257

Wakely, P. (1986) 'The devolution of housing production: support and management', *Habitat International*, 10(3): 53–63.

Wakely, P. (1988) 'The development of housing through the withdrawal from construction: changes in third world housing policies and programmes', *Habitat International*, 12(3): 121–31.

Wakely, P. (1998) *Focus on DPU: A Quarter of a Century of Innovation and Achievement in UCL*, DPU News 35.

Wang, Y.P. (2004) *Urban Poverty, Housing and Social Change in China*, Abingdon: Routledge.

Wang, Y.P. and Hague C. (1992) 'The planning and development of Xian since 1949', *Planning Perspective*, 7(1): 1–26.

Wang, Y.P. and Murie, A., (1996) 'The process of commercialisation of urban housing in China', *Urban Studies*, 33(6): 971–89.

Wang, Y.P. and Murie, A. (1999) *Housing Policy and Practice in China*, London: Macmillan and New York: St Martin's Press.

Ward, P. (ed.) (1982) *Self-help Housing: A Critique*, London: Mansell.

Ward, P. (1996) 'Contemporary issues in the government and administration of Latin American mega-cities', in Gilbert, A. (ed.) *The Mega-city in Latin America*, Tokyo: United Nations University Press.

Watson, V. (2005) 'The usefulness of normative planning in the context of Sub-Saharan Africa', in Stiftel, B. and Watson, V., (eds) *Dialogues in Urban and Regional Planning 1*, London: Routledge.

WCED (1987) *Our Common Future*, Oxford: Oxford University Press.

Webber, A. (1899) (1963) 'The growth of cities in the Nineteenth century', Ithaca, NY: Cornell University Press. From Smith, D. (1996) *Third World Cities in*

Global Perspective: The Political Economy of Uneven Urbanization, Boulder, CO: Westview Press.

Weerapana, D. (1986) 'Evolution of a support policy of shelter – the experience of Sri Lanka', *Habitat International*, 10(3): 79–89.

Wegelin, E.A. (1994) 'Everything you always wanted to know about the Urban Management Programme (but were afraid to ask)', *Habitat International*, 18(4): 127–37.

White III, L. T., (1982) Non-governmentalism in the historical development in modern Shanghai, in Ma, L.J.C. (ed.) *Urban Development in Modern China*, Boulder, CO: Westview, Special Studies on China and East Asia.

Williamson, J. (1990) 'What Washington means by policy reform', in J. Williamson (ed.) *Latin American Adjustment: How Much Has Happened?* Washington, DC: Institute for International Economics.

Wong, S.L. (1988) 'The application of Asian family values to other socialcultural settings', in Berger, P. and Hiao, H.M. (eds) *In Search of an East Asian Development Model*, New Brunswick, NJ: Transaction Books.

Wong, T. and Yap, A. (2003) 'From universal public housing to meeting the increasing aspiration for private housing in Singapore', *Habitat International*, 27: 361–80.

World Bank (1984) *CHINA: Problems and Strategies of Long-term Development (Main Report)*, Beijing: Chinese Financial and Economic Press.

World Bank (1991) *Urban Policy and Economic Development: An Agenda for the 1990s*, Policy Paper, Washington, DC: World Bank.

World Bank (1993) *Housing: Enabling Housing Markets to Work*, Policy Paper, Washington, DC: World Bank.

World Bank (2000a) *Entering the 21st Century: World Development Report 1999/2000*, Oxford: Oxford University Press.

World Bank (2000b) *Cities in Transition: A Strategic View of Urban and Local Government Issues*, Washington, DC: World Bank.

World Bank, (2000c) *World Development Indicators, 2000*, Washington, DC: World Bank.

World Bank (2001) *World Bank Development Report 2000/2001: Attacking Poverty*, Washington, DC: World Bank/Oxford University Press.

Wu, F. (1996) 'Changes in the structure of public housing provision in urban China', *Urban Studies*, 33(9): 1601–27.

Wu, F. (2001) 'Housing provision under globalisation: a case study of Shanghai', *Environment and Planning A*, 33: 1741–64.

Wu, L.Y. (1986) *A Brief History of Ancient Chinese City Planning*, Kassel: Urbs et Regio.

Wu, W. and Yusuf, S. (2004) 'Shanghai: remaking China's future global city', in Gugler, J. (ed.) (2004) *World Cities Beyond the West: Globalisation, Development, and Inequality*, Cambridge: Cambridge University Press, pp. 27–58.

Yeung, Y.M. (1996) 'Introduction', in Yeung, Y.M. and Sung, Y.W. (eds) *Shanghai: Transformation and Modernisation under China's Open Policy*, Hong Kong: Chinese University Press.

Yeung, Y.M. (1997) 'Planning for Pearl City: Hong Kong's future, 1997 and beyond', *Cities*, 14(5): 249–56.

Yeung, Y.M. (ed.) (2002) *New Challenges for Development and Modernization: Hong Kong and the Asia-Pacific Region in the New Millennium*, Hong Kong: Chinese University Press.

Yuen, B. (1996) 'Creating the garden city: the Singapore experience', *Urban Studies*, 33(6): 955–70.

Yuen, B. (2004) 'Planning Singapore growth for better living', in Freire, M. and Yuen, B. (eds) (2004) *Enhancing Urban Management in East Asia*, Aldershot: Ashgate.

Yuen, B. (2005) 'Romancing the high-rise in Singapore', *Cities*, 22(1): 3–13.

Zhou, T.H. (1984) *Contemporary Chinese Economic System Reforms*, Beijing: China Social Science Publishing House.

Index